Discovering Cultural Psychology

A Profile and Selected Readings of Ernest E. Boesch

a volume in
Advances in Cultural Psychology

Series Editor:
Jaan Valsiner, *Clark University*

Advances in Cultural Psychology

Jaan Valsiner, Series Editor

Discovering Cultural Psychology

A Profile and Selected Readings of Ernest E. Boesch

by

Walter J. Lonner
Western Washington University

and

Susanna A. Hayes
Western Washington University

INFORMATION AGE
PUBLISHING

Charlotte, North Carolina • www.infoagepub.com

Library of Congress Cataloging-in-Publication Data

Boesch, Ernest Eduard.
 Discovering cultural psychology : a profile and selected readings of Ernest E. Boesch /
[edited] by Walter J. Lonner and Susanna A. Hayes.
     p. cm. -- (Advances in cultural psychology)
 Includes bibliographical references.
 ISBN-13: 978-1-59311-746-7 (pbk.)
 ISBN-13: 978-1-59311-747-4 (hardcover)
 1. Ethnopsychology. 2. Psychological anthropology. 3. Cognition and culture. 4. Boesch,
Ernest Eduard. I. Lonner, Walter J. II. Hayes, Susanna A. III. Title.
 GN502.B64 2007
 155.8'2--dc22

                                                                    2007009426

ISBN 13: 978-1-59311-746-7 (pbk.)
          978-1-59311-747-4 (hardcover)
ISBN 10: 1-59311-746-9 (pbk.)
          1-59311-747-7 (hardcover)

Printed in the United States of America

CONTENTS

C. MESSAGE THROUGH THE OTHER

SERIES EDITOR'S INTRODUCTION

The Gracious Complexity of Culture:
Striving Toward Humanity

This book is a landmark in contemporary cultural psychology. Ernest Boesch's synthesis of ideas is the first comprehensive theory of culture in psychology since Wilhelm Wundt's *Völkerpsychologie* of the first decades of the twentieth century. Cultural psychology of today is an attempt to advance the program of research that was charted out by Wundt—yet at times we are carefully avoiding direct recognition of such continuity. While Wundt's experimental psychology has been hailed as the root for contemporary scientific psychology, the other side of his contribution—ethnographic analysis of folk traditions and higher psychological functions—has been largely discredited as something disconnected from the scientific realm. As an example of "soft" science—lacking the "hardness" of experimentation—it has been considered to be an esoteric hobby of the founding father of contemporary psychology. Of course that focus is profoundly wrong—the opposition "soft" versus "hard" just does not fit as a metalevel organizer of any science. Yet the rhetoric discounting the descriptive side of Wundt's psychology is merely an act of social guidance of what psychologists do—not a way of creating knowledge.

As is the case with most rewritings of disciplinary histories in science that are aimed at guiding the thinking of scientists, this look at *Völkerpsychologie* is historically inadequate (Diriwächter, 2004) and constitutes a limitation on gaining basic knowledge in contemporary psychology. It is a conceptual blinder of our time—legitimizing the reduction of complex and dynamic wholes of the psyche into their elementary components. Histories of psychology are symbolic tools for directing the immediate future of the science.

For Wundt *Völkerpsychologie* was an integral part of psychological science—yet one for which methods other than experimental are necessary. His setting the stage for addressing the issues of creative synthesis of new psychological phenomena has taken 100 years to slowly regain prominence. We are still far from providing adequate solutions—handling the processes of emergence is a difficult conceptual task for contemporary developmental sciences. Cultural developmental psychology has to make sense of how something—that does not (yet) exist—comes into being out of very different predecessors.

Here of course is a clear parallel with developmental biology where the hierarchic system of genetic control mechanisms guarantees the possibilities for growth of new adaptations (Beurton, Falk, & Rheinberger, 2000). Add the appealing—yet poorly defined—notion of *culture* to the developing system of humans and we have a dynamic, multilevel, and largely unpredictable drama of meaningful living in an ever-changing world. A science of cultural psychology cannot reduce human lives to a limited number of invented causal entities—such as "nature" *versus* "nurture," or five (or any other number) factors discovered through a standardized test. Instead, our science needs to conceptualize abstract processes that at the same time can be located—and studied—in the middle of the lives of ordinary human beings anywhere in the world.

Cultural psychology is a general science within which phenomena of human conduct and meaning construction that vary immensely across the world are examples of basic universal processes. Ernest Boesch's work is built over decades as such general theory of culture—in the form of symbolic ways of acting—and is thus a survivor of the avalanche of post-modernist takeover of the social sciences in the second half of the twentieth century. When viewed from the viewpoint of an active, meaning-making person who acts within one's social world, the idea of knowledge being "local" or "fragmented" makes no sense. Instead, the person is united into one—heterogeneous and highly flexible—whole. The person acts differently in different settings, as well as even in similar settings over time. Post-modernist thought failed to see the forest behind the trees—what looks inconsistent or fragmented to an outside observer is consistently adaptive (flexible) from the inside.

Boesch's intellectual heritage transcends both post-modernism of the social sciences and narrow-minded empiricism of psychology. Psychology's "mainstream" may have learned to avoid complex ideas—rendering our contemporary prevailing empirical orientations epistemologically mute.[1] That is dangerous for any science. Our contemporary move towards the study of intraindividual variability in contemporary psychology (Molenaar, 2004) may be the first step to bring the voice of the experiencing persons back to traditional psychology.

Ernest Boesch's work—definitely located outside of the "mainstream" of psychology—marks the advancement of the field of cultural psychology in the second half of the twentieth century. It is a colorful synthesis of ideas from the humanities and the sciences. It ranges from the beauty of the sound of the violin, and from the disturbing appeal of Picasso's paintings to unifying ideas that only currently begin to be recognized in contemporary neurosciences. His work is the best example of serious scholarship in psychology—where basic philosophical ideas meet the phenomena of deep human experience, and where the superficiality of "standardized methods" that is so much in vogue in psychology—is not allowed to eradicate the human condition of our deep desire for meaningful being.

Boesch's work has had major impacts in different areas of psychology. He is honored in cultural psychology as well as in its more traditional counterpart—cross-cultural psychology. His ideas have led to new inquiries in both domains of developmental psychology (Baltes, 1997, 2001) and in the new area of the study of dialogical self (Hermans, 1997; Simão, 2001, 2005; Simão & Valsiner, 2006). His work has led to the innovative action theory of Lutz Eckensberger that transcends the limits of the often too general arguments of activity theories (Eckensberger, 1997), and has motivated the semiotic approaches to environmental psychology (Lang, 1997). Perhaps the most important feature that these different areas can borrow from Boesch's work is the focus on the phenomena of living—perhaps best called the aesthetics of ordinary being.

In Ernst Boesch's work one sees his ideas guide his own theory building—he is the best example for his own theory. The unity of striving for the far and unknown (*Fernweh*) and its opposite—striving for the feeling of being at home (*Heimweh*)—are closely acting together as the reader of this book will soon discover. There is always ambiguity in moving—any step taken from the previous stable stance towards the expected new one is inherently ambiguous (Valsiner, 2007). Human beings may have hard times with ambiguities—yet all life depends on them. There would be no new discoveries if this ambiguity were absent—no Columbus would take off to the stormy seas in the search of a promised land, no discoveries would happen in any science—innovation in any sphere of life would be impossible.

Ernst Boesch's ideas have developed carefully over decades—and have gained from his experiences in Europe and Asia. In his meticulously elegant ways he has created a real example of a science—in the sense of *Wissenschaft*—of culture as it abundantly guides the human *psyche*. There are no artificial boundaries of disciplines for his inquiry into the basics of being human—psychology, anthropology, sociology, art, literature and philosophy all are parts of the never-ending inquiry. His science is deeply poetic in its core—quite opposite to the prevailing tendency of twentieth century psychology that has largely become a version of rational accounting practices of small behavioral or cognitive elements. What easily gets lost in that computerized rationalism is the depth and dynamics of human aesthetic feelings—be those in creating music, reading literature, or enjoying a painting.

The poetry of everyday life is very prominent in Boesch's theorizing. His work is only now—after the first exposition of the symbolic action theory (Boesch, 1991)—for the first time available in its fullness to the readers in the English language. Walt Lonner and Sue Hayes deserve our utmost gratitude for making this possible. Translating Boesch's ideas into English is a very complicated task—as the texture of thought in the Continental European tradition has *Gestalt*-qualities that tend to disappear as they travel across the English Channel or the Atlantic. The authors of this volume have succeeded admirably—working as a team with the enthusiastic and ever-youthful Ernest Boesch himself—in bringing the present collection of major contributions to the international readership.

This book is an intellectual dessert—to be enjoyed like a glass of good wine, or a slice of cake—at a sophisticated dinner. It is for the lovers of deeply intellectual *gourmet* experience. The reality of all of the complexity of the human life is held in highest reverence in this work—independent of the social and institutional trivialization of basic knowledge that we can observe in our contemporary academia. Ernest Boesch's message is free of all "impact factors" that we nowadays learn to consider as canalyzers of science. Neither is it published—nor publishable— within the mechanistic market of "peer reviewed" journals. Our contemporary social scientists often replace the focus on innovative ideas by one on the renomé of where they get published. Nothing can be more damaging to science than such displacement of focus.

The work represented in this book is a testimony to quality of complex and elegant theorizing. It takes profound life experience to be free from the fads and fashions of each of the decades—and on this 90th birthday of Ernest Boesch we can see the prevailing value of his ideas making their ways in many directions within psychology in the twentieth century. Cultural psychology is fortunate to be the leader in the build-up of new psychology—and the ideas presented in this book are at the forefront of the science in the making.

Jaan Valsiner
Worcester, Massachusetts
October, 2006

NOTE

1. It is tempting to compare the state of affairs in contemporary psychology with that in chemistry in the second half of the eighteenth century. At that time in chemistry, theory-free practical empirical orientation prevailed. General abstractions were devalued, and systematic efforts to establish general knowledge were those of what had been empirically established—rather than allowing for prediction of where new substances might be found. Lavoisier changed that (Roberts, 1991, p. 123), but it took another century until chemistry arrived at the predictive powers of the Mendeleev's Periodicity Table (see Brush, 1996 on its first reception). Psychology in our time is still far from similar synthetic power.

REFERENCES

Baltes, P. B. (1997). Ernst E. Boesch at 80: Reflections from a student on the culture of psychology. *Culture & Psychology, 3*(3), 247-256.

Baltes, P. B. (2001). Boesch at 85 on cultural psychology: foreword. *Culture & Psychology, 7*(4), 477-478.

Beurton, P. J., Falk, R., & Rheinberger, H. -J. (Eds.). (2000). *The concept of the gene in development and evolution.* Cambridge, MA: Cambridge University Press.

Boesch, E. E. (1991). *Symbolic action theory and cultural psychology.* Berlin, Germany: Springer.

Brush, S. G. (1996). The reception of Mendeleev's Periodic Law in America and Britain. *ISIS, 87,* 596-628.

Diriwächter, R. (2004). Völkerpsychologie: The synthesis that never was. *Culture & Psychology, 10*(1), 179-203.

Eckensberger, L. H. (1997). The legacy of Boesch's intellectual Oeuvre. *Culture & Psychology, 3*(3), 277-298.

Hermans, H. J. M. (1997). Commonalities in Boesch and Murray: bridging between a European and an American thinker. *Culture & Psychology, 3*(3), 395-404.

Lang, A. (1997). Thinking rich as well as simple: Boesch's cultural psychology in semiotic perspective. *Culture & Psychology, 3*(3), 383-394.

Molenaar, P. C. M. (2004). A manifesto on psychology as idiographic science: Bringing the person back into scientific psychology, this time forever. *Measurement: Interdisciplinary research and perspectives, 2,* 201-218.

Roberts, L. (1991). Setting the Table: The disciplinary development of eighteenth century chemistry as read through the changing structure of its tables. In P. Dear (Ed.), *The literary structure of scientific argument: Historical studies* (pp. 91-132). Philadelphia: University of Pennsylvania Press.

Simão, L. M. (2001). Boesch's symbolic action theory in interaction. *Culture & Psychology, 7*(4), 485-493.

Simão, L. M. (2005). *Bildung,* culture and self: A possible dialogue with Gadamer, Boesch and Valsiner? *Theory and Psychology, 15*(4), 549-574.

Simão, L. M., & Valsiner, J. (Eds.) (2006). *Otherness in question: Labyrinths of the self.* Greenwich, CT.: Information Age Publishers

Valsiner, J. (2007). *Culture in minds and societies: Foundations of cultural psychology.* New Delhi, India: Sage.

PREFACE AND ACKNOWLEDGMENTS

During the last half of the twentieth century psychology has witnessed a robust ascendance in the psychological study of culture. Whether under the aegis and influence of cultural psychology, cross-cultural psychology, psychological anthropology, indigenous psychology, or related facets of research and scholarship, the study of many complex dynamics between human psychology and human cultural contexts has flourished as never before in the history of modern psychology. A relatively small number of individuals served as major leaders of these theoretically and experimentally innovative areas of the discipline. One of these individuals is Ernest Eduard Boesch, a Swiss-born psychologist whose distinguished career has spanned over 65 years of scholarly activity. This book features highlights of his development as a cultural psychologist. To provide readers with examples of his scholarly contributions, we present 11 of his previous publications in Part II of this book.

We chose the words, "Discovering Cultural Psychology," as part of the title because they describe the "journey of discovery"—a description Ernest frequently used to describe his professional career—that he pursued without a clear and well-reasoned plan. When Ernest Boesch started his career, he had no intention of becoming a "cultural psychologist." In fact, he told us during our interviews that when studying at the University of Geneva with major figures such as Jean Piaget and Andre Rey, he did not remember hearing the word "culture" in his lectures and discussions with faculty and students. Ernest was simply preparing for a career in psychology without knowing how he might apply his education after completing his exams and thesis. He and many of his peers who were greatly distressed by the horrors of World Wars I and II hoped that psychological studies which they and others might initiate would lead to greater human understanding and empathy so that society could be liberated from unbridled aggression.

Through his participation, in the mid-1950s, in UNESCO meetings that often addressed the educational needs of "underdeveloped" nations, Ernest, as a new professor of psychology, was offered the opportunity to direct a major research program in Thailand. By choosing that direction in his journey, he unknowingly found himself on the path to cultural psychology. He mastered the work of experimental psychology at Geneva, practiced and refined his skills as a school psychologist in the Canton of St. Gallen, and then directed one of the earliest of cross-cultural research projects in Thailand. It was during this sojourn of 3 years that Ernest found himself questioning how culture influenced the behaviors of his team of researchers and their subjects. Thus he went from experimental psychology to school psychology to cross-cultural psychologist to cultural psychology. At age 90, his intellectual life continues to be transformed, but always in the direction of commenting on and hoping to do something about trenchant human problems. In short, he continues to be a deeply concerned cultural psychologist and humanitarian. This book examines the nature of his transformation and, as noted above, offers a sampling of his writings that are reflective of his professional development.

Ernest Boesch is probably best known as the architect of his particular approach to cultural psychology known as symbolic action theory, a perspective that he developed over many years. Most of the readings we have included feature, in various ways, elements of his symbolic action theory. Chapter 3 of this book was largely written by Ernest and provides a concise overview of some major elements of his theory.

We hope that the book will do justice to what we consider to be the more important parts of his professional development. One of our hopes is that it will be influential to advanced students in psychology, and possibly budding scholars in other fields as well, as they prepare for careers that will lead to further insights into the importance of human cultures in this era of social and economic globalization. The meaning of "reality" is constantly being challenged. Many scholars are meeting these challenges by pursuing the elusive goal of understanding how person and culture define each other.

A number of people merit our sincere thanks and acknowledgment. First, of course, is Ernest Boesch. Personal interviews of considerable depth as well as friendly visits, along with innumerable e-mail exchanges, were essential throughout the process of producing this book. The patience he showed, especially with his failing vision, was remarkable. The second person to acknowledge and thank is Ernest's wife, Supanee.

Her quiet and charming presence, infectious smile, and subtle humor, were always sources of comfort. She also found a number of photographs of the type that belong in such a book. We are pleased that many of them have been included. We thank Robert B. Textor, a close friend of both Ernest and Supanee, for accepting our invitation to write chapter 4 for this book. The fact that Bob Textor was in Thailand for some time with Ernest, witnessing the transformation that Ernest was experiencing, provides important information about an interesting career in transition. We wish to thank a number of people who were involved with Ernest as students and colleagues. Either directly, but most of the time indirectly, these individuals provided valuable information about Ernest, especially during his long career at the University of the Saar. The late Paul Baltes, Lutz Eckensberger, and Hans-Joachim Kornadt, genuine and globally-recognized scholars in their own right, are the most prominent of a number of erstwhile informants who have worked and studied with him. All who wrote articles for the special issue in 1997 of *Culture and Psychology*, titled "The Legacy of Ernest Boesch in Cultural Psychology," informed us in important ways. That special issue contains many of the papers that were given during a December, 1996 Festschrift in Berlin celebrating Ernest's 80th birthday. Interestingly, 10 years later this book may be viewed, in part, as a way to help Ernest celebrate his 90th birthday on December 26, 2006.

We wish to thank a number of individuals who were instrumental in helping to make it possible to include certain articles in Part II. They include the following: S. Karger publishing company who allowed us to print "The Bangkok Project, Step One"; Cigdem Kagitcibasi, a well-known cross-cultural psychologist, whose effort lead to the inclusion of "Cultural Psychology in Action Theoretical Perspective"; Michael Cole, a renowned cultural psychologist who gladly and generously paved the way to include "The Sound of the Violin" and "The Seven Flaws of Cross-Cultural Psychology," both of which appeared in publications of the Laboratory of Comparative Human Cognition. We also thank the publisher of the *Journal de la psychanalyse de l'enfant* for permission to include "Reality as Metaphor" and to Virginia Geck who assisted Ernest Boesch in translating it from the original French version. Sage Publications kindly granted permission to include "Why Sally Never Calls Bobby "I", a brief article that appeared in *Culture and Psychology*.

We want to thank Jürgen Straub and Arne Weidemann for contributing an informative and rich commentary on Boesch's contributions to the field. Professor Straub has a firm understanding of symbolic action theory and may be its most active proponent. The recent book he edited with D. Weidemann, C. Koebl, and B. Zielke, titled *Pursuit of Meaning*, is a most welcome contribution to the growing literature involving the interface between psychology and culture.

Jaan Valsiner merits our special thanks. When he responded enthusiastically that the new series he was editing for Information Age Publishing Inc. would "certainly" take the book, we were pleased and so, we might add, was Ernest Boesch. To have a well-known cultural psychologist like Valsiner endorse the project so enthusiastically validated our belief that the book can, and we hope will, influence students who want to learn more about the lives and contributions of people whose careers they have admired. It is important that the book appears in a series that we believe will have a long life and a long reach in the academic community. And we thank Information Age Publishing, and its founder, George F. Johnson, for leadership shown in publishing books like this so that others may discover cultural psychology and all that it has to offer.

We wish also to thank Kay McMurren, a secretary in the Department of Psychology at Western Washington University. She continued to show her typical patience and perseverance in transcribing many audio tapes that we made during our interviews with Professor Boesch.

Walter J. Lonner
Susanna A. Hayes

INTRODUCING THE AUTHOR OF THE IDEAS

Getting to Know Ernest Boecsh

The Authors

The psychological study of culture is not new. If one were to wade through an immense volume of psychological literature, starting with the ancient Greeks, one would find a large number of books, essays, treatises, research projects, and so on that focused in some way on "culture" and all of its behavioral and philosophical permutations. What is relatively new, however, is the astonishing *rate* at which such efforts have appeared during the past half century. Often guided and inspired by the works of anthropologists, linguists, and other scholars, hundreds of psychologists have devoted a good part of their careers to the complex and challenging study of the many and diverse influences of human culture on the core of human psychological growth and development. One of the scholars who has devoted much time and effort in the study of culture is Ernest Eduard Boesch. This book is about him and his contributions. As such, we think it provides an interesting and useful psychological perspective on how we might attempt to understand people whom we consciously recognize as culturally different from ourselves.

As authors, we have both been deeply involved with cross-cultural and cultural psychology for most of our professional lives. Academically and experientially, we might be described as "seasoned." Hayes has been focused on Native American populations since 1964. She taught and counseled in elementary schools on the Colville Indian Reservation in Northeastern Washington and has remained in contact with members of that community to the present. Lonner's career has focused on many aspects of cultural and, especially, cross-cultural psychology. His primary involvement has been with the International Association for Cross-Cultural Psychology and as founding editor of the *Journal of Cross-Cultural Psychology*. As major elements in his career, these and related activities have allowed him to meet many leaders in the field of cultural and cross-cultural psychology. In addition to their independent work, the authors have collaborated on various projects for a number of years. Both are among many like-minded individuals who are interested in the study of human culture, an important part of one's identity. We enjoy the challenge of trying to determine what culture means to people everywhere, how it shapes lives and thoughts, and what can be done to understand it to the point of being effective in different cultural contexts. Lonner readily admits that when he began his "formal" academic career in the mid-1960s, he was naïve with respect to the numerous contributions that many scholars made for decades to help practitioners and theoreticians understand the delicate interface between psychology and culture. He is not alone in that naivete. It was quite common for psychologists who were in graduate school during the first 70 years of the twentieth century to have had essentially no formal and sustained exposure to "culture" in their required course work. Of course, nearly everyone who is affiliated with the social sciences and humanities knows of the influence of Margaret Mead and Ruth Benedict, and several other anthropologists. Lonner was vaguely familiar with the names of John and Beatrice Whiting, well known because of their "Six Cultures" project. The Whitings's use of what they called a "psychocultural model" qualified them as pioneers in the field of psychological anthropology, a term and orientation for which the anthropologist Francis Hsu was well known. The names of Sir Frederick Bartlett and Wilhelm Wundt, both eminent psychologists, were also somewhat familiar because of their excursions into the topic of "culture". But it was quite rare that universities, especially those in the United States, offered complete courses in the *psychological* study of culture. Ask professors or colleagues in psychology over the age of 50 if they heard of people like psychologist W. H. R. Rivers of the famed Cambridge expeditions in the early 1900s to the South Pacific, or of the "carpentered world hypothesis" that was introduced in Segall, Campbell, and Herskovits's *The Influence of Culture on Visual Perception*, published in 1966. Chances are that the names evoke vague familiarity if they are recognized at all. Because of this, most psychologists were never fully introduced to any of the scholarly orientations where culture was a primary focus of inquiry and investigation. Consider, for example, how Michael Cole (1996) began chapter 1 in his influential 1996 book, *Cultural Psychology: A Once and Future Discipline*:

> According to the mythology propagated in standard American textbooks, the discipline of psychology began in 1879 when Wilhelm Wundt opened a laboratory in Leipzig. What was new about this "new" psychology of the 1880s was experimentation. Students of human psychological processes in laboratory settings used ingenious 'brass instruments' to present people with highly controlled physical stimuli (lights of precise luminance, sounds of precise loudness and pitch, and so on) and to record the content, magnitude and latency of their split-second accuracy. Mind, it was believed, could now be measured and explained according to the canons of experimental science.
>
> Less often noted—the topic received only a single sentence in Boring's (1957) tome on the history of psychology—was that Wundt conceived of psychology as necessarily constituted of *two* parts, each based on a distinctive layer of human consciousness, and each following its own laws using its own methodology.
>
> In recent years interest has grown in Wundt's "second psychology," the one to which he assigned the task of understanding how culture enters into psychological processes (Farr, 1983; Toulmin, 1980). My basic thesis is that the scientific issues Wundt identified were not adequately dealt with by the scientific paradigm that subsequently dominated psychology and the other behavioral-social sciences. As a consequence, attempts by psychologists working within the paradigm of twentieth-century experimental psychology to reintroduce culture as a crucial constituent of human nature face insuperable, unrecognized, difficulties. (pp. 7-8)

Having spent several years studying the ideas of Vygotsky, Luria, Bechterev, and others in the so-called Russian school of thought about culture, and helping to introduce terms such as the "zone of proximal development," Cole was one of several influential scholars who encouraged psychologists to explore the world beyond their borders. Fueled by a growing and sometimes impassioned plea by many to help rectify this unfortunate situation of perfunctory coverage, authors of introductory psychology texts—and/or their publishers—made some attempts to infuse "culture" into their broad, survey-like coverage of topics, all of which are affected by culture. Attempts to enter culture into the equation were often dismally shallow, stereotypical, somewhat "obligatory", and embarrassingly repetitive. For example, 20 years ago Lonner (1989) conducted a detailed analysis of about 35 of the most widely used introductory psychology texts in the United States (and also widely used in other countries). The purpose of the analysis—essentially a master's thesis under his direction by a German graduate student, Elke

Rumpel (now Murdock)—was to document the nature and extent of "cultural" coverage. That is, when, where, and how were terms like "culture," "ethnicity," "global," "universal," "race," and so forth, used in the texts? The most striking finding was that only three topics or "factoids" concerning culture were found in *all* texts in the sample: (1) the Whorf-Sapir hypothesis which dealt with linguistic relativity, (2) the Darwinian-oriented research by Ekman and others on the universality of the facial expression of emotions, and (3) the ongoing debate about cultural or "racial" bias in IQ tests. Moreover, many chose exactly the same quotes, photos, and citations when using these brief examples in an almost perfunctory and obligatory manner. A range of other topics were briefly mentioned in most of the texts, but they were barely noticeable and often served as "fillers." And some of the texts did not even mention culture.

It may be slightly unfair to "pick on" introductory texts in this context. They generally do a fine job of covering mammoth amounts of material. However, when one considers that approximately 1.5 million university students in the United States alone take introductory psychology each year (it is an extremely popular course), a golden educational opportunity seems to have been missed for many years. Elke Murdock and Lonner plan to replicate the study in 2007-08 to determine the extent to which the current generation of introductory psychology texts include "cultural content."

Consider also the general status of the psychological study of culture just prior to the development of the seminal six-volume *Handbook of Cross-cultural Psychology* (Triandis et al., 1980). The preface to these books said, in part

One of the key facts about psychology is that most psychologists who have ever lived and who are now living can be found in the United States. About 50,000 psychologists live in the United States and several thousand more graduate each year. The rest of the world has only about 20 percent of the psychologists that are now or have ever been alive. Moreover, psychology as a science is so overwhelmingly the product of German, French, British, Russian and North American efforts that it is fair to consider it an entirely European-based enterprise (with American culture considered the child of European culture). Yet, science aspires to be universal. Cross-cultural psychologists try to discover laws that will be stable over time and cultures, but the data base excludes the great majority of mankind who live in Asia and the Southern Hemisphere. Are so-called "psychological laws" really universal? Are theories merely parochial generalizations, based on ethnocentric constructions of reality? (p. ix)

Motivated to help correct this gross imbalance, cross-cultural psychologists wished to help develop a truly human psychology that would be as valid in Addis-Ababa, Beijing and Zimbabwe as it is in Athens, Boston, or Zanzibar. They wanted to contribute to the forging of a psychology "writ large," and in the process help explain human behavior in its innumerable exotic contexts.

Those were exciting times. However, the more that both of us became involved with the "new" cross-cultural movement, the more it validated the words of pioneering cross-cultural psychologist Gustav Jahoda, voiced some years ago, that cross-cultural psychology has a long past but a short history. In other words, it was the "new kid on the block." What JCCP and IACCP did, more than anything else, was to institutionalize cross-cultural psychology and encourage the discipline to "study all that is human," which was a slogan used to help define the scope of cross-cultural psychology. Since those early years, when IACCP began making solid contributions, we, the authors, have learned a great deal more than we ever thought we would about the "long past" that Jahoda mentioned. For centuries, psychologists and other scholars have been interested in the customs, beliefs, values, and virtually all aspects of the lives of people who lived across the river or over the next mountain range.

There are an incredible number of more or less specialized "culture-oriented" books in psychology that have appeared within the last 35 years. And in these books we learn much more about psychological methods and perspectives, as well as their origins. A number of people who identify more with cultural psychology than with cross-cultural psychology or psychological anthropology have made major contributions to the psychological study of culture. We have utmost respect for these scholars, for in many ways we consider them our mentors or intellectual guides. In addition to Michael Cole and Gustav Jahoda, already mentioned, we have been enriched with the works of such scholars as Richard Shweder, Jaan Valsiner, James Wertsch, Jürgen Straub, Hazel Markus, Shinobu Kitayama, and others who strongly identify with cultural psychology. Most importantly in terms of the focus of this text, we include the name of Ernest E. Boesch as one whose influence has been unique and substantial.

Ernest Boesch made lasting contributions to cultural psychology as a staunchly independent and profoundly deep thinker. Many years ago Boesch recognized the important influence of social and ecological contexts on human motivation and action. As already noted, he has often described his career in this field as a "journey of discovery." While he may have heard of similar work by other scholars, and while he was heavily influenced by the famous constructivist, Jean Piaget and other scholars at the University of Geneva, and also by his training in and practice of psychoanalysis, Boesch assiduously and painstakingly probed various aspects of human behavior on his own terms and in his own manner. Ernest Boesch's early career, as noted earlier, was essentially "orthodox."

After his formal lectures and exams in Geneva, he worked as school psychologist while completing his dissertation which addressed the assessment of children's learning. He was well on his way to having a productive and probably brilliant career as a journeyman researcher, whose work Piaget admired. However, Ernest was attracted to applications of psychology in real life settings. He became interested in the early work of UNESCO (see chapter 3) and eventually became the director of an extensive cross-cultural project in Bangkok, Thailand. Thus, in 1955 at age 39, the erudite Swiss-born Ernest Boesch left the familiar and comfortable European climes of academic life for a new world of applied research in a country that was completely new to him and was scarcely on anyone's psychological map.

This study of Ernest's life and work is largely about his Thailand experience and how it shaped his academic and personal life. He is an extraordinarily observant and concerned scientist. World events, especially the many tragic conflicts and disasters that make the daily headlines, have always captured his attention because they obviously reflect on humankind's winding journey toward intercultural awareness and respect. With scholarly and humanitarian zeal, he painstakingly developed a theory of "action-in-context" or, as it is more formally known, symbolic action theory.

It has been our honor and privilege to work on this book for nearly 5 years. We thank Ernest for his generous sharing of insights, information, and suggestions that have been offered throughout this project from the first interviews to the final proofreading of chapters. It was our good fortune to have traveled to his home near Saarbrücken, Germany, for detailed video-recorded interviews, and for pleasant lunches and dinners with Ernest and his wife, Supanee. They are both kind and considerate hosts. Being with them, even for short periods, is an education in its own right. We have both learned and benefited as a result of our interactions with them.

We know of no other book quite like this one. To our knowledge, extensive biographies of major contributors to the fields of cultural and cross-cultural psychology do not exist. Surely some books cover aspects of the lives of such scholars, but not in much detail. While this book is not a complete biography, we believe it contains important background information about EEB that is useful and important for those who are beginning as well as advanced students of cultural psychology. In this volume we have covered the main currents and themes of Ernest's life and a sample of some of his pivotal and insightful works. Spread across several topical areas, these readings demonstrate Ernest Boesch's rich intellectual breadth. We think this book will motivate and inspire those individuals who, like Boesch, want to discover for themselves the rewards, and the perils, awaiting them as they grapple with the fascinating complexities of culture.

BACKGROUND FACTORS IN
THE DEVELOPMENT OF THIS BOOK

The Saarland is among the more pastoral regions in Germany. Its modest per capita population, among the lowest density in the country, adds to its distinctly rural atmosphere. Historically, it has often been at the center of border struggles. Juxtaposing the Alsace-Lorraine region, for a significant period of time the area was practically controlled by France with which it shares a lengthy border. From 1919-1935 it was under the control of the League of Nations and was then returned to German administration. Many of the Saarland's long-term citizens are bilingual; the more highly educated are trilingual (German, French, and English). It is not uncommon to hear Letzeburgish, the official language of Luxemburg, on the streets and in the shops. Luxemburg is the only other country that shares a border with the Saarland.

The region was the setting of fierce ground and air battles during both world wars, especially during the weeks after the D-Day invasion in June of 1945 that ushered in the end of the Second World War and the fall of the Third Reich. In late 1944 General George C. Patton's 3rd Army slogged through the Saarland on its push toward Berlin. Nearby, there are separate and solemn military cemeteries for both Germans and their wartime enemies. The Saar region, with significant industrial capacity such as coal mines and steel mills, was bombed heavily during World War II, and has frequently experienced hard economic times. Nevertheless, the region's undulating hills, farms, and world-famous vineyards make it quite peaceful and livable, despite the ravages of war and economic downturns.

The Saarland's *Hauptstadt*, or main city, is Saarbrücken. A medium-sized city, it contains little of special interest to tourists. Because of its proximity to the Saar, Mosel, and Ruwer rivers where some of the world's finest white grapes are grown on steep riverbanks and adjoining hills, many sojourners who are motoring to Paris, or whose aim is the ancient Roman city of Trier with its famous *Porta Negra*, stop at one of the numerous vintners in search of bargains in white wines. Saarbrücken is the home of the excellent University of the Saar which was founded in 1948 by the French at a time when Saarland was a politically independent state but under strong French tutelage (1945-1959). Many of the university's buildings housed important parts of the German *Wehrmacht*. The postwar intent was for the university to become a European institution.

Approximately two kilometers from the university is the small *Stadtteil* (suburb) of Scheidt. A community of well-kept homes, Scheidt is a quiet and serene setting. Near the end of one of the short cul-de-sacs is a flat-roofed house with an attractive glassed entrance. Its address is 8 Drossel-weg and is the home of Professor Dr. Ernst Eduard Boesch and his wife, Supanee. While this manuscript is primarily about Ernest, as he usually calls himself in English and French, Supanee's indirect presence in these pages is strong. As wife and homemaker, she has assisted this accomplished scholar through her attention to careful and meticulous eating habits that have contributed to his living for more than 90 years and counting. Her deep dedication to Buddhism is impressive, and has contributed to a home that has a peaceful and unrushed ambience.

Upon entering their home, one is captivated by the rich collection of art and artifacts from various cultures, on Supanee's devotion to (and Ernest's deep interest in) Buddhism, as evidenced by numerous paintings, carvings, and sculptures of Buddha. The home reflects simple, comfortable, and contemplative living. There are no trappings of ultramodern urban life except for the high-tech television set that Supanee enjoys much more than Ernest. Until recently, a grand piano graced one corner of the spacious living room. Once the object of Ernest's respectable musical skills, he recently gave it to his son Christophe and his wife Hedwig. Their children will no doubt learn to play it.

Their private garden, completely visible through large windows, features a pond that many frogs call home much of the year. The garden is neat and manageable, and, consistent with Buddhistic thinking, looks natural rather than manicured like one would find in much of the Western world. Gracing the wall above a semicircular staircase leading to the lower level of their home is a striking painting of a bright sun trying to squeeze its rays through a stand of crimson barked trees.[1] Near the foot of the staircase one sees many books on well-kept bookshelves. Two rooms occupy most of the downstairs. One of them features Ernest's sauna, a health sanctuary that he religiously uses for at least an hour almost every night of the year. The other is well-equipped with exercise machines. The sauna, the exercise room, and meticulous and careful eating habits (mostly Supanee's Thai food that they usually prepare together, and Ernest's penchant for his homemade dark bread), punctuate Ernest's and Supanee's quest to take exceptional care of themselves. A moderate "heart incident" in 2004 contributed to Ernest's hypervigilance about his health.

Returning to the main floor, we step down the hall and, after passing a few small bedrooms, we enter Ernest's comfortable office. Immediately struck with the character and feel of the room, one senses that it is the pantry of ideas and the workroom of a reflective and productive intellectual. In short, one knows that a vital and dedicated scholar works there.

The bookcases, the walls, the specially designed desk with numerous cubbyholes used for sorting out correspondence with colleagues from many countries. An imposing and well-known photo of Jean Piaget, with his beret and trademark meerschaum pipe, is clearly visible on one of his bookshelves. Classic, and we suspect rather rare, books by Freud, Pierre Janet, Claperede, and other European scholars fill the glass-encased bookshelves. The books, with their bent spines and worn covers, testify to their frequent use for many years. There are valued collections of Asian and European art as well as sentiment-bearing art strategically arranged in the study. A numbered lithograph of a Picasso painting is well-placed. Considerable and sophisticated music appreciation is part of the sanctuary of ideas as well, but it never interferes with his writing. The absorbing activities of writing and listening to music are too intense to be done effectively at the same time, he says. Ernest loves Bach, Mozart, Chopin, Brahms, much of Beethoven, and so many more. He is less fond, however, of the more modern composers, although he appreciates some jazz legends such as Dave Brubeck and Oscar Peterson.

What we have here, then, is a comfortable home that has been a haven for Ernest and Supanee for many years. Since Ernest's retirement in 1986 at age 70, they seldom travel, and when they do it is usually for short distances. Ernest's failing vision places severe restrictions on nearly all of his activities, including reading. Fortunately, during the process of writing this book he was still able to use e-mail and see the monitor, provided the print was larger than normal and the background was set for maximum white on black contrast. Their home, carefully planned by both of them, specifically suits their life style. It is also the setting for the continuation of a love story involving two people from strikingly different cultures whose paths happened to cross during Ernest's first research stay in Thailand from 1955 to 1958.

Why have we chosen to describe the home on 8 Drosselweg in more detail than might be expected or warranted in a biographical sketch? Quite simply, the peaceful setting, the layout of the house, and its numerous artifacts and accoutrements are vitally important to the people who live there, and tell much about their lives and the meaning they attach to their belongings. In one of the documents we included in Part II, an essay titled "A Meditation on Message and Meaning," Ernest poignantly explains this meaningfulness. In that essay he describes the setting in his inimitable way (see chapter 15). One's home is indeed a reflection of one's character and priorities in life. In that room every item has meaning to Ernest. Most of the meanings are fairly trivial—for example, a book that he recently ordered or a bill that he intends to pay—but many are saturated with meanings that only he, and perhaps Supanee, can understand completely. His lengthy description also provides an excellent example of the kind of complex thinking that has gone into his life-long desire to explain the vicissitudes of human desires and potentials, all of which culminates in his major theoretical contribution, symbolic action theory.

One could, of course, go on and on with Ernest's descriptions and reflections of his belongings. To a cultural psychologist, understanding a person's surroundings and their intensely personal meanings to that person are essential to understanding the highly personal and idiosyncratic world of "person in context."

Lonner's Initial Involvement With Ernest Boesch: A First-Person Commentary

I knew the name, but hardly anything else, of Ernest Boesch for several years before I met him. He is well-known in some psychological circles as the founder of the so-called "Saarbrücken School of Cultural Psychology," and it was through that connection that I could roughly place him in the "family tree" of psychologists who are interested in the study of culture. His name is most closely associated with symbolic action theory (SAT), of which he is the chief architect. SAT is especially well-known among a relatively small but influential international group of scholars who identify with cultural psychology. Professor Boesch served as teacher and mentor of several psychologists who themselves have made major contributions to the field.

I first met Ernest in the Fall of 1984, shortly after arriving at the University of the Saar for a sabbatical year, with the aid of the Fulbright program and support from the Deutsch Forschung Gemeinschaft (DFG), which is the counterpart of the United States' National Science Foundation. My main sponsor was Professor Dr. Hans-Joachim Kornadt, who, like me, considered himself to be a cross-cultural psychologist. Professor Kornadt had previously worked in a research project of Boesch's Center, and although later engaged in a different area of psychology at the university, he and Boesch were collegially close. Shortly after my arrival in the Fall of 1984, I met Ernest for the first time. He was director of the Social-Psychological Research Center for Development Planning. At the same time, Robert B. Textor, then a professor of anthropology at Stanford University and now professor emeritus, was also visiting Saarland. He was working with Ernest on various mutual interests, including futuristic studies, still one of Bob's research interests. They had met earlier in Thailand, and had bonded there. The three of us quickly reached a high level of mutuality in our focus on the elusive concept of "culture." We decided to meet on a weekly basis to discuss both our common interests and to learn more about the different perspectives they represented in the study of culture. Thus, for periods of 2 to 4 hours, at least once a week, we met, we talked, and we thought. Representing cultural psychology (Boesch), cross-cultural psychology (Lonner), and cultural anthropology (Textor), the concept of culture was our common denominator. Our views were often quite different and challenging, but always interesting and mutually edifying. From the beginning of my relationship with Ernest Boesch my expectations were confirmed: that he was a dedicated, serious, and first-class scholar. I recall describing him to my wife, Marilyn, immediately after our first meeting. I told her that I finally met Ernest Boesch and exclaimed that he is a "gentleman scholar in the finest European tradition." I was impressed with his impeccable grooming, his multilingual fluency, his sincere politeness, his quiet graciousness, and the overall aura of intellectual excellence that radiated from a face that strikingly resembled the countenance of the famous French oceanographer, Jacques Cousteau.

Our weekly discussions tended to focus on Boesch's orientation to the psychological study of culture—that is, his approach to cultural psychology—and especially its unsettled relationship with cross-cultural psychology. As our sessions progressed, it became increasingly clear that his perspective on culture and human behavior needed to be presented to a much broader audience than they had been. Previously, his rather complex and detailed explanations of human behavior were known only to a relatively small number of his colleagues and former students. I urged him to consider writing a book that would articulate his unique views on the specific ways that one's cultural context influences all thought and behavior. Reluctant to do so at first, Bob Textor joined me to persuade Ernest to write the book. Thus, several years later, *Symbolic Action Theory and Cultural Psychology* (Boesch, 1991), was published. Bob Textor and I had the pleasure of writing an introductory commentary for the book, and Gustav Jahoda, the eminent scholar of culture mentioned earlier, wrote its foreword. I had the pleasure of working with him on the book, declining his occasional kind invitation that I join him in the effort as coauthor. Flattered by the invitation, it seemed impossible for me or anyone else to articulate his views on the intricate theories of an active, thinking, and reflective psychologist whose life intersects the complex workings of a specific culture at a specific juncture in time and space. I was learner, he was teacher—then, now, and always.

Our collegial friendship blossomed into a more personal relationship. Ernest and I have stayed in touch since our meetings in the mid-1980s, doing so largely via e-mail. Occasionally either I alone or my wife and I would visit him and Supanee for a day or two during trips to Europe. It was such an occasion in March, 2002 that I asked him if anyone had ever suggested or offered to write in some detail about his life and career.

Somewhat surprised that no one had (except for a few relatively brief autobiographical accounts), I asked him if he would allow me the opportunity to give it a try. He was flattered by the offer and I was immediately challenged by what I knew would be a daunting task. However, I strongly believed that he had an important story to tell. A profile that captured some important biographical details about his life and work would be helpful to others, particularly as an interesting contribution concerning the origins of cultural psychology.

Further impetus for this work resulted from a discussion I had with Elliot Aronson, the eminent social psychologist and professor emeritus at Stanford University, and Carol Tavris, who is probably best known as an author of introductory psychology texts as well as other writings. I asked them what they thought was the most important part of effectively writing about the life and times of a colleague. Almost in unison, they said that anyone who takes on such a task must feel deep and profound respect, sometimes awe, and an utter interest in the person being profiled. I do have profound respect for Ernest Boesch and have enjoyed listening to his interpretations and explanations of complex human behavior. He seems to reach his stride when he explains, usually spontaneously, the nature of some contemporary human foible or problem. A devoted humanitarian, one of his goals in life has been to give to others that which we expect ourselves—respect and understanding. Sometimes he reminds me of an elegant Swiss watch with its meticulous inner workings and reliability. His compassion, his dedication to scholarship, and his eloquent fluency in several languages are very impressive. It was an honor to see them act in unison.

In many ways I consider Ernest Boesch to be a mentor whom I met well after the midpoint of my career. Some academics argue that everyone needs a mentor who, early in one's vocation, is such a strong role model, intellectual advisor, and personal "super-ego" or omnipresent intellectual humunculus that he or she has a powerful effect on one's way of approaching the world and consequently one's professional development. Such a person should inspire, sometimes cajole, and continually influence one's thought and behavior within the context of his or her career, always in a supportive and caring manner. The fact that I cannot think of anyone who has served as my mentor suggests that I have never come close to having one. I have admired and have been strongly influenced by many "senior" psychologists and other academics with whom I have studied, and with whom I have "bonded." But I was never fortunate enough to interact with any of them in a close and supportive relationship for more than a few formative years. Thus, perhaps I saw in Ernest Boesch a person who could serve as the kind of "later in life" mentor or alter-ego that I had never experienced in my earlier academic career. Was it my longing for a mentor that motivated me to get involved in this process? If so, why get involved in such a time-consuming project at this time of my life? I retired from teaching and other routine academic duties in June, 2001, about a year before I offered to write about his life and contributions. After all these years why not cut back on my work? Is such dedication part of the nature of the love and admiration that one must have for another person prior to embarking on a biographical profile of him or her? These are interesting questions, personally. Denizens and budding mavens of the much younger generation might want to reflect on them from their own, highly personal, perspective.

Few people were aware that I made the commitment to launch this effort during the March, 2002 stopover at Professor Boesch's home. My wife, Marilyn, did, of course, and so did Ernest's wife Supanee, for they were present when we first discussed the project. My closest colleague at Western Washington University, Susanna A. Hayes, knew about my plans a few months after I made some initial progress. I knew that Sue had written a brief biography of Emmett Oliver, a well-known educator and elder of the Quinault Indian tribe of Western Washington, and I have known that case-study type documents, with the depth and breadth they require, were among her favorite ways to approach the understanding of people and their times. I thought of Sue as the perfect person to join me in this project. Thus, approximately a year after I committed myself to take on this task, I asked Sue if she would consider joining me. My invitation was prompted by the knowledge that her skills, insight, and compassion would help immeasurably in the project. Realizing that I would be discussing parts of my writings with her anyway, it was logical for her to join me. I am immensely pleased that she accepted my invitation. Thus, while this biographical profile was initiated by me and the collection of materials was my responsibility during the beginning, Sue and I are coauthors in every sense of the word. Fortunately, Sue has met Ernest and Supanee (see below), and now regards them as dear friends. The feeling is mutual. On two occasions, Sue and I traveled to Germany specifically to interview Professor Boesch and learn more about his life and career.

Structuring the Project

The material for this project came from a variety of sources. Like any excellent scholar, Ernest Boesch has written extensively. We had access to nearly all of his work, including many publications that are in German and French. His complete *Schriftenverzeichnis* (bibliography) is included in this book. We used many of these references, of course. In addition to his voluminous writings, we collected many hours of both audio and video recordings and interviews. On four different occasions, for a total of about 70 hours over 16 days, he was interviewed in his study. The first of these interviews was during my 4-day visit with him in December, 2002. My second meeting was in July, 2003, when my wife and I stopped by for a 3-day visit. On both occasions, I used a small portable tape recorder. The third meeting was in March, 2004, when Sue and I spent 5 days in Scheidt, commuting the short distance from Hotel Seewald in the neighboring town of Dudweiler. During that meeting both the tape recorder and my camcorder were used. Sue and I traveled again to Scheidt for our fourth meeting in late October 2005. During that meeting we carefully reviewed the drafts of the first few chapters, making necessary corrections and noting where revisions and additions would be necessary. Fortunately Sue has excellent note-taking skills that would be the envy of an accomplished foreign correspondent. The audio and videotapes for the first two meetings were then transcribed by Kay McMullen, a secretary in Western Washington University's Department of Psychology. In addition, there has been much e-mail correspondence involving the three of us. This often included the sharing of files as attachments.

The interviews were conducted entirely in English. German, of which I have a reasonable level of reading competence and enough "street" German to be dangerous, would have been a better mode of expression for Ernest because, as he told us several times, he believes he can express himself best in that idiom. French may have worked just as well. Fortunately, Ernest is perfectly able to express himself in English, as evidenced by the large number of works he has published in the only language that Sue and I know well.

Early in the writing of this profile of a scholar we were faced with a decision that all biographers, regardless of the depth of coverage, must face: Does one focus primarily on the *works* of the person being profiled, the *person* him or herself (as in a characterological study) or both? Because most of his works are available, especially his 1991 *Symbolic Action Theory*, we decided to focus more on the person and how his life has interacted with his theoretical and applied contributions rather than simply the latter. However, chapter 3, which was written in close collaboration with Ernest, focuses more on the theoretical and academic aspects of both his career and unique contributions as well as how his work can be understood in a broader context. Our view is that Boesch's work can be understood best against the backdrop of various experiences and choice-points in his life than merely a summary or litany of his scholarship.

Sue Hayes and I invite the reader to explore and enjoy this profile of Ernest Eduard Boesch. No biographical treatment, not even massive works written to cover the lives of such titans as Beethoven, Bach, Churchill, Darwin, and many others, have ever been complete. However, we hope that our attempt to profile Ernest's life in sufficient detail to explain his professional development will enhance the meaning of his contributions. In cultural psychology it goes without saying that no thoughts and actions in anyone's life are context-free. Whether considering one's biological and genetic background or one's environment, no study of a person can be complete without considering both. This book, then, is the result of our admiration of a remarkable and profound thinker whose life spanned most of the twentieth century. Ernest told us many times during our interviews that his perspective on human behavior led to various paths during his travels, with new elements and insights entering his thinking as he experienced the world and reflected on contemporary struggles. As a dedicated constructivist in the mold of one of his major influences, Jean Piaget, Professor Boesch readily admits that his views can, and have, changed in ways that his experiences suggested they should. In the same way, the experiences that Sue and I have had over the course of this project have changed, and especially with respect to a major question: For whom should it be written? While this profile is first a tribute to an original thinker in psychology, we hope that it will serve a much broader purpose than that. Beyond its biographical content, we hope it will serve as a document that instructs and informs students of culture. We envision this book to be one that could profitably be used in seminars and upper-division classes in cross-cultural and cultural psychology. We believe it will help explain why, and how, *Symbolic Action Theory* came into being. We especially hope that the readings we have selected, with Ernest's help, will be as instructive to hundreds of scholars as they have been to us.

As an overarching—and, consistent with much of his thinking, a polyvalent goal—we wrote it with the hope that the object of the treatise, Ernest E. Boesch, will consider our effort to be reasonably accurate. We think that what we have written captures a good portion of the core features of the personal and intellectual life of an original and unique thinker who stuck to his beliefs throughout his career and the true gentleman scholar in the grand tradition of European intellectuals that we think he represents. Ernest told us many times that he takes psychology very seriously, and that it is extremely hard work to develop anything in the discipline that will have some degree of staying power and influence. We hope that readers will appreciate this assessment and will be enriched and inspired by the life and works of a dedicated cultural psychologist and genuine humanitarian.

A Brief Overview of the Book

Beyond the informative initial material, the book is divided into two major parts. The four chapters in Part I focus on Ernest Boesch's early years in St. Gallen (chapter 1) and his enriched years in Geneva (chapter 2), where he studied under some brilliant and influential psychologists and educators. chapter 3 is exclusively devoted to what many regard to be the capstone of his career—symbolic action theory. Because he so painstakingly constructed SAT and is quite particular in how it is understood and articulated, we considered it important for him to be deeply and carefully involved in presenting an overview of his views. Knowing that he was still completely able to do so, we believe that a fitting component of this book, which is nearly entirely devoted to a profile of his life and work, would be a chapter that features the components of SAT as he wants them to be understood. Chapter 4, the "Intermezzo," is a charming essay written by Robert B. Textor, a retired Stanford University professor of anthropology who was mentioned earlier. Bob Textor was involved with Ernest in Thailand and watched him at work. They remain close friends.

Part 2 consists of 11 selected readings—book chapters, journal articles, essays—that provide solid examples of his work and how he has written about a number of topics. With just two exceptions, the readings appeared only in English. The exceptions are "Space and Time as Valence Systems," which originally appeared in German, and "Reality as Metaphor" which originally appeared in French. Both of these articles were translated especially for this book. The readings are organized somewhat thematically and, to a certain extent, chronologically. They were chosen, with Ernest Boesch's careful help, because they represent a good *durchschnitt* (cross-section) of his writings. Every one of the readings contains marvelous examples of the way Boesch thought about problems and issues, all the while trying to say important things about the nature of culture, or cultural artifacts, and what they can and should mean to caring individuals.

Concluding the book is chapter 16. In it we wished to say a few more things about Ernest Boesch, his life and times, and his legacy. Following that is his complete bibliography.

NOTE

1. This painting, with Ernest and Supanee's permission, was used for the dust cover. The painting was purchased in 1957, in a common Bangkok art shop.

REFERENCES

Boesch, E. E. (1991) *Symbolic action theory and cultural psychology*. Berlin, Germany: Springer Verlag.

Boring, E. G. (1957). *A history of experimental psychology* (2nd ed.). New York: Appleton-Century-Crofts.

Cole, M. (1996). *Cultural psychology: A once and future discipline*. Cambridge, MA: Belknap/Harvard.

Farr, R. M. (1983). Wilhelm Wundt (1832-1920) and the origins of psychology as an experimental social science. *British Journal of Social Psychology, 22*, 289-301.

Lonner, W. J. (1989). The introductory psychology text and cross-cultural psychology: Beyond Ekman,, Whorf, and biased I.Q. tests. In D. Keats, D. Monro, & L. Mann (Eds.), *Heterogeneity in cross-cultural psychology: Selected papers from the ninth international conference of the International Association for Cross-Cultural Psychology*. Lisse, The Netherlands: Swets and Zeitlinger.

Segall, M. H., Campbell, D. T., & Herskovits, M. J. (1966). *The influence of culture on visual perception*. Indianapolis, IN: Bobbs-Merrill.

Toulmin, S. (1980). Toward reintegration: An agenda for psychology's second century. In R. A. KIasschauand & F. S. Kessel (Ed.), *Psychology in society: In search of symbiosis*. New York: Holt, Rinehart and Winston.

Triandis, H. C., Berry, J. W., Brislin, R. W., Draguns, J. G., Heron, A., Lambert, W. W., & Lonner, W. J. (Eds.). (1980). *Handbook of cross-cultural psychology* (Vols. 1-6). Boston: Allyn and Bacon.

CHRONOLOGY OF ERNEST E. BOESCH'S LIFE

December 26, 1916   Born in St. Gallen, Switzerland.

September, 1921   Enters elementary school, highly motivated as a reader, musician.

September, 1928   Enters Latin branch of high school.
Parents divorce, mother and sister leave home. Ernest lives with his father.

1930   Transfers to commercial branch of high school. Studies English, French, Spanish. Economic depression brought about effects of poverty. Paternal Grandfather dies. Grandmother moved into the home with Ernest and his father. Returned to Latin high school and completed his studies with excellence.

1936   Served required military time in medical corps as conscientious objector.

October 1939   Began studies in Geneva at Institute Jean Jacque Rousseau at University of Geneva (Arrival at Geneva experienced as a second birth, a new beginning). Faculty members included: Edouard Claparede, Pierre Bovet, Jean Piaget, Andre Rey, Richard Meili, Gertrude Dworetzky).

1941   Meets Claire, a student in interpreter's school, in Geneva.

August 1942   Married Claire.

August 1943   First child, Andreas, born.

1943   Moves from Geneva to St. Gallen and begins his career as the Canton's school psychologist.

1943   Successful defense of dissertation, Andre Rey, primary faculty advisor.

Chronology continues on next page

Chronology of Ernest E. Boesch's Life Continued

1951   Receives and accepts call to Chair of Psychology at newly founded University of the Saar.
Christophe born in St. Gallen.
Begins to participate in UNESCO meetings on child psychology.

1952   Published a revision of his dissertation on assessment of children, based on his experiences in St. Gallen.

1953   Monique, third child, is born in Saarbrücken.

1955   Departs for Bangkok to direct the International Institute on Child Studies Meets Supanee, his Thai language instructor.

1958   Returns to Saarbrücken, his family, and University teaching.

1959   Divorces Claire.

1960   Returns to Bangkok, marries Supanee. Returns to Saarbrücken with Supanee. Claire and Children leave for Paris, eventually on to Geneva. Published *The Bangkok Project, Step 1* (described UNESCO research program).

1986   Retired from University of the Saar. Invited address at the 1986 meeting of the International Association of Cross-Cultural Psychology, Istanbul.

1991   Celebration of 80th birthday in Berlin at Max Planck Institute.

1996 to present   Continued writing on many topics (see bibliography).

INTRODUCTION INTO IDEAS

Experience, Method, and Dynamic Self: Prefatory Comments on Ernest E. Boesch's Contributions to Cultural Psychology

Jürgen Straub and Arne Weidemann

"The symbolism of action … is indeed pervasive and complex. Lacking the conventional constancy of signs and icons, it is likely to vary according to individuals, situations and cultural inputs. This variability creates methodological problems, but commerce and politics, fashion and art, even religion, all make use of it—pragmatically, and often to our detriment. Therefore, cultural psychology should not shy away from its complexities. Much in our world, pleasant as well as worrying events, can be understood only by understanding its symbolic intricacies."

—(Boesch, 2001, p. 482)

THE UNITY OF BOESCH'S PSYCHOLOGY

The reader of an academic disquisition expects an instructive lesson. Such readings can be rather prosaic affairs. Where is the student who would still expect to be "educated" by such specialized literature? Who would expect an experience that not only requires intellectual presence but that addresses, challenges, and perhaps even changes the "whole person?"

Usually, scholars and students do not read academic publications as a source of "dynamic self-knowledge" or as a means to test and expand the limits of their selves. They are rather modest and only expect an increase in their factual knowledge and an improvement in their theoretical and methodological expertise. To study means to accumulate expert knowledge in a very specific academic field. Such knowledge can be tested easily in exams. Even in the humanities such knowledge—unless it is philosophical in nature—can be easily and systematically represented, perhaps even in symbolic forms such as graphs, diagrams, and charts. It is relatively easy to teach and memorize such knowledge. Classes at universities and colleges serve that purpose and so do textbooks, which repeat and expand the material taught in class. As an academic discipline, psychology is no exception to this academic rule. The balance sheet of its disciplinary achievements is drawn regularly; the academic state of the art is constantly reviewed. In classes and textbooks, confirmed findings are discussed side by side with outdated and innovative research methods as well as with old and new theories.

Ernest Eduard Boesch's list of publications is impressive (see bibliography). It documents the continuous creativity of an agile mind. However, Boesch never wrote a "textbook" introducing the basic theoretical tenets of his thought and research, but he did outline his approach at a somewhat advanced level (Boesch, 1991). Sporadically, he would systematize his own positions and contrast them with competing positions and perspectives (e.g., Boesch & Straub, 2006). Nor has anybody, to this day, penned a book that is based on Boesch's work and could justifiably be categorized as a challenging "textbook." Critical responses to Boesch's psychology are still negligible (and often meaningless or unconvincing). Moreover, the criticism does not represent the growing recognition of an outstanding work. Only recently have Boesch and the Saarbrücken tradition in cultural psychology (Valsiner, 1997) started to win the recognition and the public tribute that they deserve.[1]

The few existing studies on symbolic action theory and cultural psychology are restricted to a review of the most basic elements of a way of thinking as it evolved over a period of 5 decades. Usually these studies concentrate on a few, select aspects. Nevertheless, such contributions to textbooks (e.g., Cranach & Tschan, 1997) and journals (e.g., Baltes, 1997, 2001) provide a first impression of the originality and creative power of a "grand old man" of scientific psychology in the twentieth and twenty-first century. Boesch continues to expand his body of work that reflects his efforts to clarify and refine his thinking. Therefore, it is difficult to characterize his contributions to the discipline fully.

These investigations are far from providing a comprehensive survey, one that would do justice to all the manifold elements and facets of Boesch's work. They particularly tend to elide the results of Boesch's extensive empirical research, one that can be called an "empiricism of its own kind" (more on this below). At best, extant writings present small examples here and there, which illustrate the significance, function, and benefit of the theoretical concepts found in Boesch's work. This obvious deficiency is particularly unfortunate since in Boesch's empirical studies various aspects of his thoughts and his experiences form a productive liaison. Closely interwoven, symbolic action theory and cultural psychology are both products of and indispensable prerequisites of his work. The same is true for the phenomenological (descriptive) and the hermeneutic (understanding), in short, for the *interpretive methods* that fit the theoretical foundations to which they inextricably belong (more below). As Boesch's empirical studies demonstrate, theory, method and empirical research form a unity, which if ignored can result in grave misunderstandings. Part of this unity is the aspiration of Boesch's psychology to make a difference and *say something to people*. For his readers, Boesch's texts embody what many scholars and students have been looking for as "food for thinking." Those who partake of this "food" run a two-fold risk: they are instructed and, consequently, extend their knowledge; but they may also feel the need to work with and change their selves.

THE THEMATIC PLURALITY AND LINGUISTIC WEALTH OF BOESCH'S EMPIRICAL PSYCHOLOGY

Boesch's psychology represents the entire palette of our life-world experiences and expectations. Nothing human is strange to it, or rather, nothing shall remain strange to it. It approaches the fields of experience and the horizons of expectation in a cautious (on these terms see Koselleck, 1985), interested, and concentrated manner. It does so based on a concept of "experience" which transgresses and ultimately overcomes the limits of the modern idea of scientific empiricism. That is why we spoke earlier about an "empiricism of its own kind," which does not refer to something that is unknown or absolutely new. On the contrary, the methodological shaping of experience as it typically occurs in symbolic action theory and cultural psychology is reminiscent of the Aristotelian concept of "experience," at least in principle (and that is what we are concerned with at this point!).

When Aristotle said $\varepsilon\mu\pi\varepsilon\iota\rho\iota\alpha$ (Greek: empeiría; Lat.: experientia; Eng.: experience; German: Erfahrung, Empirie), he was not thinking of something that could be *produced* under the standardized, controllable, and reproducible conditions of the laboratory. Aristotle was not concerned with producing anything at all. His idea of a specific form of knowledge was radically different from scientific empiricism that emerged in the modern age. As a result of the so-called Galilean paradigm shift, which revolutionized the sciences by introducing new methodologies, "empiricism" (in the Greek sense of $\varepsilon\mu\pi\varepsilon\iota\rho\acute{\iota}\alpha$) became a rather restrictive form of research. Only a methodology that relies on the feasible, controllable, and calculable, scientists said (and many would still say today), promises to yield "truly scientific" results. According to this approach, access to new knowledge depends on clearly defined conditions under which such knowledge can be *produced*. It is not a secret that this kind of research serves the purpose of subjecting nomological theories to empirical tests in order to prove their validity. To a large degree, contemporary psychology is indebted to this modern concept of empiricism. Boesch's approach moves away from the empiricist ideal of producing knowledge under experimental conditions, without deviating from the claim of pursuing a methodically conducted, empirical science! Yet Boesch does not deny the value of experimental research. Quite to the contrary, he considers it absolutely imperative for certain purposes. His own psychology, however, pursues other goals and is based on concepts of experience and empirical research that are different from the ideal of the experiment that is upheld by the nomological sciences.

Like Aristotle, Boesch is interested in the life experiences of human beings, and in the ways they think and talk about their experiences with others without the influence or direction of scientists. His psychology studies the kind of experience we all have as members of groups or as individuals, and which we often articulate in slightly awkward and inaccurate ways. In one way or another, we continuously have and "process" such experiences, consciously or unconsciously. Experiences refer to past events. Expectations anticipate hoped-for or feared experiences. Nothing that can be included in the realm of the everyday reality of human life and action is excluded from Boesch's psychology. On the contrary, everything can be interesting and relevant, regardless of whether scientists have a methodological key to it or not. It is not the routinely available scientific methods that define what will become the subject of scientific research; rather, symbolic action theory and cultural psychology concern themselves with "the burning issues" of human life as they occur.

The methodological repertoire of Boesch's psychology must be adjusted to these issues and to the phenomena these issues address. At times this means that his work has to develop suitable methods in order to pursue its scientific interests, and sometimes must fall back on an unconventional modus operandi, which is unconventional only when compared to the tenets of modern methodology. Not every step on the path toward scientific knowledge can be strictly regulated. As indispensable as methodological rationality is, it still has its limits. These limits are marked by life-world experiences and expectations, which appear and change every day, but which can never be *produced*, particularly not under the standard-ized, controlled, and reproducible conditions of the laboratory.

At the core of Boesch's thinking and research is the truly complex existence of human beings in a field of action. This surfaces in much of his writing, but perhaps not as obviously as in his most recent books (Boesch, 1998, 2000, 2005). Theories and methods make only a marginal appearance in these texts. Instead, Boesch deals with all kinds of phenomena, describing them carefully, analyzing them meticulously, and reflecting upon them sagaciously. When all is said and done, the reader of Boesch's work encounters a rather incredible variety of themes. The ordinary and inconspicuous is considered as important as the extraordinary; the profane is of no less interest to him than the transcendental, the numinous, and the sacred. Picasso's "manic relationship to work" and his complicated relationship to women are as fascinating to Boesch as the visual arts, music, literature, and poetry. In Boesch's work, gender relationships, sexuality, and the many forms of love, as well as their often unexpected, unplumbed depths, repeatedly appear as subjects of detailed analysis. In addition to the "dramatic" ups and downs of our existence, he is equally interested in rather banal actions, ranging from buying a fountain pen to talking to oneself while working. This psychology addresses human desires, hopes, and moments of deep satisfaction as well as the suffering of rejection, disappointment, misery, and death. His texts move the reader from reflections about the boundless human desire for optimizing the self-world relationship to passages about the omnipresent threat to the human potential for action. The pursuit of well-founded knowledge and the need for rationality are as present in Boesch's works as are faith and religion and the entire range of emotional modes of approaching the world. In Boesch's action theory and cultural psychology, human creativity is treated on equal terms with aggressiveness and destructiveness. Love and hate are equally important subjects. When Boesch speaks about responsibility and welfare, he may also consider it important to reflect deeply on violence and terror that are ever present in human life past and present. This deep and intense approach to the study of psychology cannot be executed with expectations of obtaining measured and testable results as is often the case in empirically-oriented scientists. Boesch's writing is deeply anchored in the "humanist" interest in enlightenment, without sharing the exaggerated rationalism or the naïve optimism of the belief in progress of past eras. For Boesch, "culture" is a site of ambiguity and conflict. It is "Janus-faced" (Boesch, 2005, p. 96), simultaneously representing the inextricable network of good and evil. From a psychological perspective, the appealing and the repulsive, attraction and revulsion are much more closely related than we humans like to admit. We see the foreign and the other (and all its variations and nuances) as simultaneously fascinating and frightening. This applies not only to the other and the foreign *outside* of one's own self, but, as Boesch points out again and again, particularly to the self *as* foreign and other.

Symbolic action theory and cultural psychology serve as instruments for the investigation of the broad variety of cultural life forms, language games, and practices, of their commonalities *and* differences. Boesch's psychology almost always starts from a concrete, life-world phenomenon: a peculiar thought or disconcerting sensation, an intimate or a frightening desire, an odd idea or simply from an ordinary "praxic" action. Like Sigmund Freud, he scrutinizes that which appears to be obvious and natural, and focuses his attention on inconspicuous details, hidden interconnections, and contra-intuitive correlations. Like Freud, Boesch is endowed with a talent for linguistic expressiveness, one which is rare in the field of psychology. His writings give impressive evidence of how deeply the skill of the observer depends on the opulence, complexity, and precision of the descriptive *language* at his disposal.

Many of Boesch's psychological studies exemplify the fact that this science, as soon as it is dedicated to life-world phenomena, demands a multiplicity of research skills. The "receptive senses," as well as the keen eye and open ear of the experienced observer, are indispensable, as are his or her gift for empathy and flexibility. The cool rationality and the analytical gaze of a theoretically and methodologically skilled thinker are as important as the sensitivity, fantasy, and imaginative powers of a writer who depends on the medium of language for articulating his or her insights and, thus, often *struggles* for the appropriate form of representation. Boesch's approach to the discipline reminds us of a fact that is all too willingly "forgotten" in modern psychology, namely, that some psychological knowledge can only be accessed through the author's literary competence. Many psychologists, particularly those who are influenced by neurosciences and work in the dominant field of "biopsychology," still suggest that scientific progress arises out of the availability and professional use of new technological apparatuses and procedures. In some areas of psychology, technology may indeed be indispensable; in other areas, however, progress depends on other approaches (Laucken, 2001).

In symbolic action theory and cultural psychology, researchers need an extraordinary amount of linguistic sensibility and creativity and Boesch's writings demonstrate this. Neither is it surprising that his own books are rich in elucidating metaphors, unusual analogies, and daring comparisons, and often display an elaborate narrative structure. In Boesch's symbolic action theory and cultural psychology, one often "stumbles" over such innovative (and hardly translatable) terms as *Fantasmus* (fantasm),

Gewahrnis (the state and moment of a realization), or *Schemen* (shadow/specter) which Boesch developed to articulate his theoretical views.

Boesch has repeatedly insisted on foreign language competence. Those who want to understand a form of life that is neatly interwoven with language games, especially one that is completely alien, needs to be able to speak the language that belongs to this life form. Boesch himself learned Thai in Thailand (and encouraged his collaborators to follow his example). He even pointed out that his thoughts show traces of the language in which they first came into shape. Many of Boesch's publications were written in German, some were authored in French or English.[2]

No matter in what language this brilliant author wrote, his own life makes an appearance in all of his texts. Often it is hardly noticeable, sometimes it is hard to miss. Many of Boesch's examples originate from his own everyday life, which constantly changed over the many years he spent on different continents. They reflect an unusual life story that was defined by concentrated work and which is the subject of the present volume.

Attentive readers will have no problem realizing what Boesch's texts are all about. They will relate the stories, observations, and analyses offered by Boesch to their own (perhaps not yet understood) experiences and expectations. Even though Boesch draws his examples from the wealth of his own experiences, his psychology, almost without exception, speaks about "things" that concern us all. He moves actions and the human potential for action into the center of our attention (see chapter 3). He takes seriously that which impairs or threatens, which fosters and enriches this potential. One of the recurring themes in Boesch's psychology is our human ability to navigate through a world structured by signs *and* symbols, to act in the material, social, and cultural world, to achieve or not to achieve one's goals and realize one's action potential. Everything that moves and haunts people, that motivates, inhibits, or paralyzes them—this is what his psychology is interested in.

NORMATIVE CLAIMS, LIFE-WORLD FOUNDATION, AND THE LIMITS OF UNDERSTANDING: NOTES ON READING THIS BOOK

Occasionally, Boesch's writings display opinions that are based on values, beliefs, and personal perspectives which the author is not willing to yield. He upholds the scientific ideal of objectivity and is open to all kinds of possibilities in terms of moral and political perspectives and values. But he is far from being morally or politically indifferent. Boesch does not shy away from expressing strong opinions, which adds a "touch of cultural criticism" to symbolic action theory and cultural psychology. (Boesch's discourse on listening to music may serve as an illustration here; see Boesch, 2005, pp. 107-112, and particularly pp. 165-168). Readers will notice Boesch's critical stance in this book. And they will have to deal with it and to use and sharpen their own sense of judgment.

So far, students who wanted to draw a broad and accurate picture of symbolic action theory and cultural psychology were referred to Boesch's writings. Yet for novices, who commit themselves to the study of psychology, his texts are challenging. Anyone who has ever made an effort to teach Boesch's psychology to students and discuss his texts in seminars will agree with what the author himself said about many of his thoughts and insights: "This sounds simple, but it is not" (Boesch, 2001, p. 481). Sometimes a text that appears to be perfectly lucid and comprehensible turns out to be hard to understand—particularly in all its prerequisites, implications, and consequences.

Saying this, we are not only referring to the theoretical and methodological finesse that is a trademark (and, in fact, a prerequisite) of Boesch's psychology. This psychology is demanding and based on a fairly large array of prerequisites, not the least because it processes, reflects, and integrates complex experiences which its author had *in real life*, not vicariously through reading books. Boesch's research and thinking is firmly anchored in the everyday world of real life. It is marked by the life experiences of a man who knew how to combine mobility and flexibility with continuity and persistence, and that over many decades. Not all readers share this wealth of experience, which would make it possible or easier to understand what Boesch has to say. The difficulties of reading Boesch and the limits of understanding his psychology lead us to an insight which, although it may be uncomfortable, we would be ill-advised to ignore: Not everybody can learn (or teach) everything at every time, and with no effort at that. Learning is a process that is possible only if the learner meets certain preconditions, (which, of course, can be provided, at least in part), and if she or he is willing to put some effort into it. Sometimes this may require "external support."

Walter J. Lonner, Boesch's American friend, and Lonner's colleague Susanna A. Hayes, took the initiative and shepherded the creation of this text. It will promote and broaden the awareness of and the reception of Ernst Eduard Boesch's work. It will introduce Boesch's work to many who are interested in the evolution of his approach to the study of cultural psychology. For this purpose and for good reasons Lonner and Hayes have presented information about Boesch's personal and academic development that will allow readers to understand how he arrived at his current place as one of the founders and major contributors to cultural psychology. This interrelationship is the focus of chapters 1 through 3, but it also appears in Robert Textor's "Intermezzo" (chapter 4) and other parts of this volume. Often it was so-called "critical life events" that touched and moved Boesch along the course of his long, varied, and productive life. By reflecting and thoroughly processing such "life events," Boesch saw himself encouraged, if not compelled, to review and, if necessary, revise his scientific theory and methodology. This provided new insights which had a lingering effect on the style of his psychological thought and research.

In the following sections of this introduction, we will concentrate on a few other aspects which we think are necessary for understanding symbolic action theory and cultural psychology. One of the central concepts in Boesch's work is the *systematic function of experience*. This term refers not only to the intricate relationship between the author's biographical experiences and his scientific interests and sensibilities, but also to his style of thought and research. We also included this term in the title of this introduction because it points out the differences between empirical and cultural approaches to the study of psychology.

Work as complex as the theory and methods of cultural psychology—and more specifically the theory and methods of Ernest Boesch—offer many opportunities for expansive coverage. Many particular topics can be the point of focused study. The following parts of this introduction are written to enrich the readers' understanding of the work of Professor Boesch. We hope this content will complement the basic assumptions of Boesch's symbolic action theory as he described it himself (Boesch, 1997, 2001). In addition, the following will serve as an introduction to the work of Lonner and Hayes as they present elements of Boesch's life and works (with Boesch's endorsement and approval).

POLYVALENT ACTIONS:
SOME THEORETICAL CHARACTERISTICS

The concept of goal-oriented and purposive action is central to Boesch's psychology. Unlike other psychological action theories, which may at first appear to be similar, symbolic action theory and cultural psychology go beyond the theoretical scope of intentionalist and teleological models of action (e.g., Boesch, 1980, 1991). Students of his "material" analyses will easily recognize a recurring discussion of actions, actions which are always goal and purpose oriented, and which appear either to be enormously complex or sometimes not even recognizable. This, however, constitutes one of the as-yet underestimated strengths of symbolic action theory, which overcomes the one-sidedness and narrowness of many action theories that have come to dominate psychology since the late 1970s (see Straub, 1999).

Initially, Boesch's action model (see chapter 3) was based on the cybernetic model of a feedback loop and assumed that every action serves one goal or purpose. Over the years, the goal-orientations became more and more complex. Moreover, the theoretical idea of polyvalence undermined the basic structure of the intentionalist model in so far as *meanings* are not the exclusive result of goal-oriented and purposive action (they can also evolve from cultural and social rules or from narratives and myths). As time passed, symbolic action theory and cultural psychology gradually assumed an ever more differentiated and complex character. This was not the least due to the fact that the *semantic structure* of actions increasingly moved to the center of theoretical attention.[3] One could describe Boesch's theory as a psychological pragma-semantics of human action. Its terms and concepts are coined for the meaningful praxis in which we are entangled on a daily basis. This applies not only to the concept of polyvalence (which has already been mentioned several times), but also to concepts such as myth and fantasm, the concept of the symbol (which is different from that of the sign), as well as to many other basic concepts (see chapter 3). Boesch's *symbolic* action theory refers to an extremely complex mesh of cultural, social, and individual as well as denotative and primarily connotative *meanings,* which form pragma-semantic networks. Boesch speaks of "networks of meanings," which can be examined by dint of a method known as connotational analysis. It is exactly these *meanings* that the discipline of psychology has to address if it wants to arrive at substantial statements about actions. In its critical reception, this fundamentally important theoretical and strategic decision is far too often ignored or marginalized. If the human world is conceptualized as an inevitably meaningful reality, then psychology is obligated to use hermeneutic, interpretive, and empathic methods, traditionally known in the German-speaking world as *sinnverstehende Methoden*, "methods of hermeneutic understanding" (Habermas, 1967/1982; 1981, pp. 114-203; Straub, 1999).

Boesch did not tire of demanding the application of these methods again and again. This call can also be heard in the contributions to this book as well as in the publications of other, like-minded authors. We would like to mention one of those authors here because his action and cultural psychology displays rather astounding similarities to Boesch's approach, although the two "grand old men" of twentieth and twenty-first century psychology never met or otherwise communicated with each other. In one of his most important books, with the telling title *Acts of Meaning*, Jerome Bruner observed in a rather casual, incidental manner that his action and cultural psychology was "an interpretive psychology, in much the sense that history and anthropology and linguistics are interpretive disciplines" (Bruner, 1990, p. 118). These disciplines each dedicate themselves to the meanings that people attach to their actions and their lives, a task that connects them, regardless of all other differences. Their interest is in phenomena—such as, for example, actions—which are already hermeneutically-mediated in the everyday fabrix of life. Anthony Giddens (1976), who insisted on a methodological difference between natural sciences on the one hand, and the humanities and social sciences on the other, aptly described the basic methodological structure of these disciplines as a "double hermeneutic."

It is exactly this demand for an analysis of meanings that met and continues to meet with a certain degree of resistance in academic psychology. This is because such an analysis carries considerable methodological consequences. To begin with, such an analysis requires a "nonrestrictive," unprejudiced form of scientific empiricism, one that is open to the experiences of others and strangers (see above). Then it necessitates the application of interpretive, hermeneutic, or empathic methods (see also Straub, 2006; Straub & Weidemann, 2006). But this is something that to some representatives of the discipline is nothing short of blasphemy. If interpretation and understanding become the name of the psychological game, then, as some psychologists see it, the authority of objectivity and certainty will soon dwindle. And this is correct: There is no "objective knowledge" (in the sense of irrevocable and uncontested findings) if all knowledge is (and must be) acquired through the employment of interpretive methods. Every interpretation is dependent on contingent, that is, social, cultural, and individual preconditions. This is not the place for absolute knowledge. However, this is not to conclude that interpretive disciplines, in turn, foster absolute subjectivity and arbitrariness, and that everyone could just do and say whatever comes to their minds. Interpretation also needs to follow certain rules. And no one can evade the duty of rationally explaining and validating his or her statements. Interpretive methods need to guarantee that the development of scientific experiences and knowledge are understandable and controllable by other researchers.

The human world is a world of meaningful, cross-referential signs and symbols. It is a world of dynamic, semiotic, and symbolic systems meshed with the practical reality of history. "A broom is a broom is a broom," Boesch once quoted, but only to show the meaninglessness of such simplistic realism by a careful analysis of the polyvalent enmeshment of a broom, which occasionally even made it a symbolic apotropaic object (Boesch, 1983). Culture is a symbolic praxis. Its elements, including its objectivations, have a meaning because humans, in groups and as individuals, *give* meaning to them. Psychology is enmeshed in this process as well, but not unknowingly. On the contrary, it is anxious to fulfill methodological requirements when engaged in the analysis of meanings.

And how do symbolic action theory and cultural psychology fulfill these requirements? We will briefly discuss this question in the following section.

Connotation Analysis

Connotation analysis is a method applicable in many areas of empirical research and is an integral part of Boesch's symbolic action theory and cultural psychology (see e.g., Boesch, 1982, 1991). In 1976/1977 he for the first time wrote at length about this method that is based on Freud's technique of free association (Boesch, 1976b, 1977). Boesch (1991) has expanded the use of connotation analysis beyond Freud's free association technique, but of course in his research work he used various other methods as extensively explained in two chapters published in 1971. However, he upholds a systematic relationship between "biotic" (qualitative) and experimental methods: The first should make full use of careful observation, while experimental investigations should follow and control with more precision—where amenable—certain finds of biotic, or cultural, research (p. 364). This little publication— reprinted with an additional introduction in spring 2006[4]—being of special importance, shall here be considered a little more comprehensively. Boesch describes the application and the benefits of this method in different contexts. He extensively explains how he taught connotation analysis to university students. Attention was often focused on their associations, imaginations, and waking dreams.

The results of connotation analysis, however, do not exclusively refer to aspects of an individual's personal existence, or his I-world relations, but always to "transindividual" psychological contexts and psycho-socio-cultural relations as well. This becomes very obvious in works of his such as the analyses of famous works of art such as Picasso's painting "Guernica" (Boesch, 1991, pp. 279-294), of poems like Rilke's "Cornet" (Boesch, 1982), of literary narratives and travelogues like those by Cees Noteboom or Adolf Muschg (Boesch, 2000, 2005, pp. 169-222), but also of ritual as well as everyday objects and actions (see Boesch 1982, 1987, 1991, 1998, 2005). Student's associations were also analyzed in this way.

For instance, Boesch interprets a student's fantasy that revolves around death as follows:

The idea of death as the satisfying young lover, as the true love that promises complete emotional security, is a mytheme which has become suspect to our rational minds, but which, if McClelland is correct, still lives on as a fantasm. (Boesch, 2006, p. 42)

Boesch further maintains "that the reality of death (and perhaps of suffering) is superimposed by a fantasm in which an unfulfilled childhood desire for security mingles with unsatisfied erotic fantasies and a self-denying resignation resulting from emotional disappointments" (Boesch, 2006, pp. 42-43). Again, these words clearly emphasize past life experiences and developments which may have had a lasting impact on an individual. But at the same time, Boesch articulates a general insight from the reservoir of the action and cultural psychology of death (and suffering). Death is a natural occurrence, a (social) mytheme, and a (subjective) fantasm (a self-fantasm, a partner-fantasm, etc.), all at the same time. As an inescapable event in the life of every individual, death is part of the natural order of things. But it is also part of the collective and individual world of valences. It is polyvalent. The palimpsest of meanings is present in many different actions. And connotation analysis enables one to recognize this.

Always paying attention to "structural constancies," the interpreter looks for recurring themes and, in the course of the analysis, forms an ever more precise picture of the relevant connotative relations between fantasms and myths. Thus, as in the analysis of the student's above-mentioned waking dream, the interpreter talks about the "relationship between the state of threat and security," "forlornness" (also in a metaphorical sense), the "inadequacy of one's own efforts," and about many other things (Boesch, 2006, pp. 28-31). Boesch organizes these themes and analyzes them in terms of their situative, functional, and analogical symbolics (Boesch, 1976a); he then constructs his connotation analyses in such a way that the inner consistency and coherence of the interpretations become more and more prominent. When analyzing Picasso's 'Guernica' he thus speaks of Picasso's "need to overcome the threat felt in his narcissistic fantasms by transforming them into myths" (Boesch, 1991, p. 294). Here, too, like in other of Boesch's texts where Picasso and his work play a prominent role, the aim is not to provide a complete and all-encompassing psychogram of the artist but rather to highlight the indissoluble interweaving of myth, fantasm and other layers of meaning. It is not the objective (or the objectively measurable) "world of facts" that is of interest here but the subject's "world of valences." Connotation analysis does not aim for the cognition of objective issues and facts. Rather, it has an eye for subjects and their relationship to themselves and the world. Taking this as its starting point, Boesch's psychology is capable of recognizing psychological phenomena that form the basis for intersubjective comprehension and consensus.

Boesch distinguishes between manifest and latent meanings, with the latter being the primary subject of connotation analysis. The networks of connotations, which comprise our fantasies, our imaginative as well as our praxic actions (Boesch, 1991, pp. 73-86), are not there for all to see. Their reconstruction is a labor-intensive process, one that relies on the hermeneutic procedures of connotation analysis. This method requires a considerable amount of life experience and scientific skills on the part of the interpreter. But it also draws on other sources of knowledge, interpretive perspectives, comparative horizons, and last but not least on references to the realm of "culture." Our actions are always cultural phenomena, and *as such* they are meaningful. Conversely, culture cannot exist or change without human action.

Our earlier remarks about death as a mytheme and a fantasm can be transferred to numerous other phenomena: they belong to a world of valences, whose individual components exist in a complex frame of mutual referentiality. The elements of these "systemically" structured, semantic networks are as polyvalent as are their relations to each other. Connotation analysis can present semantic contents in a methodologically regulated way and, if they are conducted *lege artis*, claim validity. However, due to its principal character, this kind of analysis cannot lead to objective, absolute knowledge or definitive insights. Inevitably, striving to understand means having to choose *one* of many possible "paths of understanding" (Jauß, 1994). In the interpretive sciences, knowledge is never final but open to competing perspectives and readings.

Boesch refuses to work with a registered inventory of fixed symbolic meanings (see e.g., Boesch, 2006, pp. 51-65, 67), which is why he is skeptical of a psychoanalysis that is too fixated on such symbolic meanings and, on top of it, "sexualizes" all meanings for theoretical reasons. For Boesch this signals a theoretical bias that easily leads to premature interpretations and empirical short circuits.[5] Connotation analysis is an elaborate procedure which does not allow any shortcuts, but requires both intensive and extensive readings. It is a "method for the specification of experienced connotations of images and ideas as well as concrete perceptions and actions" (Boesch, 2006, p. 67). The search for structural constancy, coherence, and consistency is obligatory. It is a method that suggests exploring all the possibilities of interpretive analysis and "travel[ing]" seemingly digressive side paths, as one of Boesch's metaphors has it:

> Our experience of reality is enmeshed in fantasms, and no other method is
> a more reliable instrument for highlighting the fantasmic components of
> our relationship to reality. (2006, pp. 67-68)

Understanding reality as experienced reality and experience as an event enmeshed in collective myths and subjective fantasms entails the application of a methodological approach identical with or similar to the one recommended in Boesch's connotation analysis. It means accepting the fact that this method is intentionally not standardized and that the data collected by way of its application "escape formalized evaluation" (Boesch, 2006, p. 69). This does not automatically mean a methodological "disadvantage." Rather, it simply indicates a necessity, an unavoidable condition of an otherwise methodical form of knowledge formation in symbolic action theory and cultural psychology.

Dynamic Self, Paradoxical Equilibrium of the Psyche: Aspects of a Concept of the Human

The theoretical foundation of Boesch's psychology is not only based on his account of action and cultural psychology in the stricter sense. Like other psychologies, his approach is backed by a certain concept of the human or *Menschenbild*. The concept of the human as it is understood by symbolic action theory and cultural psychology does not tally with any of the versions established in other psychological approaches; it is different from the concept of the human in psychoanalysis, behaviorism, cognitive psychology, or those action theories that are known for their "rationalism" and "individualism" (Herzog, 1984).

The center of Boesch's concept of the human holds a seemingly simple idea. In many of the empirical studies this idea is clearly visible. The contemplation of inconspicuous, ordinary actions, the analysis of religious rituals, the creations of an artistic "genius," altruistic deeds, but also the excessive violence that only enemies can exert against each other—they all draw attention to *one* central motive: humans strive for so-called *interior-exterior balance*, for *equilibrium of the psyche*.

Time and again, Boesch's psychology is concerned with an "intimate accord of existential dimensions," a harmony of self and environment which is fundamental to "our ego, our sense of reality, and last but not least to the way we make a place out of the world" (Boesch, 2005, p. 83). Boesch assumes that humans want to experience themselves as an integral part of a larger whole, that they intuitively assume the existence of such a whole, and continuously integrate their actions into such an intuitively constructed world. This intuition of wholeness Boesch calls a *Gewahrnis*, a state of being aware, that resembles a syncretic impression [*Anmutung*] rather than a full consciousness. Even the simplest action, Boesch maintains, is amalgamated into such an experienced wholeness of the world, and the individual perceives his or her actions as a contribution to the preservation of this wholeness and to a certain degree of "harmony."

This wholeness may assume various shapes, Boesch argues. We speak of it as the fatherland, western culture, nature, or human dignity. Such frames of reference stabilize one's sense of self and offer an orientation. As soon as these frames cease to exist and we are forced to act in unfamiliar configurations we feel a sense of the uncanny. This is what is important: The self is anxious to form a coherent and consistent relationship to the world. This motive, of which the actors are vaguely, incompletely, or not at all conscious, contributes decisively to the *dynamics* of human life and actions. At first it may seem paradoxical that this motive forms the core of a disquiet that can never be calmed and that exposes the permanence of happiness as an illusion and a psychological chimera. In Boesch's psychological anthropology humans appear as *creatures "doomed" to imperfection but permanently striving for perfection and happiness.*

Let us take a closer look at this. For Boesch, the normative ideal of a life in pursuit of perfection and happiness is an anthropological-psychological necessity, although it may differ in shape and design, depending on individual and cultural conditions. What is for some a goal of all endeavors for others may be a horror or, at best, of little interest. In one form or another, however, the ideal of reaching perfection can be found in every human life, functioning as a rather basal motive which "arches" over many concrete motives and conscious intentions. The actions of individuals give as much evidence of this fact as do collective practices. The insatiable longing for perfection reigns everywhere, be it in religious faith, in art, or even in the seemingly banal activities we perform in the monotony of our daily lives. This longing and striving, these aspirations are described by Boesch, in the prosaic language of his theoretical psychology, as an unstable and fragile *balance between "interior" and "exterior."* This balance is regulated by the "target values" of action.

In his ecologically- or culturally-oriented approach, as Boesch calls it, the concept of *balance* means "a relationship between a self-compliant modification of the exterior and an environmentally compatible adjustment of the interior" (Boesch, 2005, p. 81). He perceives this as an interactive procedure in which interior and exterior structures are intertwined, and, at the same time, capable of shaping and changing each other. The exterior as an other forces itself upon us in much the same way we impose ourselves on the exterior. We change it as it changes us. These changes include material and social as well as "purely mental interpretations of our view of the world" (Boesch, 2005, p. 81). Interior-exterior balances emerge in many different ways and may always be rebalanced. The scope extends from "emotional tunings, semantic interpretations, and the acquisition of skills to technological or artistic changes of the exterior"

(Boesch, 2005, p. 82). Last but not least, such balance can be artificially induced, e.g., by using drugs.

This active striving for self-environment balances that which Boesch identifies as "culture." Cultural achievements always correspond with such balances. Consequently, Boesch defines culture as an "incessant attempt to produce, consolidate, and improve a livable interior-exterior balance" (Boesch, 2005, p. 117). Which does not mean, of course, that in realizing this attempt we do not permanently also produce imbalances.

Boesch often speaks of the pleasant, the friendly, and the perfect. Yet he also wonders whether the ominous and the resistant are not only just annoying and frightening (and, hence, spark the desire to remove or transform them), but are also fascinating. Whether, in other words, there is not also a desire for the horrible and the unwholesome. Boesch, however, does not diagnose such an antagonism [which Freud anchored in the topological dualism of Eros and Thanatos, the sex (life) and the death drive] but looks at the concept of the perfect (pleasant, familiar, etc.) itself *in its ambiguity.*

Boesch's *psychological* concept of perfection is a heuristic *ideal type* (and, as such, indispensable). It refers to an aspiration, a "nonreifiable," nonfixable state. Basically, it marks the nonidentifiable vanishing point of thinking, feeling, longing, desiring, wanting, and acting. Moving toward this point, the goals of the actor change and the point itself changes its position. While acting, one may *experience* the path one took as goal-oriented; in certain moments, atmospheres, and moods one may even have the unmistakable impression of having reached the goal. Everyone experiences moments of deep satisfaction, fulfillment, and contentment, albeit to varying degrees and in different ways. However, such feelings of happiness, states in which, as Boesch says, self and world are experienced as a unity, are only transitory. This experience is of great importance in Boesch's approach to psychology.

For the record: At the core of Boesch's psychological anthropology is a *psychological paradox.* The equilibrium one desires and pursues is not a "given," ongoing state. Yet at the same time, human beings cannot choose to *not* long for and pursue this equilibrium. Banal and extraordinary, inconspicuous and eccentric, profane and sacred activities all give evidence of this. People who, in happy moments, feel in balance with themselves and the world also feel the transitory, vanishing character of this feeling. The equilibrium one feels in certain moments, atmospheres, and moods comes in the paradoxical gestalt of a state that vanishes in its subjectively experienced presence. In other words, it "exists" in the mode of withdrawal.

The concept of "equilibrium" in Boesch's interpretation also possesses a normative meaning. It is part of a theoretical vocabulary created to enable critical analyses and diagnoses of culture. For Boesch the drive to perfection is a general human motive, one whose effectiveness is rather limited. Usually, one contents oneself with compromises. One is content with substitutes. Today, as Boesch notes in one of his critical analyses of contemporary culture, such substitutes are provided by consumer goods, which represent perfection. For Boesch, compensations lurk everywhere and they undermine and sabotage "the strive for perfection through which a culture becomes humane" (Boesch, 2005, p. 106).

As this last quote may finally demonstrate: symbolic action theory and cultural psychology, as a framework, is not content with defining the human being. It is interested in what human beings can make of themselves, and is never uncritical about or indifferent toward that which has already been achieved and that which still appears to be possible.

NOTES

1. See Lang and Fuhrer (1993), *Culture & Psychology*, 1997, *3*(3); *Culture & Psychology*, 2001, 7(4).

2. It is noteworthy (and a reflection of Boesch's position in German-language psychology) that, thanks to the initiative and active support of his American friends Walter Lonner and Robert Textor, there is an extended French edition of his 1991 opus magnum *Symbolic Action Theory and Cultural Psychology* (Boesch, 1995), but that to this day there is no German translation

3. Symbolic action theory and cultural psychology rejected the claim to absoluteness common in deductive-nomological and in inductive-statistical models of explanation. Last but not least, they reject the idea that psychological explanations of human actions need to be monocausal. The theorem of the polyvalence and overdetermination of human action is not compatible with the idea that an action is always "produced" by only one cause. Even more so, it challenges the scientific theorem of causality as such.

4. In the following we quote from this reprint. The introduction added to the reprint consists of pp. 3-10.

5. Freud, by the way, would have shared this opinion, which explains why it took some time for him to integrate mere symbolic interpretations into his own work; they only appear in a later edition of his famous book, *The Interpretation of Dreams*. Even so, Freud mistrusted symbolic interpretations throughout his life, insisting instead on the necessity of free associations, particularly in his criticism of Carl Gustav Jung, who, in turn, held a firm trust in the universal meaning of specific symbols.

REFERENCES

Baltes, P. B. (1997). Ernst E. Boesch at 80: Reflections from a student on the culture of psychology. *Culture & Psychology, 3*(3), 247 - 256.

Baltes, P. B. (2001). Boesch at 85 on cultural psychology: Foreword. *Culture & Psychology*, 7(4), 477-478.

Boesch, E. E. (1976a). *Psychopathologie des Alltags. Zur Ökopsychologie des Handelns und seiner Störungen*. Bern: Huber.

Boesch, E. E. (1976b). *Konnotationsanalyse. Zur Verwendung der freien Ideen-Assoziation in Diagnostik und Therapie*. Saarbrücken: Arbeiten der Fachrichtung Psychologie, Universität des Saarlandes.

Boesch, E. E. (1977). Konnotationsanalyse - zur Verwendung der freien Ideenassoziation in Diagnostik und Therapie. In P. Hahn & E. Herdieckerhoff (Eds.), *Materialien zur Psychoanalyse und analytisch orientierten Psychotherapie, Heft 4* (pp. 6-72). Göttingen & Zürich: Verlag für Medizinische Psychologie im Verlag Vandenhoeck & Ruprecht.

Boesh, E. E. (1980). *Kultur und Handlung: Einführung in die Kulturpsychologie*. Bern: Huber.

Boesch, E. E. (1982). Fantasmus und Mythus. In J. Stagl (Ed.), *Aspekte der Kultursoziologie. Aufsätze zur Soziologie, Philosophie, Anthropologie und Geschichte der Kultur; zum 60. Geburtstag von Mohammed Rassem* (pp. 59- 86). Berlin: Dietrich Reimer.

Boesch, E. E. (1983). *Das Magische und das Schöne*. Stuttgart: Fromman-Holzboog.

Boesch, E. E. (1987). Zur Psychologie des Magischen Handelns. In J. Albertz (Ed.), *Wissen-Glaube-Aberglaube* (s. 171-189) Wiesbaden: Freie Akaemie.

Boesch, E. E. (1991). *Symbolic action theory and cultural psychology*. Berlin, Heidelberg, New York: Springer.

Boesch, E. E. (1995). *L'action symbolique. Fondements de psychologie culturelle*. Paris: L'Harmattan.

Boesch, E. E. (1997). Reasons for a symbolic concept of action. *Culture & Psychology*, 3(3), 423-431.

Boesch, E. E. (1998). *Sehnsucht. Von der Suche nach Glück und Sinn*. Bern: Huber.

Boesch, E. E. (2000). *Das lauernde Chaos. Mythen und Fiktionen im Alltag*. Bern: Huber.

Boesch, E. E. (2001). Symbolic action theory in cultural psychology. *Culture & Psychology*, 7(4), 479-483.

Boesch, E. E. (2005). *Von Glaube und Kunst zu Terror. Über den Zwiespalt in der Kultur*. Göttingen: Vandenhoeck & Ruprecht.

Boesch, E. E. (2006). Konnotationsanalyse - zur Verwendung der freien Ideenassoziation in Diagnostik und Therapie. In P. Hahn & E. Herdiekkerhoff (Eds.) *Materialien zur Psychoanalyse und analytisch orientierten Psychotherapie, Heft 4* (pp. 6-72). Göttingen & Zürich: Verlag für Medizinische Psychologie im Verlag Vandenhoeck & Ruprecht. (Reprint with a new introduction 2006)

Boesch, E. E., & Straub, J. (2006). Kulturpsychologie. Prinzipien, Orientierungen, Konzeptionen. In G. Trommsdorff & H. -J. Kornadt (Eds.), *Kulturvergleichende Psychologie. Enzyklopädie der Psychologie. Serie VII, Themenbereich C „Theorie und Forschung"*. Göttingen: Hogrefe.

Bruner, J. (1990). *Acts of meaning*. Cambridge, MA: Harvard University Press.

Cranach, M. v., & Tschan, F. (1997). Handlungspsychologie. In J. Straub, W. Kempf & H. Werbik (Eds.) *Psychologie. Eine Einführung* (pp. 124-158). München: dtv.

Giddens, A. (1976). *New Rules of Sociological Method*. New York: Basic Books.

Habermas, J. (1981). *Theorie des kommunikativen Handelns. Band 1: Handlungsrationalität und gesellschaftliche Rationalisierung*. Frankfurt a. M.: Suhrkamp.

Habermas, J. (1982). Ein Literaturbericht: Zur Logik der Sozialwissenschaften. In J. Habermas *Zur Logik der Sozialwissenschaften* (pp. 89-330). Fifth, enlarged edition. Frankfurt a.M.: Suhrkamp. (Original work published 1967)

Habermas, J. (1988). *On the logic of the social sciences*. Cambridge, MA: MIT press.

Herzog, W. (1984). *Modell und Theorie in der Psychologie*. Göttingen: Hogrefe

Jauß, H. R. (1994). *Wege des Verstehens*. München: Fink.

Koselleck, R. (1985). "Erfahrungsraum" und "Erwartungshorizont" - zwei historische Kategorien. In R. Koselleck *Vergangene Zukunft. Zur Semantik geschichtlicher Zeiten* (pp. 349-375). Frankfurt a.M.: Suhrkamp.

Lang, A., & Fuhrer, U. (Eds.). (1993). Cultural Psychology-Kulturpsychologie-Psychologie Culturelle. *Schweizerische Zeitschrift für Psychologie, 52(2)*, 65-147.

Laucken, U. (2001). Wissenschaftliche Denkformen, Sozialpraxen und der Kampf um Ressourcen – demonstriert am Beispiel der Psychologie. *Handlung, Kultur, Interpretation. Zeitschrift für Sozial- und Kulturwissenschaften, 10*, 292-334.

Straub, J. (1999). *Handlung, Interpretation, Kritik - Grundzüge einer textwissenschaftlichen Handlungs- und Kulturpsychologie*. Berlin, New York: de Gruyter.

Straub, J. (2006). Understanding cultural differences: Relational hermeneutics and comparative analysis in cultural psychology. In J. Straub, D. Weidemann, C. Kölbl, & B. Zielke (Eds.), *Pursuit of meaning: Advances in cultural and cross-cultural psychology* (pp. 163 - 213). Bielefeld: Transcript.

Straub, J., & Weidemann, D. (2006). Psychology, culture, and the pursuit of meaning: An introduction. In J. Straub, D. Weidemann, C. Kölbl, & B. Zielke (Eds.), *Pursuit of meaning: Advances in cultural and cross-cultural psychology* (pp. 11-20). Bielefeld: Transcript.

Valsiner, J. (1997). Editorial: The Saarbrücken tradition in cultural psychology, and its legacy. *Culture and Psychology, 3(3)*, 243-245.

PART I

ERNEST EDUARD BOESCH— THE JOURNEY OF DISCOVERY

CHAPTER 1

THE EARLY YEARS OF
E. E. BOESCH

The Authors

When first meeting Swiss cultural psychologist Professor Ernest Boesch, a distinguished scholar and major contributor to his discipline, one is impressed by his intense presence and focused attention. He looks like a scholar; dignified in his bearing, highly observant of his environment, and thoughtfully attentive and responsive to those he meets. Born during World War I and living through most of the twentieth century, he has witnessed some of the most difficult and innovative times in modern history. He is the ever-questioning and searching thinker, often allowing his deeply poetic spirit to influence his spoken and written language. He appreciates and respects the depth and range of human cultures and accomplishments.

One cannot meet Professor Boesch without becoming aware of the importance of Supanee, his beloved wife and partner who brought her Thai culture and traditions into his life. They met in Bangkok in 1955 when Professor Boesch was appointed the director of UNESCO's International Institute for Child Study (IICS) while on leave from his faculty position as the chair of psychology at the University of the Saar. Along with many of his colleagues, Professor Boesch participated in and contributed

Discovering Cultural Psychology: A Profile and Selected Readings of Ernest E. Boesch, pp. 3–23

to UNESCO's international education conferences on children's learning and development. He was recognized for his knowledge of educational testing and ability to identify factors that influence children's learning. The new and challenging position as IICS director in Bangkok allowed Professor Boesch's interest in cultural psychology to flourish.

From his perspective as a sojourner, it was important to study and learn the Thai language. This could enrich the significance of the Institute's research through his increased awareness of the people and his ability to communicate with them, particularly those who worked at the Institute. Supanee, a member of a prominent Bangkok family, had studied Thai language and literature. She was also familiar with English and had acquired some knowledge of French. Several members of her immediate family were in the medical professions, and some had studied abroad. As a staff member of the Institute, Supanee was chosen to teach Thai language to Professor Boesch. This assignment led to a friendship that unexpectedly became a lifelong relationship. We will look more extensively at Professor Boesch's stay in Bangkok in the third chapter of this book and in the Selected Readings section.

The longer Professor Boesch lived in Bangkok the more he noted numerous remarkable contrasts between life there and in European cities. He knew that learning Thai was a key to understanding the culture and executing his responsibilities as the director of the Institute especially since many employees were Thai. In addition, Professor Boesch was fascinated with the culture and lifestyles he observed. He was impressed by the social openness and warmth of the people, a far different context than that of Europe. For him life in Bangkok was a period of rebirth (his arrival at Geneva was also described as a rebirth). He was fascinated and pleased with his new cultural and geographic surroundings.

There is much information to present in a profile of a scholar of such extensive and diverse experiences as those of Ernest Boesch. He chose to follow interesting and challenging pathways often in response to intuitive as well as rational inclinations. His early years, beginning in St. Gallen, provided the formation that led to his explorations and enquiries into the complexities of human learning. This chapter focuses on Ernest Boesch's childhood experiences within his family and the schooling received in his home community. The social context of his early life was importantly shaped by his relationships with his parents and grandparents, his teachers and peers at school, the economic strife of the times, and family hardships. Even for a citizen of Switzerland, the vicissitudes of two world wars greatly disrupted the national and regional sense of peace and well-being.

As a student, Ernest Boesch and his peers were deeply concerned for the people in surrounding nations, particularly those who were unjustly and violently targeted by the genocidal criminals who perpetrated death and destruction with little internal censure. The following account of his early life is based primarily on the information he shared during extensive interviews and written communication from 2002 to 2006. The interviews took place at his home in Saarbrucken and were recorded and transcribed for the authors' reference. Ernest was most cooperative with his response to follow-up questions. He also provided detailed reviews of the multiple drafts of the chapters included in the following biography.

ST. GALLEN: AN IDYLLIC CITY

In keeping with Ernest Boesch's psychological perspective that environment is influential in shaping human thought and action, the following is a brief overview of the history of St. Gallen, birthplace of the Boesch family, including grandparents. Many cultural psychologists and other social scientists hold that early experiences have long standing influences on subsequent life experiences and expectations. Similarly, the past often provides the framework for creating one's future (Boesch, 1991).[1] In addition the natural and cultural characteristics that are commonly associated with the people of Switzerland have persisted to this day. The natural beauty and serenity of Switzerland's lakes, rivers, mountain ranges, and rich fertile valleys are greatly cherished.

St. Gallen, or St. Gall as it is often referred to among English and French speakers, is the capital of the canton. The region's rolling pine covered hills gradually lead to the mountains. Naturally beautiful and with a moderate climate, the area attracts visitors year round. Currently, it has a population of approximately 75,000 inhabitants who speak a Germanic dialect of Alemanic. For the entire canton, the population is approximately 300,000. It is interesting to note that St. Gallen is named for an Irish monk, Gallus, who arrived in the area about A.D. 612 as a missionary who followed the route of Columbanus, another Irish monk well known for his extensive missionary travels. The region was primarily wilderness at that time. Gallus built a small retreat for himself near the Steinach River. A year later, he founded a monastery that thrived until A.D. 646 when he passed away.

Many years later, another monk, Otmar, founded a school for scribes and translators at the monastery. It soon became a famous center for the arts and religious studies. Pope Adrian I sent Benedictine monks from Italy to St. Gallen at the request of Charlemagne, who ruled most of Europe (the Holy Roman Empire) from 800 until A.D. 814 St. Gallen grew as a center for scholars after the monks founded a library around A.D. 830.

When St. Gallen was threatened by invading Huns between the years of 924 to A.D. 933, the library's precious texts were moved to the Abbey of Reichenau on Lake Constance. When the Huns departed most of the texts were returned after a new library was built.

By the thirteenth century, St. Gallen had a reputation as a growing and important trade center for fine linens that were produced in the region. The city's notoriety for trade soon exceeded its recognition for scholarly endeavors. Most of the people of the region were involved in some aspect of linen and embroidery production. St. Gallen was the only Swiss community in that period with trade representatives in distant cities such as Lyon and Nuremberg.

With the growth of commerce, serious tensions developed between the lay people and the governing abbots. Eventually, dissension within the church and the formation of new sects resulted in opposition to the rule of clerics directed by the pope in Rome. Gradually, a majority of St.Gallen's population converted to Protestantism, the religious persuasion of Professor Boesch's grandparents. The Boesch family also participated in the tradition of fine embroidery design (personal communication, March 2004).

A printing press was installed at the St. Gallen Abbey library in 1630. This contributed to the monks' renewed social and educational influence in the area. It also led to more religious conflicts culminating in the pillage of the library. Most of the books and manuscripts were carried away to Zurich and Bern.

After Napoleon's military campaigns in Switzerland in the late eighteenth century, the imposition of French law influenced the political structures of the canton. A francophone persuasion remained even after the region was returned to local control. French became the second most important language of Switzerland, and was taught in St. Gallen's schools. An orientation to French language was evident in the scholarly interests of Professor Boesch, particularly when he chose to enter the University of Geneva as a young man (personal communication, March 2004).

The ancient city and the bustling modern city that grew around it have become popular tourist destinations in contemporary Switzerland. The University of St. Gallen has achieved an international reputation in economic sciences. In the twentieth century, the production of fine linen and embroidery was replaced by the manufacturing of optical goods, pyrotechnics, chemicals, and pharmaceuticals.

GROWING UP IN ST. GALLEN

Ernest Boesch was born on December 26, 1916, his parents' first child. His mother was 20 years old and his father was 21. St. Gallen had an estimated population of about 60,000 (personal communication, November 2004). At that time, Switzerland was surrounded by nations engaged in World War I. As a neutral country, the Swiss were somewhat isolated in terms of geo-politics, trade, and economic vitality. Food supplies were strictly rationed since the nation's farmable land barely yielded enough sustenance for the population. Consequences of wartime hardship definitely affected all of the Boesch family. For most of his life Ernest suffered serious dental problems due to the lack of calcium and other important nutrients during his early development. Not at all inclined to romanticize the past, he referred to his childhood as economically and personally difficult. As part of the family tradition, Ernest's father made his living as a freelance embroidery artist.

Because of nearsightedness, Mr. Boesch was not drafted into the army that defended the Swiss borders against invasion. However, he was required to serve as an auxiliary medic during the influenza epidemic of 1918 that took over 20 million lives world wide. He attended to the sick and dying in makeshift hospitals in the region but managed to avoid falling ill himself. Professor Boesch wondered to what degree his father was psychologically impacted by seeing so many die an agonizing death, particularly the infants and children. Although he had very little memory of that period of his life, Ernest recalled seeing his father dressed in his medic uniform that included a Red Cross emblem and a long bayonet that hung from his belt. That weapon frightened the young child. His parents told Ernest the bayonet was used to chase away or kill the threatening beings that were known in fairy tales and imagined as possible enemies to his father. While this explanation was well intended, Professor Boesch speculated that it probably added to his fear of the creatures and other armed men. This may have led to his anxious feelings in later life and were related to the religious teaching he received. Those feelings stayed with him for many years.

The first home of the Boesch family was on the outskirts of St. Gallen. However, when Ernest was four, the family moved closer to the center of town near St. Leonhard church. A nearby park provided young Ernest a place to play with neighborhood children. Professor Boesch remembered that as a child he was intrigued by the pigeons that perched in the nooks and crannies of the church. He wanted to catch one of the birds, perhaps because of his fascination with their color or peculiar pattern of movement and sound. His father told him that if he could get close enough to sprinkle salt on a bird's tail, he could catch it with his hands.

Having no reason to doubt this bird catching strategy, before leaving home for the park one day, young Ernest put some salt in his pocket. When he saw the birds on the ground in front of the church, he ran toward them, trying to get close enough to sprinkle salt on their tails. As he chased the birds, he heard his father laughing and realized that he had fallen for a ruse. When he reflected on this experience, Professor Boesch laughingly mused that maybe this was a first time he learned to distrust the word of adults. Of course, such situations may occur in every child's life.

There were also occasions when he experienced his father's protective-ness. When an older boy bullied young Ernest, his father ran after him, caught him, and took him to the family apartment. The boy was scolded for behavior that was considered deserving of punishment. He agreed with Mr. Boesch and offered his cheek for a slap. No punishment was given, but Ernest recalled being impressed by the way his father demon-strated concern for both himself and the boy. He was also impressed by the boy's courage.

Another recollection of those years was of neighborhood boys flying paper airplanes at the park. Young Ernest had no airplane but his father designed one for him. They experimented with the model in the hallway at home. However, Ernest told his father the flight of his plane was less beautiful than those flown in the park. This remark left the young son feeling guilty for sometime afterward, although his father appeared to take his expressed disappointment in stride.

Ernest 's father was a strict disciplinarian. Until about the age 10, he applied harsh measures to bring his son's behavior into conformity with rules that were not always clearly communicated. "He provided me with toys suitable for my age, protected me, if needed, against bullies in the neighborhood, but if I misbehaved, he applied a punishing ritual I greatly feared. Fortunately, the beatings were rare." When they happened, he was ordered to his father's study, was told to lower his pants and then was beaten on the buttock with a rod or belt until black and blue. This was not done angrily on the spot, but coolly as though the ritual was a normal response of a father to his child's unacceptable behavior. For instance, on a family outing, if Mr. Boesch would say to his son "wait until we return home," he knew the ritual would be applied. While "sparing the rod and spoiling the child" may have been a common rubric of child rearing at that time, the treatment remained a hurtful and sad memory for Ernest.

When he was age 3, a sister was born; however, Professor Boesch has no recollection of this event. Neither did he have any recollection of his first 2 years at primary school. In the third year he was transferred to a differ-ent school, St. Leonhard, where he recalled a strict teacher who punished students sternly. When students did something inappropriate or out of form, the teacher told them to put out their hands. This was an ominous command. The children knew he would strike their fingertips with a rod as many times as he thought fitting for the particular violation. Professor Boesch remembered being hit by the rod-wielding teacher. Like his peers, he refused to show any reaction to the pain. Eighty years later he remembered this as a contest of wills with a male authority figure.

In terms of exposure to religious teachings, when he was a child, Ernest's grandparents took him to local services at the Baptist Church. He remembered that the gatherings were rather boring and the atmosphere at church was stuffy and disagreeable. When he was given books to look through, they offered stilted descriptions of heaven and hell. God was portrayed as a stern and continuous purveyor of everyone's behavior. He meted out suffering and torture to evil-doers. In retrospect, Ernest was rather convinced that those church experiences as a young and impressionable child had fostered a tendency toward religious anxieties.

As a student at St. Leonhard school for Grades 3 to 6, Ernest mainly enjoyed the handicraft classes in paper and woodworking. When he announced that he wished to sit for the entrance exam for the Gymnasium, the teacher told him he was not ready due to lack of demonstrated diligence. Nevertheless, a determined Ernest took the exam and passed. During these years, the Boesch family also moved to a different apartment in the center of the town and then, reflecting the increased income that Mr. Boesch earned as a successful designer, to an even larger and brighter place. There was room for an embroidery design studio where Mrs. Boesch and a young apprentice worked as assistants to keep up with customer requests. Curious and observant, young Ernest spent many hours in the studio watching and learning details of his father's artistic techniques. The family was able to afford a piano that Mr. Boesch, a gifted musician, played to accompany his wife when she sang favorite songs from Schubert and other composers. Ernest remembered sitting under the keyboard at his father's feet listening and enjoying the music (see chapter 15 "A Meditation on Message and Meaning"). In addition to the piano, Mr. Boesch played the oboe, flute, and bassoon. Although the family did not attend concerts outside the home, nor invite others to join their informal sessions, music had an important place in their daily life. This consistent and happy exposure to creative work and musical expression has remained with Ernest. His writings reflect the importance of art and music throughout his life to the present.

Ernest was about 8 years old when his family experienced increased economic prosperity as the embroidery business thrived. Ernest was given a bicycle, and his father bought a light motor bike, a rare possession for the times. The family home was nicely furnished (personal communication, October 31, 2004). They enjoyed favorite outings that included picnics on the shore of Lake Constance. Ernest found delight in the many ring snakes near the lake, elegantly drawing their curves in the ponds of the area. I remember catching one, carrying it by the tail and being scolded by nearby bathers about hurting the creature. Of course, I let it go again without harming it. I am still fascinated, up to now, by the elegant beauty of these animals.

Extended Family Influences

Since Ernest's paternal grandfather also worked in the embroidery industry as an enlarger, Ernest saw much more of his father's family than his mother's. He referred to his maternal grandmother as "an imposing woman I did not feel drawn to, and I did not have close contacts with her brother and two sisters living in St. Gallen." There were two additional granduncles, one for whom Ernest was named. They lived just outside of St. Gallen but infrequently interacted with the family.

Recalling time with his paternal grandfather, Ernest remembered that he taught him the craft of bow making and shooting. In the Spring of the year, his grandfather sometimes took him into the forest to cut May-pipes from hazel tree branches. These were simple musical instruments with a limited tonal range. This homely exposure to craftsmanship and traditional woodworking skills taught young Ernest to be resourceful and find enjoyment in carving simple objects in his adult years. Suggesting the lasting impact of his forest experiences, many years later when he wanted to build a home, Professor Boesch chose a site that was near a wooded hillside in a quiet suburb of Saarbrucken. During his career as a professor at the University, he regularly walked along a quiet wooded path that led to his office and lecture hall. He cherished and was inspired by the beauty of nature throughout his life. In the spirit of the *Philosophen Weg*, immortalized by some of the greatest thinkers of Europe, Professor Boesch enjoyed the freedom to think and reflect while surrounded by the natural world.

Ernest remembered his paternal grandmother as a person of warmth and hopefulness. "she never lost her good humor and confidence in life—she was a strong-hearted, kind, and courageous woman." A Catholic by upbringing, she married a protestant and attended his church services. When her former priest scolded her, she only answered: "It is the same God!" Ernest's grandmother also took her grandson out into the woods to gather wild berries, modeling a way to find happiness in simple activities. These experiences with her were remembered as enjoyable. They offered Ernest a safe retreat from disciplinary harshness. As an indication of her close and agreeable relationship with her family, after the death of her husband, grandmother Boesch lived with her son and grandson. She energetically and generously tended to cooking and household tasks. She was happy with her life and made the best of all circumstances.

COMMUNITY LIFE IN ST. GALLEN

The wider community of St. Gallen also contributed to shaping Ernest's education and recreational experiences. At Carnival time, children dressed in brightly colored costumes for parades and festivities. Young Ernest chose a costume of a "red Indian" consisting of a feathered headdress and red coloring on his cheeks. Many children selected a similar costume since it was relatively easy to assemble. This exciting event was, however, not without some anxiousness caused by older boys who sometimes looked for younger ones to tease and bully. Other community wide festivities were the annual Kinderfest, marked by parades, flags, and musical performances by students. Most certainly, Ernest also enjoyed the big and famous St. Gallen sausages.

Another popular community celebration was the Swiss national holiday of August 1. This event commemorated the liberation of the original cantons from Austrian occupation. Historically, as the castles on the hill were taken over, the victors lit fires to signal their success. According to tradition, on the night of August 1, children and adults walked up the hills to gather around the huge bonfires that lit up the night sky. These events afforded exposure to a kind of primal experience and an exciting time when family and community members honored their historic roots.

The winter season was fondly remembered for the beautifully illuminated Christmas trees Mr. and Mrs. Boesch decorated for their children according to the local custom. The trees provided brilliant light in contrast to winter's intense darkness. In those days the family created their own music together as well. These relatively easy and happy times unfortunately ended in 1929 when Ernest's parents divorced.

While still in primary school young Ernest was an avid reader of Karl May's very popular books about Native American adventures. He remembered reading late into the night, fascinated by the exciting stories. The school librarian also introduced Ernest to less adventurous readings. One of the books titled *Die Höhlenkinder im heimlichen Grund* (*The Cave Children in the Hidden Valley*) portrayed the life of an isolated brother and sister who mastered various wilderness survival techniques. The text was a kind of pre-history and a step toward more serious literature.

Professor Boesch recalled that it was around the lower secondary grades that he wrote his first poems, thereby indicating an unusual interest and skill in writing. However, his parents had no literary penchant nor did they have books at home that were of interest to him. Fortunately, the school librarian was aware of Ernest's reading interests and was able to offer him a range of alternative books to enjoy. As he grew older his interests also ranged widely. Such emotional and psychological distractions are common during preadolescence especially for very intelligent males who may find the confines of school less than inspiring.

At age 12, Ernest received a Swiss pocket knife, and recalled hearing the message, "Every Swiss man has to have his pocket knife." Among other uses, he remembered cutting small branches from trees to fashion bows and slingshots, the later being used to launch annoying attention toward the girls in his school. Again, this rather harmless kind of mischievous behavior would be recognized as typical of 12-year-old boys by most teachers and parents (personal communication, November 6, 2004).

Later in high school, Ernest joined the marching band where he first played the piccolo and later was the lead trumpet, marching at the front of the parades. He remembered playing joyful tunes as the band moved through streets that were brilliantly decorated with flowers and flags. These musical performances offered him a rewarding and meaningful sense of enjoyment while being socially engaged with his peers and the community. His father took responsibility for encouraging his son's musical interests. He gave him a recorder when he was about 10 and also provided him with piano lessons. Gradually, Ernest advanced to playing the flute and the piccolo and became very proficient. Eventually, he also learned to play the guitar that he used to accompany himself when he sang.

This range of musical interest and ability indicated Ernest's talent, motivation, and self-discipline as well as the encouragement received from his parents, band leaders, and music instructors in the community. One can surely ask how different his life might have been if he had been instructed at a level commensurate with his talents. The major obstacle to receiving more training was the limited family budget. However, despite his great love of music Ernest stated that he did not recall ever having a desire to become a professional musician. He was much more serious about expanding his ability as an effective writer of prose and poetry.

Traumatic Changes and the Life Altering Consequences

Although his family's occupation of a spacious apartment in the center of town was an advantageous move, Professor Boesch termed it as "fateful." He remembered the place as "a comfortable bourgeois building" with a large staircase and broad wood railing that he sometimes liked to slide down. He had very few specific memories of his mother during those years. Mrs. Boesch was described as an attractive woman who, unfortunately, also attracted the attention of the house owner's son, who occupied a flat above the Boesch family. This son was described as "an amateur cello player without any serious professional formation." He was "a flirtatious charmer too, and so my mother got entangled with him." This relationship was eventually discovered by her husband who then, in spite of her pleas for forgiveness, pushed her away. The stressful situation led to much anger and castigation. It was seriously traumatizing to Ernest and his sister.

Even though adultery was considered a serious offense at the time, Ernest's father apparently did not take into consideration the effects of marital break up and divorce on his children. Thus, the family's life was seriously and harshly disrupted. Mrs. Boesch and her daughter moved out of the apartment. Ernest remained with his father according to the ruling of the divorce court. Due to the father's strong feelings of hurt and anger, he made it very difficult for any visiting between his son and his daughter and former wife. Ernest was largely isolated from his mother and sister until his early adult years.

These difficult times occurred when Ernest was 12 years old. Another important transition that year was Ernest's entrance into the Latin branch of the local high school. "I was bad at Latin, disliked it, and after two years, transferred to the commercial branch of the high school." There, modern languages were taught and Ernest studied French, English, and Spanish. Yet his school problems did not stop there because much of his trouble was related to his family situation. Although for a time Ernest's behavior was so unruly he risked expulsion. Eventually he adapted and proved to be capable of excellent work, eventually finishing high school with excellence. In these respects his development conformed to what might be considered typical adolescent unpredictability.

The Role of Literature and Music

In Grade 12, Ernest performed outstandingly. He maintained high standards of achievement in both mathematics and the liberal arts. He was an exceptionally accurate speller in both French and English. Recognized for his brilliance in languages and literature, he wrote stories and poems, some of which were later published in one of the yearbooks of his town. He spoke with fond remembrance of his literary and musical friends of the time.

In the development of his musical talents, even though he was ready for advanced instruction shortly after he began playing the flute, he was not able to have lessons until he was in his late 20s. Then, for a brief time, he studied with Andre Jaunet, a famous flautist. Opportunities to perform at school and in the community allowed Ernest to develop his talent and confidence as a musician. The camaraderie of his musical peers served as strong encouragement. The range of musical instruments he mastered was a remarkable achievement for a young musician who was largely self-taught. However, enjoyment of music provided an important balance in contrast to the unhappiness experienced in Ernest's family relationships.

Until 2005, a beautiful grand piano occupied a place of prominence in the main gathering room of Professor Boesch's home in Saarbrucken. Because of deteriorating eyesight, he decided to give the piano to his son Christophe's family. Christophe enjoys playing and also has children who can benefit from having their grandfather's piano at home, thus contributing to a new generation of music lovers.

To keep his love of music part of his daily life, Professor Boesch has an extensive collection of carefully selected CDs. An excellent sound system fills his study with Bach, Mozart, Brahms, Schubert, Chopin, and others when he takes a rest in his leather reclining chair after his morning schedule of writing and correspondence. Although he once listened to music when writing and reading, he now never has music playing while engaged in his work. He finds that careful listening to great composers is incompatible with concentration on reading and writing. If he plays Bach, for example, he finds that each note has meaning and requires his full attention. But music also conflicts with the rhythm of language that is important in his writing. Thus, he works in silence during the mornings and listens to music mainly in the evening.

Times of Social and Economic Chaos

World political and economic conditions deteriorated into contentiousness and insolvency in the late 1920s. The Boesch family, dependant on the flourishing of the embroidery industry, was profoundly impacted by its break down. Fashions changed and seriously reduced the demand for embroidered linens and attire. Nearly everyone in St. Gallen was unemployed due to market changes. At the time there was no social security system to provide even minimal support for those in need of basic food, medical care, and shelter.

The atmosphere of widespread economic depression added to the heavy burdens that devastated the Boesch family. For a 12-year-old, Ernest's emotional distress and confusion was clearly reflected at school with the interspersion of somewhat marginal academic performance and mischievousness with glimmers of scholarly brilliance. When his mother married the landlord's son, the finality of his parents' divorce made hopes for reconciliation futile. Separation from his mother and sister became more definite.

Economic conditions forced Mr. Boesch to move to a much smaller and more modest apartment. To earn a living, he tried to build a new career as a textile color print maker. Additional income was earned in Carnival season when he was hired to decorate the walls of local restaurants with colorful landscapes. While the income was welcomed, it was scarcely enough to pay for lodging and food even when meals often consisted of coffee and some fruit cake. If funds allowed, perhaps they could enjoy a plate of eggs and bacon. The meals were served at coffee houses frequented by persons who also suffered economic hardships. Sometimes there were days when nothing but coffee and dry bread served as meals at home. This restricted diet was doubtless insufficient and imbalanced for a teenage boy. Even though he needed dental care, there were no funds to pay for services of a dentist. To quell the pain of toothaches, Ernest's father simply administered pain medication. As might be expected, Ernest's health declined leaving him with little resistance to colds and other common ailments. He remembered becoming rather seriously ill with health problems that were easily avoided by others who were more robust.

An added difficulty was encountered when Mr. Boesch found a new lover. Their sexual relationships could of course not go unobserved in a small apartment, and caused much conflict in the mind of a sexually uneducated 14 year old boy. This may also have had an influence on his school problems at the time. When his grandfather died, Ernest was 16. In his view, sexual disturbances turned into death anxieties which he admitted remained with him during the greater part of his life.

From the perspective of educational psychology, there is little wonder that these social, emotional, and economic upheavals in daily life strongly impacted the school performance of a stressed adolescent. Ernest described his behavior as a student in the commercial high school as "unruly and disturbing." He was on the verge of expulsion until a "sympathetic" teacher helped him to change his behavior by making it clear that he had the ability to be an excellent student. "Somehow, miraculously, I turned into a model student and passed the best matriculation examination of my class."

The deeper psychological problems persisted due to the fact that at that time there were no professional counselors or psychologists in the school or community that he could turn to for assistance. He had to deal with his problems himself. Reading and writing were his preferred forms of "therapy." He wrote a novel that was titled *Eine Wegstunde* (*An Hour of the Way*), an early attempt at prose. Eventually, when Ernest was 20, the novel was accepted by a local publisher. This achievement affirmed that his writing ability was valued by someone in a position to render an objective assessment.

In a continued search for a means to earn a better living, Mr. Boesch began preparing for another career change. Expanding on his training and experiences with the Red Cross during the flu pandemic of 1918, he gathered resources to study herbal medicine and early forms of homeopathy. He self-published a small text that summarized the results of his research. Because local law prohibited the practice of medicine without a license, father and son moved to a village approximately 20 kilometers from St. Gallen in the adjoining Canton of Appenzell where nonlicensed healing practices were allowed. For over a year Mr. Boesch was a *naturarzt* or naturopath. Ernest commuted by street car into St. Gallen each day to attend high school. He recalled that living outside of town where he could practice his trumpet without concern about disturbing the neighbors was enjoyable. He was free to hike in the hills during summer and ski during winter. There was little or no money earned as a result of his father's career change, but for Ernest, living in a small community was a beneficial change of scene. He could put a physical and perhaps psychological distance between himself and the city that reminded him of the distressful times experienced there.

Father-Son Relationship Strengthens

Despite the hardships in his life during the 1920s and early 30s, there were some positive developments that offered glimmers of hope for the future. The father-son relationship evolved into that of an elder and junior companion. "He was kind, not overbearing, taught me chess, to play piccolo and the flute. He himself had salvaged his bassoon from his bankruptcy, one of the few possessions which had not been taken away." Occasionally, father and son went into the woods to collect reeds used to manufacture mouthpieces for the bassoon. The cost of buying them was prohibitive at the time. This was one example of how Ernest learned the importance of being self-reliant and resilient in the face of adverse circumstances, a lesson that became a life long asset.

In retrospect, Ernest Boesch tried to understand the social and emotional stress his father experienced. He acknowledged that according to social norms of post-World War I in St. Gallen, the humiliation of career losses and the social distress over the infidelity of his wife and the subsequent divorce were burdensome. Such insight may have been impossible for a teen aged boy to grasp sufficiently. However, given his keen intelligence and observational sensitivities, young Ernest may have been quite aware of his father's humiliation. A fall from the status of successful artist and businessman to that of a part time decorative painter who could barely feed himself and his son had to be profoundly frustrating.

With his father as his primary source of support, Ernest was torn between coping with the wrath expressed toward his mother and managing his own feelings about his relationship with each of his parents and his sister. During the crucial time of adolescent development, Ernest experienced separation from his mother and sister, the loss of the family's home and livelihood, and the sudden death of his grandfather. Clearly, there were multiple sources of considerable intra and interpersonal turmoil. Added to this were the political and cultural tensions that existed across Europe in the aftermath of World War I and preceding the outbreak of World War II.

It is important to consider the effects of major shifts in childhood that Ernest experienced. Dissolution of family life and economic poverty were deeply saddening and stressful. Although Mr. Boesch had been brutally strict at times, he was also eager to teach his son and encourage his musical talents. Ernest never said he hated his father, but it was clear that living with him was deeply ambivalent. Furthermore, Ernest had to cope with the communicative and emotional barriers between himself and his mother and sister.

With his penchant to be reflective and analytical, these experiences only enhanced his tendency to try and understand his own and other's emotional life. Later, these experiences certainly provided the basis for his cultural interests. In Part II of this book, particularly chapter 14 titled "The Enigmatic Other," Professor Boesch's deep awareness of the complex nature of intra- and interpersonal relationships is clearly articulated.

Regarding the level of influence his childhood experiences had on his professional development, Professor Boesch saw no particular events that explained his eventual focus on cultural psychology. Yet, from his viewpoint, it is possible, even likely, that a series of traumatic experiences fostered a tendency to search for new horizons and life conditions. His curious mind searched for evidence that people could live very differently than he observed in his family. In fact, when he arrived in Geneva as a 23-year-old university student, and later in Bangkok as a professor and researcher, he referred to the excitement and newness of these opportunities as a "rebirth." Perhaps his father's resilience in the face of social and economic hardships provided Ernest with encouragement to look beyond difficult times for hopeful possibilities.

Cultural Context and Individual Behavior

Contextually, it is important to consider the many burdens that hung over Switzerland in the period between World War I and the start of World War II. Although the Swiss were not directly engaged in the wars, the reports of destruction and horror in surrounding nations were regularly covered by the media. The many hardships of economic depression and fear of invasion by German troops were all very real to Ernest and his community. He stated:

> all of that filled my childhood, adolescence, and early adult years with an atmosphere of uncertainty and threat of human atrocities. To grow up in the European culture of that time would likely give rise to longing for a different world. Thus, personal and cultural circumstances combined to determine a life-long orientation of thinking and acting. (personal communication, October 2005)

As one who read, observed, and felt deeply about hardships others endured, life in early twentieth century Europe presented great social, intellectual, and moral challenges. It was a time when personal determination to find intelligent solutions to human problems motivated many to look for hope.

In his autobiographical article published in *Culture and Psychology* (Boesch, 1997), Professor Boesch stated that he had no answers as to the life experiences and observations that may have influenced him to choose a career as a cultural psychologist. Yet, experiences in his family and community led him to realize that life held many disappointments and hardships. He witnessed his father's struggles to make a living and experienced the hopeful attitude and loving care of his paternal grandmother. Born during "the Great War," Ernest's formative years may have stimulated his desire to seek an understanding of humankind's capacity to be generous and loving rather than violent and destructive.

High School: A Mix of Conflicts and Successes

As indicated above, Ernest experienced a period of rebelliousness in his teens and narrowly escaped expulsion from high school. Thanks to the kindness and understanding of a geography teacher, he received a message that reaffirmed his academic potential. Without rod or harsh language, the teacher reminded Ernest of the abilities he could put to good use that would benefit his future. Such encouraging messages from persons outside his family captured his attention. There were choices a talented student could make that would afford him a positive future.

Ernest acknowledged that during high school he expressed his fear and anxiety in various forms of rebellion. When presented with the options of the educational curricula, there was no personal role model to help find a pathway. While he demonstrated his capabilities in modern languages and literature, he had reason to be concerned about securing an education that would result in reliable employment. In that regard, there seemed to be little value to the study of Latin, a requirement for the gymnasium. Moreover, the commercial curriculum prepared students for careers in the trades that afforded a range of attractive occupational benefits including travel opportunities. Thus the commercial curriculum seemed a good choice especially considering the family's financial hardships.

Having begun to experiment with writing poetry while still in grade school, when he was about 15, Ernest dedicated considerable time and effort to writing. Many years later, The St. Gall Yearbook of 1942 printed some of his poems. In retrospect, he looked back and evaluated this work as rather clumsy. However, with continued refinement his writing improved. The rewards of others respecting his work, membership in the school band and the symphony, provided Ernest opportunities to belong to important community groups. He was largely self taught, but took advantage of whatever instruction he found along the way.

After completing high school he became a member of "The Young Poets," a group who met and reviewed each other's work. These scholarly and artistic orientations that seemed natural to Ernest would eventually override his decision to follow a commercial career rather than enter a university. In high school, his main interests were German Literature, French, English, and mathematics. His language teachers often taught students songs as a way to encourage their acquisition of new vocabulary. Ernest discovered that he enjoyed playing the guitar and singing so much that his classmates nicknamed him "Song." Creative outlets positively counter-balanced the more stressful aspects of his life.

When he completed the commercial certificate, Ernest applied for a job as an assistant with a large carpet manufacturer. Based on his scores on the qualifying exam, the employment manager met with Ernest to tell him he was far too talented for a mundane job in the carpet business. Ironically, he was advised to reject a full time job because he was over-qualified despite the fact that his primary objective was employment and an income. His father recognized the talent of his son and supported his preparation for university studies as much as he could. Additional support came from his mother and sister.

This preparation for university implied the study of Latin, a requirement for university admission. Elsa Nuesch, a high school language teacher, tutored Ernest for 2 years. When he mastered the required skill, he was admitted to the last year of the gymnasium. He learned easily, met two good life-long friends, and graduated as the top student in languages and mathematics. During that time, another life-long friendship was begun with Andreas Juon, an organist and composer who taught Ernest to appreciate Bach's music. As to his study plans, he expressed a desire to dedicate his talents to humanitarian purposes, given the existence of unprecedented violence.

In 1936, shortly after his commercial matriculation examination, Ernest was called to military training for four months, an experience that confirmed his complete loathing of warfare. When he refused to bear arms as a conscientious objector, he was transferred to a medical unit, implying a second period of military training. As Germany's goal of military dominance became increasingly obvious, the threat of invasion griped the Swiss. Professor Boesch recalled that many citizens, including his fellow students and teachers, became vehemently anti-Nazi and fearful of their unbridled aggression.

When Hitler emerged as a political force in Germany, Ernest was 16 years old. He heard his public speeches on the radio and became weary of the military force Hitler was building. His rise to power and the widespread support he gained among the German populace destroyed human trust for many Swiss. In Ernest's perspective, the Third Reich clearly demonstrated human capacity for aggression. Many of his peers became skeptical about the future of Europe given the masses of people who enthusiastically embraced the Nazi beliefs.

The Swiss government recognized their best defense against invasion would be to heighten Germany's awareness that waging war in the Alps would be difficult and costly. Fortunately for the neutral Swiss, they posed no threat to the German regime. Allied Forces were far more worrisome with their land, sea, and air combat powers. Shortly after Ernest completed the gymnasium, the Swiss army was mobilized to secure the nation's borders and fortify the Alps for a retreat in the event of an attack despite the national declaration of neutrality. At the time, there was no confidence that any European nation was safe.

Reflections on a Century of War and Psychological Advances

Sixty years after the end of World War II, Professor Boesch acknowledged how deeply he was influenced by its effects. In his view Hitler's ruthlessness and that of his many followers greatly eroded the cultural and historic relationship between the Swiss and German people. Even though St. Gallen was close to Lake Constance and the German border, the Swiss usually chose to avoid close interaction with their neighbors. The written language of the Northern Swiss was German, but their spoken dialect was similar to that found in Alsace and in the southernmost regions of Germany. In most Swiss high schools, students were taught high German. Yet, in Ernest's view, most of the Swiss do not like to speak or hear the language because it sounds stiff and clumsy to them. He offered the following statement as his impression of Swiss-German relationships. "Our attitude towards Germany was always ambivalent. We might admire their literature but reject their mores. We feel them to be arrogant, inflexible, not natural."

Ernest's disillusionment with the German writers who aligned with the Nazis did not change his desire to become a writer. However, to be a good writer he thought it important to choose a career that was as close to real life as possible. A doctor whom he greatly admired, Hans Carossa, was also a writer. This led him to think that he too could study medicine, and eventually become both a physician and writer.

When reviewing Professor Boesch's writings, his ability to create vivid images is striking. When describing human thinking and behaving, he strives to identify interior and exterior values and beliefs that may influence the individuals whom he studies. His careful consideration of social and physical contexts on individual behavior may have lead to his awareness that cultural orientation is intricately woven into all that is perceived, felt, and generated. The main elements of Professor Boesch's penultimate work, symbolic action theory (SAT), are derived from the basic principle that each person perceives and experiences the world from both an idiosyncratic and shared perspective. Stated existentially, no two people are the same and every person is constantly transformed through daily experiences. A detailed review of SAT is contained in chapter (3 or 4) of this text.

Geneva: Professor Boesch's "Second Birth"

At age 23, with two high school curricula successfully completed, the young scholar set out for Geneva to begin his university studies in October of 1939. Geneva offered many attractions including its beautiful setting, and a friendly population and atmosphere. The University had an excellent reputation in various disciplines, including medicine. Situated near the French border, the influence of that language and culture was pervasive. To Professor Boesch's satisfaction, Geneva was as far from St. Gallen as he could travel and still remain in his neutral homeland.

When speaking of his first arrival in Geneva, he remembered that as the train approached the Lake it passed through a dark tunnel and emerged into the view of the water sparkling in the sunlight. Eventually, when he arrived at the central station, Ernest felt like he was beginning a new life. He had limited financial resources but he had hope, freedom, confidence, and determination to carve out a meaningful path. For the first time in his life, his social and physical environment was completely new and he felt as though he was "reborn" into a world of new opportunities.

SUMMARY

Born during World War I, and growing up in the din and destruction of that and World War II, Professor Boesch knew the worst of human destruction and violence. As the first child in a family of traditional St. Gallen artisans, Ernest was challenged by domestic conflicts and economic hardship. He had to grow up and make meaning of his social and physical environment with little support from the adults in his world. When he spoke of those who offered him unconditional regard, those most immediate were his paternal grandmother and a few kindly teachers who recognized and encouraged his unusual academic abilities. The feelings that dominated his early childhood were those of anxiety and fear that resulted at first from his father's harsh disciplinary practices and his vivid interpretations of gruesome fairy tales and children's stories. The atmosphere of war and violence also were pervasive for Ernest and all of his family and peers.

Fortunately, the counterbalances to these difficult conditions were found in Ernest's love of music, literature, and art with his earliest orientations occurring at home. His father and grandfather served as the primary models, teaching Ernest what they knew and encouraging his musical talents. He played in school bands and symphonies and learned from his peers and instructors. The joyous musicians whom Ernest led through town during community celebrations afforded a wonderfully free form of expression. Similarly, as his interests in literature and poetry developed, a society of young poets welcomed Ernest and supported his literary creativity.

When disheartened by economic hardships, family separation due to his parents' divorce, and the threats of war, Ernest thought he would enter a trade and give up on scholarly aspirations. Ironically, his potential employer recognized the unusual talents of the young man who planned on becoming a carpet salesman. He told Ernest and his father that anyone scoring so well on his company's screening test needed to be in a university. With scholarships and the little financial support his family could scrape together, the young scholar decided he would test his abilities at Geneva with a tentative hope of becoming a pediatric psychiatrist. Although his life was marked by many personal hardships, Ernest learned that if he wanted a different outcome for himself it was up to him to carve out his personal niche. Thus, he traveled to Geneva and became a "reborn" man.

NOTE

1. All references in the introductions can be found in the bibliography.

CHAPTER 2

PREPARING FOR A PROFESSIONAL CAREER

Ideological Growth and Searching

The Authors

INTRODUCTION

This chapter will trace Ernest Boesch's years in Geneva and his early discoveries in the field of psychology that were enhanced by his work as a research project director that was sponsored by UNESCO in Thailand. He studied with some of the greatest thinkers of the twentieth century, thriving on the rich atmosphere of intellectual vitality that was personified in Jean Piaget and his colleagues. Important decisions were made in these years, some of them absolutely life-shaping in major ways. Just as Ernest characterized his arrival in Geneva as a "rebirth," his years there launched his professional career. Socially, Geneva was the place where he met his first wife, Claire, who became the mother of their three children André, Christophe, and Monique (the first later becoming a computer

Discovering Cultural Psychology: A Profile and Selected Readings of
Ernest E. Boesch, pp. 25–43
Copyright © 2007 by Information Age Publishing
All rights of reproduction in any form reserved.

25

expert, the second an internationally known primatologist, the third a child psychiatrist).

Considering all the political, social, and intellectual developments of the pre-mid-twentieth century, Ernest and his university cohorts faced many challenges that were the result of individual and collective decisions that defied many traditional human conventions. To describe these as chaotic times is a gross understatement. Europe faced enormous political, social, and economic challenges that deeply affected Ernest and his peers. What unfolds is the story of searching for a life that reflected the honoring of traditional European scholarship and humanitarian values. There are also early manifestations of the emergence of a new order of thinking about the meaning and dignity of life as lived by all people of all cultures worldwide. This became most clearly evident in Ernest's extensive sojourn in Thailand from 1955 to 1958 (which will be described in chapter 3).

Surviving an Era of Desperate Ruination

Starting in 1939, Europeans were consumed with the growing momentum of war that eventually engulfed the continent. Ernest remembered his great distress when reading daily reports of the loss of thousands of lives and wanton destruction of cities, towns, villages, and farm lands. A response of the crowd meeting at the Berlin Sportpalast remained with Ernest to the present: When Joseph Goebbels, the Nazi propaganda minister, asked: "Do you want total war?" An enthusiastic crowd cheered "JA!" The destruction of the city of Coventry, England, followed as a warning of Germany's intentions. Such events were ominous, yet the relentless war machine left the young Swiss feeling utterly powerless.

For financial reasons, Ernest abandoned his first intention to study medicine and turned to psychology, hoping that this, too, would provide for a promising future. However, as Nazi forces gained political and military dominance, people were more and more deeply concerned for their personal and professional well being. While reflecting on this period, Ernest recalled feeling very opposed to the ideologies of both Nazi National Socialism and Soviet Communism. Even after the Nazi influence waned due to Germany's defeat and Hitler's death, Ernest "still was very distrustful of everything German. And I remained for many years very distrustful of everything Russian, prejudices which I do not defend, but cannot get rid of either." Totalitarian dominance, blatant disregard for the value of human life resulting in the deaths of over 20 million people, arrogant and self-serving leaders, were all drastically opposed to the democratic and humane values of the young scholar and his close associates.

For Boesch, Geneva, with its strong French and international influences, stood for human equality, fraternity, and liberty, core values of young intellectuals of the time. The city was a center for idealists, the headquarters for the International Red Cross founded in 1864, and site for the convening of The League of Nations after World War I. Geneva also hosted many international visitors from educational, scientific, economic, and artistic organizations, thereby maintaining an historic identity as a center for humanitarian efforts. All of these historic and contemporary accomplishments as well as the natural beauty of the area enriched the student and faculty life at the University.

Origins of Geneva as a Humanistic Center

According to Louis Binz, a professor of history at the University of Geneva, the city has been inhabited for over 2,200 years. It was a military outpost of the Romans beginning in approximately 122 B.C. Julius Caesar mentioned Geneva in his commentaries on the Gallic Wars and visited the settlement in 58 B.C. after it was attacked by tribes from the North. In time, Geneva became a world class city and attracted great thinkers such as Rousseau and Voltaire. John Calvin, a French theologian and religious reformer of the sixteenth century also became a resident of Geneva. The city was set like a gem, glimmering in the light reflected by the lake with magnificent buildings and parks located along the shoreline.

Previous to the outbreak of World War II, under German pressure, Switzerland's official position was to refuse immigration to Jews from all over the continent who attempted to escape certain death during the Nazi era. This caused distress for many from all across the country. With the help of Swiss citizens and "unruly" officials, approximately 50,000 refugees surreptitiously entered the country and were offered shelter during the war. Situated near the French border, Geneva was a portal for many who needed and found safe haven. The city was a relatively peaceful place compared to most others in Europe. Ernest was a member of a medical service unit while a student, and was called upon to fulfill short periods of military duty. Fortunately, the length of service did not interfere seriously with his studies.

Enrollment in the Rousseau Institute

The University of Geneva was famous as a center of scientific studies including psychology and medicine. The building that housed the Rousseau Institute where Ernest attended seminars and demonstrations by his professors was located along the lake front. It was known as the Palais Wilson in honor of United States president Woodrow Wilson, a strong supporter of the League of Nations. To attend major lectures, he walked to the main university building, situated in the central park of Geneva opposite the Calvin Memorial.

Ernest described his first impressions and reactions to Geneva as he explored the new home he chose for himself. "It was this brilliantly dazzling city on the lake. It was so light, and beautiful, I really felt at that time like I was a reborn person." Even after 64 years, he conveyed how magical the experience of beginning his university studies was for him. While he was not sure of the career implications of his program at the Institute, he was among a relatively small group of students and faculty who created an interesting and welcoming social context. Little did he realize at the time that he was privileged to study with professors who were producing monumental work to further the relatively new discipline of psychology.

Quite expectedly for a young man who needed to carefully monitor his expenses, Ernest searched for information about the feasibility of his goal to study medicine. He calculated that to complete all course work and then specialize in child psychiatry as he wanted to do, he would be well over 30 years old. The cost of such a long course of study was far beyond his means even though he obtained a small stipend from the Free Masons and had modest support from his mother and sister who were financially better off than his father.

Ernest concluded that the program at the Institute Jean-Jacques Rousseau was his best option because it appealed to his interests and the requirements for completion seemed realistic. While he was not sure about employment options after graduation, he had confidence that his studies would be productive. His life long friend, Kurt Peter who accompanied him from St. Gallen to Geneva, pursued his initial choice, the study of medicine.

The Rousseau Institute was first directed by Edouard Claparède and later by Jean Piaget who came to Geneva in 1929 after his studies at Zurich and Paris. On the occasion of his 80th birthday, Ernest reflected on his university experiences. He acknowledged how little he knew of his major professors who lectured in psychology.

> None of these names meant anything to me, but pondering the length and the costs of medical studies (I had to live on a very small stipend), I decided on the spot to enroll in this Institute, attracted by its program, although totally ignorant of its professional possibilities—psychology, at that time, being a largely unknown profession in Switzerland. I often still wonder at the naïve confidence with which I embarked on a totally unknown path. (Boesch, 1997, pp. 258-259)

Ernest stated that he was possibly drawn to psychology because he wanted to come to an understanding of his personal difficulties. He also thought he might approximate his goal of becoming a child therapist by studying child psychology. Like many students, he selected his program of studies with little advisement. It is not difficult to imagine that he felt somewhat apprehensive about his sustainable career options as a psychologist.

Fortunately, before long the young academic realized that whatever the long term consequences, he had found his way into a congenial group of peers and scholars. His social and professional associations were encouraging and hopeful from the outset. Because it was wartime, the number of students from outside of Geneva, normally high, had shrunk considerably. The city had become a quiet place and affordable student rooms were relatively easy to find.

Studying With Psychology's Early Leaders

The student body at the Institute, most of whom were Swiss, included about 30 men and women. Paul Osterrieth, from Belgium, one of he few students from outside of Switzerland, became Ernest's close friend. As it turned out, after completing his studies, Paul became a professor of child psychology in Brussels. For all students, the severe wartime rations of petroleum products, restricted their travel options, especially by car. Therefore, most students walked from their residences to lectures and laboratories. Ernest had a room in the center of town and walked about 30 minutes along a pleasant route to the Palais Wilson.

Fellow students and faculty often gathered in what they called the *Amicale* or friendly meetings and discussions. Edouard Claparède hosted gatherings at his beautiful home that was surrounded by a park. After Claparède's death, about a year after Ernest's arrival at Geneva, Piaget hosted small groups of students at area restaurants. Later, André Rey, professor of clinical psychology, also hosted small groups of students at his home. They all participated in lively discussions about their classes and the on-going investigations faculty members presented in lectures.

Professors Bovet, Claparède, Piaget, and Rey were among the early scholars who elevated studies of child development to a central place in psychology. Ernest could hardly have been at a better place at a better time. Initially unaware of the genius of Piaget and his great contributions to developmental psychology, Ernest's respect and appreciation for him and the other great scholars deepened as he discovered more about their discipline. Educationally, he was inspired: "I entered the old venerable building (Palais Wilson) that housed the Institute with feelings of both apprehension and awe."

When Ernest reflected on the 3½ years at Geneva, he considered Piaget and Rey to be his primary role models and teachers. He found Rey's innovations in testing to be ingenious. He stated: "I worked in his consultation. Later on, I used his tests as a school psychologist. I admired him as much as I admired Piaget who was about 44 years old and had recently published his first book on a child's conception of the world. They were competing with each other."

Both psychologists were recognized as highly inventive in their unique ways and left remarkably enduring legacies in psychological theory and practice. In Ernest's experience, André Rey included students in his work and discussions more frequently than Piaget did. His thinking was precise and analytical. He taught students how to construct, administer, and interpret the tests used in clinical practice sessions. Other faculty members were Marc Lambercier, an experimental psychologist, Richard Meili, a statistician with whom Ernest played chess, and Gertrude Dworetzky who offered instruction in uses of the Rorschach test. Congenial as these student to faculty relationships were, in the university system of the time, graduate students were very much on their own. Instead of being academically mentored by senior faculty, even when planning and completing their theses, students had to make their way independently.

Graduate Studies and Improved French Language Skills

French was the language of Geneva and Ernest had limited experience with advanced spoken and written French before arriving at the University. During his first year, he worked arduously to improve his language skills. With keenly focused attention, he attended all the lectures and experimental exercises of both Claparède and Piaget so he could grasp as much information as possible and simultaneously improve his French. Later, as an alert and diligent student who perused local bookshops, Ernest found and purchased several books by Claparède, Piaget, and Pierre Janet—a French psychiatrist who would become very important in Ernest's later work. The texts were used at the time and for many years throughout Ernest's career. Claparède's publications were especially helpful in the development of his experimental skills. Claparede's innovation in his method of client interviewing, *la reflexion parlée* ("thinking aloud" while solving a problem), and his use of the Binet-Simon test were of great interest to Ernest. He regarded Claparède to be, in some ways, a follower of the American pragmatists in the importance he attributed to individual behavior. Ernest and his peers greatly respected Claparède, for his warm personality and innovative scholarship. Claparede was also admired for his outspoken opposition to Nazi aggression and the cowardly reaction of Swiss politicians in the face of it. For Ernest, Claparede's book, *Morale et Politique*, remains an example of how psychologists should engage in public discourse in times of political danger and confusion.

One telling personal incident that Ernest recalled addressed the deference students were expected to demonstrate toward their professors. At a seminar conducted by one of Piaget's teaching assistants, Ernest made comments that the assistant interpreted as critical of Piaget's ideas. The assistant became angry and made it clear that it was not a student's place to criticize a distinguished professor. This response greatly bothered Ernest, leaving him feeling somewhat guilty. He went to see Piaget at his office and asked to be excused for his remarks. Although Piaget could be exacting, his response was to laugh and generously dismiss any concern about the questions raised.

This represented a refreshing and new dynamic in Ernest's relationships with a senior and powerful male adult. When meeting with students informally, Ernest remembered that Piaget could be friendly, even comradely. "I recall one common outing of the Institute in a Geneva restaurant where, sitting beside me, Piaget filled his dark, chewed meerschaum pipe and, handing it to me, said "Boesch, fumez-la! (Boesch, smoke this!). It was an honor difficult to refuse, but not very appetizing" (Boesch, 1991, p. 259).

Students' Clinical Modeling and Practice Sessions

As part of his clinical training, Ernest and his peers replicated the "clinical interview," a technique demonstrated by Piaget as he conducted diagnostic assessments of kindergarten children. They also observed and experimented with Rey's assessment techniques in laboratory sessions. The goal of the observers was to familiarize themselves with their professors' techniques and then replicate them in experimental settings when the students independently tested children. Little did Ernest know how important this training would be to his career immediately after graduation. He was offered a position as a school psychologist for the Canton of St. Gallen where testing all students referred by teachers due to questions about their cognitive abilities was his primary responsibility.

By the end of his first year at Geneva, Ernest wrote and passed his first major university exam for the *Certificat de Pédagogie*. The pressure he felt to perform well within a short time was so high that his work of preparation was accompanied by painful intestinal cramps, a disturbance he endured occasionally during many years of his adult life. Fortunately, health problems did not interfere with his diligence, and he passed the examination with excellence.

An example of the range and depth of Ernest's thinking about psychological questions can be deduced from a situation that occurred when a group of students and a professor from the Institute were visiting the city zoo. Ernest visually studied an antelope with an elegant white marking along its spine and commented to the professor that it was beautiful. In response, the professor asked: "why is it beautiful?" Ernest could not provide a ready answer but never forgot the question. Later, when reflecting, he commented that it focused his attention on the subtle problems of aesthetic perception. It elicited a particular type of inquiry which contributed to one of Ernest's most important publications in 1983 titled *Magic and Beauty*.

Rather than glossing over a comment that reflected aesthetic appreciation, an expression that may reflect a great deal about a person's mode of thinking and feeling, an astute psychologist encouraged careful and focused analysis of the rationale, motivation, and contextual prompts that may influence a person's voluntary expression. From Ernest's perspective, such probing exchanges can generate new information about unconscious values, perceptions, thoughts, and feelings. Whether one is conscious or unconscious of one's early cultural formation, a well placed question may initiate a new level of self awareness. Without apologies, Ernest stated that asking pertinent questions is an art that many psychologists fail to practice. He has found that too many scholars and therapists ask only the questions they have been directed to ask by professors and clinical supervisors. In Ernest's view of professional practices, this may result in research and therapy that is quite superficial and ineffective.

Another reflection that indicated the growth Ernest experienced due to his attentiveness and discussions with professors, particularly in the case of Piaget, was stated as follows.

> His lectures opened to me a way of thinking which marked me for life; in the seminars, his unassailable reasoning not only impressed, but also awed me—I remember saying that I felt him to be like a giant mountain one cannot hope to climb. What impressed me too was his skill in interviewing children in front of the class. It convinced me at an early age that we have to convey the skills we want to teach by doing and not only by lecturing. (Boesch, 1991, p. 259)

Later, Ernest applied his student experiences when he served as a school psychologist and as research director of the UNESCO Bangkok project (see chapters 3 and 5). Instead of guiding subjects to desired answers by preformed questionnaires, he wanted to engage them in conversations with open-ended questions. However, when working in

Bangkok, he realized this goal only partially due to the insufficient training of his research assistants. The open-ended interviews encouraged informants to respond in ways that reflected their unique thoughts and reactions rather than providing researchers with easily tabulated lists of data that often led to questionable, if not error prone, research reports. Simply put, Ernest began to consider qualitative research as an important complement to quantitative work. This was important when testing individuals, but was particularly important when studying cultural and cross-cultural phenomena.

Not only did Ernest benefit from models of scholarly excellence, but he also learned from the comradely exchanges that were part of university life at that time. This is exemplified in his account of the following encounter. One day as he made his way from his residence to Palais Wilson, he met up with another student from the Institute. He asked her why she was studying psychology. Without hesitation the woman replied that she wanted to try and save humanity (see chapter 12, Part II). In Ernest's view, most cultural psychologists tend to be idealists. They desire to increase knowledge and understanding of cultural influences on human behavior. The notion that psychologists have a responsibility to focus their studies on finding ways to benefit people of all cultures was a commonly shared belief of himself and his peers.

The clinical and theoretical demonstrations and lectures Ernest witnessed undoubtedly implied that culture was part of human motivation and behavior in laboratory as well as naturalistic settings. However, culture was never overtly discussed at the Institute (Boesch, 1991). Theoretically, Piaget's constructivism and Rey's clinical processes presumed the interaction between clients and their social and physical environments as well as intrapersonal dynamics. Commenting on the contrasts between the world of psychology then and now, Ernest observed that a number of contemporary psychologists tend to realize that cognitive and emotional behavior is deeply reflective of cultural influences. Why the connection between culture, motivation, thought, and behavior was not overtly addressed earlier may be attributed to the relative newness of psychology as a discipline. It was one of many areas waiting to be explored by an increasing number of scholars and scientists.

In Ernest's view, he was fascinated with the training in constructivism and interviewing techniques that he developed further when working as a school psychologist, and then as a professor and cultural psychologist. As a faculty member whom Ernest respected highly, Professor Rey practiced a rational, very sophisticated approach to testing and assessment. To his students he was kind and supportive, encouraging their independent work. He created nearly all of the tests and methods that were used in his seminars and in the Institute's child consultations. To complete his students' applied training in testing strategies, including report writing, Professor Rey had each student present and discuss reports on the tests they used in examining a child. Ernest and his peers found that Professor Rey was a person with whom they felt a close and positive connection. He was easy to contact and a stimulating intellectual who encouraged and enjoyed open discussions among students when he hosted them at frequent gatherings at his home. When Ernest conducted research for UNESCO in Thailand, he used and adapted both Dr. Rey's and Piaget's methods of gathering information in the cultural context.

Regarding the nature of his studies with Piaget, Ernest spent the second year attending his lectures on cognitive development, later to be published in many works on the intellectual development of children. In Ernest's third year at Geneva, Piaget's lectures focused on emotional development, leading to the book *La Formation du Symbole Chez L'enfant (The Language and Thought of the Child)*. It was during this year that Piaget began to study perceptual illusions. He carefully designed experiments to prove that perceptual illusions were not an inborn characteristic of visual perception, but were a result of the way individuals constructed visual space. As a student assistant to Piaget during that year of research, Ernest was directed to test kindergarten children with the Delboeuf Illusion. Piaget failed to explain the rationale for the study to his assistant, and Ernest found the testing and documentation process quite tedious and boring. However, after the fact, when he learned the purpose of the work, he found it a fascinating contribution to the discussion of Gestalt psychology.

An Important Offer Declined

Before completing his studies, Piaget offered Ernest a position as his assistant on the perceptual illusions project. Although it became an important effort, it was focused on very detailed and relatively abstract experimental testing. Piaget's invitation was a distinct honor and indicated the esteem with which he regarded Ernest's talents as a young psychologist. However, Ernest was eager to do more practical work with children. When another career option became available that better suited his interests, he declined Piaget's offer. This decision, considered in retrospect, was crucial to Ernest's academic career (Boesch, 1991). Pondering "what might have been," remaining at Geneva may well have resulted in many research projects coauthored by Piaget and Boesch as well as those by Piaget and Inhelder.

Professor Bärbel Inhelder who was also born in St. Gallen in 1913, was a recent graduate student of Piaget, and the first school psychologist in the Canton of St. Gallen. In her professional practice, Dr. Inhelder used the tests and methods of Piaget and Rey. When she decided to leave St. Gallen and return to Geneva as Piaget's assistant, she offered Ernest her position. He traveled to St. Gallen to discuss the details of the assignment. After he agreed to accept the offer, Dr. Inhelder returned to Geneva where she continued her highly productive collaborations with Piaget, and Ernest prepared for a new role that began in Spring, 1943.

When Boesch submitted his report on the Delboeuf experiments to Piaget, it was accepted as a diploma thesis (*diplôme général de psychologie*) and resulted in the assistantship offer. Reflecting back on his decision, Boesch thought that turning down Piaget's offer may possibly have been a "stupid" mistake. Yet, he somehow felt that over and again life led him to decisions which, although perhaps appearing irrational at the moment, later proved to have been reasonable or even fortunate.

A semester after receiving the general diploma, Ernest was granted the *diplome de psychologie appliqué aux consultations pour enfants* (a degree in applied psychology for childhood consultation). During the last term at Geneva he prepared *L'examen de doctorat* (the doctoral exam) which was an oral review of three areas; psychology, education, and philosophy. After successfully completing this exam, students were able to fully dedicate their time to writing their doctoral dissertation. Once completed, the results of the work had to be defended at a public discussion. In Boesch's experience, preparation for the doctoral exam was the most demanding learning period of his life. He had never attended a philosophy lecture, and had very little exposure to the education professors. He had to make up for these deficiencies by an intense study of literature. Finally, he passed the exam with high marks.

School Psychologist: Canton St. Gallen

During Boesch's meetings with Dr. Inhelder regarding the nature of the school psychologist position, he learned that the work included a demanding schedule of assessments and extensive travel to communities that ranged from remote mountain villages to small towns. The pupils came from a wide range of economic backgrounds, differing religious traditions, and spoke different variations of the local dialect. He definitely had not chosen a position that was easy or predictable. His position was full time, and there was also a dissertation to be completed and defended. In his doctoral thesis he planned to identify the problems, methods and organizational solutions to assessing children's academic and psychological functioning in schools. In his practical work, he sometimes employed psychological tests commonly used at the time, but included also those demonstrated at Geneva. This presented some problems since the tests developed at Geneva were based on experiments conducted with French-speaking subjects. Students in the Canton's schools generally did not use French as their first language and therefore the performance norms established in Geneva had to be adapted to the Alemanic Swiss area. Thus, Boesch, being new in the field of school psychology, was confronted with various practical as well as methodological problems.

To adapt assessments to his clients in the Canton, was necessary since language, religion, and social-economic factors made a difference in children's responses to test items. Students born and raised in remote mountain villages had little exposure to large or diverse communities. As Boesch indicated, he had no training to work in schools nor was he familiar with life in remote villages (Boesch, 1997). He was on a steep learning curve himself.

With determination, Ernest proceeded with his work and eventually gained national and international recognition for his accomplishments. As a service to parents and teachers of the Canton, he published regular articles in the local newspapers on child development concerns. He also founded a Society for Mental Hygiene for the region of Switzerland he served (Boesch, 1997).

A DISSERTATION: OBSERVATIONS OF AN APPLIED PSYCHOLOGIST

From the beginning of his career as a psychologist, it was obvious that Boesch oriented most of his scholarship to practical applications of psychological principles and techniques. His doctoral dissertation of 1946 that identified issues and techniques for clinical assessments of children was read by Professor Maurice Debesse of the Paris Sorbonne University. He consequently came to visit Boesch in St. Gallen and asked that he write a book on the exploration of child personality. The book was subsequently published in 1952 with the title *L'exploration du caractère de l'enfant (The Exploration of the Character of the Child)* and gained much attention in France. The year before, the University of the Saar in Saarbrucken, Germany, a university founded in 1948, offered Boesch the chair of psychology which he accepted after careful consideration. The position presented many challenges including the fact that Boesch was the only psychology professor. However, Ernest was attracted to challenging situations.

Thinking about the varied professional experiences of his young adult and later life, Ernest stated that a major element of his theory of human behavior, symbolic action theory, centered on understanding the interaction between individuals and their culture. His thinking was based on Piagetian constructivism, but he came to recognize that thoughts and feelings are not necessarily conscious, but often exist at an unconscious level. Observable behavior was the result of multiple and complex internal processes as well as interactions between the individual and her/his social and physical environment. As psychologists of the time began to study the totality of human behavior in naturalistic contexts, the new discipline of cultural psychology gradually made its way to the surface of scholarly recognition.

On the basis of his multiple research experiences, Boesch progressively elaborated his views on the interpenetration of culture and individual behavior. The result of his many years of teaching and writing, this in-depth analysis of the person-within-a-culture became known as the Boesch approach to cultural psychology. The words of Professor Paul B. Baltes, one of Boesch's eminent students, add important insight into his professional distinctiveness. "Anyone reading his major works (e.g., Boesch, 1976, 1991) must be impressed with his skill of observing others and himself. Although Boesch definitely aimed at the conjoint use of experimental methods, the dominant part of his evidence is observational and hermeneutic. And like his mentors Andre Rey and Jean Piaget, Boesch is a gifted and careful observer (Baltes, 1997, p. 253). Further describing the Boesch approach even more specifically, Professor Baltes stated:

> Concepts such as beauty and aesthetics, action planning, action space, the unconscious, defense mechanisms, the role of action-guiding beliefs, identity, the self, feelings and fantasms were part of the substantive agenda; they made Boesch search for the complete meaning of psychology and a holistic account of human functioning. (Baltes, 1997, p. 250)

Boesch often heard Piaget refer to the works of Pierre Janet with great respect. While searching in a book store, Ernest found two volumes of Janet's main work, De l'angoisse à l'extase (From Agony to Ecstasy). He carefully studied Janet, and his ideas became an important contribution to Boesch's theoretical concept of action. By way of contrast, when Boesch read a book by Kurt Lewin, an early field theorist who was born and educated in Germany and a graduate of the University of Berlin, he stated that he found it impossible to understand the work. Perhaps this was related to the fact that Piaget and his colleagues seldom referenced German psychologists other than the Gestaltists. The avoidance of a German scholar may have been intentional due to the strong anti-Nazi persuasion of the professors and students at Geneva.

In his private life, Boesch began to face problems, which certainly intensified his existing introspective tendency. Reflecting back on this period of his life, he recognized that his intense self-scrutiny was in part related to early manifestations of conflict in his marriage to Claire. When attempts to resolve his problems were not helpful, he turned to the psycho-analyst Oskar Pfister, a friend of Sigmund Freud but yet an independent thinker. Later in his career, Boesch also practiced as a psychoanalyst for several years.

As a school psychologist, Ernest saw how widely family influences varied among the population he served. There was considerable variance in the behavior that fell within the range of "normal." The title of his school psychologist office, *Fursorgestelle fur Anormale,* translated as the "Office of Assistance for the Abnormal." Immediately recognizing the derogatory and discouraging implications of this title for parents and students, Ernest changed the name as soon as he started his work. "School Psychological Services of the Canton of St. Gall" conveyed more clearly the function of his office for the elementary schools of the Canton (excepting those within the city of St. Gallen). The area he had to serve as the sole psychologist was 2,026 square kilometers.

The limited time available for the examination of referred students was an ongoing concern. Seldom was it possible to schedule interviews with parents, especially the fathers who were away from home during work hours. Roads could be treacherous, especially in wintry conditions. Trying to do a comprehensive assessment was analogous to putting together a complex puzzle in a brief time span, and often without the necessary pieces available. Students had to be tested in schools, mostly empty classrooms or teacher recreation rooms—certainly less than desirable for putting a child at ease. For parent interviews, Boesch had to go to their homes, often distant farms guarded by sometimes hostile dogs. The most commonly used test was the "Biasch test series" an instrument somewhat like the Simon- Binet, but developed for Swiss children. However, Boesch also always used the assessment materials of Rey. Piaget's tests which included the use of scales, water glasses and other testing materials, were the most commonly used assessments. This meant that Ernest carried substantial materials with him as he traveled to the schools.

Ernest met farmers in the Rhine Valley, mountain villagers, families of strong Catholic and Protestant persuasion, and students who spoke a Swiss dialect different from his own (Boesch, 1991). While these experiences with diverse populations may have sensitized Ernest to the influences of culture on behavior, he still did not explicitly associate differences in thought processes with different cultural orientations. Later in his professional life, particularly when conducting research in Thailand, the influences of cultural variations became more prominent and important to his thinking.

When trying to understand how cultural differences were not recognized sooner than they were, Boesch identified two main factors. Neither cultural anthropology nor social psychology was addressed in his seminars and lectures at Geneva. Piaget did not mention the influence of culture when he was examining children's cognitive processes, their responses to experimental games, or their interpretation of symbols such as pictures, carvings, medallions (Piaget, 1962: Sugarman, 1987). Secondly, as a new practitioner, Boesch was very careful to follow exactly the experimental procedures prescribed. Most likely, if Piaget or Rey had discussed the effects of culture, Ernest would have tried to identify cultural variables that may have influenced his clients' test-taking and classroom behavior. As it was, his days were filled with multiple school visits, testing sessions, and as many home visits as possible. Usually, he left home early in the morning and often returned late in the evening. There was little time to enjoy leisurely activities with his family.

The larger context of these 8 years in St. Gallen is important to consider. In the early and middle 1940s, Europeans struggled to cope with devastating losses and the immense challenge of rebuilding their physical and social communities. Boesch learned about the conditions of the continent from refugees and journalists who witnessed and reported on post war trauma. Civilians who survived attacks by air and land fought to reclaim what they could of their families and homes. Young mothers searched for food and shelter for their families wherever possible. The massive trauma of death was all pervasive (Boesch, 1991). As a newly trained psychologist, Boesch realized that he and his cohorts faced immense challenges as helpers even in neutral Switzerland. So he did not hesitate to cooperate as an advisor with Ursula Gallusser, a younger colleague from Geneva, who had accepted the post of psychologist at the Village Pestalozzi, a foundation for war orphans from various countries that was located near St. Gallen.

While conducting interviews and tests, Boesch progressively discovered that the subjective elements of science (e.g., personal perceptions of researchers and subjects) are linked to the objective results, such as of measuring intelligence or memory span. These experiences nurtured his distrust in mere numerical scores on test results. Thus, when he found unusual results for apparently 'normal' students, he applied a clinical method which he called "testing the limits" (published later during his work in Saarbruecken). The longer he worked, the more he realized that life circumstances affected test-taking behavior. Therefore, test results could be relatively meaningless without additional information about students' holistic development and educational backgrounds.

However, these insights did not deflect Boesch's theoretical interests. At that time, Piaget thought that intellectual development had reached the limits of structural completion at about age twelve. During his testing of children, Boesch came to doubt this and obtained permission to carry out a study of problem solving among children aged 12 to 14. He was able to show further progression of abstract structure formations. He shared this report with Piaget, but due to complications in correspondence during the War, the report was never published and became lost. Yet, for Boesch the results were an important source of intellectual encouragement.

When she left St. Gallen, Professor Inhelder gave Boesch a copy of her dissertation titled: *The Diagnosis of Reasoning in the Mentally Retarded*. It was based on her research as a school psychologist on the usefulness of Piaget's experiments as diagnostic methods. For Boesch, this book became a very important guide in testing the intellectual development of children, and it paved the way for the above mentioned "testing the limits." Eventually, Dr. Inhelder also became aware of culture's influence on psychological processes. She conducted a study in Africa on the effects of malnutrition on the intellectual development of children. Jerome Bruner also arranged for her to spend several months lecturing at Harvard. Her 40 year collaboration with Piaget and other noted psychologists earned her international recognition.

In the 1940s, when he identified students with special needs, Boesch had a narrow range of educational alternatives he could recommend. Some students could profit from altered instructional techniques. Boesch tended to recommend the *enseignement individualisé* (individualized teaching) propagated by Professor Dottrens in Geneva. Students who had test results in the range of mental retardation had to be transferred to schools for the "feeble minded" located in specialized institutions. Boesch always found it difficult to make such recommendations since it implied a separation of children from their family. Yet, at that time, special classes for mentally retarded children only existed in a few localities. Looking at the amount of problems and challenging work he had to face, Boesch felt inadequately prepared. He stated: "Although considered one of the top students, my studies were too brief to provide a solid all-around education. I had insufficient clinical experience." Understandably, for one who had never taught in an elementary school, suggesting alternative teaching techniques to experienced teachers was difficult.

Major Life Transitions Into Adulthood

For a person with a penchant for philosophical reflection, the lasting impacts of two world wars within a span of 50 years led Boesch to question the future of Europe and human life generally. There was deep distrust for almost everything German due to the atrocities committed in the course of their military and ideological campaigns. The motivation to make a positive difference in human conditions was a central theme in his life and work.

When Boesch was asked about his view on contemporary psychology, he identified the search for scientific objectivity as its major focus. Yet, citing the behaviorist approach, he stated that its methodology and results, although of interest, were of limited value. Scientific measures aiming at quantifying behavior did not lead to a realistic view of human life and were of only limited use for its improvement. Boesch considered understanding the human person as a responsible actor, with anticipations, motivations, and evaluations that occurred in a cultural context to be the most needed and major focus of psychological investigation. He questioned, for example, how effectively contemporary psychologists were helping to resolve conflicts, and in particular the violence between culturally different groups.

Early in his career, Boesch strictly adhered to the experimental psychology that was demonstrated at Geneva. Yet, he eventually discovered that objective measures, such as of children's memory, did not account for the many psychological factors that, uniquely impacted each child's recall and other behavior patterns. In a sense, his clinical experience and psychoanalytic interviews led him to become a "cultural psychologist" although at the time he did not yet call it thus.

Boesch's deep interest in art, literature, and music, together with his psychoanalytic and cultural experience, made him gain a particular interest for the importance of symbolism in human psychological functioning. He recognized the important place of symbols across cultures, but also became particularly aware of the pervasive symbolism in human action.

He concluded that very few behaviors can be measured in isolation. Psychologists could surely measure the amount of time it takes a 10-year-old to solve a specific puzzle. In contrast, Boesch concluded that it is very difficult not only to identify and measure motivations and feelings, but also the biographical and social influences on behavior. For him, it was not useful to quantify what is done without also qualifying why a person, in a specific situation and context, chooses one behavior over others. Boesch finds many basic and important psychological questions still unresolved. To that purpose, not only do experimental measures need improvement, but all possible sources of information need to be considered when trying to understand any and all forms of human behavior.

Marriage and Career: A Difficult Balance

In the Fall of 1941, in the pension where he had rented a room, Ernest Boesch met two sisters from France. Lorraine, the elder of the two, was a pianist, and Claire, the younger was learning to be an interpreter and was an amateur violinist. Ernest felt attracted to Claire and eventually, they married in August, 1942. They spent an agreeable year in Geneva, meeting often with their friends Paul and Catherine Osterrieth. At this time, Ernest was working very hard to prepare for his doctoral examination. After successfully completing the exams, Boesch accepted the school psychologist position in St. Gallen. The young couple moved there in 1943. They found an apartment, pleasantly located in front of the central park. In August 1943, a year after their marriage, their first son Andreas was born. While care for Andreas occupied much of Claire's time, Ernest was focused on his professional duties and writing his dissertation. Other than the music they played together at home or in an amateur orchestra, the young couple had little time together.

A Dissertation Well Noted

In 1946, Boesch successfully defended his dissertation under the direction of Professor André Rey. His work, addressing the problems of assessment faced by school psychologists was reviewed by other European scholars. It particularly attracted the interest of Maurice Debesse of the Sorbonne, and, as already mentioned, Debesse encouraged Boesch to write a text on the psychological study of children. The book appeared in 1952, and very likely influenced Debesse and Piaget to recommend Boesch for the faculty position at the University of the Saar in 1951.

The University of the Saar offer was attractive, because it meant considerable professional and financial improvement. The town of Saarbrucken, although still burdened by heavy damage due to the war, had the advantage of being located near the French border and not too distant from Switzerland. The decision to accept the position at the Saar opened a new and crucial chapter in the life of the Boesch family. In 1951, a few months before moving to Saarbruecken, their second child, Christophe, was born, and shortly afterward, in 1953, their daughter Monique was born. The closeness of these two births may have contributed to the increasing tensions in their marriage.

A New Opportunity: Research Director for UNESCO Study

During the first years at Saarbrücken, Boesch became known as a child psychologist. He was invited to attend, as an expert, UNESCO sponsored conferences on educational problems in post-World War II Europe and Asia. His contributions were well received. As a result, in 1955 he was offered to direct a research institute organized in Bangkok by UNESCO and the Thai Government. The purpose of the institute was to study the influence of culture on the development of children. With the permission and even the encouragement of the rector of the Saar University, Boesch accepted the offer, his first experience of living and conducting research outside of Europe.

With a wife and three young children (Christophe and Monique at home, Andreas at a boarding school in Switzerland), the decision to leave for Bangkok was, of course, emotionally charged. Given the tensions in their marriage, Ernest and Claire speculated that a period of separation might be beneficial. In 1955, Ernest went to Bangkok and Claire remained in Saarbrucken with their young children. The 3 year sojourn was a major turning point in both his personal and professional life. How it affected Boesch's further work and development, will be reflected in subsequent chapters.

REFERENCES

Baltes, P. B. (1997). Ernst E. Boesch at 80: Reflections from a student on the culture of psychology, *Culture and psychology, 3*(3), 247-256.

Boesch, E. E. (1997). The story of a cultural psychologist. *Culture and psychology, 3* (3), 257-275.

Piaget, J. (1962). *Play, dreams, and imitation in childhood.* New York: Norton & Company.

Sugarman, S. (1987). *Piaget's construction of the child's reality.* New York: Cambridge University Press.

CHAPTER 3

SYMBOLIC ACTION THEORY AND ITS APPLICATIONS[1]

The Authors in Collaboration With E. E. Boesch

"It is the dilemma of psychology to deal as a natural science with an object which creates history."

—Boesch, 1971, p. 9

In the preceding chapters we sketched the background and early development of Ernest Boesch. The purpose of this chapter is to present his contributions to psychology and therefore to clarify why we consider his work to be worthy of a biographical profile. His professional life can be quickly summarized. His basic schooling was in St. Gallen, followed by studies at the University of Geneva. For 8 years he was a school psychologist in the Canton of St. Gallen, a time of rich field experience. In 1951 he accepted a position as Professor of psychology at the new University of the Saar. An offer from UNESCO to serve as Director of the International Institute for Child Study (IICS) was accepted in 1955. In 1958 Ernest Boesch returned from Bangkok a substantially changed person both professionally and personally. In 1962 he founded at the University of the Saar the "Socio-Psychological Research Center for Development Planning," a unit for research in developing countries. In the years to come he assumed the

Discovering Cultural Psychology: A Profile and Selected Readings of Ernest E. Boesch, pp. 45–79

double function of teaching at the department of psychology and, as director of the Research Center conducting research projects in Thailand. In 1987 he retired, the author of 14 books and more than a hundred articles on a broad range of topics.

Maintaining remarkable mental acuity at nearly 90 years of age, he continues to be engaged in writing. This range of professional activity, after all, is not basically different from the lives of other cultural psychologists. But his scientific contributions are. They present an original, encompassing theory of human action in relation to and interaction with culture. His original contributions are the focus of this chapter.

Before continuing, however, we want to make it clear that Ernest Boesch participated substantially in this chapter. The reason for this is quite simple. Boesch developed his contribution to cultural psychology, symbolic action theory, through his observations and reflections during and after his years of research and teaching. He did so in increments during his "journey of discovery," starting with a strong foundation in developmental psychology and insightfully employing interpretations of human behavior as a Piagetian constructivist. Because he is still an active and engaged scholar, we thought that he should be accorded this unprecedented opportunity to explain the process as he lived it and remembered it. Through his words and recollections, and not our interpretations of his works, we believe the substance of this chapter will help immensely in the understanding of what he has done and why he did it. We edited Ernest Boesch's commentaries and added explanations and clarifications when deemed necessary. Throughout the chapter we tried to pursue the essence of information Ernest shared during interviews and expanded upon in voluminous e-mail correspondence. For these efforts we are deeply grateful, especially given challenges he now experiences with progressively declining vision.

We join Ernest Boesch in stressing that he was not a member of a "movement" or a "school" of cultural psychology. When he began his work, cultural psychology as well as cross-cultural psychology and psychological anthropology—a trilogy of somewhat interrelated fields—did not yet exist in any organized form. Historically, this precluded formal contact with organizations or groups that may have, even if in some nascent form, provided some semblance of a theoretical anchor or orientation. He started his work as a creative scholarly endeavor and only progressively established contacts with other scholars and their emerging ideas in the field. The contacts he made shall be mentioned in due course.

Ernest Boesch has presented his theory in many publications as it developed from tentative beginnings to a complex system of thought and observation. Following is a sketch of this development and then a more detailed description of symbolic action theory (SAT). This cannot be done here as extensively as Boesch did in his text, symbolic action theory and cultural psychology (Boesch, 1991). However, the readings in Part II do provide insights into his views as they were presented over his long and distinguished career. A bibliography of Ernest Boesch's works is included in this text for those who wish to consult a more diverse range of his original works published in English, French, and German. Whenever possible, readers are urged to consult the original sources to enrich their understanding of SAT and its applications.

Jürgen Straub (2005) wrote in his foreword to Ernest Boesch's latest book that "from the start Boesch's action theory and cultural psychology was ahead of his time" (p. 7). Indeed, when, in 1951, he started teaching action theory at his university, to our knowledge, and more importantly his, most other psychologists in Europe would have rejected the term "action." It could not be operationalized and measured, and, much worse, it may have sounded teleological, therefore making it patently unscientific. Yet Boesch, influenced by Piaget and the French psychiatrist Pierre Janet, taught it and started a research program that focused on the regulation of action in space in 1952. Delayed by his Thai assignment, he published that early research in 1971 in the chapter "Organisation und Regulation" of *Zwischen zwei Wirklichkeiten* (*Between two Realities*). In these years, his interpretation of action theory was relatively simple. It centered on single goal-oriented actions, a kind of cybernetic model of goal-process anticipations and feedback regulations between "is-values" and "should-values." Not yet related to culture, it was, however, the germ of an idea waiting to be nurtured.

RESEARCH IN BANGKOK: 1955-1958

Ernest Boesch's early years at the University of the Saar were unexpectedly interrupted in 1955 when UNESCO offered him a position as director of the newly founded "International Institute for Child Study" (IICS) in Bangkok. This was a decisive event in his life, and he described it quite candidly in an article titled "What kind of a game in a far-away forest?" (1997a). For one thing, Ernest Boesch had never been to Asia, say nothing of living there apart from his wife, young children, and the familiar European context. Not unlike many of his European colleagues and other professional peers throughout the highly industrialized and "psychologized" world, he was a well-trained psychologist who was unfamiliar with the vast majority of non-European cultures.

His assignment was to study the impact of culture on the development of children, and to train the Thai staff of the IICS. Boesch was offered this post on the basis of his reputation as a child psychologist, despite the fact that he lacked any knowledge of cultural psychology and anthropology. Thus, during his first year in Bangkok he had to work hard at filling these gaps of information, in addition to training the six staff members in child psychology and experimental-diagnostic techniques. Planning the details of a research project to be carried out in the Bangkok schools was an added dimension of his responsibilities. What "free time" he had was given to learning the Thai language with admirable dedication and a strong desire to enter as intimately as possible into the Thai culture. By the summer of 1956 the research plan was ready. It contained a theoretical presentation of action theory and of main psychological terms used, plus detailed instructions for tests which he thought to be more or less "culture-free", the interview schedules for the parents, and a theoretical justification of the methods proposed. (The term "culture-free" was freely used many years ago, but Boesch soon had to discover its questionable claim, and it was eventually also seriously challenged by methodologists in both cultural and cross-cultural psychology.) The introduction to the research plan indicated its aim, which at that time was original and still unique: to facilitate the coordination of research among departments of child psychology in order to collect data from different cultures. That was, of course, UNESCO's intention, and this first Research Plan attempted to give it a concrete methodological and theoretical framework. It served as the blueprint for the teaching and research at the IICS.

In terms of the daily schedule, Ernest Boesch was very busy yet the work was accomplished satisfactorily, presenting, of course, the usual problems in cross-cultural groups, made easy however by the open goodwill of the Thai staff. The stress Ernest felt came rather from his attempts to operationalize "culture" as the independent variable in his research scheme. This, of course, was his main assignment, but how could any scholar successfully operationalize "culture" given its complexity and multidimensionality? The literature he consulted, both anthropological and psychological, did not provide much help. He avoided the easy choice to concentrate research on a single variable, as for instance Piaget had proposed or as one or the other of the UNESCO research fellows at the IICS preferred. He assumed that the "impact of culture on child development" was broad, with different forces influencing many functions. Therefore, he assumed, a first study should cover a broad spectrum of meaningful topics. The breadth of his research plan, which even by today's standards was acceptably sophisticated, resulted from these considerations.

Implementation of the plan from late 1956 to 1957 was not easy. The staff members of the IICS, all educators by training and experience, had previously received only a minimum of exposure to psychological methodology and commensurate research experience. Although the first year was mainly devoted to their training, the time was of course too short for making them skilled experimenters, and so the experiments undertaken in the Bangkok primary schools were far from well done. However, the results could be presented at the 1958 "Expert Meeting on Cross-Cultural Research in Child Psychology" which Boesch organized on behalf of UNESCO in Bangkok. For this meeting, he wrote the main working paper entitled "Problems and Methods in Cross-Cultural Research." It contained the first public presentation of Ernest Boesch's action theoretical view of culture. We believe that the working paper he wrote was perhaps the first of its kind, coming as it did from that meeting. In retrospect, it is a validation of Straub's recent assertion that Boesch was indeed "well ahead of his time" with the presentation of his views on action theory and cultural psychology.

However, before that conference, a crucial event occurred that had a strong bearing on the further development of his action theory. Following is his account of what happened.

> While driving on the main road to the Bangkok airport, a "samlor" (a tricycle riksha) turned unconcernedly, without the driver's looking around, from a side road directly into the path of our car. It was only by a rapid braking that we avoided an accident. Pondering this incident, I was suddenly struck by the thought that for this riksha driver a side road and highway formed a different structure than for me. For me, at the junction between the two lay an invisible barrier, forcing me to slow down and to ascertain the safety of proceeding further. Space, over and beyond its physical layout, was mentally structured, containing limitations for our actions which, I presumed, varied by culture and, probably, also by individual. (Boesch, 1991, p. 9; 1997, p. 8)

Boesch (1997a) then commented,

> although an apparently simple insight, it had important consequences. Action theory, which I had professed at my university since 1951, became cultural-ecological. Our world as we live in it is both structured by action and structures our action. It is an uninterrupted feed-back system which, after all in 1957, before cybernetic thinking entered psychology, was not that obvious a thought. (p. 8)

The event described here resulted in a paradigm shift and eventually a substantial revolution in how Boesch (1997a) perceived, studied, and explained the relationship between human beings and culture. He commented further about this discovery as follows.

> This insight did of course not provide me with a "general factor," a formula explaining Thai culture, but it had an advantage over other definitions of culture. It handed me so-to-say my proper key to unraveling the cultural

texture, but it consisted of more than just rational understanding. Karl Bühler would have called it an "Aha-Erlebnis," a "that's-it experience." Such an experience possesses a highly subjective valence. It marks our mental "action potential," the one that masters a complex problem, or brings an end to a situation that is perplexing and full of doubts. Being able to find what I have just called a key increased my confidence in being able to unravel the maze of cultural intricacies, to arrive at an intelligible structure. That, of course, was only a hope, but it gave me a direction. (p. 9)

The event occurred too late to have any impact on the research program, but it had a profound influence on the theory. What was it that made it so important? In Ernest Boesch's mind, insights never occur out of the blue, and neither are they merely intellectual. For events to be meaningful, they have to meet some kind of emotional readiness, as unspecific and unconscious as this may be. In fact, one might notice that already the 1952-53 experiments mentioned above allowed Boesch to realize that space is organized according to action. Yet, he needed the Samlor incident to trigger both, a decisive theoretical insight, and a personal reorientation. Thus, asking what gave the incident such importance to Ernest Boesch may help to understand not only the Thai man's behavior, but also why, after completing his obligations in Thailand, Ernest Boesch did not simply return to his Western-based, pre-Bangkok psychology. He had arrived at the realization that he was a new cultural psychologist.

Let us look more generally at Ernest Boesch's (1997a) experiences in Thailand. They are described as follows.

Thailand was the complete opposite of my past. The climate was hot and sunny in contrast to cold St-Gall and gray Saarland. The people were friendly, smiling, and relaxed in contrast to the purposefully serious Europeans. Thais knew a compassionate tolerant religion and they gathered in warmly colored temples. By contrast, Europeans experienced a strict and rule-oriented Christianity in gloomy churches. Thais had a teeming and vital nature in contrast to the secretive one of Europeans. This captivated my interest. For example, in my Thai house and garden I encountered termites, stinging black and burning red ants, turtles, six different kinds of snakes, tuckaes, house geckos, bats, all kinds of birds, toads, and frogs. I found the food to my taste, acquired new habits of socializing, dressing, and grooming. I even learned more spontaneity, curiosity, and a fresh awareness. It would have been interesting to examine how I changed and how I remained constant. However, it is likely I changed and remained constant in every respect, although *to varying degrees.* (p. 6)

Thus learning the Thai language acquired a more than practical meaning. Ernest Boesch wanted, he writes, "to belong" or, as he called it, "to be one of them." This did not mean that he wanted to identify with any specific person—what he wished for was rather to participate in that "Thai-ness" which came to him as an unexpected fulfillment of his private "fantasms" (a term that will be explained presently). In this vein, the event with the samlor driver, "uneducated and dumb," as Ernest's driving companion labeled him, may have gained somewhat symbolic meaning as a confrontation with "Thai-ness," in a situation the structure of which was relatively easy for Ernest's curious mind to understand. At that point, after close to 2 years in Thailand, he had developed sufficient familiarity and openness to have an unbiased perception of the event. Some years later he published this insight in the article "Space and Time as Valence Systems." The article became the basis for a developmental-constructivist theory of man-culture interaction. Although published twice (1963 and 1971) it did not appear to receive particular notice in the professional literature. European psychology was still unable to regard humans as cultural beings. The "Seven Flaws" article in the selected readings section of this book is also relevant to this point.

Post-Bangkok: The Path to SAT

On leaving Bangkok, Ernest Boesch wrote, he felt nostalgia and profound disorientation. In a state of what some might refer to as "culture shock," or perhaps more specifically "reverse culture shock" he felt like a stranger in Europe, an estrangement both professional and private. In his private life, his marriage, already seriously compromised before Bangkok, ended in divorce and, as a result, too, the painful separation from his three young children. Two years after his return to Germany, he married the daughter of a respected Bangkok family of minor nobility. The upheaval in his personal life added to the cultural conflict that Ernest Boesch experienced after his sojourn in Thailand.

As mentioned earlier, Boesch (1997) experienced a definite professional change that could be called an uprooting. He described it as follows.

> From child psychology I had turned to cultural psychology, and this was more than just a change of label. At that time, behaviorism dominated our science, yet, while I never had been a behaviorist, my new approach, "emic" rather than "etic," hermeneutic more than nomothetic, put me squarely outside the respectable circles. But I also carried back the prestige of "one who had been there" (p. 9)

At that time, assistance to developing countries counted as a political priority. However, Germany lacked experienced experts. Given his experience, Ernest was invited into the advisory council of the German Ministry for Economic Cooperation, a position he held for several years. Universities were also requested to contribute to this policy. Therefore, the University of the Saar founded a Center for Development Assistance (later called "Socio-psychological Research Centre for Development Planning—RCDP) and appointed Ernest as its director.

It was this Center that kept Boesch in Saarbrücken for his entire career, in spite of honorable calls from two other German and two Swiss universities. None of these would have offered him the opportunity to continue his psychological work that deeply involved culture. The Center was fortunate also in other respects: It was given its own building, located ideally in the clearing of a forest, about a 10-minute walk from the main campus. A self-contained unit, it consisted of a staff of four permanent assistants, two secretaries, and temporary assistants whose number varied according to the requirements of particular projects. However, because it was not given its own research stipend or budget, all projects had to be funded by external sources.

The charge given to the RCDP was to conduct psychological research into problems of development in Asian and African countries. That meant primarily applied studies, such as one that dealt with German vocational schools in Afghanistan and Thailand. However, in his dual function as head of the department of psychology and director of the RCDP, Ernest tried to find research problems that were both useful to planning developmental programs and generally relevant to psychological theory. He finally opted to address problems of social change.

Forty-one years ago he published *Psychologische Theorie des sozialen Wandels* (*Psychological Theory of Social Change*, Boesch, 1966a). This was a very elaborate, detailed presentation of—not yet symbolic—action theory applied to concrete events in the social "field." Again, there was practically no response from the scientific community. It was an article of about 80 pages (half the length of the original manuscript due to editorial limitations) published in a voluminous *Handbook of Development Policy*. The venue may partly explain the poor reception the paper received given that it was somewhat beyond the scope of usual professional psychological literature. However, it became the blueprint for four of the major projects that Boesch implemented in Thailand.

The first two studies were based on the hypothesis that new knowledge and skills were first acquired by educated groups in a community and would then progressively filter down to those who were less educated. The first study tried to assess the attitude towards social innovation of administrative cadres in official agencies. A report on this appeared in 1970 under the title *Zwiespältige Eliten* (Ambivalent Elites, Boesch, 1970). A more important second study was funded by the Deutsche Forschungsgemeinschaft (German Research Foundation). It concerned communication between doctors and patients. This presented a paradigmatic situation of interaction between highly educated professionals and less informed groups, each having to make adaptations when attempting to communicate. Thus the overall rationale was to investigate not only general communication problems, but specifically also the transfer of new information by the doctors to their patients—one might have called it the doctor's educational role. This project forced Boesch to enlarge the concept of action by asking in which sense illness could also be considered an action. At the same time, wary of questionnaire studies, Boesch recognized the opportunity to closely observe the communication process. In about a dozen Thai hospitals his team was allowed to install recorders in the consultation rooms. Doctor and patient interviews completed the data thus collected. A parallel study in villages explored the attitude of farmers toward illness and traditional healing. Boesch (1997a) commented on this Doctor-Patient study as follows.

> Here, the structural view induced by the "samlor incident" became enlarged by a dynamism of interaction between unequal partners, one able to heal, the other needing to be healed. This did not replace the structural view: We were going to study a social space with its own distances and barriers and techniques of approach; but within this structural system we conceived a dynamism of take and give, of mutual influences and dependencies (because, in subtle ways, the doctor was dependent on his patient, too). Culture, as a field of action, was considered here in both its structural and dynamic dimension. Finally, the doctor-patient interaction, although focused around an illness, constituted an intersection of two different goal systems, self-conceptions, beliefs and social loyalties. Thus, the denotational content of the interaction differed as to connotations, or meanings; the specific action, by its cultural imbeddedness, became also symbolic. (p. 10; for a report on the project see Boesch, 1977)

Later, Ernest Boesch noted that neither at the time of designing the project nor during the data analysis were all the implications fully recognized. In part, he was occupied with the practical execution of the project. The German research assistants were not highly motivated to learn Thai even though they were given the opportunity to study the language for a whole year. Therefore, they were not very efficient in training and supervising the Thais who had to carry out the actual interviewing. Still, the research offered many valuable and complex observations, incentives for further theoretical development. During the study Boesch became more acquainted with thinking patterns of farmers, with magical thought and procedures, with the polyvalence of goals, or with the impact of beliefs on practical action. An experience he considered to have fundamentally furthered his theoretical work.

The next two innovative studies were conceptually somewhat different. They concerned, as Ernest Boesch (1997b) wrote, "the being-between-two-worlds of the farmer." The first study was on the appeal which the big town, Bangkok, had for the villager, intending to understand the attraction of its facilities, fashions, and even seductions. The second study was focused on how farmers anticipated the possible impact of the future on their present lives (p. 11). It was influenced by Robert B. Textor's "future anthropology" but aimed at studying the threat rather than the promise that changes might hold for the farmers. Both studies, although with a different emphasis, were intended to analyze the impact of social innovations on less informed groups.

Methodologically, however, the projects initiated a radical change. The doctor-patient study made obvious the vital importance of researchers' mastery of the language and a detailed familiarity with the theoretical frame of the investigations. The study had also demonstrated that learning about the attitudes and thoughts of the "subjects" required time, meaning a situation of mutual confidence, and of familiarity with their living conditions. Therefore, the two new projects were planned as a full year of observation and interaction in each of the villages. The researchers were Phornchai Sripraphai, a Thai sociologist and his wife, Cathleen O'Hearn, an American psychologist. After receiving extensive training in the rationale of the project, they stayed together in the selected village, participating in many daily activities and avoiding formal interviewing until the very last period of their stay. They gathered information concerning the problems of the project during many informal conversations at various occasions. The observational data may not lend itself to rigorous statistical treatment, but is incomparably richer and more valid in content than data obtained in formal interviews.

Ernest Boesch called these research methods "biotic" and gave them priority over experimental research: "unobtrusive interviewing in natural settings will have to be developed as a special skill and will have to precede, accompany—and often also to follow up—more formal questioning (see 1991, p. 364 ss). However, he provided the following advisement:

> the main methodological requisite will be an adequate theoretical framework ... of cultural forms and conditions of action.... (This will guide the interviewer to decide) whom to interview on what.... Therefore, in planning as well as performing research, our most frequent question was: What kind of action is this for the actor within his specific context and situation?... Thus, when planning an investigation on future anticipations of Thai villagers (Sripraphai & Sripraphai, 1988), we had to specify under what conditions a person started future planning, in which form and along which dimensions. We had to ask, too, what it meant to talk to an investigator

about future anticipations (this being an action in its own right); which, then, brought up the question of how, when, and why an individual tended to protect his private imaginations, fears, and hopes. Inquiring about the nature of an action will necessarily lead to action networks within an action field. (1991, p. 365)

All these insights and experiences provided by the research activities of the RCDP were supported and deepened from a very different perspective, that of Ernest Boesch's studies and practice of psychoanalysis. For about fifteen years, although on a limited time scale, he practiced psychoanalysis and daydream techniques. This was because, in part, in the Department of Psychology he had to teach introduction to psychotherapy, but more so also for gaining additional insight into the private functioning of minds. This experience certainly contributed much to his thinking about the symbolism of action and objects. Freud's writings were an important source of information for Ernest Boesch; while not following Freud's biological determinism, he found his method of free association to be a valuable method of investigation. Their use requires, however, caution and skill, and before all the awareness that free associations are actions, too, influenced, therefore, by momentary circumstances and purposes no less than by deeper sources.

Symbolic Action Theory

The research projects of the RCDP and teaching in the Department of Psychology were a more than full-time assignment which left Ernest Boesch little time for writing. However, in 1969 the university added first a second, then soon additional professors to Boesch's department. His work load diminished, the period of his main theoretical publications began. In 1970 he wrote a small, 87 page booklet with the title *Zwischen Angst und Triumph; über das Ich und seine Bestätigung (Between Anxiety and Triumph—on the I and its Confirmation)*. The work did not correspond to the spirit of the time, and so it was published only in 1975, mainly because the lector in the publishing house Boesch worked with happened to be a poet receptive to the aesthetic reflections in the manuscript. Yet, it contained essentially all the ingredients of his symbolic action theory, albeit not yet in the later terminology: goal orientation, action sequences, immediate and superordinate regulations, polyvalence, action potential, symbolism. Most important perhaps, it contained a fully-fledged theory of aesthetic experience and thus opened a problem area which would gain much importance in Boesch's work.

Already before publication of the 1975 booklet, Ernest Boesch started writing his first major presentation of action theory, openly symbolic although not yet labeled as such. It appeared in 1976 under the title *Psychopathologie des Alltags—zur Ökopsychologie des Handelns und seiner Störungen* (*Everyday Psychopathology—On the Eco-psychololgy of Action and its Disturbances*); see Boesch, 1976. The title and the thematic orientation of the volume were influenced by circumstances. At that time, Ernest Boesch was considered for a chair in clinical psychology at the University of Geneva. He would succeed his former teacher, André Rey. He greatly coveted the post, but for several reasons he finally turned down the offer. Yet, it was this situation which made him use the term "psychopathology" in the title of the work, although, by adding "everyday," he reduced its scope to mostly normal disturbances of action and its regulation, such as fatigue, annoyance, anxiety, stress, or guilt. In the subtitle "eco-psychology" he clearly manifested his cultural interest (culture, he wrote elsewhere, is the ecosystem of man). Thus, the book centered on the eco-cultural embeddedness of action, different affective regulations, and a description of various "fantasms," a term here used for the first time. In 1980 a shorter summary of his theory called *Kultur und Handlung—Einführung in die Kulturpsychologie* (*Culture and Action—Introduction to Cultural Psychology*), was also written during the 1970s, a very creative decade for Ernest Boesch. At that time, German psychology officially still followed an experimental ideology strongly influenced by neo-behaviorism and statistics. Therefore, these books gained limited recognition in the official circles of psychology.

However, they offered a broad and systematic presentation of action theory, symbolic without doubt, but Boesch did not yet qualify it by this term. In fact, the three publications have to be seen together. They each presented Boesch's action theory, but with partly different emphases. The first centered on the experience and creation of art. The other two strongly emphasized the ecological embeddedness of action, to which the "Psychopathology" adds, besides the disturbances of action, the new term of "fantasms." The third book not only summarized and completed the main aspects of the theory, it gave a special place to the symbolism of action and added the terms "objectivation," "subjectivation," and "myth," terms which will play an important role in the later publications of the theory. SAT, emerging and evolving since 1958, was fully present in three books of the 1970s. The next major publications of 1991 and 1995 did not basically change the theory, but summarized, concentrated, enlarged, and deepened its presentation. In addition, they were enriched by detailed analyses of concrete examples.

Action, Myth, Fantasms, Action Potential

Let us now look at some main terms of SAT and their theoretical implications. This can, of course, not possibly mean an extensive review of the theory. Boesch has analyzed the different aspects of action thoroughly in a number of publications (see the bibliography), and to summarize it all would by far exceed the space of this book. We intend to concentrate here mainly on those concepts which distinguish Ernest Boesch's symbolic theory most clearly from other action theories, which, in the meantime, have become widely accepted. Although an important distinction seems to us also the theory of aesthetic experience contained in SAT, we regret being unable to include it in this summary.

A first basic concept is of course *Action*. Action is goal-directed behavior. Goals are anticipations of future states which either attract or repulse, so that action may seek some desired state or object or may try to avoid an unwelcome situation or threatening object. Goals are "dominant" contents of mind – they enjoy a "primacy of consciousness" (Boesch, 1980, 1991, p 126ss), which often results in inhibiting most—or all—other preoccupations.

Reaching a goal demands energy, skill, attention, devotion, patience, which are all, like the goal anticipation itself, internal qualities; thus, action is always both internal and external, in other words, it implies, inseparably and simultaneously, a subjective and an objective experience —a duality which plays an important role in Boesch's theoretical work. He seems to see one of the basic human motives in the reduction of discrepancies between internal intentions, motivations, and feelings and the external conditions and effects of action. This is a problem which he considered particularly in the context of language and of artistic creation (Boesch, 1983, 1991).

Actions are never isolated behaviors. They occur within fields and specific situations which imply both material and cultural opportunities and barriers, licemcies, rules, prohibitions, even threats; they have to be coordinated with other actions the person plans or is already engaged in, as well with the actions of other persons. In addition, goals, most of the time, prepare for or lead to other actions, in other words, actions form chains of goals and systems of coordination.

Some actions are merely "instrumental," aiming at a main, or "superordinate" goal, such as exams which have no value in or of themselves; they are instrumental, in the sense o necessary conditions, for reaching the superordinate main goal, such as becoming a doctor; however, this will again serve further goals, and thus becomes instrumental in its turn, and so on. These successive goals, of course, have to take into account the effects they might have on related actions, actors and situations, they will therefore be integrated somehow into networks of diverse interests, individual and social concerns. This complex texture of action will be controlled and regulated by some "overarching" purposes, such as perhaps, for the doctor, "leading a good life" or "helping people in need" or even such a subconscious one as "defeating death"—whatever those mean in the mind of the actor. Naturally, this complex of actions is related to past experiences which may influence the actual motivation and performance in many ways. Therefore, to understand an action completely, it is not enough to look at its immediate manifest goal; one has to consider the complexity of its intentions and determinants—Boesch speaks of its "polyvalence." This term derives, on the one hand, from the double inner and external experiences with their own valences, proper to all actions, but on the other hand also from the fact that action goals are composite, i.e., mostly pursue several associated purposes, although the "direct" or main goal may mainly occupy the consciousness—the doctor acquiring healing skills wants to enhance also his social status, improve his marriage perspectives, gain or deepen friendships, plus other less obvious hopes, including even long-term ones.

Actions have to overcome distances particularly those of space and time; intention and achievement of a goal are never simultaneous. The time lag may be frustrating if the distant goal implies long waiting. It may be strenuous or even painful if the performance is hard or difficult; it may also be pleasant, even to the extent that one enjoys the path leading to the goal more than the goal itself. These processes are controlled by "should-values," such as skill, efficiency, elegance, style, speed, economy, and the actor tries to keep his performance within the limits traced by such criteria. Pierre Janet considered these controls of the course of action to be "regulations," meaning by that largely unconscious, emotional "secondary actions," a term designing the fact that those regulations are not actions in their own right, but function only for acting upon, or controlling, the goal-directed "primary action." While Janet particularly considered the regulation of the energy input, for Boesch secondary actions may be energetic as well as cognitive, unconscious as well as conscious.

Overcoming the goal distance also requires, naturally, figuring out how to proceed. This "process anticipation" will of course be influenced by past experience, successes as well as failures. It requires in particular to evaluate one's skill and means of action on the one hand, the material and social situation to be taken into account, on the other. Such anticipation may reveal inadequacies in one's—objective as well as subjective—action potential, and may thus induce special preparations, sometimes even a preparatory learning phase. To pursue a goal can thus turn into a complex of coordinated actions, possibly transforming the actor's situation, may be even himself. Of course, all this is controlled not only by the individual, but as much—or even more—by cultural standards and rules.

"Anticipation" as a concept, because of its teleological implications, was often a kind of stumbling block for those who attempted to understand and accept Boesch's theory. It sounded unscientific to behaviorally-oriented psychologists. However, although anticipations may sometimes simply project previous experience into the future, as often they conceive variations of the actual situation, innovations or even transformations of one's skills, action orientations or thinking. For Ernest Boesch, therefore, future anticipation is the realm of hope, of invention, of conceiving more appropriate forms of reality and life, in short the dimension of human creativity, and therefore corresponds to a basic orientation of human beings.

Anticipation is an action in its own right; there are persons who sometimes spend more time in anticipating what they might do rather than doing it. However, anticipation is usually a mental action, not performed materially—it is not "praxic" in Boesch's terminology ("praxic" = openly performed, distinct from "practical" = effective or successful action). It belongs to that other, important type of action which Ernest Boesch calls variably "referent," "imaginary" or "ideational." Imaginary actions are important for mainly two reasons: On the one hand, unhampered by material or social constraints, they can freely invent possible or even improbable situations, can imagine actions of all kinds, and should an imagined action appear too difficult, it can easily be abandoned and replaced. Ernest Boesch (1991) says:

> The power of imaginative action in anticipating events, manipulating reality, tentatively transforming the world according to one's wishes or fears, and creating new kinds of reality, gives imagination a pervasive importance. Imaginative aspects of action thus constitute a considerable and necessary proportion of our life.... Praxic action provides feelings of mastery which imaginative action cannot equal; yet, the latter introduces and elaborates the dimension of potentiality. Thus, the actual mastery is complemented by a potential one, and in this sense each level of action contributes in its own way to the subjective action potential. (p. 99)

Be it added that, in fact, all action is accompanied and motivated, often even almost exclusively, by imaginative contents, which will become particularly evident in the section on symbolism.

The second reason making imaginative action important is that, as an inside performance, it remains private and therefore not accessible to social control. Social constraints imposed on praxic action reduce their variability and thereby limit possibilities of innovation. This greater freedom of imaginative action may—and often does—extend to socially tolerated media of expression, mainly fiction and art, so that many social changes or revolutions have their forerunners in those media.

Let us add here, to finish this very short summary of Ernest Boesch's concept of action, that he points also at "side-actions" which may accompany the main one—such as taking a break, drinking a cup of coffee, have a chat, but also singing, whistling, or work. These may sometimes mainly serve to combat fatigue, to recover one's energy, and might then be considered to be a kind of "secondary actions," but as often they are real side actions, trying for instance to maintain contact with colleagues or with the outside world by listening to the news, having a look at the newspaper or simply thinking about some other concern. Of particular interest are perhaps the monologues accompanying action, such as murmuring to oneself "ok, that's done," "and now, let's not forget," "O God, that's difficult"—and so on. Some people do it aloud, others only silently, yet, such monologues reveal that we continuously reflect our action, confronting ourselves with it. Thus, the monologues during action do more than control the process; they relate it with our self, with the actor's total situation.

For expanding further the meaning of action in the cultural field, Ernest Boesch introduced new concepts, the main ones being "fantasms," "myth," "action potential" and the "symbolic variance" of action and experience. He is careful to stress that in coining the term of myth, he was strongly influenced by Claude Lévi-Strauss, the famous French anthropologist, founder of the structuralist movement, while Gaston Bachelard, a philosopher no less famous in France, confirmed in important ways his conception of symbolism. A conception, however, which owes much to Sigmund Freud's writings and Boesch's own psychoanalytic experience—and perhaps not least to his literary background.

"Myths" and "Fantasms"

What does Boesch understand by "myth?" He speaks of it already in 1980, but gives it much closer consideration in 1991. In usual parlance the term designates some kind of tale, like the Oedipus myth, relating to basic topics of human destiny. However, as Lévi-Strauss has shown in multiple careful analyses, different myth-tales may express a same basic structure. Boesch therefore reserves the term of "myth" to those basic structures and uses "myth-stories" for the tales and, like Lévi-Strauss, "mythemes" for particular themes relating to myths. These basic structures, binary for Lévi-Strauss (such as Yin-Yang or male-female), do however not necessarily, for Ernest Boesch, correspond to rational configurations. On the contrary, he defines myth as follows: "A myth is a system of explanation and justification for which no rational proof or deduction is or can be given. It somehow encapsulates firm and unquestioned ideas of reality, its reasons and consequences." He gives an example:

> A woman potter, while modeling her pot, might tell her on looking child the story of God moulding man from clay,... The story of "God the maker of man" is a myth, or rather; in the terminology I propose here, a "myth-story...." It explains the origin of things and of the world as a whole, implying promises (God the protector) and limitations (the commanding, controlling and punishing God).

The myth does not necessarily take the form of a story,

> For example the if-then statement "God helps those who help themselves" is a cultural "mytheme" for which no proof is given or felt to be necessary. In every culture, popular wisdom and collective attitudes are expressed in such hortatory and explanatory statements. (1991, p. 123)

Thus, "patriotism," "manliness," "womanliness" would name other myths which a child experiences concretely by manifold behaviors, pleasures, amusements, instructions, prohibitions, rewards, sanctions, disappointments, models and antimodels, stories, proverbs—and so on, differing according to situations, environments and, of course, culture. It may be noted that the term of "myth" does not, as in popular usage, imply to be "mere fiction"—excluding the question of truth, Ernest Boesch simply considers that a myth is accepted without requiring proof.

These experiences, partly congruent, partly different or even contradictory will, in the course of development, be progressively unified, similar to, but more complex than the structuring of objects; they will, of course, shape the behavior of the child, meaning that mythemes imply concrete instructions for what, when and how to act. Yet, at the same time, the child will assimilate them and thereby form his or her subjective conception of the social myth. For instance, to be brave, a mytheme belonging to the myth of "manliness," will of course be shaped individually, according to situation, past experience, hopes or fears of a boy.

Thus, the assimilation of myths is controlled not only by the actual situation of the individual, but particularly by the goals he or she tries to pursue in life. These anticipations of a personal future, Ernest Boesch calls "fantasms." He tells that he somehow intuitively caught onto the term when meeting a man with a dog strolling in the wood. What kind of fantasies, he pondered, tied this man to his dog? Did he hope it to be a protection against imagined dangers, or a companion in his loneliness, or what else? There must be some kind of filters channeling our interests, likings, apprehensions, our receptiveness or aversion towards what we meet in life. They may, of course, be due to previous experiences, conditionings, trainings, models, but those are transformed into projections of personal being, into hopes, expectations or anxieties. Thus, Boesch (1991) defines fantasms as "overarching goals which concern the nature of the antici-pated ego-world relationship, including both hopes and fears" (p. 124). They are "dominant goal patterns, guiding the direction and evaluation of actions with regard to their ego-relevance. As such they transcend actual situations, yet, they orient the ways in which we structure or assess our relationship with the environment" (1991, p. 268). If those private goal formations "conspire with myths," that is, somehow control their assimilation, naturally the inverse is no less true: Social myths strongly influence the development of fantasms. One may argue the terms, but the interaction of fantasms and myths, however one would choose to call it, doubtlessly sheds an important light on the genesis of basic motivations and allows an intimate description of enculturation processes.

Indeed, the mere knowledge of social myths does not give them moti-vational qualities. An anthropologist may acquire much insight into the belief system of a culture, yet, because he did not undergo this intimate blending of myths with his personal fantasms, he will always remain a stranger, not feeling motivated to cultural integration like a native per-son.

The term of "fantasm" is often understood to be synonymous with "fantasy," yet Boesch (1991) clearly distinguishes between the two. He clarified the difference by the following example:

> A boy climbs a tree as high as he can and imagines himself on the mast of a ship on the lookout against pirates. This I would call a fantasy, It expresses [however] a kind of basic theme: It divides the world into good and bad people and assigns to the ego the role of watching out and defending his field of action against evil. This basic theme would be called a fantasm— more specifically a "threat fantasm" combined with one of "self assertion". Obviously such a theme can be expressed in many different fantasies, emphasizing now the one, now the other fantasmic component. (p. 124)

Thus, the individual may form various fantasms which can be mutually reinforcing, but occasionally also conflicting. Most of the time he or she will not be clearly conscious of them, yet, they will unconsciously direct the person's tastes and interests, likes and dislikes up to anticipations and plans for the future. Should different fantasms conflict with each other, they might seriously unbalance the person. This is why Boesch thinks that a careful "fantasm-analysis" would not only be important in psychother-apy, but might even be helpful in education. Indeed, many neurotic reac-tions stem from disharmonious fantasms or from impediments to fantasmic striving rather, or at least as much, as from past frustrations – outlook may be more traumatizing than recollection. (As to myth and fantasm see also chapter 7, Part II).

"Action Potential"

A third overarching goal is the "action potential." Boesch, defines it as

one of those overarching goals which direct, control, or regulate specific actions, and among those it is probably the most important. I tend, indeed, to consider it to be what one could call the "basic motivation." Indeed, we continuously strive at optimizing our action potential, and this reinforcing, strengthening, or enlarging of our readiness and capacity to act appears most of the time to be more important than any specific single goal. (1991, p. 105)

What does Boesch mean by "optimizing the action potential"? There are three main points. First, it means experiencing and improving a mere "functional disposability." A person may engage in playful or pleasurable activities for their own sake, such as running, jumping, climbing, aimlessly driving around, all kinds of sport, physical as well as intellectual, sometimes even senselessly destructive. Second, action potential implies improving and enlarging one's "competence," skill, practical and intellectual "mastery." And a third meaning Boesch (1991) sees in a twofold "ordering potential," aiming, on the one hand, at "providing one's world with a consistent, transparent structure, and on the other, creating systems of explanation and justification, but also of compensation, somehow combining experienced reality with ideational and imaginary structures" (p. 107).

Thus the wish to optimize covers all action areas. Boesch (1991) distinguishes mainly two important directions of this wish. The one concerns "mastery" or competence and skill, relating to specific actions; the other aims at a "fundamental" action potential which implies a general ability to act. He explains it as follows:

(the fundamental action potential) might be defined as the extent to which one feels confident of meeting one's potential standards in any kind of situation. Mastery—subjectively defined—plays a role, yet so do emotional evaluations of one's energy potential, one's capacity to suffer, or be happy, one's feeling of being worthy of other people's love and respect, one's luck in circumventing perils and hazards, and possibly other appraisals which do not fall under the terms of competence or mastery. (p. 108)

Thus, "functional proficiency, goal-mastery and structuring potential all contribute to the fundamental action potential, albeit in partly different ways." However, among those the structuring potential is of predominant importance:

> We experience our world dichotomically: there is the inner experience of being a subject, versus the one of the external world. This I-world relationship is continuously structured in an "ordered," "transparent," "consistent" way. Obviously this structuring activity of our mind consists of a functional skill which entails experiences of "the power to understand" and thus yields intrinsic satisfactions of its own which easily irradiate into a general kind of self-confidence."
>
> Thus, structuring serves an over-all concern of orientation and justification: it will certainly be performed on the basis of special experiences, but aims at integrating them into overall structures. In this sense, the structuring activity becomes of primary importance for the constitution of our fundamental action potential: the understandable structure of our "subjective universe" facilitates confident action anticipations, while the experience of one's "functional potential," the ability to establish structures, is a potent self-reinforcer. (p. 109)

It is the "need for transparency" which Boesch introduces here as an overarching goal, and it can plausibly be considered to be a fantasm. Action potential, we might conclude, may aim at specific proficiencies or general strength, but those, basically, contribute to realizing, defending and maintaining the individual myth-fantasm structures. In this sense, the strengthening of the fundamental action potential serves indeed self-reinforcement and self-maintenance. Boesch is careful to point out that even the specific mastery or competence are perceived and evaluated according to the individual's value system—meaning his or her myth-fantasm structures. And although they appear to be concrete and situation specific, they always also imply anticipations of future action possibilities or difficulties, and thereby generalize into the fundamental action potential. Of course, this is not because the individual would expect identical action situations, but they somehow symbolize possible outcomes. This symbolism of actual occurrences does not require phenomenal similarity, so that even the throwing of a coin might increase the confidence for a future action (see 1991, p. 109).

This would of course bring up the problem of the *self*. The self is, in the subjective experience, a relatively stable structure, in spite of changing moods and varying action experiences. This implies that the self needs to be stabilized, and therefore the individual selects and interprets, may be even transforms actual or remembered experiences, endeavoring to adjust their meaning to his or her overarching goals. This necessarily requires some instance which directs and controls these processes, in other words, some kind of constancy within the actually occurring variations. Boesch calls it the "I", which allows him to justify at the same time both the variability and the constancy of the person. He has devoted to this problem a fascinating chapter in his 1991 book "From I to self" (p. 297ss). Two of the original articles included here may give some ideas concerning this problem which regretfully cannot be discussed adequately in the space of this chapter (see chapters 9 and 10, Part II).

We have seen that, in order to strengthen and stabilize the fundamental action potential, the individual selects and interprets her or his experiences, whereby their symbolic quality plays an important role, since actual experiences are analogues, but never similes of projected events. So let us turn now to Boesch's conception of the symbolism of action.

The Symbolism of Action

Ernest Boesch has written extensively on the symbolism of action. In this chapter reference is made primarily to his 1991 text, *Symbolic Action Theory and Cultural Psychology*, since it was published in English. Other references can be found in publications of 1975, 1976, 1980, 1983. Following the thinking of British anthropologist Raymond Firth, he distinguishes between "symbols" and "signs." Indeed, much of what usually is called a symbol, is in fact a sign—such as flags, mathematical "symbols," traffic or commercial "symbols." Signs, he explains, are arbitrary structures which point at commonly accepted meanings. Language is a prime example, words being signs which, although with no qualitative resemblance to their denotations, are understood in a similar way throughout the linguistic community. They, however, can acquire a symbolic meaning, as will become clear in the following passage.

As authors of this biography, we often consulted with Ernest Boesch about different facets of his theory. In an e-mailed question early in 2005, he was asked to expand on his views on why symbols and symbolism are so important in understanding people from other cultures. His answer summarizes in a clear way the main aspects of his concept, so we quote it here:

He begins by asking

What is a symbol? Definitions have been offered and discussed by philosophers, theologians, linguists, anthropologists, psychoanalysts, sociologists and others, and so it might be vain to raise the question again. It would, at any rate, not be very helpful to enter into a discussion of the different definitions on the market—definitions of terms are always somewhat arbitrary. Yet, having coined the term of "symbolic action"—for good reasons, I believe—it might be useful to justify again the term and its significance for psychology. Let me start by one or two examples.

The Thai alphabet contains several different signs for the same spoken consonant. That makes the orthographe rather difficult because one cannot trust one's ear for spelling (the same, of course, is true for English, French, German, but for different reasons). There are, for instance, three letters for the sound "ch." One of them, called "chor-chur" (the Thais name their letters) is used very rarely, has a complex form which a learner can easily confound with three or four other letters. When I learned Thai, I asked my teacher "why not drop this letter—it has the same sound and function as the "chor-chaang?" She answered: "Oh no! I would pity this beautiful letter!" Certainly it was an astonishing, very irrational answer. And in fact, Pibul Songkram, the dictator who ruled Thailand after World War II, utterly failed with his attempt to reform the Thai writing by excluding the many apparently superfluous homophonic consonants. The Thais "felt pity" for them.

This gives food for thought. A letter, of course, is a sign. A sign is an object which, by convention, is given a specific meaning. Thus, this "chor-chur" signifies, for every Thai, the sound "ch." In linguistics, this is called its "denotational meaning." Which, however, implies, too, the function of the sign? The function of this "ch" is to be combined with other letters in order to form a word. This indeed is also common knowledge relating to the sign.

This, of course, applies to any object. The object I see on my shelf, by its size and form is a sign, too, meaning "a book." And, again, this sign has a function, it contains information. The function somehow encloses the limits within which the sign maintains its meaning. In the case of the "ch," the function is strongly limited: It can form only those words to which it is assigned by the orthographe, and those, in this case, are not numerous (my dictionary lists only nine). The function of the book is broader, yet limited too: It can contain only information formulated by words or other printable signs. Yet, however that be, it is "denotation." Thus, everything we know in our world has this denotational sign quality. It is a quality which, of course, is cultural. An illiterate nomad from an African desert might not know a book, as I did not recognize a book in a longish bundle of palm leaves when I first saw one in Thailand—however, every Thai, Burmese, Khmer or Laotian would perceive it as a book of religious content.

Now, there are qualities not included in the denotation: A book can be burned, sullied, torn, can be respected, even revered, its content can be enjoyable or boring, true or false. It may belong to the collection of a famous publisher or may be a cheaply printed mass product. All these qualities would be called "connotations," meaning the qualities which derive from the intrinsic properties of the sign-object; including also actions and experiences directly related to these connotations—I may like the binding, the printing or the paper of the book, I may like it for bedtime reading or need it for my work. The connotations of glass are, among others, to be transparent, to be breakable, to injure if handled without care, the connotations of a car are all the qualities of speed, safety and comfort announced in the advertisements, and so on. Thus, there are two threads of meaning related to a sign, the one consisting of the "objective connotations", which include cultural ones, the other of the "subjective" ones, which express the direct relationship of a person with properties of a sign."

Let us include here, for additional clarification, another example of object connotations which Ernest Boesch gives elsewhere, an even less conspicuous one than a book: the familiar common broom. The broom, he says,

stands at the intersection of various meaning clusters. One cluster concerns its material – wood, bristles, hair, all taken from living organisms and thereby relating to vitality. By its form, it may evoke stick-like or cross-like objects, and by its function it relates to both dirt and cleanliness, in the literal as well as the figurative sense. These properties, alone or in combination, can induce various connotative meanings. They can range from the child's play horse to the witch's mount, from sexuality and womanhood to apotropaïc, i.e., protective magic, according, of course, to regional cultural traditions. (1991, p. 231, also in 1983)

This leads back to symbolism and to continue the above quoted passage.

The saying of my Thai teacher "I pity this beautiful letter" may also be of an entirely different order. It seems to refer not to the quality or function of the sign, but to a more complex personal relationship with it. For instance, its difficult form may have presented a challenge to the first or second grader in primary school, so that mastering it, being praised for it by the teacher, meant an early triumph in childhood."

These kinds of subjective connotational qualities integrate object and subject in a complex net of experience—I call those symbolic. The distinction may appear artificial; yet, it seems to be important to distinguish between connotations immediately related to the nature and function of the object, and those which relate it to the actions and experiences of the subject. These second ones may indeed extend far in time, they may connect the object or event both with situations and actions already experienced, and with plans, hopes, fears of a sometimes conscious or more often unconscious quality."

There exists a Haiku by the Japanese poet Basho which expresses this subtle, only vaguely conscious symbolism:

"Even in Kyoto
when I hear the cuckoo
I long for Kyoto."

The first Kyoto, is the denotational reality, which includes the sound of the cuckoo—which symbolically evokes the second Kyoto, the imagination of a not yet or no longer existing place of subjective experience. Kyoto, the real, thus, is subliminally also symbolic, and this symbolism—dormant in a sense—is awoken by the sound of the cuckoo. Which, of course, is possible only because this sound carries a symbolism of its own—related to some meaningful memory. The longing for Kyoto expressed in this Haiku wants to transform the real, actual town into a dreamed one. In other words, symbolism may have—in fact often has—a motivational strength.

Of course, we all have our Kyotos, subliminal qualities which relate our representations not only with previous experiences, but also with plans and hopes or fears, and thereby make them motivational. I meet a person and shake hands with him or her. Unconsciously, I register firmness of pressure, texture of skin, duration of contact, and although I do not register all that, a host of other handshakes flares up in my unconscious mind, related to personal interactions, and make me wish to continue the contact, to intensify it, or to let it simply pass, or even urges me to wash my hands afterwards. The simple gesture of a handshake integrates the contact into more complex I-other relationships, experienced as well as envisioned ones."

Thus, symbolism relates. We have seen that the material and functional qualities of a sign constitute its denotation; this is somehow completed by connotational meanings, relating to various aspects of the sign, aspects, however, directly connected with its denotational properties. To these now symbolism adds an integrative dimension. Indeed, it integrates the sign (i.e., the object, event, action) into the individual's history and outlook. I have in previous publications enumerated a number of dimensions along which this integration takes place: "Situational," connecting the sign with situations of which it had been a part; "functional," evoking the subjective (proprioceptive, emotional) experiences related to the sign; "analogical," pointing at formal, functional or meaningful analogues; "ideational," relating the sign to ideas, beliefs, theories; "alternative," including opposites or alternatives to the meaning of a sign; and finally, "self-evaluative" qualities. Such an enumeration may not be very helpful; it can neither be complete, nor is it sufficiently dynamic. Its use is rather to point at the multidimensional meanings of symbols, or, in other words, at the complex ties a symbol can establish with an individual's biography."

We never experience or handle objects as such—we always act in situations, which, again, relate to other situations—past, present or anticipated ones. Of course, these situations also include ourselves—acting as an individual as well as a member of a culture. Psychoanalytic experience makes this particularly evident. Analyzing, by free association, any content of mind, be it a dream, a recollection or an anticipation, it will unavoidably lay open complex individual and cultural constellations, a "symbolic variance" which not only integrates the individual most intimately in his culture, but also with his or her past and outlook, including hopes, fears, and self-other-conceptions."

Of course, this should not be misunderstood. I do not say that action is a symbol, but only that it is symbolic—in other words, it has both a factual and a symbolic variance. Whereby the factual variance usually enjoys a "primacy of consciousness" (Boesch, 1980, 1991). We tend predominantly to be conscious of our goals and the means to reach them, but rarely only of the symbolic qualities of our actions, representations and outlooks – those rather hold a "primacy of motivation." Even should we try to understand our motivation, we probably never realize the complexity of its symbolism. Yet, although barely conscious of it, symbolism controls considerably the dynamism of our action.

The conclusion is simple: Without insight into the symbolic dimension of human action, we will never be able to understand neither individuals, nor groups. That is what I tried to show by multiple examples in my writings of the last twenty years or more—yet, I am afraid, with not much success.

This passage, we think, contains the essential definition of action symbolism. Concepts or denotations establish structures, implying objective relationships, while symbols establish structures of a subjective nature, inserting actions and objects in an individual history. Of course, many details from the long chapters devoted to symbolism had to remain omitted, in particular the many examples of simple daily objects—such as a clay vessel, a broom, a pen, an apple, meat, a glass of wine—the symbolism of which Ernest Boesch carefully explains in various places (see several chapters in Part II, especially chapter 15). All this shows the importance of the concept, and it is therefore astonishing that, while there exists ample anthropological literature on symbolism, psychologists seem to eschew the subject (with the exception of psychoanalysis which, however, tends to define symbols more restrictively). As, by the way, psychologists do so also with culture. Where, in later publications, (as in the three-volume revision of the *Handbook of Cross-Cultural Psychology* by Berry et al., 1997) the word "symbol" is cited, it is used in places where Boesch would prefer the word sign. For psychologists, symbols remain occasional structures in particular contexts, like dreams or rituals, and so they fail to recognize their pervasive function of motivation and biographical integration.

We have now covered the concepts of myth, fantasm, action potential and action symbolism, but by far they do not exhaust Ernest Boesch's action theory. His theoretical publications consider carefully, among others, the embeddedness of action in its ecological and social contexts (e.g., Boesch, 1976, 1980), the time and space dimensions of action (Boesch, 1976), the phases of the action process and the difference between "praxic" and "referent," that is imaginative, actions (Boesch, 1976, 1980, 1991), the coordination of actions both within the subject and between social partners, conflict of action (Boesch, 1991); he carefully specifies the different levels of consciousness of action, from emotional regulations to reflective thought (Boesch, 1980, 1991); as mentioned above, he describes disturbances of action (Boesch, 1976). In various publications he treats problems of language, and of course the question of objects—from simple everyday objects to aesthetic ones—occupied particularly his attention (Boesch, 1975, 1976, 1983, 1991, 1998, 2005). To cover all this, as important as it may be, would of course by far exceed the space available for this biographical profile. We hope that the articles referenced in this chapter will at least allow glimpses on the rich texture of this theory.

Culture in Symbolic Action Theory (SAT)

What, then, would make this symbolic theory also a cultural one? One thinks, of course, first of the ecological embeddedness. Thus, in a first, broad definition Ernest Boesch considers culture to be an "action field" which, by its opportunities and barriers, its rules, permissions and limitations not only forms the actions and thoughts of its inhabitants, but is continuously also formed and transformed by them. Occasionally, Boesch calls culture the "biotope" of humans, by which he wants to emphasize more than the close interrelatedness of people and nature. Of course, each natural object, when perceived, handled or evaluated, is also cultural, but in extension this is true for all that surrounds human beings: Each object in their world is not simply an object, but a carrier of cultural meanings. In this sense, action theory is "ecological" as well as "cultural," the two terms differing in orientation and emphasis rather than in essence.

In a narrower definition, Ernest Boesch says that culture starts when people build shelters, huts and houses. Those constitute the "fix points" for structuring the external space and world, and provide "centrality" to the various actions of the inhabitants, a place of permanence from which to start out and to come back, a secure haven for resting, restoring, dreaming. It shelters important private experiences, but allows also undisturbed planning and preparing of outside ventures. Among all places, the home will be the most transparent one, and by the rules and values practiced inside, it will become the nucleus of culture.

Boesch has therefore devoted detailed chapters to the significance of the home, both as a shelter of privacy as also a limitation of one's range of freedom—thereby being paradigmatic of culture in general. The farther away from home, the less transparent will be the situation, the material surroundings becoming less known, the social habits and rules more uncertain, opportunities as well as dangers one had imagined may turn out to be wrong. Thus, cultural structure changes with distance, the village being less transparent than one's home, the distant town less than one's village and so on. There may be isolated islands far away, familiar again, but to a lesser extent, like a holiday resort, yet, on the whole, away from home, culture becomes more and more an imagination and a construct. In other words, distances are not only geographical, but also experiential and symbolic. Thus, feelings such as national pride, patriotism, and a sense of national identity are mythical more than realistic, based on stories, customs, and traditions, and where they lead to images of self-confirmation, they turn into fantasms.

The individual acts in situations, and situations are always cultural, one can not step outside one's culture. Even if a girl swims in a solitary lake, a boy climbs a tree in a lonely wood; their actions as well as their surroundings are cultural. The time chosen for swimming, the swimming itself, the coolness and depth of the water, all have their cultural connotations, as does, for the wood climber, the tree, the wood, climbing and so on. Yet, in spite of that, the action itself is not experienced culturally—the pleasure, effort or fatigue of the movement, the freshness or cold of the water on a naked skin, the singing of birds in nearby trees, all that is individually lived. The individual action is embedded in culture so naturally that it does only rarely register consciously.

Thus culture, as a field of action, contains opportunities and barriers, provides promises and prohibitions, encouragements and threats, enticements and frustrations. Yet, its content is much richer than the individual can exploit; therefore, culture, for each person, centers around his or her experiences, which progressively condense into individual frames of reference, perception and evaluation of culture, but also into those conceptions and projections of oneself we encountered as "fantasms". In this sense, culture is a construct, concretely verifiable in the near surroundings, but becoming more and more imaginative with increasing distance.

The subtleness of this individual-culture-interaction is difficult to describe in the artificial categories of language. In his essay entitled "Culture-Individual-Culture" (see chapter 9, Part II), Boesch illustrates by an example this mutual influence and shaping between individuals and their cultural surroundings. Each action a person performs is cultural, and thereby confirms culture, each action, however, introduces also variations based on individual choice, taste, and even inventiveness. Thus, an individual can feel in harmony, but also in discord with what he or she imagines to be their culture. Yet, individual variation is important, both for the harmony between individual and group, and for allowing innovation. Therefore, culture has to provide

> leeways, degrees of freedom, which individuals may fill out according to their inclinations and orientations. Of course, the gifted ones, the privileged ones, will enjoy more of those opportunities than others, yet, potentially, human beings are, within limits, creators of situations. This is the deeper sense of the concept of action. Action implies the possibility of choice and the potential of the actor to effect those choices.... Such a con-

ception, necessarily, implies responsibility.... Man is the perceiver, interpreter, transformer and to some extent also the maker of his world and so
he becomes also responsible for it—each in his or her smaller or bigger
ways. (Boesch, 1991, pp. 368-369)

Referring to culture as a field of action is consistent with Ernest
Boesch's definition of culture as both a structure and a process (Boesch,
1991, p. 37ss). Indeed, the cultural contents are both material and
ideational, in other words, they are meaningful facts. Of course, human
creativeness can change material facts as well as their meanings. That of
course is common knowledge; culture is the product of people. Given this
widely accepted view, Ernest Boesch finds it surprising that psychologists
all too often do not show much interest in culture. For many of them
culture is simply an "independent variable," a system of conditioning,
constraints, and models to which individuals have to adapt. Contrary to
this stance, such passages stress the humanistic concern underlying
Boesch's theoretical work. He even more clearly expresses this in his
publications demonstrating the application of SAT to concrete questions.
With Ernest's guidance, let us now turn to those.

Application of SAT

A theory can be explanatory, if the independent variables, the conditions of their impact and their result can be clearly defined and objectively measured. This, except perhaps in the stricter natural sciences, is
rarely the case, and in no way applies to SAT. SAT would rather belong to
the type of theories which we may call "descriptive"; it aims at detailed
descriptions of the observed processes, of their regularities and variations,
in space as well as in time, without attempting to reduce them to the for-
mat allowing experimentation. What then is the use of such a theory? It
sharpens observation, and by that also empathy (which makes it relevant
in psychotherapy). Observation, in order to be realistic and useful, naturally needs direction, therefore it will start with a preconception of the
phenomena to be observed. That, of course, forbids too narrow or biased
cadres of observation; they have to remain open to as many of the potential influences which can be hypothesized. This openness Boesch claims
for SAT, and he tries to test this assumption on various concrete examples.
He did so extensively in works of 1980, 1982, 1983, 1991 and the three
late publications of 1998, 2000, and 2005. The results are rich and sug-
gestive, both for the understanding of concrete situations, as also for the
deeper insight into the theory. Space allows us only a limited considera-

tion of this aspect of SAT, but some detailed examples can be found in section II of this report.

Let us start with the major among those publications, the 1983 *Magic and Beauty*. Ernest Boesch considers it to be one of his most important works. It is indeed a masterful demonstration of the psychological meaning of objects, and counts among the major contributions to psychological aesthetics (Allesch, 1987). Of course, Boesch has over and again manifested his interest in objects, starting with the symbolism of the house in 1980 (see chapter 15, Part II) and then covering various objects, from a simple broom to a mask or a violin. But in this 1983 book he concentrates on magical and aesthetic objects. He justifies this choice by two considerations: First, more practically, when working in alien cultures, the use and meaning of magical and art objects often requires to be understood; second, more theoretically, objects of magic and art appear to be paradigms of the two basic orientations of humans: To master the outside world (magic), and to structure the self (art). Both, of course, attempt this by symbolic means; thereby they also exemplify the impact of symbolic representations and rituals on thoughts and actions. Adding to it the 1975 publication "Between Anxiety and Triumph," the two books present to our knowledge an encompassing—and unique—action theoretical conception of art on the one hand, and, on the other hand, a psychological interpretation of magical thinking and ritual which usefully completes anthropological theories.

Ernest Boesch frequently considers the meaning of art objects. His interest started with the simple and ubiquitous fact that many utensils of common use are decorated. Why did already prehistoric women decorate their clay vessels? What is the function of objects apparently produced for no other reason than to please the eye, like a painting, or the ear, like a tinkling bell? The answer is complex, related mainly to the balancing of the I-world-relationship, as Boesch explained in many studies. Some of the articles included here may explain this more thoroughly: For instance, he analysed in great detail the connotations and symbolism of his home—a very personal demonstration of the fruitfulness of SAT for understanding a person's life and values (chapter 15, Part II); the essay on the sound of the violin (chapter 8, Part II), or the one on sculptures which Picasso liked to make from discarded materials (4-7) are other examples of such object analyses, as are also, in other publications, the studies on Carnival masks (Boesch; 1998) or on the symbolism of money (Boesch, 1991).

These "applied" studies, however, also pursue a methodological aim. In 1977 Ernest Boesch had published an article on "Connotation Analysis." In this paper he demonstrated how Freud's method of "free association" could also be used with material whose authors were not available for live interviews. His solution was to select specific themes in a work, and search in other works of the author or his biography for related contents. The "common variance" of similar themes occurring in different contexts could then shed light on its "meaning." Boesch (1982a) demonstrated this method first by the careful analysis of a poem by Rainer Maria Rilke; then he applied it to Picasso's famous painting "Guernica" to which, in his works of 1991 and 1995, he devoted long chapters. Picasso's *Demoiselles d'Avignon* caught his attention later in a different context (Boesch, 2005). Picasso, whose life and work he has studied over years, served Boesch in several publications to assess the use of SAT for understanding surrealist art. Finally, in an article on "Telling Stories" ("Homo Narrator," in 2005), Ernest Boesch applied connotation analysis for studying the development of an author's work over time. All these studies proved connotation analysis to be a valuable tool in the psychology of art and literature.

The three most recent books by Ernest Boesch (1998, 2000a, 2005) cover a wide spectrum, from *Sehnsucht* (longing) to terror, from gossip to Haikus, from carnival to literature. They analyse the psychological reasons at work in the development of the violin through history, but look also at the origin of music and the psychological function of musical enjoyment; they span the range from art to religious faith, from faith to terror; they consider anti-Semitism and racial prejudice in a new way, discuss the symbolism of consumption, language and literature, dream and poetry. These far-reaching studies not only shed a new light on many commonplace objects and actions, but they also enlarge and differentiate theoretical terms. The reader will discover the depth and width of Ernest Boesch's interests, but also his deep concern about the sociocultural situation of his time – he has, let us not forget, lived the bigger part of the twentieth century which, in the words of Leonard Bernstein, was "a century of death." In "A Psychology of Concern" (see chapter 12, Part II) he expresses this most clearly.

In Boesch's most recent book *From Art to Terror* (2005) Jürgen Straub wrote a very insightful foreword. Referring mainly to the diverse studies in the three latest works, he writes: These studies are not simply an illustration of the symbolic action theory and cultural psychology. They differentiate it and stimulate further differentiations (p. 15). In this sense, all these different concrete applications of SAT are a rich source for deepening insight into the relationship of human beings with their world, but they also—both in content and method—represent a pool of ideas and suggestions for further studies which could close the gap between psychology and the every day life of people.

Summary and Conclusions

This chapter presented a brief and succinct summary of the major psychological works of Ernest Boesch. Nine of the 11 books he considered important were published in German, 5 are out of print. Thus they could be summarized in this overview only briefly for tracing the development of his thought, while his major English publication became the focus of our consideration. In his personal perspective, Ernest Boesch has achieved much in the presence of many serious challenges. Going back to his early career as a school psychologist and advancing through his role as a University professor and research director for the UNESCO studies in Thailand, he each time had to accept his assignment without adequate preparation. His studies at Geneva were curtailed by World War II, and after eight years of work as a school psychologist, the call to the chair of psychology at the University of the Saar presented him again with only little familiarity with university life and requirements. Finally, after four years at the University of the Saar, he went to Thailand without adequate knowledge in anthropology and cultural psychology.

After returning to his University, for 10 years he was the only professor of psychology. Simultaneously, he assumed the directorship of the Socio-Psychological Research Center for Development Planning. These double functions presented a heavy work load which left him little time for cultivating outside professional contacts, little also for his hobbies of music and reading. While he regretted these conditions, in our view they were also fortunate. He had to find his way alone a great deal, but this also forced him to cultivate and trust his own observations, carefully weighing and analyzing them with sensitivity and empathy. Thus, in many respects, his work reflects his personal observations and theoretical reflections, drawing from the thinking and researching of relatively few, but prominent other scholars. Intuitive insights combined in his work with rational analysis, particularly in his studies concerning music, literature, art and magic. Thus it is not surprising to find in his writings concepts like *Anmutung*, emotional "appeal," intuition. Over time he has even developed some degree of distrust for merely rational or logical psychological theories and research. In his reflective mode he stated: "Mankind would never have survived in the primal forest if it had to trust rational decisions—an ominous noise or a shadow in the bush does not allow long rational deliberations." Of course, he also clearly recognized that by intuition alone human culture would not have advanced. Boesch neither overrates cognition nor underestimates intuition. Yet, he stresses that also in our time, decisions from every day matters to politics are often based on hunches, emotional preferences, intuitive appraisals, with rational justifications added merely as after thoughts. All through his career he saw himself as a citizen of his times, deeply concerned and critical of what he felt to be the political and social disinterest of large sections of psychology. Psychology, he was convinced, should responsibly participate in our world. It is not by chance or accident that his most recent book addresses the deep ambivalence in culture.

In his 1991 publication, Ernest Boesch very clearly formulates his beliefs about the purpose or cultural psychology. Let us quote this passage for closing this chapter:

> Cultural psychology is not infrequently considered to be a branch of general psychology applied to alien cultures. This, of course, is an error. Cultural psychology is no less relevant in our own cultures and subcultures, and in fact is already practiced to some extent under names such as "social psychology," "environmental psychology," "consumer psychology," or "political psychology." It certainly is going to make inroads, too, in clinical psychology, counseling and psychotherapy (where by the way, action theory will be of significant importance). Yet, these branches tend to be considered as mere specializations subsumable under the "basic" discipline of general psychology. It is my contention that in the future the prestige of psychological investigations which disregard the cultural context should and will be reduced to the level of biotic validity they can claim—and prove.
>
> Cultural psychology is a "systemic" science. We have seen in the preceding pages the enormously complex interrelations into which the individual action is embedded. In other words, the paradigm of "independent-dependent variables" will no longer be of great use; this use will be even less when we remember the ubiquitous and considerable symbolic variance of reality and experience which makes the "operationalization" of variables a futile endeavor.
>
> Necessarily, then, progress in cultural psychology will come about less by an increased sophistication of measurements than by a continuous interplay between observation and theory. Theory will guide observation. Observation will check and modify theory. Progress will consist of multiplying and differentiating observations which can subsequently and deliberately be integrated into a refined theoretical framework. Improving the fit between observation and theory will thus become the dominant methodological concern. This, in a nutshell, would be how I define a methodology which might be qualified as hermeneutic, provided that the term is not taken as a license for freewheeling speculation. On the contrary, this conception requires that a theory be made explicit from the outset, as a framework for specifying problems and directing observations. The interchange between findings and theory remain an "overarching goal." Action theory would, I assert, be suited for fulfilling such a function.
>
> But there is more to it. Action theory, in the constructivist conception I have proposed, is based on a dynamic philosophy of the human being. As I see it, historically psychology has tended to adopt three paradigms

of human nature, which can be succinctly formulated as follows: a first, exemplified by the Gestalt perspective, considered human behavior to be determined by the structures of the brain; for a second, behaviorism, man was the product of a succession of conditionings; and a third, psychoanalysis, saw man as being shaped by imprintings and reaction-formations during childhood. All based their scientific status on a strict determinism, and of course, all are right. The Gestalt laws are real, conditionings do occur, and we all are influenced by childhood experiences. Yet, all three are wrong in the generalization of their findings to the nature of man. Although psychoanalysis (and some Gestaltists) has tried, none of them proved able to explain the main human achievement: culture.

In constructivist action theory, by contrast, human beings interact with the environment in a dynamic way, thereby structuring the objective and social world as well as the self and its action potentialities. Of course, this ontogenetic construction is neither unguided nor arbitrary. The successive structures the human child achieves are in part determined by his constitutional endowment, following a universal course. In part, they are guided by cultural impacts. Yet there remain degrees of freedom due both to culture and to the elasticity of our endowment which individuals may fill out according to their inclinations and orientations. Of course, the gifted ones, the privileged ones, will enjoy more of those opportunities than others. Yet, potentially, human beings are, within limits, creators of situations. This is the deeper sense of the concept of action. Action implies the possibility of choice, and the potential of the actor to effect those choices. I am aware of the philosophical problems this raises—it is my choice to disregard them. We cannot solve unsolvable problems—like the one of freedom—before taking a stand.

Such a conception, necessarily, implies responsibility. Culture is a creation of human beings, a result of choices made over generations, but also a result of continuous interactions between individuals and their group and environment. Man is the perceiver, interpreter, transformer and, to some extent, also the maker of his world. Thus, he also becomes responsible for it—each in his or her smaller or bigger ways. Trying to understand man as a cultural being forced me to see the diversity of cultures as a proof of human creativity. Then, however, a strictly deterministic theoretical framework could not be appropriate anymore. For all these reasons, although having undergone quite a few theoretical influences, I unhesitatingly opted for the one which not only allows inclusion of man's creativity, but also promises to restore his dignity. (1991, pp. 365-367)

An Observational Note by the Authors

After a careful, reflective reading of this chapter and a similarly careful reading of the biographical chapters of this text, Ernest Boesch emerges as a most remarkable scholar. His legacy is that of a truly independent thinker and explorer of new possibilities for the applications of his discipline. As a university student in the late 1930s and early 1940s, his formal education and training was far different from that of most contemporary graduate students of psychology in Europe or North America. He preceded the era when psychology was intensely focused on isolating minute elements of human behavior, studying them using various adaptations of 'the scientific method', and analyzing large accumulations of data through statistical techniques. On the contrary, he had the very rare chance to be close to eminent psychologists like Jean Piaget and André Rey who not only taught theoretical psychology but demonstrated and supervised themselves its concrete application. Both practiced a subtle, nonformalistic way of interviewing and testing children (which became famous as Piaget's "clinical method"). Yet, in their ways, both somehow remained strict experimenters, and, thus, Ernest Boesch started as a strong believer in Claude Bernard's experimental "ideology" (C. Bernard, *Introduction à la médecine expérimentale*). In his beginning years as a University professor, Ernest Boesch himself taught basic statistics and experimental techniques, and, as mentioned above, initiated an experimental research project.

However, already as a school psychologist he practiced a "clinical," flexible testing of children and paid close attention to their familial and social situation. He founded a regional society for mental hygiene and tried to stimulate public awareness of educational problems by articles in the local newspapers. His encompassing method of diagnosing children led to a first important publication *L'exploration du caractère de l'enfant* (1952) which was one of the assets leading to the call to the University of the Saar.

Yet, all this remained basically within the cadre of applied psychology of his time—it was hermeneutic only as far as clinical work always has to be hermeneutic to some extent. It was only when confronted with the problems in a foreign culture that Ernest Boesch fully recognized the many methodological and even philosophical questions raised by the usual studies based on data gathered from groups of subjects via tests, surveys, and questionnaires. He recognized the biases included in statistical analysis and comparisons. While, in his previous work, he had shown empathy and subtleness in dealing with children, he now also demonstrated much curiosity and respect for cultural conditions and the courage to break with the methodological constraints within his psychological circles. He now started on his own way, disregarding the opposition it produced even within his own university and his isolation among his psychological peers. Symbolic action theory was the result, and he believed it much better suited to the study of cultural psychology than the mainstream formal methods. It is both this courage to stick to his own observations and convictions, and the deeply thought, original result of it which makes Ernest Boesch for us to be an exemplary scientist and human being.

NOTE

1. With the exception of three references at the end of this chapter, all in-text references can be found in E. E. Boesch's complete bibliography that is included in this book (see pp. 363-370).

REFERENCES

Allesch, C. G. (1987). *Geschichte der psychologischen Aesthetik* [History of psychological aesthetics]. Goettingen: Hogrefe.

Berry, J. W., Dasen, P. R., Kagitcibasi, C., Pandey, J., Poortinga, Y. H., Saraswathi, T. S., & Segall, M. H. (Eds.). (1997). *Handbook of cross-cultural psychology* (2nd ed.). Boston: Allyn and Bacon.

Sripraphai. P., & Sripraphai, K. (1988). *Future anticipations in a Thai village.* Saabruecken: Breitenbach.

CHAPTER 4

INTERMEZZO

The Ernest Boesch I Met a Half-Century Ago

Robert B. Textor[1]

Professors Lonner and Hayes have asked me for a short account of the "young" Ernest Boesch I first met 50 years ago. Here is my report, organized as follows:

1. The chronology of my friendship with Ernest.
2. Ernest's mission in 1955.
3. The general situation in Thailand in 1955.
4. A few of the cultural challenges Ernest faced.

I will confine myself to a "slice of time" approach. I will not attempt to trace Ernest's professional evolution before or since his Bangkok experience. That evolution is, after all, the principal subject of this book.

Discovering Cultural Psychology: A Profile and Selected Readings of Ernest E. Boesch, pp. 81–94
Copyright © 2007 by Information Age Publishing

CHRONOLOGY OF A FRIENDSHIP

In Bangkok, 1955-57

When I first met Ernest Boesch in 1955 I was a 32-year-old graduate student in cultural anthropology from Cornell University, and had been in Thailand since 1952, working in a variety of research capacities, and developing fluency in the Thai language. It is the tradition among cultural anthropologists that we choose a culture to specialize on when we are young, and do intensive dissertation fieldwork there. Usually the period of fieldwork is a year or possibly two. I had already been there for 3 years, principally because I was determined to "master" the language and culture, and also because I greatly enjoyed living in Thailand, where every day provided a chance to actually live my anthropology and use it to solve problems. By 1955, I had begun to regard Thailand as my second home.

There were relatively few Western social science researchers working in Thailand in 1955. We all knew each other, and before long Ernest and I met. We "clicked" immediately, and have been good friends ever since.

In 1955 I was immersed in my dissertation fieldwork on religion, magic and divination in the agricultural village of Bang Chan—often called the "Cornell village," because a variety of scholars from Cornell University, of various disciplines, have written about it in books and dissertations. Although Bang Chan was then located only about 20 miles from the edge of built-up Bangkok, it was still in most respects a fairly typical peasant village, where 90% of the people were farmers growing rice as a cash crop, and where one could still get fish for supper by netting them from the numerous canals that laced through the village. (Today, Bang Chan has been totally absorbed into the Bangkok megalopolis.)

Although my research took me to Bang Chan, I would usually spend weekends in a small house in Bangkok that I and one or two other Western scholars had rented. It so happened that one of my housemates decided to leave, so I invited Ernest to take his place and help pay the rent, and was delighted when he accepted. For some weeks thereafter, until he found a house of his own, we had numerous chances to compare notes on Thai culture. During this continuing dialogue I learned a lot about psychological research from him, and I believe he learned something about Thai culture from me.

After Ernest moved out, another member of his study group at the International Institute for Child Study, the Canadian sociologist/educator Murray Thomson, took his place. (Most of the scholars working under Ernest were Thai, but there were a few scholars from elsewhere, and Murray was one of these.) The three of us would discuss such subjects as how to organize the new institute so that it would be sustainable, and would produce good social scientists, as well as relevant, credible and useful research products.

At an International Conference, Burg Wartenstein, 1959

By 1958 Ernest had returned to Saarbruecken to resume his teaching, and I had returned to Cornell to complete my doctorate. In the summer of 1959 we met again as participants in the "International Symposium on Stability and Change in Thai Culture," sponsored by the Wenner-Gren Foundation for Anthropological Research, and held at Burg Wartenstein, the foundation's renovated castle in Austria. The Symposium brought together some 20 participants, but a serious drawback was that they were almost all Americans or Europeans, some of whom, I thought, were only marginally qualified. Remarkably, only two of the participants were Thai: Miss Supanee Na Songkhla, then Ernest's fiancée, and Dr. Tom Boonlong, a Thai business executive with a serious avocational interest in gaining a social-science understanding of Thai culture.

On the face of it, this under representation of Thais seems absurd. However, the organizer of the symposium, the late Professor Lauriston Sharp of Cornell, had in fact made every effort to pull together the best available talent. The sad fact was that, at that time, there were no Thai cultural anthropologists, and no suitable Thai cultural psychologists, that he could have invited. They simply did not exist.

Today, 47 years later, the situation is vastly different. There are numerous Thai social scientists, educated at the doctoral level, who are fully capable of dealing with Thai cultural phenomena. Among the many who can take some credit for this shift are Ernest himself, and Dr. Sharp, who was responsible for creating the Cornell Southeast Asia Program and making it one of the premier such programs in the world, and an effective one in educating excellent Thai scholars to achieve doctoral-level competence.

At a Second International Conference, Saarbruecken, 1982

In 1982 Ernest served as host and convener of the "Second Thai-European Research Seminar," focusing that year on Thai culture, and held at the University of the Saar. Thailand specialists from various European countries attended. Also, in stark contrast with the Burg Wartenstein experience 23 years earlier, a number of Thai scholars various social science disciplines also attended, and participated actively and effectively—

with, I thought, a salutary effect on the overall quality of the experience. Another interesting contrast with Burg Wartenstein was that this group apparently had a policy, at least informally, of excluding American specialists on Thailand, for some reason. However, as convener, Ernest arranged for my attendance anyway, on grounds that I was at the time physically located in Europe, teaching at Stanford's "overseas studies" program in Vienna, and was hence a temporary European! One of my Thai colleagues, the late Dr. M. L. Bhansoon Ladavalya, and I gave a joint report on our 1981 project of eliciting cultural futures scenarios from a sample of professors at Chiang Mai University, using Ethnographic Futures Research methodology.

In Saarbruecken on Sabbatical, 1984-85

In 1984-85 I spent a sabbatical year as a Fulbright scholar and as Ernest's intellectual guest at the University of the Saar. My project was to develop models and methods for use in creating an Anticipatory Anthropology (see Textor in Mead, 2005, pp. 16-28; and Sippanondha Ketudat, 1990). By good fortune, W. J. Lonner was also there for that year, and we had many productive triangular discussions about cultural and cross-cultural psychology.

In Thailand Doing Fieldwork, 1986

Thanks to funding that Ernest raised from the Volkswagen Foundation, in 1986 he and I, and our graduate student advisees, spent several weeks together in a small town and village situation in Rayong Province, Thailand. There, using an Ethnographic Futures Research methodology, we looked at ways in which villagers perceived and evaluated alternative sociocultural futures for their community or nation. Through this experience we were able to get a much firmer understanding of the methodological adaptations that are necessary in eliciting future visions/scenarios from Thai peasant or post-peasant agriculturalists—as distinct from the many Thais (and others) I had previously interviewed, who were mostly urban, educated and relatively cosmopolitan.

Copy-Editing a Book, 1991

In 1991 I offered my copy-editing assistance to Ernest as he finalized his *Symbolic Action Theory and Cultural Psychology*, which was published by

Springer Verlag of Heidelberg and New York (and 3 years later as *L'Action Symbolique: Fondements de psychologie culturelle* by Editions L'Harmattan of Paris). Credit for urging and advising Ernest to produce this monumental work goes to Professor Lonner, who felt strongly that Anglophone social scientists ought to have an opportunity to learn about symbolic action theory directly from its founder. Professor Lonner advised Ernest on various matters of scope, content, and organization. My contribution was much more pedestrian, namely to go through the manuscript line by line and make suggestions as to how his ideas could be rendered more idiomatically accessible to an Anglophone social scientist reader, especially one who is not a psychologist. Professor Lonner and I jointly authored a brief "Introductory Commentary" to this book.

At a Third International Conference, Merlingen, 1991

Also in 1991, Walt Lonner and I were guests at a "Symposium on the Cultural Environment in Psychology in Honor of Ernest E. Boesch," sponsored by the National Research Council of Switzerland, and held at a resort hotel in Merlingen. At that symposium I gave a paper titled "Tempocentrism: A Universal Phenomenon with Cultural Variations," which was my effort to link anticipatory anthropology to both cultural and cross-cultural psychology.

Since 1991 Ernest and I have remained in good touch, partly by my visiting Saarbruecken, as well as by e-mail, and phone calls every month or so. It is heart-warming to note that even now, as he approaches the age of 90, he continues to write daily.

ERNEST'S 1955 MISSION TO BANGKOK: DEALING WITH EMICS AND ETICS

As is explained in chapter Two, in 1955 a 39-year-old Ernest Boesch accepted from UNESCO a daunting assignment: to build and develop an International Institute for Child Study in a nation that he had never visited, and knew very little about. The new Institute was expected (1) to encourage and develop the field of child study in ways that took seriously into account the cultural environment in which the child grows up; and (2) to produce research results that would make possible rigorous and useful cross-cultural comparison.

In a general sense, this duality of focus—between the viewpoint of the native and the viewpoint of the outside scholar—has always been at the heart of cultural anthropology. To understand the particularities of a given culture, one must, as Malinowski put it, "grasp the native point of view." To proceed to compare one culture with several others, one must conceive and use categories that in some sense apply to **all** of those cultures. One must, in short, use both sides of the duality.

It is convenient to parse this duality in "emic" and "etic" terms. An "emic" account of behavior is a description of behavior in terms meaningful (consciously or unconsciously) to the actor. An "etic" account is a description of a behavior in terms familiar to the observer, who is often from a different culture. These two labels (derived from the linguistic terms "phonemic" and "phonetic") were brand new and rarely used in 1955, but have subsequently become common in social science research. In psychology, among the very first to use the distinction was John W. Berry (1969).

"Emics" and "Etics" in Psychology

Since anthropologists have various ways of defining "emic" and "etic," I turned to Lonner for a summary of how psychologists tend to view this distinction, and he obliged with the following statement:

Consistent with the culture-specific (emic) versus culture-general or universal (etic) distinction, here are some other characteristics that are often noted by cross-cultural psychologists (see Berry, 1969):

Emic

 Studies behavior from within the system
 Examines only one culture
 Structure discovered by the analyst and not imposed from outside (or brought in)
 Criteria used for analyses are relative to internal characteristics

Etic

 Studies behavior from a position outside the system
 Examines two or more cultures, comparing them
 Structure is created by the analyst
 Criteria used for analyses are considered absolute or universal

Other Terms or Orientations Often Used

 Ideographic and unique (emic) versus nomothetic and statistical (etic)
 Qualitative and case study (emic) versus quantitative and large N (etic)
 Constructivistic versus reductionistic

As examples of anthropological research products that are intensely focused emically and etically, respectively, see Textor 1973 and 1967.

With respect to psychology, it seems clear that cultural psychology leans toward emphasizing emic formulations, and cross-cultural psychology toward etic formulations. I would argue, however, that both of these forms of psychology, if they are to reach their full potential, need to employ *both* emic and etic formulations.

My Advice, Which Ernest Fortunately Declined

Ernest arrived in Bangkok well prepared for etic analysis, in the sense that he was deeply schooled in general psychological theory, which, in the minds of at least some psychologists of the day, was more or less applicable to people worldwide, regardless of culture. (He was, though, far from being the classic "hard-nosed" psychometrician suspicious of any data set unless it is in quantitative form.) At the same time, Ernest had a more emic orientation than many of his contemporaries in psychology, given his lifelong fascination with the uniquenesses and particularities of poetry, music and art.

Ernest's immediate challenge, however, was to decide how much of his effort to use in developing an emic sophistication with respect to Thai culture. This involved a difficult decision, since it takes years of hard work to learn the Thai language and culture.

Having personally experienced the *Sturm und Drang* of trying to master that language and culture, I offered Ernest my "sage" advice: "Look, you have only two years to spend in Bangkok, and you face a huge task of institution building. There are only so many hours in a day. It seems to me that you do not have time to do all this and also learn Thai well—even though you would start with the great advantage of already knowing several languages. So, I would suggest that you concentrate on your main assignment of building the Institute, and defer your language learning till later."

In offering this advice, I was mindful of the numerous Western technical experts whom I has seen come and go, who would arrive full of enthusiasm to learn the Thai language and culture, but who would typically fall far short of success—even though some of them used up much precious time in the effort. I didn't want my friend to make the same mistake.

Ernest pointedly did NOT accept my advice. And the world is better for it. He was right. I was wrong. As Chapter Two suggests, I had underestimated his unusual drive and aptitude, and equally, that of his tutor, namely Miss Supanee Na Songkhla, one of the scholars attached to the Institute, who eventually became his wife. In due course, Ernest could speak, comprehend, read, and write beautiful Thai. Today, decades later, whenever I visit the Boesch residence in Saarbruecken, I am struck by the fact that at all meals the conversation is *exclusively* in the Thai language, and that I am expected to comply, even though my Thai might be rusty, and I might be aching to toss in a convenient English phrase. At such moments, it is wonderfully clear that Ernest's immersion in the Thai culture has greatly enriched not just his professional creativity, but his entire personal life.

THE GENERAL THAI SITUATION IN 1955

Despite space constraints, brief mention should be made, of a few aspects of the general situation in Thailand that greeted Ernest in 1955.

Reverence for *Farangs*

Ernest embarked on his institution-building adventure enjoying an enormous built-in advantage: he was a *farang*. This Thai term, derived from *Francaise*, essentially means "Caucasian Westerner, presumably of Christian background." If Ernest had been Chinese, Japanese, Indian, Filipino or Nigerian, he would not have enjoyed anywhere nearly the same advantage.

The principal historical reason why *farangs* were (and still are) exalted is that Thailand, alone in Southeast Asia, managed to evade the colonial grasp of a European power. While the British gobbled up areas in present-day Burma and Malaysia that were at least nominally under the Thai crown, and while the French did the same in Laos and Cambodia, the core territory of Thailand, then called Siam, remained independent. The principal strategy that the Thai monarchy used to preserve its independence was to modernize (and more or less Westernize) many of its institutions, especially those of law, diplomacy, civil administration, and commerce. Thus, unlike people in many Asian nations that had become independent only during the ten years preceding Ernest's arrival (e.g., Burma, Indonesia, the Philippines) or were yet to gain authentic independence (e.g., Malaya, Singapore, Cambodia, Laos and Vietnam), intellectuals and ordinary people in Thailand generally did not harbor anti-Western animosity. Indeed, many Thais actively sought out contact and friendship with *farangs*.

Thus Ernest, arriving in Thailand as a *farang* (even though from Switzerland, a country that had never had an overseas empire) received much automatic deference. This deference was all the greater because of his sponsorship by UNESCO, since Thais in general tended to respect the United Nations.

Intellectual Dependency

An unfortunate consequence of Thailand's century of placating the West was a certain tendency on the part of Thais, even intellectuals, toward intellectual dependency, toward automatically regarding any idea put forth by *farangs* as correct and "up-to-date." One of Ernest's major challenges in working with Thai scholars at the Institute was simply to give them the training and confidence that would enable them to make useful *independent* contributions. This meant creating an atmosphere in the seminars he conducted at the Institute, in which Thai participants would feel much freer to express their ideas, than was true in their previous educational experience, where there was typically little or no questioning of the teacher's message.

Desire for Progress, Democracy, and Justice

In 1955, Thailand was seen by most people, including Thais, as an "underdeveloped" nation. It had relatively little industry, and depended for foreign exchange largely on the export of commodities such as rice, rubber, tin, and teak. Its largely rural population was somewhat over twenty million (as against somewhat over 60 million today). The Thai government had indicated a great desire for development, and was going out of its way to attract development experts, mostly from the West.

In a Thai conversation on development, a frequently heard term is *khwaam caroen*, a term sometimes glossed as "progress," and implicitly defined as a process toward greater physical ease and material comfort attained through the deployment of technology involving increased use of inanimate energy. In 1955, it seemed that all Thais wanted "progress," just as they wanted to be "up-to-date" (*than samaj*).

Along with this concept of "progress," and sometimes virtually conjoined to it, most educated Thais expressed a strong preference for democracy and justice—two broad concepts heavily influenced by Western ideas.

The pace of the American government's efforts to foster "progress" in Thailand was accelerating greatly in the mid-50s, as part of a broad "Cold War" strategy to win the hearts and minds of the Thai people, and help ensure that the Thai government remained actively anti-Communist. The Vietnamese defeat of the French in 1954, the year before Ernest's arrival, and the withdrawal of the latter from Indochina, only accentuated these American efforts. Scores of American "technical advisors," civilian and military, flooded into Thailand, promoting modernization and development in numerous ways—and, indeed, sometimes in ways that unintentionally frustrated true development.

In addition to American aid, other industrial nations were also at work in a Thailand that was humming with development programs. Bangkok became a major center of United Nations activity. Young idealistic Thais viewed development and democracy as Thailand's best destiny—and young practical Thais realized that participating in development programs could be the key to rapid career advancement.

While the International Institute for Child Study was not specifically chartered to contribute to overall development, the fact that the Institute gave promise of producing, among other things, better educational approaches and hence better educational results, was seen as contributing to overall development.

THAI CULTURAL VALUES

Ernest found traditional Thai culture fascinating, and threw himself into it. He inquired deeply into Theravada Buddhism, then as now the religion of 90% of the Thai population. As a psychologist, he was naturally intrigued by the Buddhist notion that all life is suffering, and that the ultimate solution to recurring cycles of suffering is the renunciation of all desire. As a human being, he felt (as in fact do most Thais) that renouncing *all* desire was too strict a standard.

Ernest saw Thai Buddhism as the seedbed for a variety of key Thai values—values that he would have to understand in order to fulfill his mission. Space here permits the discussion of just four such values, namely empathy, joyfulness, interpersonal harmony, and autonomy in a context of hierarchy. The brief discussion below is based on a more complete formulation available in Sippanondha Ketudat (1990, pp. 74-80.)

Empathy and the "Caring Heart"

In the Thai language, the morpheme *caj*, which may roughly be glossed as "heart," is found in well over *300* Thai terms (Lee, 1987, pp. 149-193). One wonders whether there is another culture anywhere, modern or otherwise, with so many lexemes referring to empathy and caring. To a considerable extent, these "heart" terms reflect the fundamental Buddhist principles of loving kindness (*meedtaa*) and compassion (*karunaa*).

In terms of "empathic intelligence," the Thai people are, as Ernest learned and appreciated, arguably much more highly developed than most people of Western enculturation.

Joyfulness

Sippanondha (1990) also cites as another essential feature of the Thai national culture and identity

> a certain joy in life, a playful attitude (*khwaam khiilen*), a preference for things that are fun (*sanug*), and a proclivity toward comfort (*khwaam sabaaj*) in a general sense. This proclivity is not just toward material comfort, but toward interpersonal relations that make everyone feel comfortable at heart (*sabaajcaj*) in a general sense. Along with this goes a tendency not to take the troubles of the moment too seriously. Our cultural tendency to emphasize "knowing" in a wide sense … is related to a tendency not to take any one setback too seriously, and to value the Buddhist notion of equanimity (*ubeegkhaa*). (p. 77)

While Western tourists typically find the joyfulness of the Thai people highly attractive (which helps explain why tourism is now Thailand's number one earner of foreign exchange), Westerners serving as change agents, such as Ernest, sometimes find this quality frustrating. One Western complaint is that some of their Thai opposite numbers seem to "work at play and play at work." A more balanced judgment might be that they are more likely to "combine business with pleasure," but still manage to produce good results. At any rate, here is another feature of Thai culture that Ernest had to learn how to deal with.

Harmony and Avoidance of Confrontation

Almost all Westerners who visit Thailand are struck by how pleasant the Thais are. One reason why life in Thailand is so pleasant is that Thai culture strongly disvalues direct or overt confrontation. Ernest had to learn from experience that, in leading a seminar or practicum, one does not overtly criticize a Thai scholar in front of that scholar's peers or subordinates. The Thai system does, though, provide *non*confrontational means of expressing honest criticism, and it is up to the foreign change agent to develop that skill.

This concern not to upset another person is also obviously relevant to the study of child development in Thailand, in the sense that the child is less likely, than in the democratic West, to question the teacher or other authority figure.

Decreasing Hierarchy, Increasing Autonomy

For five centuries before Ernest arrived in Bangkok—since the Thais conquered the Khmer and proceeded to borrow culturally from them—the Thai national social system has been characterized by a rigid hierarchy, which has proven helpful—and probably essential—to preserving independence and domestic order. Alongside this rigid hierarchical pattern, and in tension with it, stands a set of patterns favoring personal autonomy. As a broad generalization, one can say that a Thai youngster will typically place a higher value on individuality, than would a comparable youngster in, say, Japan or India.

In 1955, as today, Thai notions of hierarchy are strikingly in evidence in the profound, quasi-religious respect that the Thai people feel and express toward their beloved King, and in the effectiveness and decisiveness of the senior civil service—the very leadership that historically did the right things that enabled Thailand to escape colonization by any Western power.

Since the overthrow of the absolute monarchy in 1932, however, there has been a steady trend toward less hierarchy and more individual autonomy, and less emphasis on statuses ascribed by birth, and more on statuses achieved by merit. Sippanondha, writing in 1990, provides an optimistic scenario for the future of Thai culture in which this autonomizing trend will continue. He also believes that many hierarchical structures will survive, but that many of these will be more democratic in the way they function.

Ernest, Murray Thomson, and I spent hours discussing how to reach an optimal balance between hierarchy and autonomy. Ernest, coming from the role of chair professor in a European university, sometimes leaned toward hierarchy. Murray, coming to Thailand fresh from service as director of adult education for the Province of Saskatchewan, and having been a faculty member at the National Training Laboratories in Bethel, Maine, sometimes leaned toward autonomy. I typically found myself somewhere in the middle. All three of us favored maximum feasible autonomy for the individual scholar (or small teams thereof), but also recognized that the establishment of sound social science standards meant that there had to be considerable direction by Ernest, and that many Thais would actually value that. A complete *laissez faire* approach would clearly not work, but neither would a plan simply dictated by the director. Here, then, was a fourth thicket through which Ernest had to find his way.

Final Comment

This short statement has attempted to sketch some of the cultural challenges that the young Ernest Boesch faced. Much more could be said about these challenges, but suffice to say here that in my judgment Ernest dealt with them all admirably, and in the process enriched not only his own personal life, but also the subdiscipline of cultural psychology. We are all in his debt.

NOTE

1. **Robert B. Textor** earned his doctorate in cultural anthropology from Cornell University in 1960. After postdoctoral appointments at Yale and Harvard, he joined the faculty at Stanford University in 1964, taking early retirement in 1990. For the past 3 decades he has worked at developing theories and methods for the practice of anthropology in an anticipatory mode. Two of his recent publications are:

    Margaret Mead and the World Ahead: An Anthropologist Anticipates the Future. This is a compendium of 25 selected writings and lectures by Margaret Mead in which she engages in anticipatory anthropology. Edited, with an introduction and commentaries, by Robert B. Textor. It is volume 6 of a seven-volume series for the Margaret Mead Centennial, under the overall editorship of William O. Beeman. New York and Oxford: Berghahn Books (2005, p. 376).

    Die Zukunft Oesterreichs: Chancen und Risiken im nanotechnischen Zeitalter (The Future of Austria: Opportunities and Dangers in the Age of Nanotechnology). With Ernst Eugen Veselsky as coordinator, editor, and principal author; Robert B. Textor as methodological advisor; Norbert Rozsenich as general secretary; and 21 Austrian coauthors. Vienna: Buchverlage Kremayr & Scheriau/Orac, Vienna. (2006, p. 189). An English version of this book, translated from the German by Hedwig D. Thimig, with the editorial assistance of Robert B. Textor, is available on the Internet at http://www.stanford.edu/~rbtextor/

REFERENCES

Berry, J. W. (1969). On cross-cultural comparability. *International Journal of Psychology, 4,* 119-128.

Lee, C. K. (1987) "Heart Language." In A. Buller (Compiler and Editor), *Proceedings of the International Conference on Thai Studies* (Vol. 2, pp. 149-93). Canberra: Australian National University.

Mead, M. (2005). *The world ahead: An anthropologist anticipates the future* (Robert B. Textor, Ed., with commentaries). New York and Oxford: Berghahn Books.

Sippanondha Ketudat. (1990). *The middle path for the future of Thailand: Technology in harmony with culture and environment* (With the methodological and editorial collaboration of Robert B. Textor). Retrieved 2006, from http://www .stanford.edu/~rbtextor/

Textor, R. B. (1967). *A cross-cultural summary*. New Haven, CT: Human Relations Area Files Press.

Textor, R. B. (1973). *Roster of the Gods: An ethnography of the supernatural in a Thai village* (Vol. 6). New Haven, CT: Human Relations Area Files Press.

PART II

BASIC READINGS

INTRODUCTION TO THE SELECTED READINGS

The Authors

Following are overviews and the reprinting of eleven selected papers and essays of Professor Ernest E. Boesch. These writings clearly articulate his views on the complex nature of cultural influences and interactions with human motivation and behavior. They also describe the difficulties researchers encounter when they attempt to study individuals and groups from a cultural and cross-cultural perspective. Within this collection are some of the earliest iterations of cross-cultural methodologies that compared European (German) and Asian (Thai) children whose social and intellectual development were studied under the auspices of a UNESCO institute that Professor Boesch directed between 1955-1958.

There are also more recent publications including a 2003 article from *Culture & Psychology* that addressed questions of child development. For those who wish to expand their familiarity with the range of Professor Boesch's writing, a bibliography of most of his work is included in the text. No list of publications is completely inclusive since Boesch continues to write and publish.

Tracing Boesch's interest in writing back to his high school years, he was and still is passionate about expanding and improving his ability to

Discovering Cultural Psychology: A Profile and Selected Readings of Ernest E. Boesch, pp. 97–98
Copyright © 2007 by Information Age Publishing
97

convey meaning. Reflective of his times, he is also deeply interested in the myths and legends of people from all cultures. During our interviews, he mentioned that he has kept some of his early poems, and still finds a few to be "quite good," a remarkable endorsement for one who is his harshest critic.

While Ernest Boesch has focused more on academic than creative writing throughout his career, a sample of the following works clearly indicate that he applied all of his talents to his writing, largely because he believes there is a close link between form and content in all types of human expression. In his creative writing, particularly after he became aware of the many legends in Thai culture, he enjoyed writing fantastic stories that were based on his interpretations of traditional Thai dragon stories. Remembering his early childhood exposure to fairy tales about witches and goblins, Ernest was interested to see if there were parallel themes and morals that children might take from these stories that were created and sustained by elders of their culture. His ability to read and speak Thai has greatly enriched his ability to discover indigenous meanings attached to the folk legends. His mastery of language, a major reflection of cultural norms and patterns, reflects his holistic and ecological approach to studying human psychology.

We hope the selected readings serve to inform and educate our readers about the many challenges Boesch and his peers faced as pioneers of cross-cultural and cultural psychology. Remembering that Ernest was a young adult when World War II raged, he became committed to studying psychology to better understand human behavior, both positive and negative. As a Piagetian constructivist, he believed that people learned primarily through modeling. He saw how ruinous unbridled aggression could be. Furthermore, he believed that war was not an inevitable result of human desire for power and security. Professor Boesch continues to be deeply committed to his early goal of using his knowledge and experience to promote the psychology of human concern, respect, and empathy. His words trumpet his stance as a citizen of the world with undying interest and compassion for his fellow citizens of the world. No one can convey who Professor Boesch is better than he can. Reading a sample of his works affords a meaningful encounter with this great scholar, artist, and humanitarian.

A. GETTING INTO ACTION

INTRODUCTORY COMMENTS TO CHAPTER 5

"The Bangkok Project, Step One"

The Authors

Chapter 5 includes Professor Boesch's assessment of the complex problems encountered while directing the UNESCO research program in Bangkok. The program required 2 years of planning and was a major undertaking of the International Institute for Child study. There were three primary goals underlying the research conducted by Boesch and his colleagues: (1) to collect information about the intellectual development and education of Thai children; (2) to train and support a research team that included both Asian and Europeans; and (3) to develop a research plan that would facilitate international cooperation for conducting parallel and comparable studies around the world. Step one refers to the first phase of research that lasted from 1956 to 1958. Professor Boesch described this research as "one of the most important and challenging undertakings in modern psychological research." This statement suggests that the study was recognized as a major initial effort

Discovering Cultural Psychology: A Profile and Selected Readings of
Ernest E. Boesch, pp. 101–103
Copyright © 2007 by Information Age Publishing
All rights of reproduction in any form reserved.

in cross-cultural psychology replete with methodological and philosophical complexities.

RESEARCH QUESTIONS AND METHODS

Two questions that were frequently asked by those who were aware of the project were whether Asian children were as intelligent as European American children and what tests were used to measure intelligence. Here the major element of cultural differences clearly influenced that entire project. As Professor Boesch defined it, intelligence is generally the way a person structures his/her behavior. The implication is that behavior is chosen according to what one might deem appropriate and effective in any given context. In this respect behaving intelligently is determined by both the situation of the person and her/his motivation. Cultural norms contribute to how anyone behaves consciously and unconsciously. Therefore, comparing the results of intelligence tests of children from different cultures, even if "culture-free" tests are used, is extremely complicated and of questionable value in Boesch's experience.

For those who conduct research in a culture that differs from their own, there is a challenge in trying to determine what particular elements or agents of that culture influence the behavior of the people being studied. To describe the difficulty of this research, Boesch analyzed how a European might struggle to listen to and appreciate Thai music. For Europeans, one's expectation of musical sound is learned by listening to what is played or sung and approved as meaningful by large segments of the local culture. When Europeans begin listening to Thai music, the sounds are so different and dissimilar to what they are used to hearing; they may find it strange and unappealing. It takes time and retraining to appreciate the different way Thais compose and perform their music. Similarly, Thai people must work at appreciating European music because it is so different to them. However, something specific within the culture is reflected in the music of the people. A researcher is challenged to identify just what that something might be.

Testing the Children

As might be expected, selecting a population sample for the research was replete with challenges and uncertainty about the influence of diverse cultural factors. There were all the usual concerns about having comparable and representative samples from both Bangkok and the Saar. Even efforts to determine students' socioeconomic status proved difficult.

Issues such as variations in curricula variances and conformity to school attendance also had to be analyzed.

Next came the myriad of questions regarding the type of tests to use, the methods of testing, and various ways to interpret results. Elements of intelligence that were tested included: free drawing; graphic development; development of basic physical concepts; verbal development; free verbal expression; motor performance; vocabulary and verbal learning; and projective tests. In addition, interviews were conducted with students and their parents. Results of some of these tests were presented in the paper in both narrative and graphic forms.

Summary

Historically and practically, this paper provides an excellent example of an early cross-cultural study of children's intellectual development. Professor Boesch wrote clearly and specifically about the many limitations of the Bangkok Project. This paper added to the education of psychologists who may be involved in cross-cultural research. With his usual in-depth approach, Boesch pointed out the many ways that cultural differences must be considered when planning similar research projects. Perhaps, most importantly, Boesch dedicated two years in preparation for this study thereby indicating the care he took to organize an effective team and consider the many questions presented by this complex and collaborative effort.

CHAPTER 5

THE BANGKOK PROJECT, STEP ONE

Ernest E. Boesch

For almost two years I had the opportunity of observing two Thais studying in Europe. They were doing postgraduate work in psychological institutions and were under the supervision of experienced members of
student exchange services.

The short conclusion of these observations was that, as a safe bet, even
psychologists and qualified social workers tend to run into most serious
misunderstandings when working with Asians who are not yet accultur-
ated to Western ways of life.

The reason for it? There is a joke about an American professor, who,
while lecturing, was puzzled by seeing three Chinese girls sitting in the
front row, all looking indistinguishably alike. When he had finished, the
three girls rushed forward to ask him: "How does it happen, Professor,
that all Americans look indistinguishably alike?"

Anyone who has lived in other cultures knows that the joke is a lie.
Human beings are individuals wherever we meet them. They smile, get
angry, are happy or sad in an individual, personal way, and, furthermore,
their emotional reactions seem to us to be immediately understandable.
This similarity of expression accounts for our tendency to expect the same

Discovering Cultural Psychology: A Profile and Selected Readings of
Ernest E. Boesch, pp. 105–123
Copyright © 2007 by Information Age Publishing
All rights of reproduction in any form reserved.

of them as we expect of members of our own culture. This, however, is precisely the reason for the misunderstandings occurring between members of different cultures, because, though the basic mechanisms of emotional reaction and expression (as well as, often, the main ways of reasoning) show a [124] striking similarity, allowing immediate communication between hetero-cultural partners, there is also a whole set of psychological differences, less apparent perhaps, but very important for the structuring of action.

What will happen, then, in the hetero-cultural contact is obvious: In spite of apparently similar attitudes, the partner does not "live up to" our expectations, and we tend to judge him accordingly. Lazy, dishonest, childish, neurotic, unintelligent, unable to grasp problems, are but a few of the judgements about Asians I have heard time after time. In fact, the Thai (whom we shall take here as an example for the whole range of possible hetero-cultural partners) does not fit into our specifically culture-bound system of social expectations, and therefore any judgement relying on it is basically wrong. Yet, as long as we remain unaware of our own "prepatterning," using our spontaneous expectations, we will tend to vitiate the hetero-cultural contact.

In short, our patterns of judging frequently seem not to apply to the behaviour of non-Western human beings. This fact suggests that our psychological knowledge is only partly based on "human universals," and to some extent is a specific product of our own Western culture, valid only as far as it remains within its own limits.

This, then, is a basic challenge to psychology, and we cannot even console ourselves by considering this challenge as a mainly theoretical one, the use of psychology outside the boundaries of our culture being of only limited interest to us. For, if psychological methods and the knowledge we derive from them are a product of specific cultural conditions, we might equally meet "sub-cultural strata" within our own Western world which would, too, prove refractory to our attempts at understanding. Moreover, this course of thinking suggests that the question of "variables of personality" will not be answered as long as no sufficient understanding of the cultural (or we might call it as well environmental) conditioning of personality traits is available. We must therefore face the problem of the variability of human nature in relation to different environmental conditions.

We might put this provisionally in a short formula: We can assume that human beings possess, on the whole, the same kind and amount of "basic behaviour potentialities," varying according to a similar pattern of biological distribution. We can assume, further[125], that culture represents a set of agents with selecting and directing power. Thus the basic behaviour potentialities are activated in a process of "cultural specialization." There is little knowledge, so far, as to the *areas* in which this specialization takes place, and little knowledge, either, as to its *results*. It is likely, however, that the *process* of cultural specialization conforms to what we generally know about learning. At any rate, we meet here some basically important problems of human psychology, i.e.:

1. the cultural agents (or variables) leading to personality formation;
2. their results in terms of functional specialization;
3. their ways of acting.

Solving these problems is a relatively new adventure in our science, and the methodological difficulties are such that no claims for very substantial results can as yet be made Their solution, however, will not only prove or disprove the general validity of our psychological categories and methods and throw new light on certain problems of personality, but at the same time will be of eminently practical use in applying psychology to education and social work within different cultures.

In the light of these considerations, the "Bangkok Project" is probably one of the most important and challenging undertakings in modern psychological research. In the year 1955, after two years of planning and preparation, UNESCO and the Thai Government founded jointly the "International Institute for Child Study" in Bangkok (in the following referred to as the IICS). The main promotors of the idea were Dr. W. D. Wall, UNESCO (now director of the National Foundation for Educational Research in England and Wales) and His Excellency Momluang Pin Malakul, Minister of Education in Thailand. The IICS has devoted itself to three main purposes: (1) To gather data about the developmental and educational status of Thai children, (2) to training and promoting co-operation within an "inter-cultural" team of research workers in Bangkok, and (3) to organize a system of international co-operation for obtaining comparable parallel data from different cultures.

I had the honour and the pleasure of directing the IICS during the years 1956-1958 and of carrying through the first part of its research programme. This period will be referred to as "Step One of the Bangkok Projec," and only this phase of the programme will [126] be covered by this report. At the present moment, the direction of the IICS is in the hands of an Australian colleague, Dr. Hugh Philp, who in his turn will carry out "step two."

It is probably necessary, before describing the actual research work, to say a few words about the situation in which it was done. The first question I was asked by a high Thai official on my arrival in Thailand was whether I thought that Asians were as intelligent as Euro-Americans. And the first question I was asked by most psychologists, when I was telling about our work, was: which tests did you use? Both questions were certainly beside the point, but both, in a sense, frame our problem. Intelligence can be defined as the very general ability of structuring the different aspects of behaviour. There is no reason, however, to limit "intelligence" to certain fields and kinds of structure formation alone. It is true that we have developed a concept of intelligence shaped mainly by the nature of tasks which we use in intelligence-testing, namely problem solving. Furthermore, the validity of our testing relies to a great extent on the fact that our educational and social setting leads to a highly competitive attitude in the fields of objective and abstract performance.

This Western concept of intelligence, however, is most likely to reflect a cultural specialization which need not necessarily occur elsewhere. The establishment of objective structures of a causal-dimensional-classificatory type may be the main field of intellectual activity in one culture, and hence will produce an intelligence of the Western kind. In another culture, the weight may shift more towards the formation of "social structures," while individual problem-solving behaviour may be neglected or even partly inhibited. If this be the case, i.e., if society tends to reject the individually conceived solution of problems which deviate from established cultural patterns, and if furthermore the potentially or actually reproving agents of society are persons of a certain status and position, the real problems which an individual in such a society has to solve consist in structuring his relationships towards the groups of statusholders. Hence, the intellectual development of the individual will tend to cope with social rather than with other situations. Problems of an impersonal kind will be likely to evoke little curiosity, but probably a fine understanding and handling of human relations will be developed.

It will be obvious by now that the measuring of intelligence in the first and in the second culture raises quite different problems and that reliable results could be expected only if we had means for evaluating levels of structure formation in the different functional areas. The so-called "culture-free" intelligence tests can claim this quality only as far as their use of non-verbal and sometimes non-concrete material frees them from problems of translation and material transformation. But insofar as they declare the handling of objective and abstract material to be the main criterion of intelligence, they remain totally culture-bound.[2][127] This argument does not attempt to discredit the value of intelligence-testing—it simply states the questionable values of intercultural comparison of test results.

So, what then is the situation of the cross-cultural research worker? Let us take a simple and straightforward example for illustrating the question, borrowed from a previous account.

Most people who hear Thai music for the first time are surprised by its lack of harmony and the monotonous phrasing of its melodies. It sounds out of tune, and one never really knows whether this is so because of a different tone scale or because it is out of tune. Nevertheless, it may appeal to you, because you like the people who like it or because its strangeness is somehow exciting. But, judging honestly, one does not really like it. It is too different from European music. In other words it does not fulfill the expectations which we have for music. But one night, lying and waiting for sleep, it may happen that you hear a solitary singer, and that you are strangely moved by the quiet line of his melody. It fills you with some feeling of unpretentious, but sober beauty, alien to our code of aesthetics, but still performing what all art should: arousing fascination and emotion. You may not know what leads to this sudden liking, and it may have vanished again the next morning. But you know now that you are dealing with some unknown, but real dimensions. Dimensions which are a challenge—henceforth you will not superficially measure and judge, but you will try to "live into," to submit to the strange reality, in order really to understand. We might say that at that moment, we have discovered one of the many "cultural specializations," different from ours, for reasons which we still do not understand, but representing a problem. We could say that the Thais have little musical talent, since they have not a science of harmony, melody and counter-point, and do not enjoy music with the same aesthetic thrill as we do. Such a statement, however, is meaningless. It simply says that music in Thai society has a different position and role than in ours. We have, in fact, not advanced any further.

This simple example with a touch of unscientific romanticism shows, however, one important difficulty in cross-cultural research: The problem of discovering the relevant dimensions. We may take for granted that, when we enter a new culture, much of what is relevant in it may escape our perception just as the charm of a Thai melody eludes an unprepared listener. It is probable, furthermore, that the reaction of the foreign listener to a Thai song (even once he has got "the feeling" for it) differs strongly from the one of the native Thai. In other words, every culture develops a specific system of agents acting on the individual, and the first main task of cross-cultural research is to discover these agents. It is this which I have called the "phenomenological approach," and it corresponds to the classical methods of cultural anthropology, collecting carefully all kinds and bits of evidence and information. The organization of these data will only allow drawing a first sketchy picture of a culture, mostly in qualitative terms and, therefore, in certain respects not very satisfactory in comparative work. Yet, no careful and systematic programme of cross-cultural research can be drawn up without this preliminary observing, "living and feeling into," and collecting data related to the culture. There is some danger in modern psychology of asking questions too hastily and of relying upon statistical procedures to obtain a relevant answer. Yet, the interesting answer is much more a function of the intelligent question than of the tools of analysis. We believe that in research, like in diagnostic clinical work, results are achieved by a continuous process of narrowing the fields of question with a corresponding increase in their precision.

Keeping these reasons in mind, it seems obvious that the "step one" of the Bangkok Project could have had only a survey-function. It was carried out by a team of learners—Thai research-workers learning the methods and proceedings of psychological research, and foreign research-workers learning Thai culture and language. Our methods had to be simple and easy in order to fit the level of training of the Thai members of the team; they had, furthermore, to cover as broad a field of psychological "functions" and conditions as possible, in order to allow afterwards the construction of precise hypotheses and more precise as well as narrower questions. We shall relate here some aspects of our first research programme and try to extract from them some conclusions for further planning.

In our first period of work we could neither cope with broad geographical areas nor with too large a number of children. We therefore abandoned the first intention to work in Bangkok as well as up country and limited the investigations to Bangkok schools only. For similar reasons we could not think of large random sampling. Hence we selected (within the limits of availability and readiness for co-operation) four experimental schools in which the distributions of pupils appeared to correspond to the socio-economic situation of Bangkok population as revealed by the official census.[3] Obviously, no school in itself could be expected to contain a representative cut from the Bangkok population. Therefore grades 1 and 4 were taken from two schools complementary to one another, in order to match satisfactorily children from lower classes on the one side, from middle and upper class families on the other side. Thus, grade one and four (the first and last of the Thai primary school system) represented our main sample; grades two and three were added for the group testing only. Table 6.1 gives a summarized account of our sample:

We refrain from giving more details, but this table shows that only grades 1 and 4 approach some representativeness, while grades 2 and 3 are obviously overloaded with better income groups. We must keep in mind, however, that such a table provides nothing more than a very rough estimate, since precise statistical criteria are not available in the official reports, and the information from our sample, too, is not reliable, for reasons which have been explained elsewhere.[2]

Let us stress, furthermore, that grades 1 and 4 (on which we shall mainly concentrate in the following discussion) are composed of two classes each, the first (A 1 and A 4) coming from a lower-class school, the second (D 1 and D 4) from a Government demonstration school with bet-

**Table 6.1. Distribution of Pupils in
the Four Grades (8 Classes)
According to Income of Parents**

	Grade				
	1	2	3	4	
Middle and higher income group	36	53	56	28	(N)
	50	78	73	44	(%)
Lower income group	36	15	21	35	(N)
	50	22	27	56	(%)

ter educational facilities and smaller numbers of children per classroom. Both schools were co-educational and slightly more than half of the class members were boys.

In Thailand compulsory schooling begins at the age of 7 years. Earlier schooling, however, is allowed, if the head-master and teachers agree. A glance over Table 6.2 shows immediately the effect on education of the different social status of parents in our schools. There is obviously a strong tendency to earlier schooling in the well-to-do families, especially noticeable in the school D (a school with mostly children from higher and middle Government officials), hence a lower average age and a narrower range of age-distribution. The data from our interviews confirmed the greater interest in and concern for education among,'parents of children in school D.

The sample described above was used for the first step of our investigations, the group testing. For the second step (see Table 6.2), only grades 1 and 4 were used; however, in the meantime children had been promoted to grade 2 of primary and grade 1 of secondary school. While the lower grade children remained mostly the same, a quite considerable proportion of the higher grades changed and had to be replaced by a new group, tested by the same methods. By this replacement the shift towards the better income groups in the higher grades was slightly accentuated. Since the details of the second sample remained otherwise largely the same, they are not reported here. It may only be added, as a further indication of educational differences, that in both groups the socio-economic status affects also the number of siblings of our children; the ratio of siblings per subject in both schools (A:D) is roughly similar, namely 1.7: 1.02.

The various research steps of our first investigations were grouped as follows:

(A) Group Testing
   I. *Graphic Development*

Table 6.2.   Age Distribution in the Experimental Classes

School Age-group 1		2	3	4	5	6	7	8	9	Total
A1G(irls)		8	13							21
B(oys)		4	7	6	1					18
DIG		9	4							13
B		11	8							19
B2G										—
B		17	9	7	2	1				36
C2G		8	17	3						28
B		1	3							4
B3G										—
B			27	5	3					35
C3G		1	16	22	2			1		42
B										—
A4G					3	8	11	1	2	25
B			1		2	7	5	5		20
D4G				5	2		1			8
B				11	5					16
Total G	9	21	46	30	7	8	12	2	2	137
B	11	30	46	30	13	8	5	5		148

(Age-group 1: 5;9-6;8 years; age-group 2: 6;9-7;8 years, etc. until age-group 9: 13; 9-14; 8 years).

    I.1. Free drawing:
        1. Drawing of a house, a tree and a person.
        2. Drawing of a plan o£ the inside of the child's home.
        3. Drawing of the child's family, including the subject himself.
        4. Drawing of a good and a bad dream.
    I.2. Formal aspects of graphic development:
        1. Drawing of simple graphic elements on dictation.
        2. Copy of forms of increasing complexity.
        3. Segregation of entangled forms.
        4. Copy of forms in inverted positions.
        5. Representation of spatial superposition of forms.

    II. Development of Basic Physical Concepts
        A form-test examining constancies of spatial directions, weight and volume, as in problems used by *Piaget.*

    III. Verbal Development
        III.1. Formal aspects:

1. Vocabulary test.
2. Test of logical-verbal relations (Foucault test).
3. Sentence-construction test.
4. Understanding of kinship-terms.
III.2. Free expression: Sentence-completion test.

IV. Development of Interests and of Social Orientation
1. Interests and wishes.
2. Sociogram.

(B) *Individual Testing* (only grades 2 of primary and 1 of secondary school)

I.   *Motor-Performance:* Tapping test.
II. *Learning*: Verbal learning.
III. *Projective Tests: 1.* Rorschach.
                 2. TAT (special form for cross-cultural purposes).
IV. *Individual Interview,* mainly centred on:
                 1. Family-relations.
                 2. Self-evaluations and aspirations.
                 3. Interests and activities.
                 4. Social relations.
                 5. Moral judgements.

C. *Parent Interview,* covering the following main areas:
    I. Socio-economic status:
                 1. Type of dwelling.
                 2. Number and relationships of inhabitants.
                 3. Occupation and monthly income.
    II. Physical and mental development of the child (subject)
    III. Role of the child in the household (activities, social relations)
    IV. Educational practices and aspirations related to:
                 1. Work and play.
                 2. Social relations.
                 3. Sex.
                 4. Moral, religious and superstitious attitudes.

It is impossible to relate here all the observations made in the course of these investigations, and too early, too, to expect a total analysis of the results. Part of the results have been published in mimeographed from, others are still in process of analysis (see bibliography). In the following pages we shall try to present some of the data now available and to mention the main problems raised by them.

Unlike, for instance, Javanese children, our Bangkok sample shows little special graphic ability. On the contrary, graphic development seems to be slower and less original than that of children elsewhere. We may recall that our first age-group (grade 1, resp. grade 2) includes mainly children from 6-9 years of age, while the fourth (resp. fifth) grade children were mostly between 10 and 13 years old. We generally accept, for Western children, that between the ages from 6 to 11 the child slowly moves from "intellectual realism" to "visual realism" (Luquet), which means elimination of transparencies, abandoning of "rigid schematism" (representation with simple graphic elements, like circles, triangles and rectangles) and acquisition of perspective, movement and correct relation of details. In the house-drawings, however, only a small proportion of our sample uses perspective, while the majority, up to the higher age-group, persists in using simple schematic forms. Similarly the tree- and the person-drawings remain relatively schematic, and where they leave the schema it is often only to reproduce some common pattern of a Western fashion journal. The copy of a rhombus (diamond), generally taken as a test for 7 year olds, is performed accurately only at the grade 4 level; however, if incorrect angles but general correct relation of sides is accepted, too, we get 60% of "correct" solutions at grade 2, and over 80% in all the following grades. Other copy-of-forms-tests corroborate these results: the children of our sample seem to be relatively slow in handling graphic forms. Special tests for checking operative (and not representative) dealing with forms seem to indicate, however, that Bangkok results do not differ very much from European [133] results; this, however, can only be a vague hint, since no precise parallel data are at the moment available for these tests.[11, 19, 21] This seems to indicate that the slowness and unoriginality of graphic development which we observed in Bangkok children is much more a function of a lesser degree of exercise than an indication of genuine slowness in mental growth.

As far as can be approximately judged, the verbal development does not seem to show similar retardation. The increase of abstract words in the vocabulary of children seems, on the contrary, to be rather quicker than has been found in the Saar.[13] While at the ages of 9, 12 and 15 the percent of abstract words found in a vocabulary test with Saar-children is resp. 1.9 and 14%, grade 1 in Bangkok begins with 7% and increases to 21.5% in grade 4. The other verbal tests (Foucault, Sentence-Construction) similarly seem to follow the usual pattern of Western children, although here, for the moment, we do not have exactly comparable data at our disposal. This, by the way, may surprise the reader, since both of these tests, although in a slightly different form, have already been standardized in Europe. The reason for it is simply that they have been standardized according to a scoring system which we could not apply in Bangkok and, therefore, the exact comparison has to wait until European data have been scored in the same way.

Let us not look into all the details of the available results. Lacking for the moment precisely comparable data, we would only risk overloading these pages with material of as yet undetermined meaning. But what has already been shown permits a first conclusion: it seems that, compared with Western children, Thai children do not develop in an entirely parallel way. There are retardations, correspondences, and it is safe to assume, too, advances in comparison to the developmental rhythm of our children. A first, simply descriptive task of cross-cultural psychology lies, therefore, in determining precisely the areas of slow and of accelerated development. We have found that such an area of slow development seems to be the mastering of graphic forms. We have then to ask the question of why such a functionally underdeveloped field exists. Thus, logically, a second task of cross-cultural psychology lies in explaining these retardations and advances, which point either to constitutional factors or to factors of environmental pressures and incentives. Do we get indications concerning these factors from our material?

Any cross-cultural assumption of constitutional mental differences has to remain unchecked for the moment. We do not have sufficient means at our disposal to test such an hypothesis. Cross-cultural psychology may itself, one day, contribute at least a partial' answer to these questions, be it per exclusionem or per confirmationem of environmental influences. So we have to concentrate, in the present situation, on problems of environmental conditions of psychological development. That is why a relatively large part of our research work was devoted to interviewing and to projective tests. Unfortunately, most of these data are still in the process of analysis, so that, again, we can only cast some scattered light.

A first indication might be given by contents of imagination. We have collected drawings of good and bad dreams from our subjects. Since graphic expression seems, as we have seen, not to be a special strength of Bangkok children, their dream-telling in a drawing did not provide many highlights on their inner life. Some indications might be given by the larger distribution of themes in good and in bad dreams, in the tendency to exclude the dreamer's self from bad dreams, but to include it more frequently in the good ones, and in certain types of themes. Thus frequent themes of good dreams are making trips, having fun and receiving things or money. This last category is not without interest: while only 4.8% of the first grade children include the "receiving-themes" in their dreams, in grade two the percentage already rises to 28.2%, in grade three remains on the same level (27.1%), and in grade four rises to 43.2 of children whose good dreams tell about getting money, gold, winning in the lottery or getting a car, a house and similar themes! The mere motor joys and activities like fishing, swimming, riding, walking, constitute almost 38% of the first grade themes but fall to 3.7% in grade four (grade 2 : 23.1%, grade 3 : 13.6%). These two opposite "slopes" reflect in a nice way not only the developmental shifts in interests, but also the increasing concern of the children with economic problems. Most of the bad dreams tell about being attacked by ghosts, human beings or animals (37% in grade 1, between 60 and 63% in grades 2-4). Seeing accidents or exciting things or killing oneself is a second group of themes, although of lower frequency (1: 18%, 2 : 22%, 3 : 18%, 4: 14%). The more numerous different themes in good dreams might indicate that good dreams are more frequent than bad ones—however, as long as it is not checked by individual interviews, this remains a [135] mere guess. The high incidence of being attacked (ghosts, etc.) might certainly be a cultural index, since not only the fear of ghosts, but even more the fear of powerful human beings is a fairly common trait in Thai personalities.

The TAT's and sentence completions would be a valuable complement to these dream-data, but unfortunately their analysis is not yet finished. The Rorschachs, however, have been analyzed as to their formal aspects, but no striking differences between Bangkok and Swiss results were revealed. A more detailed study of the Bangkok Rorschachs together with those of other cultures is under way in our institute.

As to the observation of concrete child behaviour, only one piece of systematic data gathering was done in connection with some sociometric tests. A group of collaborators studied the behaviour particularities of over-, under- and average-chosen pupils in four classes of primary school. Their data, interesting in themselves as to the different behaviour characteristics of these three groups, give some hints as to the educational situation of the children. All observations were class-room observations showing, in European terms, a relatively high amount of interaction between children in the class-room, of which only a small amount (1.8%-4.3%) was of an aggressive or otherwise rude kind. This would fit into the general observation that on school-grounds, during recesses, an astonishingly small amount of aggressiveness is displayed by the children, in spite of there being sometimes very little adult supervision. This suggests a relatively low degree of repression of individual activity during teaching and, therefore, a correspondingly low explosion of repressed forces after working hours. A hopeful picture of relief for those accustomed to European school-ground noises.

We might obtain some better clues for our initial problem of disparities of development between Western and Bangkok children by some interview data. One part of the children's interview was concerned with the self-evaluation of our subjects. A discussion of this in some detail will help us to clarify the problems of this kind of work.

The more we worked in Bangkok, the more we tended to see the really important problems of cross-cultural psychology in the field of attitudes. Self-evaluation in comparison with one's group members can be used as one indicator for the development of [136] attitudes. We used a very simple device, asking the children to rate themselves in different school subjects and in some physical or behavioural qualities (general school success, writing speed, writing neatness, skill in arithmetic and drawing, physical strength, good behaviour, physical beauty). The children had to assign a rank to themselves and to express their aspirations in these areas; they had, in addition, to guess which ranks the best and the poorest student would assign to themselves if they were asked the same questions. All the questioning was done individually, with 59 children of primary school grade 2, and 55 of secondary grade 1; of this last grade a group of 12 unfortunately had to be eliminated, since their results showed a strong bias introduced by an unskillful interviewer. Exactly the same questions have been asked since with Saar children of the same age, one younger group of 20 (average age 9 years) and one older group of 20 (average age 12 years). The Bangkok sample as well as the Saar sample included both boys and girls. The results are expressed in Figures 7.1, 7.2, and 7.3

We can summarize certain general developmental characteristics: Increase of self-criticism with age and change of aspirations are probably processes of growth which all children in the world go through. On the other hand, our results express some cultural peculiarities: the greater tendency towards central evaluations of Bangkok children, the greater decrease of aspiration with age, and, most of all, the consent in question 2 (older group) that good students should not "show off"; answers of the children like "he doesn't like to show himself" or "he pretends that Amphon is stronger, because (otherwise) Amphon might feel hurt" illustrate this tendency. We find in these two aspects of our results (general growth processes and cultural peculiarities) an example for what has been said previously in this article, i.e., that culture selects amongst the possible forms of behaviour and specializes in them.

It would naturally be possible to extrapolate such findings. We won't do it, keeping in mind not only the tentativeness of our results due to the small groups examined, but also the danger of any extrapolation in genetic psychology. It is safe to say, however, that the developmental processes, expressed in the above graphs tend towards some adult

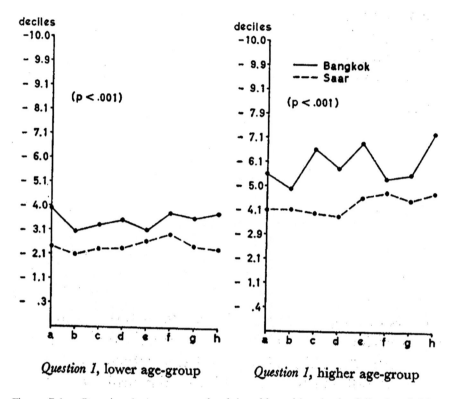

Question 1, lower age-group   Question 1, higher age-group

Figure 7.1.   Question 1: Average ranks claimed by subject in the following fields:
a = general school success, b = writing speed, c = writing neatness, d = arithmetic, e = drawing, £ = physical strength, g = good behaviour, h = beauty. The
real class ranks have been converted into deciles. p computed according to X°-test
for k independent samples (see Siegl, S.: Nonparametric Statistics for the Behavioral Sciences, New York 1956).

pattern and it is, in a sense, nothing else than these adult patterns
which, in their totality, we call "culture." Seen in this way, cross-cultural psychological research boils down to a very simple formula: We
have to know the "adult matrices" and the ways and means in which
they influence processes of growth. In our case, no precise adult
matrices are available for comparison. However, every student of Thai
culture knows that obedience, gentleness, sparing of others' feelings
are much more important values than in Western culture, while initiative, individuality and criticism, so much valued in the West, are of
secondary importance. The "limits of tolerance" within which a Thai
may distinguish himself from others in clothing, behaviour or think-

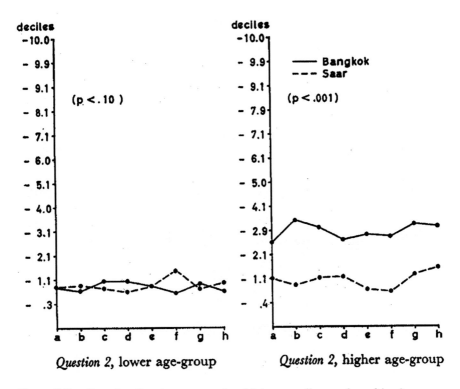

Figure 7.2.   Question 2:   Average ranks which, according to the subject's guess, the best students would assign to themselves in the same fields.

ing, seem to be much narrower than in Europe and America. Thus, we may say that the above results move clearly towards the two different types of adult matrices and, therefore, express the process of "developmental acculturation."

An additional hint might be extracted here from our results: while it seems that the adult world builds up special rules for good behaviour and limits for its display, the same seems not to apply for bad or unskillful behaviour. No distinctive cultural features, indeed, seem to differentiate our groups in question three, and this seems to corroborate our everyday experience: Society says that we should be good, and how we have to behave if we are good; it says, too, that we should not be bad, but fails to say what to do if we are bad.

Thus, this short review of the still incomplete results of Step One of the Bangkok Project has led to some conclusions useful for further work. They may be roughly summarized as follows

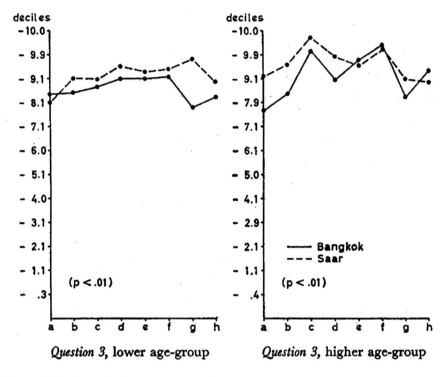

Question 3, lower age-group   Question 3, higher age-group

Figure 7.3.   Question 3:   Average ranks which, according to the subject's guess, the poorest students would assign to themselves in the same fields.

1. Personality development of children in different cultures is not simply parallel, but shows areas of retardation and acceleration according to the cultural mould.

2. These differences are due (hypothetically) to the variations in universal growth processes through cultural selection and specialization.

3. The whole question of differences in functional ability must, therefore, give way first to the question of differences in the building up of motivations and "frames of reference."

4. The programme of cross-cultural research, therefore, centres on the following main problem areas

    4.1. description of adult-matrices

       2. types of influences on the growing-up (pressures, incentives, examples, etc.)

       3. universals of growth processes

4. cultural variations of growth processes.

Such simple formulations tend to obscure the methodological difficulties ; which, in cross-cultural research, are multiple. They lie not only
in the accessory (but not unimportant) fact that a cross cultural research
worker always has to rely upon native collaborators and that the co-operation with them, in a sense, implies in advance the knowledge of all one
is on the way to discover. Many of our difficulties in Bangkok were simply due to the naive assumption that the motivation for, and the idea of
research work were the same in Thailand as in Europe. But the main difficulties of cross-cultural work lie in the fact that methods of working
and the whole framework of thinking in our science are strongly tied up
with Western culture. Cross-cultural psychology means, without any
doubt, a rethinking of psychological terms, a restructuring of our usual
approach to problems. But these are questions which lie outside the
scope of this article and which will be followed up elsewhere.

The work begun in Bangkok is going on now in a double way. It is
going on in Bangkok itself where, after the first survey-study, special problems are under investigation. And it is going on in the Saar university,
through further analysis of the present data, through further investigation
and collection of parallel data, and, finally, through methodological and
conceptual studies of problems in cross-cultural psychology. About all
these we hope to be able to report in due course.

SUMMARY

The author sketches the importance of cross-cultural psychology for personality theory and for applied psychology. He then describes the main
working features of the "International Institute for Child Study" in
Bangkok, an institution for comparative research in child psychology.
After showing the problems he met as a director of this institute, he gives
the main outline of the first research step, carried out in the years 1956 to
1958. Based on the survey of results available up to now, methodological
principles and important problem areas of cross-cultural research are outlined.

ZUSAMMENFASSUNG

Der Verfasser unterstreicht die Bedeutung kulturell vergleichender Psychologie sowohl für die Theorie der Personlichkeit wie auch für die

angewandte Psychologie. Er beschreibt dann die Eigenart des oInternationalen Institutes fur das Studium des Kindes» in Bangkok, einer Institution mit der Aufgabe, vergleichende entwicklungspsychologische Untersuchungen durchzuNhren. Nachdem er auf die Probleme hingewiesen hat, die er als Direktor dieses Instituts antraf, gibt er einen Überblick über das erste Untersuchungsprogramm, das in den Jahren 1956 bis 1958 durchgeführt wurde. Die Diskussion der bis heute vorliegenden Ergebnisse führt zu einer Formulierung methodologischer Prinzipien und wesentlicher Probleme kulturell vergleichender Forschung.

RESUMÉ

L'auteur souligne d'abord l'importance de la recherche en psychologie comparée, pour la théorie de la personalité aussi bien que pour la psychologie appliquée. It décrit ensuite les aspects principaux du travail de « L'Institut International pour l'Etude de l'Enfant» A Bangkok, institution créée dans le but de faire des recherches comparatives du développement de l'enfant. Après avoir esquissé les problemes rencontrés comme directeur de cet institut, it présente un apercu général des premières recherches, effectuées de 1956 à 1958. La discussion des résultats principaux étudiés jusqu'à présent conduit à préciser un certain nombre de problèmes importants et de règles méthodologiques en psychologie culturelle comparée.

NOTES

1. The numbers in [] indicate the page numbers of the original article.
2. * Thus, as an example, we would suspect the "Culture-Free Intelligence Test" of Cattell to be heavily culture-loaded. The fact that Cattell is able to provide promising statistical data from other cultures stems simply from the process of continuously extending the range of "test-readiness" of people in other cultures through Western forms of schooling. See for instance Xydias, N.: R. B. Cattell's intelligence test. In: Social Implications of Industrialization and Urbanization in Africa South of the Sahara. Unesco, Paris 1956.
3. Central Statistical Office of Thailand: Economic and Demographic Survey 1956, Municipality of Bangkok.

BIBLIOGRAPHY

We list here the mimeographed publications related to Step One of the Bangkok Project. A limited number of copies of them are still available, most of them through the IICS, some also through the Institute of Psychology in Saarbrucken.

1. *Boesch, E. E.:* Introduction. Research Bulletin of the IICS, Bangkok 1958.
2. *Boesch, E. E.:* Survey of the first research plan and of the results analyzed up to Oktober 1957. Research Bulletin of the IICS, Bangkok 1958.
3. *Boesch, E. E.:* Problems and methods in cross-cultural research. Working Paper I, UNESCO Expert Meeting, Bangkok 1958.
4. *Boesch, E. E.:* First research plan of the international institute for child study, Parts II and III. Working Paper III, UNESCO Expert Meeting, Bangkok 1958.
5. *Boesch, E. E.:* Results of the Rorschach test with Bangkok children. Working Paper IV, UNESCO Expert Meeting, Bangkok 1958.
6. *Boesch, E. E.:* Some data concerning the self-evaluation of Bangkok children. Working Paper, Conference on Stability and Change in Thai Culture, Burg Wartenstein 1959.
7. *Charoenying, Boonying* and *Miake Kazuo:* The results of the test of family relations. Working Paper VI, UNESCO Expert Meeting, Bangkok 1958.
8. *Dharmagrontama, S.:* The results of the Tapping test. Working Paper, UNESCO Expert Meeting, Bangkok 1958.
9. *Dickinson, P.:* The results of the drawing of house-plan test. Working Paper VIII, UNESCO Expert Meeting, Bangkok 1958.
10. *Dickinson, P.:* The results of the drawing of good and bad dreams test. Working Paper IX, UNESCO Expert Meeting, Bangkok 1958.
11. *Ertel, S.:* The results of the copy of forms test II. Working Paper VII, UNESCO Expert Meeting, Bangkok 1958.
12. IICS: Research Bulletin I and II, Bangkok 1958.
13. *Kamnuasok, N.:* The results of the word-learning test. Working Paper XI, UNESCO Expert Meeting, Bangkok 1958.
14. *Korn, S.* and *Tapkantchana, S.:* Bibliography for cross-cultural research in child development. Working Paper 11, UNESCO Expert Meeting, Bangkok 1958.
15. *Limtrakool, Arporn:* A study of the logical verbal relations of children in four primary schools in Bangkok. M. A. Thesis, Bangkok 1958 (typewritten).
16. *Pisespongsa, T.:* A study of the development of interests of children in four primary schools. M. A. Thesis, Bangkok 1958 (typewritten).
17. *Prabandhakomala, Phewchantana:* A study of some characteristics of the over-average and under-chosen pupils in four primary schools in Bangkok during school hours. M. A. Thesis, Bangkok 1958 (typewritten).
18. Pratatsoontornsarn, Waroporn: The drawing dictation test. M. A. Thesis, Bangkok 1958 (typewritten).
19. *Sasajomarn, P.:* The transparency- and the inversion of forms test. M. A. Thesis, Bangkok 1958 (typewritten).
20. *Sirmpongsa, S.:* The sentence-construction test. M. A. Thesis, Bangkok 1958 (typewritten).
21. *Tapkanchana, S.:* The copy of form test I. M.A.Thesis, Bangkok 1958 (typewritten).

INTRODUCTORY COMMENTS TO CHAPTER 6

"Space and Time as Valence Systems"

The Authors

Space and time are phenomena that surround us constantly. As such, they are naturally interesting and important concepts for psychologists and others to study in general, but particularly in a culturally-informed manner. As ubiquitous concepts, space and time have been such essential parts of how human beings structure their lives that it probably would be impossible to act without them. When social and behavioral scientists study space, it of course normally does not mean "out there" with the asteroids and astronauts. Rather, it means the more or less local or regional ecological space. As such, it can be both "real" space such as measurable physical distance between family members or neighbors, for example, or between entire nation-states. And of course it can be psychological, or subjective, space as perceived by the beholder. The latter has included studies of "proxemics," a subfield that looks into such things as "appropriate" distances between people in social gatherings or during

Discovering Cultural Psychology: A Profile and Selected Readings of
Ernest E. Boesch, pp. 125–128
Copyright © 2007 by Information Age Publishing
125

conversations, or "proper" seating arrangements in diplomatic situations, where status or seniority define where one sits at the table.

Time can be similarly partitioned into "real" time as measured by a variety of chronometric devices (clocks, hour glasses, calendars, cycles of the moon, planting seasons, etc.) or by temporal phenomena that are clearly more subjective and, therefore, sources of variation between individuals. Subjective perceptions of time, therefore, have interested many psychologists as well as anthropologists. They have asked many questions about the very nature of time and how it varies as a function of age, specific experiences, remuneration ("time is money"), and of course culture. If culture is the "software of the mind," as cross-cultural psychologist Geert Hofstede has defined it, then it follows that culture "programs" the mind to experience the physical world in highly subjective ways. Many have debated whether time is "linear," or "non-linear" and perhaps even "circular" like a pool, or indeed whether time even exists beyond the ways in which people have tended to structure it for their own convenience. Thus, exactly what space and time "really" are and what they mean to people can embrace a large number of questions.

Against the backdrop of such questions, it is therefore perfectly understandable why Ernest Boesch studied aspects of space and time during his 3-year stay in Thailand and after his return to Europe. It must have been quite a contrast for him when, in 1955, he set foot for the very first time in a part of the world that was obviously different from anything he ever experienced. Here was a psychologist, born and nurtured in Switzerland, a country known for its precise clocks and its rigid structuring of time and space (think of cuckoo clocks and its fastidious train schedules), who was suddenly enveloped in a culture where the rules of life and therefore the perception of space and time may be radically different.

As reported in chapter 4 in this book (a chapter almost exclusively written by Boesch), he reported having had one of those "aha" experiences. It is worth repeating the essentials of that experience here:

> While driving on the main road to the Bangkok airport, a "samlor" (a tricycle riksha) turned unconcernedly, without the driver's looking around, from a side road directly into the path of our car. It was only by a rapid braking that we avoided an accident. Pondering this incident, I was suddenly struck by the thought that for this riksha driver a side road and highway formed a different structure than for me. For me, at the junction between the two lay an invisible barrier, forcing me to slow down and to ascertain the safety of proceeding further. Space, over and beyond its physical layout, was mentally structured, containing limitations for our actions which, I presumed, varied by culture and, probably, also by individual. (Boesch, 1991, p. 9; Boesch, 1997, p. 8)

Boesch commented further on this event:

> although an apparently simple insight, it had important consequences. Action theory, which I had professed at my university since 1951, became cultural-ecological. Our world as we live in it is both structured by action and structures our action. It is an uninterrupted feed-back system which, after all in 1957, before cybernetic thinking entered psychology, was not that obvious a thought. (1997, p. 8)

A few years later, Boesch (1963) wrote a chapter for an edited book concerning dialectics and dynamics of the person. The title of the chapter was "Raum und Zeit als Valenzsysteme" ("Space and Time as Valence Systems"). It was reprinted in 1971 in Boesch's *Zwischen zwei Wirklichkeiten* (*Between Two Realities*). We include the chapter here, translated into another language, English, for the first time. We consider it important enough to appear in its entirety in this section.

Although Boesch wrote the original chapter when he was in the early stages of articulating the components of his symbolic action theory, he noted on several occasions that the "samlor experience" contributed significantly to a paradigm shift and eventually to a substantial revolution in how he "perceived, studied, and explained the relationship between human beings and culture." Here, paraphrasing from personal communication, is how he described the "mindset" he had at the time and how his "space and time" chapter should be understood: It explains a development of conceptual structures starting from action experience with slow progressive conceptualization—a view that did not exist in developmental psychology at that time. Also, it sketches a theoretical approach which permitted an explanation of cultural differences in a genetic perspective.

Boesch commented further on what might be called major theoretical epiphany:

> Such an experience possesses a highly subjective valence. It marks our mental "action potential," the one that masters a complex problem, or brings an end to a situation that is perplexing and full of doubts. Being able to find what I have just called a key increased my confidence in being able to unravel the maze of cultural intricacies, to arrive at an intelligible structure. That, of course, was only a hope, but it gave me a direction. (1997d, p. 9)

In his major book giving the details of his symbolic action theory, Boesch devoted an entire chapter to space and time. He noted that space is a topological system of valences while time is a sequential system of valences. He also pointed out that "objective space," which he also called "textbook space," is usually geographical or mathematical. By contrast, he referred to "subjective space" as that which is experienced in the course of action in the everyday world. "Action space" was defined as the "spatial area and its action structure either of individuals, or of groups. The two terms differ in emphasis, subjective space stressing experience of space, action space stressing the structure our actions give to space" (1991, p. 145).

On the topic of time, Boesch had this to say in his preamble to further discourse on the topic:

> Time experience is based on the experience of the course of action; the distance separating a goal from our present situation must be overcome by the progressive steps of action, and it is this progression which constitutes a necessary condition for the formation of time as an existential dimension. (1991, p. 159)

Two final notes about "Space and Time as Valence Systems" are offered. First, Boesch made good use of published research on space and time when he wrote the chapter. For instance, Fraisse's *La psychologie du temps* was an importance reference as was a book by Evans-Pritchard, who studied these topics, and others, among the Nuer of Sudan. He also studied Kluckhohn's "state-of-the-art" chapter on culture and behavior. As part of the 1954 *Handbook of Social Psychology*, Kluckhohn's chapter was a major source of information to Boesch when he was thinking about the ways in which space and time might fit within the context of his emerging symbolic action theory. Second, we wish to point out that in using such words as "oecology" and "valences," Boesch was well aware of, and creatively used, some ideas developed earlier by psychologists Roger Barker and his mentor, Kurt Lewin. Thus, for those familiar with the work of Barker and Lewin, terms such as "behavior settings" (Barker) and "life space," "topological space," and "goal valences" (Lewin), will provide solid linkage with theoretical and practical systems that have much in common. The most important thing they share is the way in which they deal with the human being as the main factor in a complex field of action, or specific cultural settings.

CHAPTER 6

SPACE AND TIME AS VALENCY SYSTEMS

Ernest E. Boesch

Psychology is defined as the science of behavior and its regularities. The psychologist himself may want to think about this definition when, as in comparative cultural psychology, he is searching for a systematic framework that would permit him, conceptually, to capture behavioral differences that may be frequently observed. Only then may one notice that psychological work is predominantly limited to capturing behavior in artificial experimental situations. It is probably for this reason that psychology, still only clumsily and improvisationally, deals with behavioral research *in situ*. Undoubtedly, the one-sidedness of our science is understandable; we have tremulously acknowledged the methodological inadequacy of many previous projects and try, with some trepidation, to hold on to those areas and problems that can be packed into clean experimental designs and measured with neat statistical criteria. Certainly we have gained much by this; however, it is equally certain that we are in danger of glossing over some things simply because the methodological precision cannot be implemented at all times and in all stages of scientific work by the same method. Simple phenomenological description, collection, and interpretation precede the stage of designing experiments. Moreover, the

Discovering Cultural Psychology: A Profile and Selected Readings of
Ernest E. Boesch, pp. 131–146
Copyright © 2007 by Information Age Publishing
All rights of reproduction in any form reserved.

cliffs of risky extrapolation and, frequently, speculative interpretation must follow, provided one does not have the will to sacrifice the richness of existential problems at the altar of pristine methodology.

This specifically applies to relatively new areas of psychological research, such as cultural psychology. We know that it is dangerous to transfer our European psychological system of concepts, as well the entrenched testing methods of our culture, to other lands. Questionnaires measure dimensions that differ from our own wherever the social significance of the discussion changes; deviations of experiments have an unusual significance for us where individual performance is not a social value, and the desire for usable behavioral criteria is more urgent where linguistic communication difficulties initially exist.

Social psychology surely owes something to the methodological aids of modern research. Despite this, we are still far from the goal of applying them to all important behavioral areas with equal success. The attempt to describe behavior at least logically, therefore, presses on with perhaps the optimistic hope that we may reach respectable starting points for systematic behavioral studies in a cultural comparative framework. The following observations of space and time are parts of such an attempt. These may be easily and effortlessly dismissed as a speculative collection of everyday events; is it, therefore, more logical not to concern ourselves with such everyday occurrences? For example, for years psychological attempts were made to test vehicle drivers for their suitability. However, it has not been considered that the widespread availability of individuals' motor vehicles has changed so much with respect to space and time, as we will see, that it could be assumed that we are confronted with one of the most psychologically important phenomena of Western history. A banality? That is generally up to the observer. However, let's devote ourselves to our problem.

"Space is a snapshot of time," says Piaget (1995), "and time is space in movement" (p. 14). Indeed, as long as we strive for the metric systems of space and time, as Piaget did, we may observe them as complementary phenomena. However, if we in the meantime begin to observe them as valency systems of behavior, their complementarity can no longer be so easily formulated. Surely Piaget is right when he defines metric time as a "coordination of movement": "If this designates displacement or movement or inner movements, as only represented by planned, anticipated or reconstructed acts, which are three-dimensional in structure; time again and again plays the same role as space in reference to unmovable objects" (p. 14). Time as a valency system, however, relates to internal stimulus rhythms with their own model frequencies and it no longer concerns the coordination of current or potentially three-dimensional movements, but instead the coordination of another type, which is the intent of these pages. And if metric space can be defined as a system of positions, behavioral space is a system of valencies—which, as already noted, will be explained in more detail below.

Surely close relationships exist between the valency period and the valency space, because all behavior occurs simultaneously in both, and measurements of a timely nature are used liberally for space as well as time.

The period of experience relates its quality not only to the coordination of three-dimensional movements, but also to organic stimulus rhythms, energetic regulation processes and action tendencies. The behavior period is more elementary while the action space is more physical. Despite this, we will begin our observations with space, because the variations of relevant questions will be clarified by using it as an example.

VALENCY SPACE

For geometric space, it is given that a section, AB, is homogenous and that it remains identical and independent from the direction in which it will pass (therefore, AB = BA). That this does not apply in the case of behavioral space is obvious—the way back is not the same as the way there, and the last segment of a stroll appears longer and more difficult than the first. Geometric space is a system of positions; but behavioral space is a system of interpretations, attractions and repulsions. Positional relations permit a three-dimensional orientation; valency relations, on the other hand, determine the type of actions that are appropriate within it.

Topology and valency, however, are not independent from each other. If a person wants to manage in a strange city, he or she must restructure a series of successively perceived locations and create a system of related positions. This is not always successful; the passenger in an automobile generally processes the surroundings more slowly than does the person at the wheel; the common pedestrian walks more slowly than the student who is searching for a room. A location that arouses no interest has less of a chance to be coordinated with others because a potential behavior target must remain; in other words, the tendency to return is what motivates three-dimensional structuring. The permanence of behavior targets, however, is a function of three-dimensional valencies. Consequently, the structuring of dynamic as well as factual space are closely related. We will therefore define behavioral space as a topological system of valencies and will attempt to restate this position more precisely.

Examples of space valencies are numerous. Height, depth, width, and proximity, as well as closed and open space, have different attraction values that range from indirect positive and negative appearance qualities to social, artistic and cosmological space symbolisms. Entire cultural eras are defined by variable space preferences—consider, for instance, architectural styles, social trends, sports types (such as mountain climbing!), the preference for certain vacation locations; yes, even vacationing as such is tied to space valencies and their alteration.

All of the above are examples of the valency characteristic of space. We would like to differentiate between locations, spaces, distances and directions for a more systematic consideration of evolving problems.

The space we experience is neither homogenous nor continuous; it contains locations and intermediate spaces. Behavior objectives reside within the location; intermediate space, however, contains no objectives. It is only distance. The air traveler, for whom two locations are frequently separated only by wide and almost empty spaces, experiences this more intensely. In such a situation distances do not correspond to any specific local behavior and are bridged by trivialities, such as reading, eating and sleeping. Location and intermediate space are very mixed when walking, wherein the path may trigger a series of playful behaviors. These behaviors, unlike the actual action objective, are not planned, but were at least included as potential objective categories when the entire action was conceived. Location and intermediate space may be, but do not have to be, constant qualities of various parts of the behavior field.

Location and intermediate space, meanwhile, are not the only aspects of one's action space. Intermediate space can be defined as the connection between two or more behavior locations. There are also spaces which are themselves unstructured and contain no clearly definable behavior objectives; however, they do not lead to a certain location, and therefore, in contrast to intermediate space, do not have precise endpoints. The adventurer who sails off into the sea with an unknown destination enters such a space; this also applies to the child who dares to set foot in an unfamiliar forest. Let's just simply call such areas the "open space." We will consider this again, along with intermediate space, when discussing the problem of "distances." Presently we would like to limit ourselves to the problem of location.

Psychological locations contain positive and negative behavioral objectives. In the former they are actively sought (action centers) while in the latter they are strongly avoided. Action centers satisfy a number of requirements. They may be for activity or enjoyment, company or solitude, security and quiet, or they may for the stimulus provided by endangerment. Locations with an accumulation of permanent positive valencies are structured relatively differently; they contain a minimum of unknown or intimidating features and therefore are not only zones of satisfaction, but also of security. The location with the highest degree of satisfaction and security is the "home." A series of more or less constant satisfaction zones are generally to be found near the home—shopping locations, walking areas, entertainment zones, for example. Next to these are areas with positive obligation valencies, specifically the workplace or school. Finally, negative features can be observed in this behavior center in the form of the "prohibited areas." These can include, for example, the cemetery, disreputable parts of the city, ugly and foul-smelling sections and, yes, even within the home a dark basement or an attic may become a prohibited area for a frightened child. All of these valencies can be constant as well as variable. A satisfaction zone during the day may become a prohibited zone at night; what is enticing in the summer may be repulsive in the winter. Just as we know of territorial maps with "passes" for animals (see Hediger, 1954), individual behavioral maps can also be set up for the "human territory" with a three-dimensional distribution of valences of various strengths and qualities.

Anyone removing himself from the familiar behavior center and therefore from the "territory" will naturally not enter an empty space. The valencies are mostly generalized by psychological locations, so that, for example, the positive quality of the playing field is transferred to the "field in general." Nevertheless, the locations with positive valencies generally become sparser the further one is removed from the familiar behavior center, while in the meantime the qualities of insecurity and the ambivalences of the unknown tend to increase. Somewhere there is a "border"—what exceeds this is either intermediate space or an open space. A favorite vacation resort again can be structured as far removed within this sense as an individual behavior center—whatever is in between is merely distance.

Let us cover the problem of the border or, better said, the periphery. The periphery consists only of the area of the behavior change. More precisely, the psychological location consists of a system of different locations with intermediate border zones. House, garden and surroundings, for example, are divided into areas of a variety of different types of behavior. One does not, for instance, eat in all of these places with the same degree of naturalness; there are limits, which are not exceeded in pajamas, in slippers, without a tie or when unshaven, and if it is exceeded anyway, the result is a feeling of insecurity, of being "not proper." Everyone knows that such areas are culture-bound—just think of a map of Europe, based on the different local frequencies with which women may be seen in the dairy stores before noon in robes and hair curlers.

Peripheries can be undefined zones, such as the aforementioned "robe area." However, they can also be relatively clearly defined, such as the stairway or the waiting room, in which one adjusts to new forms of behavior. While the locations themselves appear to be selective for behavior, the periphery results in a behavior change; hence it is of an ambivalent nature. It can increase or decrease the speed of behavior.

The modification of behavior occurs most visibly where clearly defined locations share borders, such as the juxtaposition of a schoolyard and school building, or a dark and frightening cellar shares a border with a playground. Occasionally, the ambivalency of the adjustment process can be clearly expressed, for example, in a mixture of good conduct and ironic comments during an unpleasant obligatory visit, or in a mixture of unconcern and discomfort when "unshaven" in the marginal zone outside one's home.

One is hesitant when entering an unfriendly area or when leaving an especially pleasant area, and every rider knows the slowing or accelerating effect of the peripheral field from the behavior of the horse when leaving the stable and when coming home.

Since the locations are selective in reference to behavior, they can appear to be as periphery in unadjusted behavior and as location in adjusted behavior—the bedroom, for example, is a location, while the living room is a periphery for the child in pajamas. The necessity of adjusted behavior in "conditional prohibited locations" appears to be especially noticeable. Not all prohibited areas are completely avoided; for example, there are those that lose their danger only if the correct behavior is adhered to. When not entering the church with a "devoted heart," it can appear dangerous—if the condition, however, is fulfilled, it has a positive valency. The area around a Thai spirit house is avoided. However, with an adjusted proper attitude and with offerings and reverence, it will be observed as a location of hope and security. Depending on the nature of one's attitude, the periphery of the location either decelerates or accelerates ones valencies.

The boundary leads us to the problem of distance and open space; however, it cannot only form the transition to another location, but also the transition to "distance." Evans-Pritchard (1940) characterized the problem of distances from an ethnological aspect in a manner worth reading:

> It would be possible to measure the exact distance between hut and hut, village and village, tribal area and tribal area, and so forth, and the space covered by each. This would give us a statement of spatial measurements in bare physical terms. By itself it would have very limited significance. Oecological space is more than mere physical distance, though it is affected by it, for it is reckoned also by the character of the country intervening between local groups and its relation to the biological requirements of their members. A broad river divides two Nuer tribes more sharply than many miles of unoccupied bush. A distance which appears small in the dry season has a different appearance when the area it covers is flooded in the rains. A vil-

lage community which has permanent water near at hand is in a very different position to one which has to travel in the dry season to obtain water,
pasturage, and fishing. A tsetse belt creates an impassable barrier, giving
wide oecological distance between the peoples it separates (p. 133), and
presence or absence of cattle among neighbors of the Neur likewise determines the oecological distance between them and the Nuer (pp. 132-133).
Oecological distance, in this sense, is a relation between communities
defined in terms of density and distribution, and with reference to water,
vegetation, animal and insect life, and so on.

Structural distance is of a very different order, though it is always influenced and, in its political dimension, to a large extent determined by oecological conditions. By structural distance is meant, as we have already
indicated in the preceding section, the distance between groups of persons
in a social system, expressed in terms of values. The nature of the country
determines the distribution of villages and, therefore, the distance between
them, but values limit and define the distribution in structural terms and
give a different set of distances. A Nuer village may be equidistant from two
other villages, but if one of these belongs to a different tribe and the other
to the same tribe it may be said to be structurally more distant from the first
than from the second. A Nuer tribe which is separated by forty miles from
another Nuer tribe is structurally nearer to it than to a Dinka tribe from
which it is separated by only twenty miles. (pp. 109-110)

Distances, therefore, are valency-relevant. Distances, however, depend
on the nature of any intermediate spaces. Locations have a remote quality,
and this has a double meaning: on one hand, it expresses the difficulty of
reaching a goal; the remote quality would, therefore, be determined by
the ratio of distance-valency to the goal-valency within this scope. Secondly, however, "the distance" means the potential to break away from
current ties and securities, and within this scope is defined by the ratio of
the goal-valency to the home-valency. An increasing distance, therefore,
acts within double the scope—valency-reducing (because of the difficulty
of reaching and the reduction of security), as well as valency-increasing
(because of the increase of the feeling of freedom and the change of stim-
uli).

The distance quality, as we have seen, depends on geographic as well as
ecological and social distance. It is, in the meantime, more than only a
distance index: it is a characteristic at the same time. For example, for a
German, Paris is a remote location even if he is in Paris, and his behavior
at such a "distant location" is not the same as at home. This distance quality naturally varies and depends on the length of the stay, on the company
one is with, and other factors. If in the meantime a "distant location" can
lose its distant quality, the home location will on the other hand—perhaps
even after an absence of many years—not become a remote location in
this sense; the distance here only expresses the difficulty of reaching it,

but does not provide the location with a distance quality. Many vacation resorts make a living from this distance quality and attempt to emphasize it in different ways, for example, by defining resorts as "exotic" or by highlighting some other unusual feature.

The valency of the distant location is therefore contradictory: the possibility of new forms of life, the hope to fulfill desires, the stimulation by a number of new impressions; all of these are aspects that enter into the positive valuation of distant locations. The more or less threatening quality of the unknown, as well as the problems and endangerments on the way there, are negative values. The manner in which a person evaluates these factors limits his reaction to distance, his wanderlust or even his obsession with distance, his fear of travel or his fear of distance. The negatively or positively felt qualities of the hometown naturally influence the distance assessment in a contrary sense. "Il lui suffisait de se dire: je ne serai plus ici; je serai ailleurs. Ailleurs: c'état un mot encore plus beau que les plus beaux noms" (Beauvoir, 1954).

This *ailleurs* as expression of the obsession with distance is opposed by "homesickness," in which the negative qualities of a remote location predominate.

The allure of distance and the security of home are qualities that vary, and this can especially be clearly observed in children: mother scolds and hits the child, therefore increasing the child's negative valuation of the home; at the same time the positive quality of the distance increases and the child runs away. The transition of nearness to distance is also frequently clearly demonstrated by children, and the periphery at which the child begins to become restless and scared can almost be defined as the distance or area in which it cries and asks to go home. Nearness and distance are also frequently defined as a function of the visual distance from a person. Person distances, by the way, are also common among adults; they are more clearly apparent in people who have unpleasant habits and get too close to "breathing distance" during conversations; however, an optimal speaking distance seems to exist for most people, and this is only conditionally adhered to without their knowledge.[1]

Optimum space sizes and distances are not only found in the distance from the partner, but also in space arrangements, space distributions in buildings (compare today's penchant for large areas with yesterday's living and construction trends) and in the reactions of the individual to tightness and width (including pathological reactions of claustrophobia and agoraphobia). Space, in the meantime, not only has local and distance qualities, but also directions. Directions can be defined as dynamic action qualities on one hand, back and forth, up and down. Their valuation deviates individually according to the situation: the undulations of a road will be experienced differently by cyclists and vehicle drivers; the child must climb a hill, the older person will avoid any hill. The valuation also varies according to symbolic characteristic of directions. A fear of heights and depths, for example, generally only corresponds to a superficially real danger; it is rather based on the symbolic qualities of height and depth. The symbolism characteristic is more distinct in the evaluation of cardinal points—South and East are considered to be positive and North and West as negative, and therefore unlucky, in many cultures. While the symbolism here is derived from the path of the sun, the symbolism of height is often of a social nature. Bending and kneeling as a subjective gesture, and standing as a gesture of superiority or aggression, are examples of this.

We therefore have a valency system of space, where locations, distances, spaces and directions have their various values and, according to certain laws, also change. This valency does not depend only on the individual, his action tendencies and their deviations. Instead, they are also established culturally. Hence the specific space structures of different centuries, and also the three-dimensional varied mobility of population groups. (Think of the nomads and settled populations, the greatly increased mobility of people during the twentieth century. The home ties of children and old people must also be mentioned, even if less conditional than defined in different cultures, as opposed to the wanderlust of youths.) Finally, mythological structures, from directional symbolisms to actual cosmologies, are also a part of the cultural settlement. The cultural settlement results from factual living habits of population groups; however, they can also from social analogies that are projected into space – in an extreme case, space can become an actual projective volume, and specifically where living problems of populations were and still are converted into fears of the "living space."

Let us turn briefly to the already oft-mentioned observations that space valencies change. Someone may suddenly feel crowded because of a rearrangement or new furnishings in a room, or even a change of residence; the need for vacations is frequently not only an expression of fatigue or social conformity, but also of "home oversaturation," thus creating a need for new behavior areas, new space stimulation. The possibility of such changes in surroundings, the "potential extensions," today always contributes more to evaluate a residential or vacation location. The space is therefore an actual behavior field, equal to a stimulation constellation, which is changed as needed and adjusted to the action tendencies of the individual. We not only *experience* the space with its stimulus qualities, but we also design it. It is as if the organism had a special stimulus need and selected its space accordingly. However, this leads us to the second problem, that of time.

The Valency Period

We can imagine that an animal, such as a mouse, needs three-dimensional differentiations, but does not necessarily need those related to time. A feeding station must be distinguished from a nest; a yesterday and a tomorrow, however, do not have to be differentiated. Extreme stimulation changes (light-dark, hot-cold) on one hand and internal stimulus rhythms (hunger, sleep) on the other would be completely sufficient temporal adjustments with respect to the mouse's existence. More precise deliberations will, therefore, soon show that this is not so. The spatial orientation of the mouse does not have to be based on a visual space system, but only on a chain of reactions to successive key stimulations. These critical stimulations, however, receive their significance from their position within a series, and this succession is a time-related structure, therefore the "mouse time," so to speak. We could therefore attempt a first definition, namely that elementary time consists of an order of successions. "Order" here is defined such that a series of stimulations would be coordinated with a series of forms of behavior.

An order of successions leads to certain "succession structures" or "progression structures," which, however, do not have any quality of time; the awareness of before and after, earlier and later must not be omitted. It is sufficient that each stimulation be defined by its proximity to other stimulations. Even the succession as such does not have to be realized. Time only occurs when a succession is related to another, or: A is faster than B or, while the sun moves from the horizon to the zenith, I will do this or that. Related successions are therefore the actual prerequisites for a time formation, and where one of the successions remains constant and the same, metric or physical time will develop.

Metric time spans are, also, just like geometric routes, in that they are homogenous and constant. One hour always equals one hour. If the time now becomes a measurement of the progressions, it invariably also becomes a criterion of the progressions, therefore a valency. For example, if we state that something is at a distance of ten kilometers, we have specified an objective measurement of distance; at the same time, we have also determined how far the location is within or outside of the range of our actions. The "far" here assumes a valuable significance. If we cover a path on foot, we will ask after a set time (defined by the degree of fatigue): "How much further is it?" Which means, "How much energy do I still have until I am there?" The route specification therefore becomes a measurement of resistance, which opposes that of action. This also applies for time. "This will take another half hour" is a metric measurement; however, it is also a resistance index for the action,—it designates time, which still has to be overcome. That this is not a purely metric statement is known to us, because the half hour can mean something different depending on the situation—such as the perception of a painfully short or an eternally long time span. As soon as the time statement relates to one's own action possibilities, it becomes valence. Time and space are therefore always being structured and assessed, operative as well as regulative. Paul Fraisse (1957) has provided an enlightening description and Pierre Janet (1928b) a clear definition of the problem of time-related distance and the related behavior of waiting. Fraisse say,

> Waiting and the continuity efforts are the two most important situations in which the consciousness of duration appears spontaneously. In both cases, this consciousness is the consequence of dissatisfaction. The most primitive feeling of duration therefore evolves from a frustration of a time-related origin: on one hand, the current moment does not fulfill our desires, and on the other we are referred to a hope of the future (end of waiting, beginning of action). As long as this frustration is upon us, it expresses itself also by a consciousness of resistance, therefore the interval. This results in the unexpected conclusion: currently, where time becomes a conscious reality, it appears to be too long. Indeed, a long time is only noticed if it is considered to be too long. (Bachelard, La dialectique de la duree, 1936) (Fraisse, 1957, p. 201)

The delay of gratification is not obvious. In children, it frequently leads to emotional outbursts or replacement actions or to completely abandoning the goal—until it has learned "to be able to wait." This is expressed in the perceptive definition by Janet: "Waiting is an active regulation of action; it separates two stimulations, a preparatory one and a triggering one, and it limits the action between these two stimulations to the preparation or to the erection phase" (Janet, 1928b, p. 141. Quoted according to Fraisse, 1957, p. 200). We know that the ability to wait is an individually variable capacity, or, expressed differently, that the "time-related frustration threshold" varies across individuals. Heymans and Wiersma wanted to see one of the distinctive directions of their characterological primary and secondary types. We also know that this time-related frustration threshold is deeper in children than in adults, that it is more difficult for children to establish and maintain time-related objectives. The difficulty in waiting is two-fold: for one, it is the actual suspension of the action until a specific time, for the other, it is filling the intervals: so much so, for example, that the drive becomes too strong because of the monotony and that the goal is lost because of too much activity.

It is clear that the waiting periods must be structured so that the goal is not jeopardized in order to maintain action goals, so that filling the intervals does not appear to introduce any special problems. In the meantime, there is a phenomenon suitable to emphasize the significance of the question: that of boredom. Boredom, says Janet (1928a), is "characterized as the exaggeration of a special behavior, that of searching for diversion" (p. 145). He is therefore clearly shifting it into a group of those behavior regulations which strive for an acceleration of the action (*les sentiments de pression et de l'effort*).

Boredom may not be mistaken for impatience; it is a typical feeling of the waiting period, therefore the deliberateness of action goals at a required action delay. Boredom, however, is the sensory reaction to the absence of precise current action goals; it only expresses that processes are too slow without reference to a goal.

This is an extremely interesting phenomenon. Acceleration regulations appear when an action process, compared with an action model, is too slow or if the energy potential of an individual is insufficiently used. Braking regulations, on the other hand, begin when action processes develop too quickly or if they exceed the individual's energy potential.

A time-related action model[2] can be formed by the relation of goal and need: the stronger the need, the faster the goal must be reached. The action model can also exist in a progression concept: If the current action process is stopped, accelerating regulations appear. However, where do these action models exist in boredom, which has just been characterized by missing goal and progression concepts? The assumption remains open that an action model can also exist wherein the organism anticipates a certain measure of stimulation effects or strives for a certain amount of energy output. Both can be summarized in the term of the "stimulation model," since the energy output is also measured by proprioceptive as well as exteroceptive action stimulations. Boredom develops, therefore, as an acceleration regulation wherever this "stimulation model" is exceeded.

We could experimentally introduce the term of the "psychological moment" and define it as a time span in which a need for stimulation change does not occur. It is apparent that such a defined time unit has no consistency, but instead depends on the inner as well as outer state of the individual. In a depressive patient, for example (whose need for stimulation is extremely reduced), the moment would be very long, and it would be very short in a stimulation-obsessive city dweller. Certain sensory forms would effect specific instant changes—for example, a sense of happiness would result in an extension of the moment ("how quickly the time passed"); however, fear would lead to its reduction ("it seemed to last an eternity"). The regulation that a time span appears all the shorter, the fewer changes are perceived in an action, does not contradict this (Fraisse, 1957, p. 227). The need for change and the perception of changes are two separate phenomena with the relativity that outer and inner stimulations appear to be perceived as fewer the lower the need for a stimulation change is; the long psychological moment would therefore correspond to an abbreviation of the time perception—also that time flies for lovers, someone fascinated, someone excited.

This would define an essential side of the valency time: it is based on a succession of stimulation rhythms, a situation in which the model sequence is changeable depending on the individual and the situation. Deviations of real stimulation sequences from this model sequence determine the sense of understressing or overstressing (and therefore the sense of boredom or stress) with the related regulations of the action acceleration or action repression, which must be corrected.

The valency period has been studied by experimental psychology in a number of studies regarding time perception and time deception. In these experiments the point is not to emphasize the well-known deception aspect of the time experience, but to emphasize its regulative function; the experience of time is somewhat different than the perception of time. It involves the adjustment of the organism to certain stimulation and action rhythms. The time-related "progression sense" would then be the expression of the fact that the actual action process corresponds with that of the one desired by the organism. Within this scope, it would be the expression of an action regulation, as proven by Janet, for the remaining feelings. That the time-related progression sense converts easily into a time estimate is not a counter-argument; this also applies to other types of progression senses, such as those of exertion and fatigue. Feelings are always connected with estimations and their metric conversion is always close where metrics can be applied.

If this is so, certain essential conclusions will naturally result. We are implying an active stimulation and action requirement of the organism as an essential factor in the regulation of behavior. Let us leave open the question as to what type of stimulations and actions are to which the organism adjusts; let us only observe their time-related aspect, the frequency, the rhythm and "the moment." We are assuming that there are two factors that extend the moment: adjustment and non-adjustment. In a condition of complete success—unobstructed fulfillment of a requirement—the action and stimulation requirement will be limited, at least temporarily. This also occurs, for example, if the individual no longer feels equal to himself or its surroundings, in situations of action and stimulation escapes, such as during depression. Both characterize final conditions of actions—that is, those of shorter or longer time spans—before new goals are formed.

The abbreviation of the moment, however, expresses the development of new requirements, the development of the urge for action, and the accelerated stimulation succession is experienced as an uninhibited and therefore successful action process by the organism (anticipated or current success or respective failure experiences act as action regulators during each action phase). This applies for as long as the acceleration of the time succession can be controlled by the individual. Independently controlled acceleration of the action appears to be pleasurable; forced ones, however, are exhaustive after a relatively short time.

This results in a key to understand various types of stimulation-addicted people. The joy that many who drive vehicles derive from speed is an ideal illustration of the facts mentioned previously, since it allows an increase in the frequency of stimulation and the connected success sensations, always in a relatively precise correspondence with the internal stimulation model of the organism. And since the self-worth feeling can be defined as the totality of success experiences, the great significance of this phenomenon can be easily understood. Furthermore, it is not impossible that access is found to the still little clarified question of why certain musical rhythms are tonifying and others are soothing and relaxing.

Timespans, it should be added, are not only stimulation successions, which are valued as such. They are also "intermediate spaces," which separate the now from an action goal; and just as the three-dimensional distance has a relatively lower significance, the higher the goal valency will be, the more the evaluation of time spans is dependent on goal formations. This has been described by Dorothy Lee in the following passage:

> If I walk along a path because I like the country, or if it is not important to get to a particular point at a particular time, then the insuperable puddle from the morning's shower is not frustrating; I throw stones into it and watch the ripples, and then choose another path. If the undertaking is of value in itself, a point good in itself, and not because it leads to something, then failure has no symbolic meaning; it merely results in no cake for supper, or less money in the family budget; it is not personally destructive. But failure is devastating in our culture, because it is not failure of the undertaking alone; it is the moving, becoming, lineally conceived self which has failed. (Lee, 1950, p. 12, stated according to Lindzey, 1954, p. 935)

Time as "location" and time as "distance" are different forms of experience; they not only correspond to various goal developments, but also to various types of valencies of ego and surroundings. Moment and progression valencies on one hand, goal valuation on the other, are the two poles which determine our time experience.

The influence of the valuation of goals on the experience of time not only depends on the type of goal, but also on its distance. It is all the more difficult to wait for something pleasurable, the closer the time is, since the current moment always loses more significance; the significance of the moment, in contrast, appears to increase when an unpleasant process approaches. The distance of the goal, therefore, frequently signifies a valency reduction, and this is due to the fact that time-related goals are established in connection with individual as well as social reasons.

Such goal limits are not always factually limited (such as work schedules or work rhythms of a farmer based on the climate), but are also frequently set by society or the individual. This is because reaching a goal within a specific time can become a criterion for the value of one's personality. Reaching the goal, however, receives a symbolic characteristic, which in most cases leads to a new phenomenon: the goal ambivalence, which now expresses itself in more or less pronounced unhappiness or fear components of those actions which jeopardize the subjective or social valency of the individual by the failure to reach goal.

Perhaps it becomes more understandable here that there are cultures in which one opposes the time constraint, the schedule constraints, against certain regimentations. Certainly, the more complex a society, the less it can be avoided; instead, the more the time-related behavior of the individual is controlled externally and no longer by internal sequence models, the less pleasant his relationship with time will become—and therefore, as we have seen, the relationship with himself.

Time, as viewed in general, is a system of action progressions. The system is regulated by model sequences, which are controlled by goal valencies. Expressed in three-dimensional terms, these are distances and speeds at which they have been conquered. In the meantime, there are also "time-related locations" in a certain sense. Morning, noon, evening, summer, or winter are not processes, but time-related periods of a certain type. And, like three-dimensional locations, they lead to behavior specializations, offer specific satisfaction options, have a periphery, and may have a closeness or distance characteristic. Something could be said concerning the significance of these time-related locations on behavior; however, the simple reference to them must suffice.

Valency space and valency time can therefore be treated similarly. However, differences remain. Valency time, as we have seen, relates to the regulation of behavior progressions; valency space relates to the order of behavior locations. Their reciprocality, however, is in the phenomenon of distance. In both cases, space as well as time, distance means waiting, suspense. But this also means setting and regulating one's energies. In the behavior toward distances, the individual displays his maturity; it goes without saying that it is quite difficult for a child to establish distant goals and to adjust his behavior accordingly.

"Thüng go chang, mai thüng go chang" is the onomatopoeia with which the Thai people imitate the noise of a steam locomotive—"we may arrive or not, it doesn't matter"; "I mues schaffe zom verregge" ("I have to slog until I hit the bucket") is the equivalent motto that the Swiss tell their children. These are other objectives and other "model sequences," a different sense of reality and a different living standard. It appears to me that the problem of experienced space and experienced time far exceeds the range of experiments of depth perception or time illusions. Whenever you hear a vehicle driver scold bitterly because the car in front of him forces him to "creep" instead of "driving smoothly," whenever you hear a married couple argue the respective merits of punctuality and comfort, or whoever laments the slavery of work schedules, the wide existential significance of the sketchily covered problem becomes more evident.

NOTES

1. Also compare the escape and "attack distance" of animals (Hediger, 1954).
2. We understand the concept of goal and process of an action that must be completed.

REFERENCES

Beauvoir, S. de. (1954): *Les mandarins*. Paris: Gallimard.

Evans-Pritchard, E. E. (1940). *The Nuer.* Oxford, England: Clarendon Press.

Fraisse, P. (1957). *La psychology du temps*. Paris: Presses Universitaires de France.

Hediger, H. (1954). *Skizzen zu einer Tierpsychology im Zoo and im Zirkus*. Zurich, Germany: Buchergilde Gutenberg.

Janet, P. (1928a). *De l'angoisse a l'extase* (Band 2) (Les sentiments fondamen taux). Paris: Alcan.

Janet, P. (1928b). *L'evolution de la memoire et de la notion de temps*. Paris: Chahine.

Lee. D. (1950). Lineal and nonlineal codifications of reality. *Psycho-somatic Medicine, 12*, 89-97.

Lindzey, G. (1954): *Handbook of social psychology* (Vol. II). Cambridge, MA: Addison-Wesley.

Piaget. J. (1955). *Die Bildung des Zeitbegriffs beim Kinde*. Zurich: Rancher.

INTRODUCTORY COMMENTS TO CHAPTER 7

"Cultural Psychology in Action-Theoretical Perspective"

The Authors

As one of the earliest recognized cultural psychologists of the twentieth century, beginning with his research projects in Thailand (1955 to 1958), Professor Boesch presented his theory of the complexity of human behavior and the difficulties psychologists encounter when attempting to understand the meaning and purpose of behavior within and across cultural contexts. Preceding the main content of the article, several key terms and definitions were offered. Culture was defined as a system of rules and conditions that regulate action. Rules include: moral, religious, juridical and institutional principles that members of a culture respect. Conditions include social, natural, and object constellations within which humans interact. Regulation implies that there is some impact of the rules and conditions on the nature and course of human action. Finally, action was defined as goal-directed behavior that

Discovering Cultural Psychology: A Profile and Selected Readings of Ernest E. Boesch, pp. 147–150

147

is usually intentional yet can be either conscious or unconscious in nature.

FOCUS OF THE CHAPTER

A central problem for cultural and cross-cultural psychologists is to determine the relationship between cultural variables and the constitution of action (or behavior) by individuals and groups. Action is of paramount importance since it is the means by which psychologists attempt to understand individuals and groups. Four main points were made by Boesch that are crucial for a cultural psychologist to consider. (1) Action is polyvalent, that is there are many levels of values and goals that influence behavior. Furthermore, the symbolism of action is also complex and exists at multiple levels. (2) The action that one chooses means that many other options are excluded due to a preference that excludes other actions in one's context of time and space. (3) There is a link or a connection between myths that are collective regulators of action and fantasms that are private regulators of action. (4) Objects, such as buildings, books, art forms, etc, are important to the study and understanding of actions within cultural contexts. All four areas should help convey an impression of the usefulness of action theory when applied to psychological studies.

Central to action theory is awareness of the complexity of goals and values that are implicit in all human behavior. Furthermore, behavior is sequential in so far as actions are sequential and follow patterns that are directed to goal fulfillment. Using the example of a skier making her/his way down a mountain slope, Professor Boesch demonstrated how this behavior is "polyvalent" or indicative of many values including mastering challenging physical and psychological tasks, enjoying graceful speed, enjoying the natural beauty of mountainous environments, and enjoying memories that are connected to previous skiing expeditions. Paraphrasing Boesch on the importance of polyvalence we know that it implies more than only the simultaneous presence of objective and subjective aspects of action: it also implies a coordination of "partial' goals." Actions may take on representational qualities and therefore have symbolic meaning. In the example of the skier (in the reading to follow), the act of speeding down the mountain may symbolize family unity if skiing was experienced as a favorite family activity during holidays.

In symbolic action theory (SAT), the approach to understanding behavior that Boesch developed while chair of psychology at the University of the Saar, nearly all human action, both conscious and unconscious, is considered to be polyvalent and symbolic. While one action may be a focus of psychological investigation, Boesch recognized that behavior is part of a complex network of symbols, values, goals, internal and external meanings. Therefore, it is very difficult to attempt to isolate specific acts of individuals or groups for the purpose of cultural or cross-cultural investigations. See the article titled "The Seven Flaws of Cross-Cultural Psychology. The Story of a Conversion" (chapter 11, Part II) for further clarification.

Dilemmas of Choice

When an individual selects one course of action over another, the field of options is consequently limited. The act of choosing to behave in a given way reflects one's awareness of both individual and cultural rewards that result from choosing one course of action over another. Culture provides the social context that influences both individual and group behavior. It specifies guidelines and limits of a physical and ideological nature. Cultural myths were defined by Boesch as ideological guidelines of thought that provide codes of conduct and the means by which events are interpreted. Myths then imply the values and behaviors that an individual and a culture aspire to achieve. There are, for example, mythic leaders of athletic teams, corporate enterprises, university communities, civil societies, etc. All who aspire to be leaders in these contexts are held to the mythic standards of behavioral performance and achievement. Shared myths are derived from common experiences within a cultural context where members communicate their beliefs and expectations with each other and thereby develop standards or criteria for culturally-approved behavior.

Related to myths, Boesch identified fantasms as subjective systems or guidelines that specify how individual behavior can be guided to comply with collective myths. Like cultural myths, an individual learns from multiple experiences and assesses those which are most rewarding at individual and collective levels of sociocultural meaning. The balance between myths and fantasms involves both subtle and continuous interactions whereby myths are interpreted and evaluated as useful to individual members of a culture. This is a developmental process of discovery of how one can live an effective, rewarding, and satisfying life. While group norms and resulting pressures on the individual are very influential, they do not, in Boesch's theory, override or negate the importance of individual choices.

The Meaning and Influence of Objects

Within SAT, objects in the field of action are considered highly influential. Since objects are dominant in human contexts, they affect how and where individuals and groups can act in so far as they instrumentally influence and shape action potential. Objects, particularly those that an individual uses frequently or possesses, such as a home, its furnishings, clothing, cars, etc., may also affect one's self-concept. The objects that are owned and used publicly are often factored into one's social status. Therefore much human action is focused on acquisition of objects that contribute to one's positive appearance and status. Consider the care and attention that is given to shopping for goods of all kind in most human societies. Professor Boesch used the home as a primary example of the way objects intricately and importantly influence human behavior.

Summary

In the condensed yet clearly articulated reading to follow, Boesch outlines core elements of symbolic action theory. A careful reading provides insight into the complex interaction of individual values and goals with those of the culture that surrounds all individuals. As a Piagetian developmentalist, a child psychologist, and a psychoanalyst, Boesch recognizes that behavior is a construct that reflects past, present, individual and collective values and goals. The complex network that encompasses all behavior must be carefully studied and respected when psychologists attempt to conduct cultural and cross-cultural investigations.

CHAPTER 7

CULTURAL PSYCHOLOGY IN ACTION-THEORETICAL PERSPECTIVE

Ernest E. Boesch

Culture is a system of rules and conditions regulating action. The definition is succinct, but needs some elaboration: By "rules" I understand the whole complex of moral, religious, juridical and institutional principles which an actor is asked to respect; "conditions" refer to the social, natural and object constellations with which action deals; "regulation" implies that there is some impact of these rules and conditions on the nature and course of an action; and by "action," finally, I understand goal-directed behavior, generally, but not exclusively, to be intentional.

The definition, obviously, gives the concept of action paramount importance in the framework of a cultural psychology, and it would appear that the central problem raised in such a context would be the relationship between the cultural variables and the constitution of action by individuals and groups.

It would, however, be presumptuous to deal with all the contents of the definition in a single chapter. I shall therefore not dwell upon the defini-

Discovering Cultural Psychology: A Profile and Selected Readings of
Ernest E. Boesch, pp. 153–165
Copyright © 2007 by Information Age Publishing

tion of the concept and structure of action. I shall rather concentrate on the following problems which, I believe, are of particular interest for cultural psychology: First, the "polyvalence" of action and the symbolism which derives from it; second, the fact that acting necessarily implies effecting choices. Third, I shall look at the relationship between "myths," i.e., collective regulators of action, and "fantasms," i.e., private regulators of action. And, fourth, I want to have a look at the world of objects, as important constituents of the cultural action field. The four topics in conjunction should allow us to get some impression of the usefulness of action theory for cultural psychology.

POLYVALENCE AND SYMBOLISM

Action, as I have already mentioned, is goal-directed behavior. It organizes itself in chains or sequences, and in systems of coordinated goals, which I call "action areas"—such as a family, a profession, or a religious congregation. I shall not go further into goal sequences and goal systems, but want to stress that the concept of goal itself already presents problems. Let us take the case of a skier. Laboriously he has reached the top of a slope: this, however, was not his goal, and neither is it the downward end of the slope, where he intends to go; his main intention being to slide down the slope, his goal is essentially the action of swinging down in light and elegant curves, or with thrilling speed, or in whatever way he chooses to enjoy the slide.

The example shows that the goal is not simply the end, but a whole phase of the action—which takes on a different aspect according to the type of action. Thus, for the potter shaping a vessel, the material goal is the finished product, and the "goal consumption phase" may be very short, consisting in some pleased (or dissatisfied) contemplation before starting the next task, while for the skier the "goal consumption phase" lasts for the whole period of sliding down the slope.

But let us look at the skier a bit longer. We might say that his goal of sliding down the slope has two aspects: the one is the objective motion in space; the other are all the subjective sensations related to it, the feeling of the harmonious interplay of muscles, the sensation of speed, the impression of mastery. The skier might enjoy both the "objective-instrumental" aspect of the action, i.e., mastering his skis, as well as the "subjective-functional" one, i.e., the proprioceptive experience related to it; at any rate, both are always simultaneously present: the action, by necessity, is "polyvalent."

Polyvalence implies more than only the simultaneous presence of objective and subjective aspects of action: it implies, too, a coordination of "partial" goals. The skier may not simply wish to slide down a slope, but at the same time to race his partner, to show off his skill, or to test his endurance. The goal, we would say, is "over-determined" (a psychoanalytical term, while the concept of polyvalence, obviously, stems from Lewinian theory), or "bundled," i.e., it combines a number of "sub-goals" into one single motivation.

On closer inspection, polyvalence is even more subtle. A particular slope may remind the skier of an excursion he made with his father; swinging down the slope may give him the impression of flying and bring to mind the memory of dreams in which he slid weightlessly through the air. In other words, the action takes on a representational quality—it becomes symbolic. No doubt that these symbolic "connotations" have an impact on the valence of the action, and no doubt, either, that such symbolic qualities adhere to practically all actions, be they conscious or unconscious: every action can recall other actions, be it materially or functionally, it recalls analogous situations, or the ideological frame in which it is inserted. In other words, every action commands various symbolic meanings: situational, functional, analogical and ideological ones.

No doubt that this pervasive symbolism of action has an important bearing on motivation. The anticipation of action goals and processes is, so much appears to be obvious, not simply determined by the valence of an objective goal, but by this complex network of meanings constituted, in addition, by the subjective-functional aspects of action, the bundles of sub-goals, and the symbolic connotations. Therefore, objectively similar actions may mean very different things. The cultural importance of such a statement is obvious: it implies the question how collective action is possible in spite of the fact that the apparently similar action, for the different participants, has not the same meaning. The tentative answer would be that there must be an overlap in the bundle of individual sub-goals which forms the nucleus for common motivation and which overrides—at least temporarily—the idiosyncratic components of the goal-structures (concerning these problems see Boesch, 1976, 1980).

Let me exemplify these rather theoretical considerations by a simple concrete event. In 1980, members of our staff, Dr. Phornchai Sriprphai, with his wife, were completing a one-year study of a Thai village. He announced their near departure to some villagers who brought this plan before the local village spirit. The oracle given by the spirit medium was that in departing now Dr. Phornchai was running a serious danger and that, in order to avert the threat, he would have to undergo a ceremony strengthening the life essence (*pithi suu kwan*). The ceremony consisted of three distinct rituals, the first of which was to set free a four-legged animal on a Wednesday, which, being the birthday of Dr. Phornchai, was considered to be appropriate. Dr. Phornchai was reluctant to submit himself to the ceremonies, yet, it so happened that on a Wednesday he found himself in the compound of the local temple where, again by "accident," he found a girl offering a turtle for sale. Around temples in Thailand one often sees people with captured animals, especially birds or fish, which the devotee is liberating for gaining merit. On the spur of the moment, Dr. Phornchai bought the turtle and set it free in the temple pond, silently pronouncing the appropriate invocation which, later on, he completed by lighting the required candles and incense sticks.

I shall not go into the other, much more complex rituals here (which have been treated extensively in Boesch, 1983), but want to look more closely at some action aspects of this "Turtle Ritual," which will allow, at the same time, to introduce some new notions. The ritual was not consciously planned, but we may assume, too, that this was not accidental. In spite of his conscious reluctance, he unconsciously or semiconsciously had already accepted to submit himself to the required ceremony. In other words, the oracle of the local spirit had produced a "goal conflict" which was now being solved in one direction. We may understand this goal conflict as a relationship between different, partly contradictory, sub-goals. Some of these sub-goals were responsible for his reluctance towards the ceremony: maintaining his self-respect as a rational social scientist, wanting to decide freely about his own movements, rejecting to be bound by a—possible— negative outcome of the ceremony. Other sub-goals urged him to accept the oracle: the anxiety—however unconscious—raised by the threat, the wish not to antagonize the villagers, to show his respect of their beliefs and values. Thus, at the outset, the "goal formation process" implied delicate choices and evaluations between antagonistic tendencies, and from the start, different sub-goals determined the structure of the goal. It was polyvalent at least in as far as personal anxieties as well as considerations concerning the villagers were combined in one single motivation.

The action itself consisted of different "actemes": buying the turtle from a girl, setting it free, reciting an invocation, lighting candles and incense. Actemes are parts of an action which derive their meanings from the common goal. Yet, they may have their own connotations which combine together for forming the experience of the total act. I do not intend to present an extensive review of them, but only want to stress some aspects important for our concern. In doing so, I do not know in detail all the private connotations of the actemes for Dr. Phornchai, but we may assume some of them with sufficient plausibility.

Buying the turtle from the girl is an instrumental act, necessary for the subsequent act of freeing the animal. Yet, it also may have had a meaning in itself, such as being generous to the girl. Had the turtle been a disgusting or threatening animal to Dr. Phornchai, he might not have bought it. Thus, the connotations of the animal enter into the act. We may safely assume that childhood experiences contributed to the private turtle-connotations. Every child in Thailand knows turtles as animals to play with or to be afraid of (the hissing of a turtle can be quite threatening). Thus, manipulating a turtle may symbolize overcoming one's anxiety, and in that case buying the turtle would have been quite appropriate to Dr. Phornchai's state of mind.

Freeing the turtle belongs to the class of merit-making actions. The idea is that by setting free a captivated animal, one eases its suffering, and by this mercy shown to a creature increases one's own store of religious merit. However, in the case of Dr. Phornchai, the act was more specifically instrumental. It was a first magical step for freeing himself from the threat of impending disaster. In a sense, like the turtle, he was limited in the freedom of his movements and by restoring the turtle's freedom of movement, he by the same token contributed to restoring his own. The act, therefore, was both specifically and generally symbolic, the turtle symbolizing the suffering creatures, but also the actor himself.

Note that the act of setting the turtle free very clearly demonstrates the objective-instrumental and the subjective-functional components. Taking the turtle and releasing it in the temple pond is the objective aspect; the proprioceptive components and the ideological-symbolical consciousness of the act constitute the subjective-functional one. Only in conjunction do both components constitute the action. Without the one it would have no reality, without the other no meaning.

This is also true for the actemes of pronouncing an invocation and of lighting candles and incense sticks, which demonstrates the generally bivalent quality of action. In addition, both actions are polyvalent by amalgamating different sub-goals, such as, on the one hand, reducing subjective anxiety, and, on the other, conforming to the social prescriptions of a "correct" ritual (which not only supports the anxiety-reduction goal, but also the one of social integration).

THE DILEMMAS OF CHOICE

The example was meant to make more concrete the assumption of a generally polyvalent structure of action. It illustrates, at the same time, another feature of action. Dr. Phornchai, I mentioned, was reluctant to submit himself to the required ceremony. He faced a dilemma of choice. Choosing one action always necessarily implies foregoing others. In other words, the choice implies a—conscious, unconscious or semi-conscious—confrontation of goals and their further reaching consequences. We already saw the kind of dilemma for Dr. Phornchai, maintaining his self-respect as a social scientist versus reducing anxiety or reassuring the villagers of his loyalty. We also saw that he made his choice unconsciously—he just "happened" to find himself in the temple compound on the prescribed day, but by doing so, he already had engaged in an action corresponding to one side of the dilemma. He had opted for anxiety-reduction rather than for scientific rationality.

Whenever we choose A, we decide at the same time against Non-A, or at least postpone, if that is possible, a choice for Non-A until later. This exclusion aspect of choices severely hampers our action potential and gives rise either to the well known "decision conflicts," or the equally well-known "post-decision qualms." Popular wisdom knows this and states that "we cannot have our cake and eat it."

Culture is a very important variable in the question of the choices we effect. One can surmise that Dr. Phornchai, within the context of "his" village, made a decision different from the one he would have chosen had he been at his home University. Actions always take place within cultural contexts which influence both the goals we anticipate and the choices we effect between them. The turtle ritual clearly demonstrates this impact.

MYTHS AND FANTASMS

This leads us to the next question: how to consider this impact of culture of an individual's action. This question confronts us with various problems. First, there is the problem of limits and barriers. Culture limits action both physically and, by its rules, ideologically. Second, we would have to consider permissions and opportunities: culture not only permits certain actions, but positively opens avenues for others. I do not propose to go into every possible impact of culture on action, but instead shall concentrate again on one basic problem, namely the relationship between myths and fantasms.

Cultural rules have different levels of specificity. The quality of a specific rule, such as the prohibition to steal, derives from two sources. The first is the occurrence of specific events, such as jealousy, greed, and resulting thefts. The second source for a specific rule are general rules, such as, in our case, the right to private property. The rules of greeting derive from general rules of politeness, and those again from the ones of respect, social mutuality and social hierarchy.

Myths

Such general rules are partly codified, for example the constitution of a country; partly they correspond to basic guidelines of behavior which are transmitted in social groups. The latter are not codified, but "implied." To some extent the rules are based on a system of rationality, like in the case of logical thinking. In other respects they correspond to guidelines which have no rational, but an ideological basis, as in the case of moral or religious rules of conduct. There is no doubt that many socio-cultural guidelines of conduct are of this latter, ideological kind. I call them "myths."

Myths in this conception are general ideological guidelines of thought which regulate the specification of social rules and provide systems of justification of conduct and of explanation of events. As in the theory of Levi-Strauss, they are considered to be underlying thought systems, but not of a basically logical kind. Once the basic premises are accepted, logical consequences may be derived, and in this sense, science also to some extent relies upon myths (see for instance Claval, 1980).

With the exception of law and religion, myths are not codified. The individual meets them, in the process of growing up in his culture, mostly in the unsystematic forms of single rules of conduct, proverbs, stories and fairy-tales. These "mythemes" and "myth-stories" are manifold, but they always express just parts of the underlying myth. In the course of his development, the individual will have to integrate the mythemes into consistent systems of belief and of morality. To take an example, the myth of the fatherland grows out of a multitude of single events—uniforms, flags, bonfires, ceremonies and parades, to name just a few—each of which is just a symbol of the general idea. This idea will have to be constructed by the growing-up from the single instances. Obviously, apart from processes of social transmission, individual selection processes, evaluation and combination will play an important role in the constitution of myths. Not everyone is patriotic in the same way and to the same degree. The individual structuring introduces variations in to the social myth.

Two comments have to be made. The first concerns the process of myth construction. I am basically a Piagetian and believe that the adult ways of perceiving and thinking our world are the results of progressive structuring during childhood and adolescence; part of this structuring even goes on during our whole life-time. By a slow and gradual process, rules of dealing with things are elaborated from which, subsequently, the properties of objects derive. By analogy I would surmise that the myth as a system of rules for dealing with ideas and the behaviors which correspond to them, derives also from progressive structuring.

The second comment I want to make concerns the collective quality of the myth. As a psychologist I confess to being somewhat baffled by the idea of collective representation. Representations are by necessity always individual, since they can be localized only within the human brain. A collective representation, therefore, has to imply a representation shared by many individuals, whereby the word "shared" cannot mean identity, but only a large overlap. Since myths are the result of the individual structuring of mythemes and myth-stories, we have to wonder how the overlap comes into being. The answer, as in the case of the object properties, seems to be that, on the one hand the individual structuring is based in similar experiences (i.e., of the mythemes and myth-stories shared in the culture), while, on the other hand interactive communication leads to interindividual adjustments.

Let us try to exemplify this, very tentatively, with the turtle ritual we already considered. We seem to be able to distinguish several mythemes: the idea of the "kwan" or life essence of a person; the idea of freeing an animal as a merit-bringing action; the magical quality of the turtle as a symbol for long life; the idea of the magical power of prayers and invocations; the idea of communicating with the super-natural by candles and incense. All these mythemes (specified in the Thai folklore by many stories and legends) seem to relate to a central twofold idea: On the one hand, man is dependent on the intervention of super-natural powers, while o the other hand man can counter these interventions by establishing or reinforcing a certain order. Although shared by all the participants in the turtle ritual, we can safely assume that the representation of the myth and the corresponding mythemes in the mind of Dr. Phornchai was different from that held by the spirit medium or by the attending villagers (who played a role in the tow subsequent ceremonies). There is communality, but not identity.

I repeat that I surmise this communality to be a result of common experience and social interaction in the course of development. Yet, development does not only lead to collective representations, but also to idiosyncratic contents of mind. To some extent every experience is unique. In respect of the objective-instrumental quality, consensus concerning the external situation involved is likely, and in this sense the situation is "objective." However, its subjective-functional qualities, referring to the private variance of experience, remain largely incommunicable. This does not mean that these aspects are less important. Our private experience in handling stones will "objectivize" the stone, i.e., contribute to the formation of its rational concept; but they will also "subjectivize" the stone and contribute to the motivation of becoming a stone collector, an artist sculptor, a mason or a stone thrower. "Subjectivization" means to structure the relationship between the individual's action tendencies and the surroundings in which he lives. It leads to the building up of an "ego-world-relationship."

All structuring follows the same course. It starts from disconnected single experiences which, at first, are perceived both syncretically and in isolation. It gradually constructs, on the objective side, systems of reality and of rational rules. What, then, are the systems to which "subjectivization" leads?

Fantasms

Without any doubt, there are general ideas along which we try to structure and lead our lives in relation to our world. Our private ideas of happiness, success, love, the ideas of "the good life," of the person we want to be, are all general frameworks with a very quaint kind of structure. They seem to be vague and without specific contours. We often are not even really conscious of harbouring such an idea and yet, we intuitively know what kind of action or event corresponds to our idea of, for instance, happiness. Should we act contrary to it, we very clearly feel guilty or anxious. These general ideas, again, seem to be systems of rules of which we are largely unconscious. I call them "fantasms."

While myths are collectivized systems of ideas about the world, society and the individual, fantasms are subjectivized systems about the relationship between the individual and his environment. Both operate on a relatively general level, they are regulators of individual instances, but both are largely unconscious structures.

We have seen that the myth itself is not an experience, but a structure evolved from the experience of mythemes and myth-stories. Similarly, fantasms are higher order, or "super-ordinate" structures evolved from a multitude of single experiences. Therefore, the mythemes and myth-stories also enter the experiences basic to fantasmic structures. Like all experience, they are selected, interpreted and evaluated, and this is done on the basis of fantasms already present. In other words, the reception of mythic elements is influenced by the existing fantasms. The social myths, we can say, pass through the filters of individual fantasms.

The reverse is equally true. Since mythic materials pass into the structuring of fantasms, these necessarily contain mythic elements. Let me become more specific by using an example. The "achieving society" is a myth. In concrete everyday life it expresses itself by a multitude of admonitions, exhortations, encouragements, positive as well as negative reinforcements, by ideological statements, by tales of success and failure, by stories told to children (McClelland, 1961, 1967) and so on. Not all individuals receive these kinds of mythemes in the same way. Everyone selects and rejects in the light of existing superordinate structures—also the achieving society produces both achievers and non-achievers.

However, fantasm-structuring continues during the whole course of life. The fantasms, on the basis of which we operate our selection of myth material, are subtly and gradually transformed. Achievement topics, thus, are assimilated into the conception of the good life, of the aspired ego, even of love and happiness, either as positive constituents, or as negative ones, i.e., topics representing threats to one's fantasmic aspirations.

The balance between myths and fantasms has to be understood as a subtle, continuous interaction, by which myths receive individual meaning. This happens by means of fantasmic selections and evaluations operating on myths, which help making fantasms compatible with social myths. Rather than stating apodictically, as is so often done, that individuals are products of social pressure, it would be advisable to study carefully this subtle interaction between myths and fantasms. The person is a product both of collective and individual forces, the balance of which may vary according to social and individual circumstances involved.

In conclusion of this section, let me indicate in what sense myths and fantasms are related to action. Myths and fantasms are not specific action goals in themselves, but they regulate the formation of such goals. One might say that they are superordinate goal structures which coordinate single goals in a way which, in the case of myths, is consistent with social expectations, and, in the case of fantasms, consistent with long-term aspirations of the individual. Furthermore, they both contribute to the formation of the social and individual selves and their interpenetration.

THE PROBLEM OF OBJECTS

Let me now turn to the last topic, the problem of objects. It is almost impossible to find examples of action which do not, either concretely or in representation, include objects. The examples of the skier, the potter, and the turtle ritual, all illustrate a specific relationship of an actor with an object. The skier represents an instrumental relationship, the potter a relationship of producing, and in the turtle ritual we meet a symbolic object. Indeed, we produce objects, and use them instrumentally as well as symbolically. However, the role of objects in action is even more general. First of all, objects "channel" our action in two senses: spatially they determine where and how we can move; instrumentally they determine what we can do. Second, by the same token, objects influence our action potential and thereby our self-concept. Third, objects determine our social status and regulate social interactions.

Looking at these pervasive functions of objects, it is clear that objects to a great extent control the patterns along which we conceive of our world. Objects are entities for structuring our world; they are instruments and goals for structuring our action, and they are symbols for structuring relationships with others as well as towards ourselves. A detailed exposé of these three main functions of the objects would carry us too far. Instead I propose to illustrate them by the example of the house.

The house, for the inhabitant, forms the center of his action field. Human space, said Amos Rapoport (1969), has a "domicentric" structure. It is the place where outgoing action starts from and where it returns to. Outside and inside are the basic dimensions along which we organize our world. But our view of the outside includes the knowledge that there are other homes which form the center of other people's universe. In other words, the experience of one's home implies a territorial structure of the action field. This relates to a complex system of rules, including rules of propriety, of rights or prohibitions to access or trespassing, of privacy and hospitality.

The house is not simply a material object imposing structure upon our movements. It is an object with social significance and ideological implications. It determines the dimensionality of our space, but also the relationship to the spaces of other people, and thus lays the basis for the socialization of space.

The house also has an intrinsic structure and function. It protects the inhabitant from the inclemencies of the climate, but also from unwelcome intrusions from outsiders. Equally important is its internal structuring of action. It is divided into appropriate action areas—for sleeping, cooking, eating, relaxing, cleaning oneself, working, socializing and so on. In this sense the house is instrumental in various ways, by providing tools and implements, by creating appropriate circumstances and "ambiance," by protecting against disturbances. This is done not only materially, but also by establishing rules of action and interaction. Action is made easy by the structure of the house, and thus favors concentration as well as relaxation. Action being made easy, the house in important ways reinforces our subjective action potential, i.e., our feelings of mastery, of competence, our self-confidence. The "inside of the territory" is an area of security, reducing feelings of shyness, anxiety, of social inhibitions. Thus, mostly one behaves quite differently within one's own home and within the home of others.

How do we know that we are within our own and not in somebody else's home? The physical outlay of the house may be quite similar, but it is filled with a multitude of objects which, by nature and arrangement, symbolize our personal sphere. It is almost impossible to find a home which does not carry the unmistakable stamp of its inhabitants. This fact ceases to appear trivial as soon as we start asking why this is so. It may be to mark one's territory, i.e., to communicate tot eh outside the kind of persons living within its limits. However, much less than what normally is found within a home would suffice for marking the territorial extent and quality. The interior of a home is furnished according to criteria of comfort and taste; the inhabitant attempts to approximate should-values of what he considers to be the "good life." He expresses fantasms, in the terminology used here.

The interior of a home is purposely arranged for facilitating actions important to the inhabitant and for creating an ambiance furthering his well-being. In this sense it turns out to become symbolic of individuals. However, the house is also symbolic by the qualities it suggests. The door is the place where one steps from the inside to the outside and vice-versa. It represents an area where the confrontation of security and vulnerability becomes prominent. It is therefore not surprising that in many cultures the threshold of the door is a place where a guardian spirit lives, that magical protective signs are attached to the door and to its posts. It is also the place where the visitor is received, has to introduce himself and will be scrutinized for admission or refusal. It is not only marked by a name plate, a bell or a knocker, but is also acknowledged by specific rituals of greeting. By its special decorations the door is often a kind of emblem, communicating qualities of the inhabitant to the visitor.

Much more might be said about the house (see for instance Bachelard, 1957; Rapoport, 1969; Boeshc, 1980). Here it was used only as an example for illustrating the different functions of objects, i.e., material-instrumental, functional, communicative and symbolic. These functions can be shown in almost all objects with which we surround ourselves, but also can be made evident with natural objects, such as trees, rivers, woods and mountains. Also the symbolic quality of animals is often evident. Cultural psychology has to include an important chapter about the concrete as well as symbolic action value of objects.

CONCLUSIONS

In this short and sketchy presentation not all important aspects of action theory could be covered. I mainly concentrated on those parts which are relevant for understanding symbolic action. I chose to do so because usually action theory tends to become just a kind of more complex behaviorism, concentrating on concrete actions with easily definable goals. However, the concept of polyvalence of goals and processes provides us with the possibility to include in our thinking and research also symbolic actions, be it from everyday life (where symbolism, as psychoanalysis has shown, plays such an important part), be it from ritual, religion, ideology or art. A psychology which is not able to include those behaviours is, I believe, crippled. Therefore, action theory can constitute an important enlargement of our cultural awareness.

BIBLIOGRAPHY

Bachelard, B. (1957). *La poétique de l'espace*. Paris: Presses Universitaires de France.

Boesch, E. (1971). Raum und Zeit als Valenzsysteme. In E. Boesch, *Zwishen zwei Wirklichkeiten*. Bern: Huber.

Boesch, E. (1976). *Psychopathologie des Alltags*. Bern: Huber.

Boesch, E. (1980). *Kultur und Handlung. Eine Einführung in die Kultur-psychologie*. Bern: Huber.

Boesch, E. (1983). *Das Magische und das Schöne. Zur Symbolik von Objekten und Handlungen*. Stuttgart: Frommann-Holzboog.

Boesch, E. (1983). The personal object. *Education, 27*, 99-113.

Claval, P. (1980). *Les mythes fondateurs des sciences sociales*. Paris: Presses Universitaires de France.

Lévi-Strauss, C. (1962). *La pensée sauvage*. Paris: Plon.

McClelland, D. C. (1961). *The achieving society*. Princeton, NJ: Van Nostrand.

McClelland, D. C. (1967). *Motivation und Kultur* (The Roots of Consciousness). Bern: Huber.

Miller, G. A., Galanter, E., & Pribram, K. H. (1970). *Plans and the structure of behavior*. London: Holt, Rinehart & Winston.

Piaget, J. (1947). *La psychologie de l'intelligence*. Paris: Colin.

Rapoport, A. (1969). *House form and culture*. London: Prentice Hall.

B. THE REALITY OF BEAUTY

INTRODUCTORY COMMENTS TO CHAPTER 8

"The Sound of the Violin"

The Authors

This essay that Professor Boesch regarded as a possible conceptual outline for a research project begins with a simple question. What is the nature and purpose of sound in our lives? Why choose such a topic, the violin, for a cultural-psychological investigation and reflection into this question about sound? Certainly the perception of sound is an important area of psychological investigation given that much human learning is derived from aural input and interpretation. From Professor Boesch's theoretical stance, symbolic action theory, the title implies goal directed human behavior that reflects a value orientation that engages in the creation of sound to express human emotion. The motivation of one who is able to create sound (rather than noise) by playing a violin varies depending on the player. However, given the challenges the violin presents, a player may seek to create beauty that is emotionally rewarding to both the player and others who hear the sound.

Discovering Cultural Psychology: A Profile and Selected Readings of Ernest E. Boesch, pp. 169–175
Copyright © 2007 by Information Age Publishing
169

The development of the essay follows a conceptual outline that guides the reader. It is as follows. (1) The violin is identified as an object of human creation and its evolution as a species of musical instrument is articulated. (2) The ontogenesis of the violin as a played instrument is presented as an indication that many people throughout history have sought to create sound with similar materials and ingenious use of the materials. (3) The goal of the human effort is to create an image through beautiful sound. (4) By studying the sound humans have created, one can learn about the various cultures that have supported the development of musical instruments (objects) that are played by members of the culture (subjects). This indicates an object-subject relationship. (5) The essay demonstrates how an investigation into one precise area of human behavior, the creation of musical sound, is relevant to the study of cultural psychology. In this overview of the essay, the essential points of the outline are summarized.

ORIGINS OF THE VIOLIN

The violin as a man-made object has a long and enduring history in the traditions of many cultures of the world. In his research, Professor Boesch found that early models of stringed instruments were plucked like ancient forms of harps or zithers. It was suggested that curiosity may have been one source that led to fabrication of stringed instruments. Early hunters heard the vibration of their bow string when they shot arrows. Perhaps they wondered how such sounds might be made with a goal other than forcefully projecting an arrow toward a selected target. Experimentation with making sound with taut strings led to various renditions of musical instruments that became part of cultural life. While this is somewhat speculative, there is little doubt that the evolution of the violin was a complex process and represents multiple aspects of scientific and artistic discovery by many inventors from many cultures. Professor Boesch traced the early violins back to Asian origins.

For Europeans, the violin was introduced from the Near East in about the eleventh century. Arab people knew the instrument as the Rabab. Europeans did more experimenting with the shaping and styling of the wood sound box and produced what was called the Rebec. By the seventeenth and eighteenth century, the violin as it is known in the Western world reached the form that is still used today. Those who took up the tradition of violin-making seemed to relate the quality of sound produced to the beauty and shape of the instrument. As various modifications to the instrument were made, the musicians changed their playing techniques. It was noted that in China to this day the more ancient forms of the violin are still used as well as the modern iterations. The study of the violin as an object truly demonstrates the cultural genesis of a man-made object that has been improved over hundreds if not thousands of years. The verification of improvement was that the violin had a greater range and sounded better when played. This fulfilled the very purpose of the violin as a human-made instrument.

Learning to Play the Violin

For those who become competent or excellent violinists, it is important to begin the training of their sensori-motor coordination at about seven or eight years of age. At this time a child can begin to manage the essential posture control required to hold and play the violin correctly. Because it takes a long period of training to learn to play the violin, parents of young students need to provide much encouragement and support. The posture elements include holding the violin under the chin and against the collarbone. One's manner of holding and playing the violin must be coordinated by the musician.

The sound produced will vary depending on the pressure applied to the bow and the way the left hand is held on the strings. Strength of the player's fingers of the left hand, the independence of finger movement, and the precision of touch to find the correct notes is the way that volume, warmth, and vibrato are achieved. The bow is held in the right hand and it must move quickly and with correct pressure to play accurately and, furthermore, beautifully. The consistent work of learning to play the violin shapes the learner's view of her/himself as a musician. The learner, often a child, experiences the tension between the ideal self and the self who is struggling for control. These experiences are shared among musicians as they master the art of creating beautiful sound through the use of fabricated instruments.

In summary, to play the violin one must begin training of sensori-motor skills early, have a sense of rhythm, muscular strength and coordination, and keen auditory discrimination. Mastery of the violin requires long hours of practice for a lifetime. "The learner is bound by an unrelenting discipline" (p. 184, chapter 8). If the learner does not greatly value mastery of the instrument, the balance between positive and negative values of playing may shift profoundly so that all the time and effort involved in learning to play becomes a burden and the violin is given up. The player has expectations to keep improving the quality of sound created. Being satisfied with the music one creates is more important than the sound of the violin as an instrument yet the two elements are closely linked.

The Importance of Sound

Sound is a very important element of human perception. It says what words do not say even when one has developed a high level of language usage. Seldom do words adequately allow humans to explore and express the range and depth of our many subjective states. Saying the words, "I am angry" does not necessarily mean "I feel angry." However, one's tone of voice will convey the mood or attitude. "Sound conveys love or anger, acceptance or rejection, joy or fear in a way which grips immediately" (p. 186, chapter 8). The ability to make sounds is an extension of the "I."

Professor Boesch identified the contrasts between "sound" and "noise." Sound is created with intention; it has great action potential and power in our life experience. Voices of the past continue to speak through literature and myths. The voice carries meaning, feeling, deep and lasting messages that may become part of conscious and unconscious living. In contrast "noise" happens when there are accidents such as cars crashing together, sirens blaring, people screaming or shouting in fright.

Music as the Ultimate Sound

Humans have the ability to create phenomena that have strong appeal and symbolize a kind of utopia. For many, utopia is the experience of beauty. For example, when one has mastered singing or playing of musical instruments, individually or collectively, new worlds are created and shared with those who are part of the experience. "Utopia is the imagination of a world entirely in harmony with our fantasms, of reality entirely in tune with inner experience. In other words, utopia abolishes the "I" "non-I" antagonism" (p. 186, chapter 8). The power of sharing beautiful sound that expresses and creates strong emotional sensations is a great gift that is highly valued due to its rare yet wonderful occurrence.

CULTURAL INTERPRETATIONS: NOISE OR MUSIC?

The purpose and mode of expression through music has evolved over centuries and lifetimes. Some sounds, for example the hoarse singing voice of Louis Armstrong or the loud sounds of his trumpet playing, may be regarded as "noise" by some. Yet others hear it as beautiful music that evokes strong feelings. Therefore, the definitions of sound and noise have changed greatly over time and across cultures.

Consider the kinds of "noises" made in rock concerts where there is harsh screaming and shrieking into microphones amplified to high volume. Fans attending rock concerts seem to enjoy this experience. To others, such phenomena deny the purity of sound in whole or in part. Commonly, that which is considered noise is contained so that its effects are controlled and limited. Professor Boesch offered the example of traffic noises that are usually avoided or blocked out when buildings are constructed. Beautiful homes are usually built in quiet and natural settings rather than along heavily used highways. For some, noise is associated with disease and refuse. That which is defined as noise is clearly a function of cultural values and expectations, thus there exists the potential for specific cultural clashes.

There are, however, some noises that may be perceived as very pleasant; the crashing of the surf on the shore or the spirited cheers of spectators celebrating the performance of wonderful artists or athletes. In Professor Boesch's experience, only the songs of birds are naturally caused musical sounds. Otherwise, musical sounds are exclusively human-made and are cultural endeavors. Historically, many great musicians dedicated their entire lives to improving their ability to create beautiful sounds. Even going more deeply into human history, Professor Boesch stated the following. "Music, often and for a long time, was a means for approaching God. Soli Deo Gloria, wrote Bach over his compositions, and even recently Sir George Solti, the famous conductor, confessed that Mozart had convinced him of the existence of God. Introducing noise in music, hence implies rejecting the cultural mytheme representing purity, including both its social and its spiritual contents" (p. 189, chapter 8). Professor Boesch suggested that music has such purity and beauty in its meaning and sound that it was and still is considered sacred to people of many cultures. However, when noise is either mingled with sound or it is substituted for sound, the sacredness of the work may be compromised if not completely eliminated.

Those who play the violin carry on a cultural tradition of searching for beautiful sound in the ideational realm of purity. For many, the violin may symbolize the conflict between natural penchants and cultural requirements. There is the constant tension between making noise and making beautiful music with the search for beauty requiring great discipline and talent.

Summary

Professor Bosech has presented his interpretation of sound as a cultural signal that both carries messages and is the message. Pure sound or music, is much more than a signal, it is an icon. The violin player is a highly skilled and motivated messenger who broadcasts the purity of sound. By way of contrast, applause of an appreciative audience was characterized as noise that listeners make to express their evaluation of the music they hear. The power or influence of music is a spiritual symbol that requires purity of the player. By purity Professor Boesch meant that the player is one who knows and is true to the meaning of the music. Through the playing of music, a violinist is drawn into the myths of a culture and experiences their influence. The musician and the music merge with each contributing uniquely to the beauty of the sound. Both are joined in a symbolic wholeness in which the music and musician are mutually complementary.

The culture that sustains music and musicians provides the criteria for beauty that is pursued through the creation of sound. The essay, Sound of the Violin, offers a paradigmatic model of ways in which culture forms the context, provides the values and motivational inspiration for the behaviors of those who live within a given frame of reference. The systems of meaning within a culture influence the values and exterior behavioral expressions and actions of all who live individually and collectively within human and natural environments. Mastery of musical instruments or other manufactured devices reflects both artistic and scientific acumen of individuals and cultural groups. Such achievements are anchored in networks of coordinated actions, thought, beliefs, rules, and values. Just as all living beings are constantly changing due to physical and social laws, cultures too are constantly changing. Therefore, by tracing the evolutionary history of the violin, as Professor Boesch has done in this essay, a model is created for recognizing the various aspects of ever- changing cultural life which shapes and directs all forms of human behavior.

Before writing this essay, no empirical study was conducted to provide a data base for determining auditory accuracy or range of trained violinists compared to a matched sample of non-violinists. Rather, as Professor Boesch stated at the beginning of his essay, his is a unique combination of phenomenological, historical, and ecological approaches to the study of sound perception and sound generation. His approach is holistic rather than technical or statistical. While psychologists can and do study human musical perception and creation from an empirical perspective, and Professor Boesch is aware that many prefer such a mode of investigation, he has chosen the approach demonstrated in this essay for much of his academic career. He has sought to gain in-depth insight into important psychological questions. Why do some individuals and groups find the music of a violin so valuable and meaningful while others do not? Why are some people within a culture very dedicated and excellent musicians and others of the same culture have little or no musical motivation or appreciation? Why do some people find it rewarding to contemplate a natural landscape while others wish to immerse themselves in a chemistry laboratory? Both empirical and phenomenological-cultural psychologists have important and mutually complementary contributions to make in the search for human knowledge and understanding.

CHAPTER 8

THE SOUND OF THE VIOLIN

Ernest E. Boesch

SOME INTRODUCTORY REMARKS

What, you may ask, motivates me to choose such an outlandish topic for this paper? The topics respectable in psychology are conventionally standardized, and although ecological and cultural psychology have in recent times introduced the meaning and function of objects into the range of problems the psychologist might consider, the *sound* of a violin would only hesitatingly be claimed to be an object.

Yet, it undoubtedly is the intended result of an action, in other words, it constitutes a *goal*. This would make it relevant to *action theory*, but this relevance might be questioned by its being an ephemeral and certainly not very profitable goal. Yet, such goals confront action theory with particular and challenging difficulties. Actions pursuing goals like eating, clothing, constructing, quarreling and so on could all claim to aim at some specifiable result, useful within some wider context; their motivation can be understood in view of some benefit. But there are actions whose meaning is less obvious: What kind of an action is "contemplating a flower or a landscape," what is the function of actions like skiing, reading a poem, collecting stamps or Picassos—or of playing music? It is the challenge of

Discovering Cultural Psychology: A Profile and Selected Readings of
Ernest E. Boesch, pp. 177–195
Copyright © 2007 by Information Age Publishing

demonstrating the relevance of action theory even for apparently useless actions which made me consider topics of this kind.

Yet, why choose the violin? I am not a violinist myself, but was a fairly competent flutist; although the questions I want to raise apply also to other musical instruments, I feel that the violin allows most clearly to point out certain phenomena, and having collected a good amount of experience with violinists, I hope to be sufficiently familiar with the features relevant to the intended discussion. However, let me clearly say that this is an essay—it might be a conceptual outline for a research project, but it still lacks confirmation by actual research.

In the following I shall first consider the violin as an object, and more particularly its "phylogenesis," i.e., its evolution to a "species." I shall then look at its "ontogenesis," i.e., how it becomes an instrument to be played. Third, I propose to focus particularly on this strange goal image of the "*beautiful sound.*" These three points will amount to a study of a specific aspect of a "culture-object-subject" relationship, and to finish I shall discuss the relevance of this example for cultural psychology.

The "Phylogenesis" of the Violin

A violin, of course, is an object, but it is an object which in no way can be related to a natural model or antecedent: it is essentially, although consisting of natural materials, a man-made object. As such it has a long history. According to historians the first instruments with strings were of the type being plucked, like the zither or primitive kinds of harps. The bow would have been a later addition. Although the actual origins of these instruments remain unknown, they must have been complex inventions. We may imagine that a primitive hunter noticed the peculiar sound on plucking the string of his bow; another would have observed that strings of different length and tension produce different sounds; playing with such bows, someone would then have found that their sounds could be amplified by connecting the chords with a hollow object, and thus the plucking string instrument would have been invented. Somebody still would have had to discover that stroking a string with a stick or another taut chord allowed to draw out the sound produced by a string to last for a while. These three discoveries, then, were essential to the invention of the violin: the result of different string tensions and lengths, the effect of a resonance body, and the stroking bow.

The result, we can imagine, was a very crude violin, but such instruments still exist and are played in many parts of Asia. Thus, the Siamese *soo uu* still consists only of half a coconut shell covered by a piece of skin to which a simple stick of hardwood is attached, with two strings fitted to the contraption (the *soo sam sai*, as says its name, has three strings). The *soo duang* and the Chinese *hu* are similarly constructed, but their body (or *head*) consists of a hollow piece of a large bamboo stem. It is interesting to note that in these instruments (as they are known today) all the essential elements of the more developed violins are already present: the strings are supported by a *bridge*, tightened by *tuning pegs*, the sound box (coconut shell) is pierced by holes, the function of which is similar to our f-holes, and even the internal sound post of the violin (a small inside "pillar" between the upper and lower surface) finds its functional equivalence in the *thuang*, a small weight attached to the skin of the three-stringed *soo* which softens too excessive vibrations. I do not know at which time these elements were added to the primitive instruments, but I am convinced that they did not result from Western models; their presence is much more likely to indicate that controlling the sound led to similar technical solutions.

Historians say that the two types of bow-string instruments known in early Europe were imported from the Near East in the 11th century or before; the first was Arab, called *Rabab*, which engendered the European *Rebec*. It consisted of a sound box of hollowed-out wood covered with parchment; at one end the body was extended to form the neck. It was fitted with one or two strings, and thus was basically similar to the mentioned Far Eastern forms—which, as we have seen, still exist, while the Rebec has disappeared.

The second type of instrument imported to Europe is said to be a *fiddle* from Turkistan, consisting of a spade-shaped sound box with added neck, fitted with two to three strings. From these two initial forms historians derive a bewildering range of instruments with different names in spite of apparent similarities, varying in shape, size, and probably in every other detail which can be altered. For the moment let us simply retain that the original instruments from which the violin ultimately developed consisted of some kind of crude sound box with attached shaft and a small number of strings. From these started the search for improvements, lasting for several centuries, experimenting with changes of the sound box, the shaft or neck including the kind and number of strings and their tuning, and the bow, these three elements becoming variously combined "across species." This long sequence of transformations of the instruments seems to be particular to Europe, and at any rate contrasts strikingly with the Chinese-Siamese violins which, as far as we know, preserved their present forms over centuries.

In this process, of course, much *bricolage* took place, empirical trying out of different woods, their shapes, curves, thickness, the size, place and form of the sound-holes, the kind and location of the inner stabilizers, i.e., the bass bar and the sound post, the glues and lacquers to be used, the number, material, thickness and tension of strings, form, length, hair and construction of the bow; similarly, various positions for playing the instrument were tried out. By the 17th/18th century this experimentation had apparently about exhausted the available options and became limited to variations in details; from now on the typical violin as we know it, with four strings tuned in fifths (g-d-a-e) remained constant, while the competing forms, mainly the fiddle and the gamba, were abandoned. Of course, this *bricolage* often led to individual solutions—the formulas for glues or lacquers for instance—which the violin-builder tried to keep secret. Of particular interest were the constructions of violin or gamba type instruments of different sizes (resulting in the now standard set of violine, alto, violincello and contra-bass); they made possible to cover the whole tonal range by instruments of similar sound quality and thereby allowed the volume and homogeneity of sound we know from the string orchestra. It seems that this construction in different sizes of similar types of instruments constitutes another particularity of European development.

The progressive construction of the violin, of course, was guided by the available materials on the one hand, and human possibilities of handling on the other. Both, however, were not a priori determining parameters; the materials were tried out and selected, and so were different ways of playing the instrument, which in turn had an impact on its form and size. Thus, the size of a viola held on the thigh is less restricted by the length of the human arm than is a modern violin held under the chin. The latter way of playing is in fact more difficult than the former; hence, it was not always ease of handling which directed the choice of solutions. Look at the particular curve-angle shape of the modern violin: In order to allow the bow to stroke the peripheral strings, the sides of the body had to "cave in" which produced the narrow "waist" of these instruments. Therefore, a kind of 8-shape, functionally quite appropriate, was already present in some old fiddles (and tried out again on violins in the late 18th century). Thus, the practical handling cannot alone explain the peculiar shape of the modern violin. It seems that the two angular protuberances on the violin's side give an added support to its "breast" (or front) which, statically, is not indispensable (see the guitar and the fiddle), but *improves the sound*. At the same time, it realizes a perfect aesthetic harmony of the form. Somehow it appears that the old violin-builders felt quality of sound and beauty of shape to be closely related.

This is, in short outline, the genesis of a truly cultural object, invented and perfected by man. We shall have to answer the question what motivated this development. At this place, I shall only frame the question, but not yet attempt to answer it. We believe to understand easily, indeed, the development of a loom from its primitive forms to continuously higher perfection: it serves ease of handling and, thereby, higher output. The development of violins, of course, also aimed at easier and more comfortable handling—but what was its output? *Sound*, or to be more specific: *more beautiful sound*. Even the elimination, in the course of development, of older forms like the fiddle or the gamba, were due to this aim, partly even at the cost of ease of handling. Thus, the older gambas had six strings tuned in quarts and a third—similar to our guitars—and the neck was fitted with frets; with only four chords and no frets the violin became less easy to play. As to sound, however, the change made sense: the fretless neck allowed the development of the vibrato which gave the sound more warmth and suppleness, while the homogenization of instruments made the sound of the orchestra smoother and more voluminous.

Let me add another consideration. I think it reasonable to assume that beautifying the sound of the instrument was a main motif for transforming it. Yet, the pursued sound was, of course, unknown. A violin-maker might have changed some aspect of the instrument, but on trying it out, the player could remark: "It sounds better, *but that's not yet it*." What would have been this "it?" An intuition, an intangible anticipation, and although such an image became transformed over and again during the century long processes of improvement, it would have remained a *"should-value"* both inducing change and also controlling it.

This "sound-goal image" not only varied over historical periods, but differs also between cultures. Thus, as we have seen, the Siamese *soo* and the Chinese *hu* remained relatively close to a (supposed) initial form of the instrument. Of course, it, too, underwent modifications which, however, had only little impact on the sound: the "head" coconut shell was carved, the "neck" or shaft as well as the tuning pegs were partly or wholly made of ivory. Such beautifications by material or inlay were also applied to European instruments, but their purpose was one of mere decoration serving goals different from the one of improving the sound. Compare the *bridge* or the *sound post* and its equivalent of the two instruments. The bridge of the Siamese *soo* consists simply of a tightly rolled piece of cloth, while in Europe, although inconspicuous, it underwent multiple variations in form, size and position whose effect was tried out over centuries. The sound-post on the other hand, an invisible inside pillor, varied only in thickness and location, while its functional equivalent on the three stringed Thai *soo*, consisting of a small weight on its skin surface, became lavishly elaborated in precious materials, occasionally even diamonds and gold - for, of course, merely decorative intentions. It is true that beautiful sound was also valued in Thailand: it is told from the three stringed *soo*, the sound of which was especially appreciated, that, the special coconut shell needed for the instrument being rare, the owner of a coconut grove able to present such a shell to the Royal Palace was henceforth exempted from all taxes (Morton, 1976, p. 76). Yet, this *soo sam sai* was played only on special occasions and acquired no place in the Siamese orchestra. What then, we have to ask, was the reason for the long-lasting search for instruments with a more beautiful sound conducting ultimately, in Europe, to the violin? Before attempting to answer it, let us look at the ontogenesis of the violin.

The "Ontogenesis" of the Violin

"Ontogenesis," of course, is not used here as in developmental psychology, meaning the unfolding of a being from its conception to maturity; I would rather understand it in its original meaning, "the coming into being." Indeed, a violin becomes really a violin only when it can be played. Its objectal purpose, so to say, is to produce sound, and this purpose can be fulfilled only by a player.

Our modern violin is probably the instrument most difficult to play, but likely also the one offering the greatest range of expressive possibilities. However, mastering it is a long and frustrating endeavor. It is said that in order to become a good violinist, a child has to start learning at an early age—the opinions vary between six to nine years. The optimum would probably be 7-8 years when the difficulties of sensori-motor coordination have been overcome. The child will of course first be given a small violin, to be replaced by bigger ones as the child grows. At the start the child is likely to be pleased with the new instrument. He or she may see mother or father playing and, as all children do, long to imitate them. Such initial enthusiasm, however, would soon be supplanted by a rather ambivalent attitude, and in most cases it requires much parental coaxing and dragging in order to keep the child from abandoning the instrument. Indeed, exercising the violin provides at first only little intrinsic reward. It is probably fortunate that the ear of the young child lacks fineness of discrimination and that, while it acquires it, the skill of playing improves, too.

To start learning early is, of course, required in order to shape the child's motricity and perception during the forming years. This is precisely of interest to the developmental cultural psychologist: that learning to master an object implies shaping the development of the individual; while, as we saw, the object was formed "phylogenetically," the individual is led to "fit" the object in its ontogenesis.

What is it that makes learning the violin difficult? Three basic problems have to be mastered: The first concerns posture, the second the technique of the left (finger-) hand, and the third the technique of the right (bow-) hand.

Since about the end of the 18th century the violin is held between chin
and collar bone. This position, more difficult but also more proficient
than earlier ones, requires not only strengthening of the neck muscles,
but also precise coordination of their innervations with movements of the
left arm for position changes. Since too much contraction of the muscles
impedes the flexibility and precision of movements, it is important here,
too, that the muscles of the neck and the shoulder remain relatively
relaxed all the while exercising the required support of the left arm.

So much as to the main postural difficulty. Considering the finger technique of the left hand, we might point out first that the child's fingers
need, particularly at an early age, to gain strength and independence of
movement. Second, the violin not being fitted with frets, the fingers have
to be able to touch the exactly correct spot for each note, which requires
the acquisition of a precise "feel" for distances—particularly difficult since
the space separating tone intervals diminishes the more the hand moves
upwards. Strength, independence of movement and precision of touch
will become particularly important for double stops, i.e., playing two
notes at the same time. Finally, the left hand has to master the vibrato,
important for giving volume and warmth to the sound.

All this is difficult enough, but will be compounded by the bow work,
which is no less exacting. The bow is about 74 centimeters long and consists of a slightly concave wooden staff which holds the stroking surface
proper, a "ribbon" about one centimeter large made of white horse tail
hairs. The player holds the bow at one end, the "nut," and glides it over
the strings. How this is done will principally determine the quality of
sound, and is therefore of major importance.

The bow touches the strings in the space between the bridge and the
fingerboard. The nearer the bridge, the sharper the sound is said to be,
the nearer the fingerboard, the softer. To produce an even sound, the bow
should therefore, ideally, move in a steady straight line—less easy than
one might believe, because the "natural" horizontal movement of the
hand traces an arc of circle. More important for the quality of sound are
the speed of the bow movement on the one hand, the pressure of the bow
on the other. For an even sound, both speed and pressure need to remain
constant. The weight with which the bow rests on the string varies along
its length, therefore keeping pressure constant requires compensatory
regulations by the bow holding hand, and this, of course, at all speeds.
Finally, the sound quality is influenced by the number of hairs which
stroke the strings. For this reason the player will hold the bow at a
sideward inclination, which, thus, must be kept constant or varied according to the sound desired. Let us not forget that the angle at which the bow
is moved differs according to the string played—thus, for the g-string
(lowest) it is almost horizontal, for the e-string (highest) it will approach

the vertical. And, finally, the bow movements must of course be coordinated precisely with the fingerwork of the left hand. Any psychologist who has ever tested motor coordination of children will agree that such a complex interplay of movements is very difficult to learn; even advanced learners will often have to concentrate on their bow much more than on the left hand. Smooth bow work will also be hampered by straining the muscles of neck, shoulders and arms; accordingly a quite delicate balance between relaxation and activation will have to be achieved.

Thus, learning to play the violin requires sensory and motor training, development of discrimination, rhythm, muscular strength and coordination. It may astonish those who believe that psychology can be learned in four years to see that learning the violin takes about twice as long - with daily training hours definitely longer than many a psychology student is willing to spend on his books or experiments. Becoming a violinist allows no short-cuts, no jumping of chapters one doesn't like, no skipping of arguments one does not understand; ignorance cannot be glossed over by empty words. In music every negligence becomes cruelly manifest in the performance, and therefore the learner is bound by an unrelenting discipline.

The initial results of learning, thus, would not be very rewarding. The sound remains crude, harsh, often disagreeable, the strings bite the fingertips, the skin of the chin gets irritated, and even social reinforcements, after a while, may become rare—the admonition to "close the door of your room when you practice" is not particularly encouraging. In spite of that, the child will have to exercise daily, often at hours when other children play together. We can thus easily understand that the violin will become an ambivalent object, and we will not be surprised by the fact that many young learners abandon after a while. "My best birthday present would be not to go on practicing the violin," said the daughter of a friend. The violin somehow becomes anantagonistic object with its inherent discomfort and constraints, a continuous reminder of one's limited action potential, of objectal barriers and social constraints, and it may even represent the "non-I" in general, the external world basically opposed to the "I."

Yet, some children "catch on." They accept the frustrations of learning because of the positive valence of some future goal. This future goal may be to conquer an adversity, to extend and confirm the individual action potential; it may also be social—to become a famous violinist, or at least to be able to play quartet in the evenings like father. However, such explanations do not suffice to explain the reason of the child's catching on, but only relegate the problem; indeed, the reinforcement of an action potential would still have to explain why the child strives to achieve this **particular** mastery, and the explanation by social models would have to understand the motivation of the violinist whom the child wants to emulate. And if playing the violin well would earn social rewards, what then would make the public appreciate music? It is exactly the difficulty of learning to play the violin, the intentness, the frustration tolerance and the perseverance needed which make an explanation by social modeling or some unspecified mastery inadequate.

Learning to play the violin is, in the terms I use, a *dominant* or *superordinate* goal. Superordinate goals are distant in time but command actions in the present, which—as with violin exercises—may not be pleasant in themselves. It is true that distant goals are somehow reached in steps. The learner's ambition will at first be to play a Christmas carol, later, a Teleman sonata, then a Mozart concerto and, finally, perhaps the violin concertos of Brahms or Mendelsohn; he may at first want be to be praised by his family, then by his school-mates, then by the public at a local concert and would at last reach for recognition by a sophisticated audience. No doubt that applause of these audiences will provide encouragements to go on playing, but they do not suffice. The more the player advances, the more an additional audience will have to be satisfied: he himself. He or she will be critical of finger accuracy and speed, but as critically—if not more—will he watch and evaluate "*his* sound." "**His**," it is here, and not the violin's. In fact, he may be hurt when a listener tells him "You must have an excellent violin, it sounds marvelous!" He wants to feel that it is **his** mastery which forces the violin to sound well. However if, his level of expectation rising, he feels disappointed with the sound, and may start haunting the violin shops to have his instrument controlled, improved, or changed for a "better" one. Now, it has become—for a moment—the "sound **of the violin**." But even on this new instrument he will spend hours a day only to improve his sound—to reach that elusive quality of tone which he feels to be moving, "going to the heart," undefinable and yet inducing a reaction of content and fulfillment, in the happy moments where he feels to have reached it.

Sound and Noise

What then is it which makes beautiful sound to become such a dominating goal? In fact, sound is a very important quality of our perception. Sound says what words don't say. Words remain restricted to consensual taxonomies and are largely unable to express subjective states. Saying that I am angry does not necessarily mean that I *feel* angry. But the tone in which I say it will show my anger clearly. Tones betray the moods of our companions, and, knowing that, we will indeed try to control the tone of our voice—be it to express, be it to hide. Sound conveys love or anger, acceptance or rejection, joy or fear in a way which "grips" immediately.

But the meaning of sound may be deeper than that. There may be two aspects to be considered. The first is the action of *making objects produce sound*, the second is the *search for perfection of sound*. As a boy I used to tighten a blade of grass between the two thumbs and, by blowing into the thus formed interstice, produce a sharp, oboe-like sound. In spring I cut fresh branches from hazel or ash trees and transformed them into recorder-type flutes. Each time I transformed nature into culture, forcing it to produce a sound which neither existed in "raw" nature, nor would have been possible to create without nature. Yet, the pleasure was immense and can be understood only by the extension of my childish action potential; it made me a creator, albeit in a tiny area. Making objects sound, thus, is a bit like taming animals: it transforms a resistant non-I into a compliant extension of the I.

Such sounds however, although exciting and pleasing, only rarely— and by accident—fulfill any standards of beauty. The *beautiful* sound is moving, it touches our feelings with a particular intensity. Myth stories and fairy tales are aware of the miraculous power of the beautiful sound: it tames wild animals, ghosts, heals the sick and appeals directly to the angels; Orpheus' voice even opened the doors to the underworld. Could we say that producing a pure, immaculate sound provides the experience of an action potential able to realize—for a fleeting moment—something like a glimpse of Utopia? The experience is perhaps very pointedly expressed—although in the realm of color—by the British artist Ben Nicholson who writes on his seeing a painting by Picasso: "And in the cen- tre there was an absolutely miraculous *green*—very deep, very potent and absolutely real. In fact, none of the actual events in one's life have been more real than that, and it still remains a standard by which I judge any reality of my own work." (Summerson, 1948, p. 7). And Gauguin to write: "The sound of my wooden clogs on the cobblestones, deep, hollow and powerful, is the note I seek in my painting" (TIME, May 9, 1988, p. 49) The statements are surprisingly similar—a certain tone of color or sound, experienced as potent and powerful, become standards, should-values, goals of aspiration.

Utopia is the imagination of a world entirely in harmony with our fan- tasms, of reality entirely in tune with inner experience. In other words, Utopia abolishes the "I"-"non-I" antagonism. The beautiful sound, an external phenomenon, yet produced by our mastery and corresponding to—or even surpassing—our ideal standards, thus becomes a proof of our potential to create a phenomenon which, by its appeal, symbolizes Uto- pia. This is, of course, not true for the beautiful sound alone, but for any creation of beauty; hence the high valence of art. Beauty bridges the chasm between I and non-I.

Beauty, however, is neither the same for everybody, nor in each culture or historical period. For a Thai musician the beauty of sound differs from the one of an European, and at the time of Bach the sound of our modern violins might have shocked rather than pleased the listener, while his string instruments, although pleasingly soft, yet appear to us weak and subdued, lacking possibilities of expression. Today we might say that a beautiful sound has, above all, to be *pure*, meaning, on the one hand, free of noise frequencies, on the other, accurately in tune. The first sounds a beginner tries to elicit from a violin or a flute will be noisy, scratchy, raw, and tend to be out of tune; in learning to play a main effort consists in eliminating these impurities from the sound. In addition, the sound must be *firm*, i.e., of constant volume. An uneven bow movement (or in wind instruments, and uneven blow) produces an unpleasantly vascillating tone. It should, furthermore, be *appropriate to the music played*. Thus, the tone of a jazz clarinet or of a Gypsy violin would not be appropriate to Mozart's concertos, but neither would a Mozart clarinet fit into a Swiss yodel band. Finally, beautiful sound has to express *subjective standards*— whatever they be. The one will aspire towards more warmth, the other towards more strength and clarity, the one will accentuate his vibrato more than the other—there will be subtle differences between players which sometimes only the initiate, or the player himself, will be aware of.

Purity of sound has obviously been of long lasting importance in European musical culture. Thus, the violin is tuned in quints which are the purest intervals, neither consonant nor dissonant. Until the romantic period, European music favored consonant chords; dissonances, of cause, occurred (as often in Bach's polyphony), but were transitional, not "standing" chords, having to be resolved in harmony. Although the romantics began to use dissonances more freely, it is only in the music of our century that dissonance has acquired an independent standing. In contrast, in Thai music consonant chords are of no importance; Thai music is structured melodiously, it is linear, not harmonic. Consequently perhaps, the purity of tuning appears to be of lesser importance; Morton gives another reason, and both may be valid: "Since in Thai music only five of the seven pitches occur as principal pitches ..., perhaps the need for great precision in tuning is not felt," he writes, and he speaks of a " 'rough and ready' approach to precise tuning" (1976, p. 28). Yet there might also exist a more deeply founded reason: Purity of sound may have symbolic values different from ours—consider for instance the fact that in Thailand, contrary to Europe, religion played practically no role in the practice and development of music.

In *modern* Europe, however, we meet musical styles which not only do not aspire at a pure sound, but on purpose introduce *noise*. Louis Armstrong, in his trumpet, but even more so in his singing, cultivated a hoarse sound, and similarly the shrieking sounds of saxophones and clarinets in modern jazz are intended by their players, and may even also require long learning. They would not sound beautiful in every ear, but they are, in their own ways, congenially expressive.

Such examples might throw additional light on the meaning of sound. In modern rock concerts the hard sounds of metal guitars is combined with the hoarse shouting, screaming, shrieking of singers—they seem to enjoy noise, and their public does so visibly and audibly. But also modern, so-called "serious," music frequently makes use of various kinds of noise: purity of sound tends, in whole or in part, to be abandoned.

Noise is "sound dirt," and it seems to be no coincidence that rock musicians at a time also tended to cultivate a dirty look: unkempt, unshaven, ragged—or at least to affect "out of place" clothing, from torn jeans to Madonna's bras and girdles ("Dirt," says Mary Douglas, "is matter out of place" [1966, p. 35]). However, noise and dirt are normal contents of everyday life; to keep them away requires discipline, effort, and is related to much social constraint. Cleanliness is required in "good society," and purity, of body and mind, is needed in approaching sacred things and places—otherwise the approach might even be dangerous. Hence, dirt can become a threat, and so can noise—to oneself as well as to others.

In fact, the meaning of noise can differ widely. It accompanies bodily discharges and thus is directly related to dirt and disease; it marks catastrophes, accidents, disaster, war, aggression; it signals a threat from dangerous animals, and nowadays belongs as well to powerful engines roaring through our settlements. But noise can also herald happy events, the convivial feasting, the exuberant joy, the triumphant success, the exhibition of powe—easily, however, degenerating towards the noises of drunkenness. Noise (in the sense of not purified sound) can even possess aesthetic qualities: the rustling of leaves in a breeze, the murmur of water in a creek, the lapping of waves on the shore. [In German one would distinguish here between *Geräusch* and *Lärm*—a difference not existing in English.] Altogether we might say that noise tends to belong to earthly, albeit somewhat out of ordinary events. Pure sound, on the contrary, does almost not occur in nature—with the exception of singing birds. The pursuit of beautiful sound, thus, is a truly cultural endeavor, and the long history of creating instruments able to produce pure sound, as much as the individual efforts at mastering them, prove the importance we attach to it. Pure sound is a *mytheme*, corresponding to a *myth of purity* which relates the individual to a social as well as spiritual order—and which, by the same token, opposes the anti-order symbolized by noise.

Music, often and for a long time, was a means for approaching God. *Soil Deo Gloria*, wrote Bach over his compositions, and even recently Sir George Solti, the famous conductor, confessed that Mozart had convinced him of the existence of God. Introducing noise in music, hence, implies rejecting the cultural mytheme representing purity, including both its social and its spiritual contents. In other words, it means shedding off constraints and becomes the symbolic realization of unhampered freedom —somehow, it too represents Utopia, but of a Dionysian kind (as opposed to the Apollinian—to borrow Nietzsche's dichotomy). The ecstasy such music can produce in many young and less young people relies on this symbolism which is reinforced by the sensorial excitement. Sound ideals, thus, can cover a wide spectrum. Noise can be pursued as obsessionally as purity of sound, but they express different myths and fantasms.

Let us come back to the violin which, as we have seen, is the result of a culturally persistent quest for beautiful sound. It belongs to the ideational realm of purity. Hence, the young learner will from the very outset be caught between the cultural goal of purity and the natural propensity for noise and dirt. The violin, thus, may start symbolizing not solely the resistance of the non-I, but as much the conflict between natural penchants and cultural requirements. Eliminating noise in the pursuit of the beautiful sound will therefore imply overcoming a deep rooted ambivalence.

It will then follow almost necessarily that becoming involved in learning the violin must have an impact on the definition of the learner's *self*. Somehow, the child will have to side with purity, he or she will veer towards the Apollinian side of Utopia. This, of course, implies renegating those sides of the "natural self" which prefer noise, dirt, disorder, and mastering the violin then may symbolize this fight against the "darker side" of one's self. However, at the same time the violin, representing the —perhaps only anticipated, perhaps already experienced—potential of producing beautiful sound, will also symbolize the "aspired self." Thus, over and beyond simple mastering of an antagonistic object, learning the violin would mean both overcoming the rejected sides of one's self as well as approaching one's self-ideal.

All this would also influence the learner's *view of his world*. He would tend to see it divided into a "me-world" and a "they-world." The "me-world" includes all those who embrace the same values, the other violinists, the other members of an orchestra, and others who appear to be united by the same quest for the pure sound. (I don't call it a "we-world," because I want to refer to an individual's view of communality, and not to a factual social community). The "they-world" of course, are those who either do not care for, or might even loath the pure sound and what it stands for. In this more or less dichotomized world the violin becomes instrumental—not only in the sense of producing sound, but somehow also for propagating its message.

Sound, indeed, is a signal: it carries a *message*, but it also is the message. In this sense, using Raymond Firth's taxonomy (going back to Pierce), the pure sound is more than a signal, it is an *icon*, i,e "a sign that represents its object by resembling it" (1973, p. 61). The musician, thus, is more than a messenger, since he or she not only dispenses a message, but represents it. The violinist Henry Szering carried a diplomatic passport and was considered an "ambassador" of Mexico, spreading a specific cultural image of his adopted country; Yehudi Menuhin, if I remember correctly, was a "UNESCO ambassador," wanting to use his violin for bettering mutual understanding. Of course, such an ambassador role cannot simply consist in playing the violin, however well that may be; it is perceived more or less consciously as "spreading the gospel of purity"— whatever values the individual may relate with it. Somehow this "messenger" quality is ritually enacted in every concert: There are, on one side, the musicians, on the other, the public; the latter reacts to the performance with "regulated noise," i.e., applause, carefully controlled as to its kind and the appropriate moment. Note, by the way, that in none of the concerts performed in a church I attended was there ever any applause: noise definitely does not belong to sacred places. In the concert hall, however, the applauding noise appears somehow as an accepting, even submissive response to the enactment of purity of sound and its symbolic meaning; it is true that the applause may also, by its amount or kind, take on a quality of evaluation—when the performance is found wanting. The public is not entirely they-world: by the act of attendance it manifests allegiance, by its applause, its otherness. This ritual, by the way, is distinctly different from the one in rock concerts where noisy music and noisy manifestations of the public somehow create a bond of similarity between both sides.

Sound is more than a message: it may also *carry power*. In "*L'histoire du soldat*" by Strawinsky and Ramuz, the violin not only symbolizes the antipode of material wealth and might, but it conveys to the player the power of a different kind: To heal, to exorcise, to protect from evil forces. This belief in power related to the realm of purity and order is widespread. A magician has to beware of defilements in order to conserve his powers, and the ubiquitous fear of impurity—although differently defined according to culture (see Mary Douglas' analysis of pollution [1966])—is a telling expression of this belief. The power of the sound derives, of course, from its spiritual symbolism, but it also requires purity of the player: Strawinsky's soldier had to renegate his worldly wealth and subdue the devil before being able to use the power of his violin. Purity of sound, purity of heart, purity of body, thus, all belong to the same myth—although with different connotations.

In this vein, the beautiful sound both is pure, but never as pure as the idea it expresses. Hence, the pursuit of the beautiful sound aims at a goal which will always remain "a step ahead": beautiful sound as experienced is not enough, the *more* beautiful sound is the real goal. It is a sound model, a should-value, never present and yet intuited; Gauguin, of course, did not intend to reproduce the sound of wooden clogs on cobblestones in his paintings, and neither did Nicholson want to reproduce Picasso's green: the experiences implied to them an intuition of a quality which would embody perfect "meaning"—a meaning, however, they pursued without knowing it. Such quest for the "still more perfect," the "still more satisfying" object or action corresponds, I believe, no less to an European myth; it expresses the anxiety of missing fulfillment, of losing power, but also the intuitive anticipation of "realities beyond" the present.

The sound of the violin, thus, is deeply embedded in cultural myths whose impact, of course, goes beyond music—which would be worth some other studies. The individual becoming a violinist will, intuitively rather than consciously, be drawn into the orbit of these myths, will undergo their influence; their meaning, however, will be subjectively constructed and merged with subjective experiences and aspirations. The mytheme of the pure sound will be related by every individual to different kinds of "purity" and order, and the pursuit of the beautiful sound will for each carry different subjective connotations. Thus myths, somehow constituting cultural cadres of orientation, will be filled out with personal relevance and meaning by the impact of the individual's fantasmic aspirations.

Thus, we will now understand the person-violin dyad as a kind of focus within his total "I" - "non-I" relationship, polyvalent and interrelated with various areas of meaning. One aspect, however, appears to me to be of basic importance in the player's pursuit of beautiful sound: to be able, *by himself, to overcome the antagonism of objects.* The violin, we have seen, is a recalcitrant object, and to master it requires profound transformations of the individual. Yet, this accommodation of the player for assimilating the object, in the long run, promises particularly rewarding returns. Indeed, the sound felt to be perfect can be produced only by a perfect fit between instrument and player. Assimilation and accommodation cannot be separated anymore: artist and violin form a symbiotic whole, the I, so to say, blending into the object, and the object melting into the I. As long as it remains imperfect, the sound is experienced as antagonism, as a signal of scission, but when perfect it becomes the symbolic proof of unity, of a cleavage overcome—in other words, it symbolically confirms our potential to reach Utopia. Sound, now, is the objectified I, in perfect harmony both with the cultural myth and the subject's fantasmic aspirations.

Conclusions

What do such laborious, perhaps even tedious micro-analyses mean for cultural psychology? Let me summarize. We have seen the genesis of a "cultural object," from its earliest beginnings—the plucking of a bow string - to the still primitive forms of the Thai and Siamese "violins," the Arab "Rabab" and the fiddle, up to the final form of the violin. We have seen this, first, as a socio-cultural process, consisting in continuous inter-actions between violinists and artisans on the one hand, violinists and their public on the other. But my contention was, second, that these inter-actions must have been guided, over and above a concern for practicality, by a search for the most *beautiful sound*. Culture, in each of its historical stages, would provide criteria of beauty, but to search for *a sound antici-pated, but not yet heard* would necessarily require individual imagination. Without such a need, carried over generations by a succession of individual players and artisans, the transformation of the object would have remained limited by practicability on the one hand, fashion or decoration (such as carvings or incrustations) on the other. This was the case of the Thai violins, and for mere practical handling much simpler forms, like the fiddle, would have been adequate, while fashion (as demonstrated by modern rock-guitars) has little impact on the sound, as long as it does not alter structure or material of the instruments. In contrast, the laborious experimentation on kinds of wood, of glues, lacquer, form and position of the bridge and other inconspicuous aspects of the instrument hints at the basic motivation to improve its sound.

I then tried to show that this same goal of the beautiful sound con-trolled the "ontogenesis" of the instrument, i.e., the individual process of learning to play it. The violin, more than other instruments, imposes a frustrating learning experience, and we found that the maintenance of motivation over the long years to mastery could be understood only by a superordinate goal which had to be more than mere social ambition. The high appeal of the search for a perfect sound became understandable by the symbolic quality of not simply hearing, but producing the sound: it implied the symbiosis of a man-object relationship or, as I said, the bridg-ing of the "I"-"non-I" cleavage.

Finding that a basic quality of beautiful sound was its purity, we discov-ered that its meanings reached far beyond the simple mastery of a skill: It appeared to be a mytheme participating in the cultural myth of purity and its antagonism to "noise." Pure sound, thus, became the carrier of a message and of power, and somehow implied "partisanship": it had its impact on the self and world-view of the violinist.

Thus, the object is, as Lang has aptly called it (1990), an external memory. The violin as an object reminds man of potential uses, their requirements and advantages. Yet, as an object, it also relates to myths and derived values of the cultural group, and learning to master it, therefore is an action of taking sides. This action, by the same token, implies a *promise*, allowing to anticipate a not yet realized, perfected potential of action. In this sense, the actual object is just the momentary focus of a continuous process of interaction, implying improving transformations of the object as well as transformations of the subject in the process of assimilation.

I have, obviously, considered principally an isolated aspect of playing the violin which, of course, is much more than searching for the beautiful sound—although this represents one of its important aspects. I have neither considered the more complex actions of performing music, nor the extended social fabric within which the pursuit of a beautiful sound takes place. The chains of interaction and feedback stretch, indeed, over a large socioecological-cultural network: The violin builder has to find his woods, the right sheep for good strings (strings being made from lamb intestines), the tool-makers for his craft, the chemists for his glues and lacquers; the violinist will relate himself to composers past and present, to members of an orchestra or other ensembles, to other soloists whose performance he studies and evaluates, to a public which listens, applauds and criticizes, perhaps also to maecens who pay him, maybe even to a dermatologist should the skin of his chin get sore from playing; but, being a child of his time, the violinist will see his skill within a framework of fashions, tastes and, ultimately, myths, and living in particular individual conditions, he will have integrated his instrument and play into personal fantasms and action goals. All this would have to be considered, should we like to make an encompassing study or plan empirical research.

Yet, "the sound of the violin" was a paradigm for more general problems; it exemplifies the cultural as well as individual construction of objects; it demonstrates the extent to which these processes do not simply constitute some isolated mastery, but systems of meaning. Mastery is not independent of goals, and goals are polyvalent and anchored in networks of coordinated action, of thought, belief, rules and values. More than that, objects are in movement, they change with the flow of culture on the one hand, with the progress of individual actions, on the other.

Action and object, thus, concur to form combined structures; mastering the violin, we saw, will ultimately unite man and object in that intimate symbiosis resulting in the beautiful sound, and we are likely to find comparable interactions in man's use of other objects. Already the invention of an object implies objectivation: the subject transforms an idea into external reality. In mastering the object, it will in turn become subjectivized, while simultaneously the individual will be objectivized by accommodation. In addition, the creation of an object implies its socialization—it will be integrated in common frameworks of action and ideation, and hence the mastery of the object entails an enculturation of the user, but also, by the individual variations in style or ways of handling the object, an individualization of culture. The interaction circle <object-user-object> is at the same time an interaction circle <culture-individual-culture> and implies progressive transformations on all levels. Piaget's model of object construction turns out to be valid not only for physical, but also for cultural objects; the construction processes involved, however, will become more complex, both as to subject-object extensions, and to layers of meaning, and the interaction subject-object will have to include both pro-active (subject -> object -> culture) and retro-active (culture -> object -> subject) influences.

All this, I believe, will lead to much more adequate models of reality than traditional psychology could ever achieve. Cultural psychology, in this vein, would necessarily have to precede all other psychological investigations—not because cultural psychology would tend to claim more importance, but because any psychological research would require to be localized within the total networks which action creates. We may, indeed, study the sound of the violin as a limited phenomenon, yet, only by being able to make evident its multiple implications would such a study become meaningful. Paracelsus coined the maxim "*nihil humanum mihi alienum esse potest,*" and it could fittingly be a maxim for cultural psychologists; the *humanum,* however, the human ways of being and acting, constitutes complex systems, and should we go on neglecting these, as traditional psychology does, human reality will indeed remain alien to us.

SOURCES

Boesch, E. E. (1983). *Das Magische und das Schöne.* Stuttgart: Frouunann—Holzboog.

Boesch, E. E. (1991). *Symbolic action theory and cultural psychology.* Heidelberg/New York: Springer.

Douglas, M. (1966). Purity and danger. London: ARK.

Lang, A. (1990). *Kultur als "externe Seele": eine semiotischökologische Perspektive. In print.*

Lloyd, N. (1982). *Grosses Lexikon der Musik.* GUtersloh: Prisma.

Melkus, B. (1973). *Die Violine.* Mainz: Schott.

Morton, D. (1976). *The traditional music of Thailand.* Berkeley: University of California Press.

Sachs, C. (1930). *Handbuch der Musik-Instrumentenkunde*. Wiesbaden: Breitkopf und Härtel.

Summerson, J. (1948). *Ben Nicholson*. West Drayton: Penguin.

Van der Meer, J. H. (1983). *Musikinstrumente*. Mtlnchen: Prestel.

INTRODUCTORY COMMENTS TO CHAPTER 9

"Culture—Individual—Culture: The Cycle of Knowledge"

The Authors

In this essay, Professor Boesch examined the ways that individual and collective information is gained, evaluated, and interacts to change the lives of individuals within cultures as well as entire culture groups and in the process raised several important issues. He considered the wide array of and sources of information that exists in most contemporary societies. The process raises questions regarding how **information** (facts and data available through observation and experience) might become **knowledge** (assimilated information that becomes part of thinking and responding processes) that is useful to both individuals and groups.

Such reflection is particularly meaningful when the contemporary global society is living in the "information age," largely facilitated by developments in high technology. By way of contrast, many cultures of non-literate societies, past and present, relied on verbal communication to

Discovering Cultural Psychology: A Profile and Selected Readings of Ernest E. Boesch, pp. 197–199
Copyright © 2007 by Information Age Publishing
All rights of reproduction in any form reserved.

share both information and knowledge which became part of the oral tradition. Professor Boesch defined culture as a community of people and the objects, institutions, and ideas they use.

KNOWLEDGE AND BEHAVIOR

Knowledge results from individual assimilation of experiences. Boesch points out that people's behavior, including conversation with other people and use of objects, are both sources of information in all cultural environments. Everyone uses objects, whether domestic or work-related such as tools, machines, furniture, clothing, or cooking equipment. All objects of one's environment, regardless of simplicity or splendor, can be information. Objects often become sources of information while members of a culture converse about their experiences with and uses of objects. When information is shared, it becomes knowledge through assimilation into thoughts and actions. While each person is a recipient of cultural messages that shape her/his use of information, each generates cultural messages that are part of the "action structure" the individual creates within life contexts. When one is confident that knowledge is grasped, it enhances and supports one's consciousness of skills and expands one's capacity for further action potential. In this sense, knowledge is a source of individual and collective power.

Cultural Changes for Individuals and Groups

All cultures develop mechanisms that evolve over time. They offer systems of stability and constancy in daily life. Life can be stable or chaotic, depending on cultural tolerance for individual or collective innovations in the use of objects and ideas. Cultures change as a result of individual innovations that affect interpersonal interactions and the use of objects. Regarding the value of change, Boesch pointed out the difference between stabilization and stultification. If an individual or group becomes too set in one particular mode of thinking and doing, they may be at risk of imbalance and obsolescence relative to the broader global context. He stated that cultures require variation, inventiveness, and adaptability that allows for progress and the advancement of knowledge.

Mutual Transformations

From a psychological perspective, Professor Boesch noted the importance of recognizing that interactions of people within their cultural contexts are always mutually transforming. People become behavioral models for each other and the process of emulation produces change, usually it is gradual but may be more rapid depending on motivational factors.

In this respect, Professor Boesch cited his experiences as a student of Jean Piaget at the University of Geneva. While every student was exposed to Piagetian constructivism, not all of them adapted completely to this theory of human development. Using himself as an example, he became a cultural psychologist, a form of the discipline that was not overtly taught at Geneva. Professor Boesch discovered the importance of cultural influences when he applied psychological principles as a school psychologist and then as a professor and cross-cultural researcher. He identified three main elements of such transformations. (1) Each individual has a need for internal and cultural consistency; (2) Individuals need coordination with others; (3) Cultures need to maintain stability through the regulation of change. These processes are present to varying degrees in individual as well as cultural change. Boesch noted that although change is part of living, not all change is progressive or beneficial. This is where collective knowledge and information sharing is valuable when the meaning and effects of change are evaluated.

Summary

To be accepted, new information has to fit with present individual as well as cultural structures of reality. When individuals have reached the conviction, a feeling of confidence, in their mastery and assimilation of information, they have a strong desire to share the information with others. In this respect, individuals enrich their cultural group as well as themselves. There is usually some degree of daring or risk when engaged in cultural innovation. However, when there is confidence in the knowledge base that provides the rationale for innovation, feedback from the culture can guide the actions taken. Most cultural changes are evolutionary rather than immediate. It is a usually a slow and calculated process intricately tied to the need for stability as well as the desire for innovation and growth. Individual and cultural changes are symbiotic. The process engages the person and the natural and social environment. Eventually, change at the individual level affects multiple and usually modest cultural changes over time.

CHAPTER 9

CULTURE—
INDIVIDUAL—CULTURE

The Cycle of Knowledge

Ernest E. Boesch

INTRODUCTORY REMARKS

Action conveys information, both about contents of our environment, as well as about our abilities, skills, emotional attractions or repulsions, in short, our *action potential* (Boesch, 1980, 1991). Obviously, external and internal information are closely interrelated, always occurring jointly, yet leading to different kinds of "knowledge." This said, we will however, in the following pages, stress particularly the external origin of information, due to our specific problem, namely the cultural impact on the individual acquisition of knowledge.

Information on the environment, of course, is provided by *all* its contents. Thus, we derive knowledge not only from books or other storing media, but from nature and climate, streets, buildings, tools and implements, customs and habits, actions gossip and rumours by social partners

Discovering Cultural Psychology: A Profile and Selected Readings of Ernest E. Boesch, pp. 201–212
Copyright © 2007 by Information Age Publishing

(Lang, 1990). Knowledge stored in verbal or pictorial form—as we generally understand it—constitutes, in fact, just a special case of messages; people in non-literate cultures will amass large amounts of knowledge without written sources, and so, indeed, do we all.

Information as such, however, is not yet knowledge. Many of our experiences do provide information, yet are simply forgotten. Knowledge results from the individual *assimilation of experience*. Genetic psychology, particularly the Geneva school, has demonstrated that even the fundamental qualities of our environment are actively structured during the ontogenetic development. It is obvious that the qualities studied by this school of psychology are far from exhausting all the aspects of the objectal world. Our object experience embraces more than weight, volume, number or physical causality of objects; objects have a price, they are beautiful or ugly, antique or modern, are toys, tools or trinkets, and such qualities, too, determine our handling of objects. Yet, being less general than the ones studied by Piaget and his colleagues, they would be likely to result from more idiosyncratic constructions.

Thus, my *first thesis* will be that the multiple information contained in, and offered by culture will become knowledge through individual assimilation, which entails selective perception, transformation and integration in order to fit the cultural messages into the action structures of the individual.

Of course, these action structures are determined to variable extents by the cultural molds, but these too may become transformed during the interaction: we are physically nourished by our environment, but our digestion, i.e., assimilation of food, transforms the environment in the process.

Mental assimilation too, changes both the individual and his environment, and since acquired knowledge tends to be socially transmitted, the successive individual assimilations would imply a risk of "distortion" (as, for instance, demonstrated already in Bartlett's experiences on remembering, 1954), and thereby increase the dispersion of knowledge and threaten social coordination. Of course, the transmission of knowledge need not rely on verbal communication, but can as well result from actions.

My *second thesis*, therefore, would be that culture creates mechanisms of stabilization in order to contain such dispersion. Yet, let us not forget that mere stabilization would stultify culture. Culture also needs variation. A bureaucracy adhering rigidly to rules and regulations would not survive for long—inventiveness, adaptability, even daring are as necessary to culture as is stability. We would have to expect, therefore, that culture attempts in various ways to establish balances between stability and change. (The term of "culture" is used here as a contraction for a community and the structures of objects, institutions and ideas, conventions and rules which both result from its actions and in return shape and regulate them. [see Boesch, 1991]).

These balances—and that would be my *third thesis*—will regulate the individual reception and transmission of information; Let us not forget, however, that these cultural rules for individual assimilation are themselves the result of individual action and may be transformed again in the course of the individual's acquisition of knowledge.

Thus, knowledge is constructed, starting from action experiences of various kinds, be they praxic, imaginative or conceptual. This "construction of knowledge" implies transformations which will be controlled by three interacting instances: first, the individual need for *consistency* over time and over action areas (both as to environmental orientation and to identify formation—see Boesch, 1991); second, the need for *coordination with others,* and third, the *cultural mechanisms of stabilization and "change regulation."* This implies that in spite of continuous controls, the cycle of knowledge is likely to entail progressive transformations of knowledge as well as of culture—which would less represent "progress" than adaptations to the needs of individuals, groups and generations.

Let us then consider these problems in more details, profiting from an event I recently observed.

The Progressive Integration of Knowledge

The other day I saw a harvest dance of a Thai village group. There was a row of musicians playing to young women in traditional costumes imitating the movements of cutting rice and throwing the sheaves over their shoulders into the baskets carried on their backs. It all looked graceful, easily recognizable as a rhythmic rendering of harvesting.

We tend to take for granted that people all over the world perform harvest dances. Yet on second thought, is this not strange? Do we not all, after work, prefer doing something different—playing soccer, cards or chess, swimming, chatting or viewing television? Would the carpenter invent sawing or hammering dances, or the hairdresser plaiting games? Yet, harvesting dances do precisely that: repeat in the form of a play one's daily work. What then could be the purpose of such activity?

Let us first remember that adults, although not usually play working, still occasionally may introduce playful variations into their actual work. In his beautiful description of rice harvesting in an African village, Camara Laye speaks of the reapers going to the field, "marching to the rhythm of the tom-tom. The young men used to toss their glittering sickles high in the air and catch them as they fell, shouting aloud for the simple pleasure of hearing their own strong young voices, and sketching a dance step or two on the heels of the tom-tom players." "They would sing at work and even play during the periods of rest. And in the evening, they would go home contented, weary but happy. The good spirits had taken care of us; not one of us had been bitten by snakes that our trampling feet might have disturbed" (1954, pp. 46-54).

Weary, but happy: the harvest had been brought in after so many months not only of labour, but also of anxiety. The experience would be one of triumph when the yield had been plenty and no accident had befallen the workers; but in other years, where the harvest was meager or accidents occurred, it might also be felt as a defeat. So, each year, there was both hope and anxiety.

Thus, while the harvest dance would not reap a single stalk of rice, very likely it would relate directly to hope and anxiety. It might intend to express gratefulness to the spirits, or to invoke their kindness for the seasons to come. It might also, by the same token, satisfy that very human need to recall or conjure triumphs and successes, thereby reinforcing one's hope and confidence.

Obviously, playing at harvesting is an action different from the one of harvesting itself. In fact, the similarity is only superficial: while the movements performed may present some analogy, and while the dancing group may be composed in part by the workers in the field, differences certainly prevail over similarities. The participants might vary, the clothes would be different, but before all, the reaping movements would have become rhythmical, stylized, stimulated as well as regulated by music, in short, the dance would have become "merely" a symbol of the real performance. Such symbol, however, is not simply a sign, representing (for which purpose?) the "real" action, but it would have become a new action with its own intentions or purposes.

Dance is one of these. (We shall presently discover others). Dancing provides an unusual experience of one's body: internal and external rhythms are optimally coordinated, and in the synchrony between movements and music the individual experiences, both, social harmony as well as his bodily action potential. Dance, therefore, is a peak experience— feeling oneself functioning optimally and in a socially integrated way. Dancing, by its grace, symbolism and social approval, provides feelings of triumph, too (in Janet's sense).

Thus we move towards some deeper understanding of the action of playing at harvesting. Harvesting constitutes, for the individual, "praxical" knowledge. In playing at it, this knowledge is extended and integrated in new action situations. By being taken out of its pragmatic framework, it will be transformed: burdens or chores are translated into enjoyment and success. It may even be that the dance, for a girl or a boy, becomes a dominant goal, so that the cumbersome work in the field appears to be only the instrumentally necessary steps leading to it. Love and marriage may be hoped to come out of it rather than bags of rice. Thus, the dance, on the one hand, integrates harvesting into other areas of the villager's life, but will, on the other hand, affect in return the meaning of the work in the fields.

The harvesting dance, however, is just one event within a much broader process: the one of acquiring, assimilating and integrating cultural knowledge. Think of its antecedents: To start with, a young girl may simply have accompanied her mother to the field, then she would have imitated some of her movements, but soon she would also be charged with little chores, such as collecting left-over sheaves on the harvested field. She would playfully try to handle the sickle, and after a while start performing with it in earnest. All of that is practical construction of knowledge and competence, and it may go on until she is really skilled with her tool.

Note that this practical knowledge is already accompanied by extensions which integrate it into broader contexts of village life. Singing or, as in Camara Laye's example, tossing sickles into the air, are "coordinated actions" (Boesch, 1991), supporting the main action of harvesting, but by the same token serving other purposes, such as social communication and cohesion. Harvesting, however, will soon extend into other action areas. Thus, the child will learn about snakes and pests in the field, will be taken to the market for selling the rice, purchasing tools, bartering, and such activities will again be related to social interactions of a new kind, knowledge about other forms of agriculture, about prices, techniques of bargaining, ruled of joking and politeness or of dealing with strangers, and so on. Harvesting thus progressively turns into a nucleus around which cluster quite a number of practical actions and domains.

Singing and dancing, however, lead to different integrations. While harvesting itself induces a progressive extension of mastery over the learner's environment, the transformation of instrumental movements into dance steps raises the level of consciousness, transforms the valence or emotional appeal ("Anmutung") of gestures, increases social approval, and through all this enhances the self-relevance of the praxis. Harvesting as a praxis, and the harvest dance as a ritual, are now tow actions closely related, yet implying different criteria of success. In one, the number of rice-bundles reaped at the end of a day is of importance, in the other it will be the grace of one's movements, the charm of one's smiling, the qualities of the music, and we may easily imagine that a girl trained in the dance steps will afterwards also feel secretly guided by some rhythm or melody in her field work. Both actions are structured in different directions, but enrich each other.

Transforming one's work into a dance implies its own directions of extension. As a thanksgiving ritual to the spirits of the field, it relates the action to existential threats and anxieties as well as to the promised securities of religion. By exhibiting one's charm and beauty, it will connect the spheres of work with the ones of love, courting and social relationships, but also aesthetic enjoyment. Thus, while the field work would extend into the market and a network of economic concerns and knowledge, the dance would enhance subjective-functional qualities (Boesch, 1980), both in the experience of oneself and of one's surroundings. Real and symbolic action, while following their own courses of extension and integration, will complete each other and will jointly constitute an intricate knowledge of the individual's action field.

I said, "the individual's action field": of course, all these activities take place in social interaction; yet, in performing them it is the participating individuals who build up skill, consciousness, valences, meaning and action potential.

The example of the harvest dance has shown us the progressive assimilation of praxic knowledge, the rising of consciousness and reflection, and its extension and integration into other action areas. Even specific knowledge, like harvesting rice, forms complex practical as well as conceptual and symbolic networks, reaching out in to different spheres of an individual's life. But this extension implies another aspect we have to consider now: the transformation, by assimilation, of knowledge itself.

The Transformation of Knowledge

I have learned psychology in Geneva and psychoanalysis in Zurich. However, few of my colleagues would consider me, today, to be a psychologist of the Genevan school: cultural psychology and action theory is no central Genevan concern. Similarly, few would consider me to be still a psychoanalyst as I have drifted too far away from its basic theoretical platform. Knowledge I had acquired became, in the course of life, amalgamated with personal experience and thinking, and thus the contents of my teaching would certainly have drifted, too. Would then my students have become action theorists and cultural psychologists? Only a handful. Most of them, too, would have acquired knowledge by transforming it in the process of assimilation.

Let us ask what knowledge means to us. Few people acquire knowledge purely for the sake of knowing. Much more than wanting to know, we want to feel *convinced*. Knowledge we look for should be experienced to be *true*, because only true knowledge can provide feelings of action potential.

Knowledge should enhance and support our skills and capacity of orientation in a world we want to be "transparent."

If knowledge we consider to be "true" implies the feeling of conviction, knowledge we do not trust gives rise to the feeling of *doubt*. Conviction does not necessarily correspond to correct, or to "objective" knowledge (here defined as knowledge which can efficiently control action). One can, as many examples demonstrate, be convinced of quite erroneous or unsubstantiated beliefs. Similarly, the feeling of doubt does not always imply deficient knowledge—some may doubt quite correct information. Yet both conviction and doubt can be very strong feelings, as experience shows again and again.

Conviction is closely related to the feeling of triumph, as Pierre Janet (1926/28) defined it: the self-enhancement due to successful action. As triumph regulates both the cessation of ongoing and the direction of future action, so conviction terminates the present search for knowledge and regulates the direction of future inquiry or interpretation. Feeling convinced of a thing, I believe to "understand" it and therefore tend to suspend further inquiry. Conviction, similar to triumph, is a strong self-reinforcing feeling. Yet, it can always be shaken by new experiences, and therefore, welcomes corroboration. Conviction, consequently, would be likely to foster two kinds of behavior: first, the openness towards confirming and reinforcing information, coupled with the rejection of contradicting one; second, the search for social approval and confirmation, implying selective social orientations. But there appears to be a third type of behavior related to conviction: *proselytism*. Conviction wants to convince, and this wish may go as far as eliminating—symbolically or even factually—those who refuse being persuaded. Indeed, doubt can be a nagging, self-diminishing emotion; infringements on our conviction threaten our action potential, and consequently our self. Proselytism, then appears to be a self-protecting, defensive type of action.

It becomes understandable, thus, that we tend to defend our convictions as long as conflicting information can be avoided, refuted or repressed. There may, however, arise occasions where we no longer are able to shun contradictions—the "cognitive dissonance" has become too strong, or new action valences are imposed by situative changes. In such cases, often painful compromises and reorientations will take place, but occasionally we may also observe quite sudden "conversions": it seems as if people, wanting to conserve a *feeling* of conviction, would rather sacrifice its *content*.

Since, as I said, conviction need not be based on "objectively true" knowledge, we would have to ask what, then, determines our convictions or doubts. What we have seen so far suggests that the new information should appear to be, on the one hand, consistent with existing *systems of orientation and thought*, and, on the other hand, should be congruent with, or even support, *anticipated action*.

What, however, are these "existing systems of orientation and thought?" They imply, first, the environmental structures as known by the individual; second, they would (as far as the individual is aware of) include ideational systems according to which a cultural group explains, justifies and directs action (what I called "myths"); third, such systems of orientation would of course also comprise of subjective experience and anticipatory action structures (which I called "fantasms"). We often are not aware of the complex constellations involved in the perception and assimilation of information. Our concept of "storing information" induces the belief in a registration-recall concept of memory which is certainly at odds with the realities of behavior. Selections, eliminations and even distortions of information, rather than being deficiencies, result from action-related assimilation of experience—"action," here, not being limited to the pursuance of a single goal, but to the over-arching systems within which an individual places his or her goals (as to some perhaps less familiar terms used here, see Boesch, 1976, 1980, 1983, 1991).

Thus, new information has to fit present, individual as well as cultural, structures. Yet, it may also appeal not by its consistency with current frames of orientation, but by its divergence from them. Action also strives for newness, variation, alternatives instead of familiarity. Everyday culture may be perceived as a rigid structure and, hence, foster tendencies to escape, or at least to extend its limits. The emotional qualities related to this kind of orientation are "curiosity" and "daring" in their diverse forms.

In such cases, *"otherness"* rather than congruence will determine the appeal of new information, and again, this otherness will not necessarily have to offer "better" or "truer" knowledge, but will often simply attract by its newness. Much innovation and social change, rebellion and evasion will result from this appeal of the different, the deviant, the promise of improvements, enhancements, or simply excitement.

Knowledge, thus, is not simply "received," absorbed, but assimilated, thereby undergoing multiple processes of selection, transformation and integration into individual systems of action. We have to wonder then, why such idiosyncratic acquisitions of knowledge would not lead to ever greater divergences, ultimately producing chaotic cultural dissonance. We know that this may indeed occur occasionally, but on the whole it seems that cultures succeed in maintaining some sort of internal constancy. Let us therefore look at these processes of equilibration.

The Feedback of Knowledge

It seems that individuals in a cultural group, to a considerable extent, *share* knowledge of a congruent kind. The "subjectivation" just described, therefore has to imply additional processes leading to common structures of knowledge. These appear to be mainly twofold: first, social interaction induces mutual accommodation of knowledge. These "processual" accommodations would, however, produce common structures only within the frameworks of particular interactions. Therefore, we have to expect superordinate cultural "channelings" and "objectivations" of knowledge.

Social intercourse requires coordination of practical action and its cognitive reflection mainly in a denotative sense: for joining forces in a team we need agreement as to procedures, tools, timing, while each member may retain the private meanings he or she connects with the common action. In other words, homogenization of knowledge concerns praxic action and the "signal function" of concepts, but not subjective connotations or symbolism. People may, therefore, cooperate for very different motifs, may derive from the action different kinds of satisfaction or frustration, may integrate it into different superordinate action systems, yet all the aspects needed for successful common action would become coordinated; the meanings of an action for the participating individuals would overlap in their practical variance.

Yet, where practical coordination is less important, where meanings relate more strongly to individual systems of order and orientation than to actual praxis, major divergences may indeed occur; think of the cleavage between believers in the biblical Genesis and in Darwinist evolution in American society, or of the divergence between modern esoterical and scientific ideologies. But there are less extreme examples. Two professors of psychology would not lecture similarly on Piaget, and neither of them, presumably, would present a "true" picture of Piaget's thinking: They would have assimilated it through their own "mental lenses." Their divergence would be even greater were it not for cultural mechanisms of stabilization.

Indeed, cultures introduce safeguards against too much distortion. These however, may very considerably. Before being written down, the teachings of Buddha were transmitted orally for about five hundred years. During this incredibly long time, they were embroidered by many legends of the master's life, but there seem to be reasons for believing that the teaching as such was quite faithfully preserved. Similar records, although perhaps for shorter time-spans, exist for the conservation of myths, legends or historical records in non-literate cultures. If we think of Bartlett's experiments on the sequential oral communication of stories (1954), such faithfulness is astounding—but these experiments belong to a different culture. Faithful oral transmission, we might assume, is likely to go hand in hand with what Mary Douglas (1973) would call "strong grid and strong group," i.e., high coherence of a group's world view, as well as high pressure to conform to it. Such coherence of a cultural world view tends to entail a particular valuation of the teacher: the teacher would represent the ultimate authority, and therefore the disciples would strive at acquiring his knowledge as faithfully as possible. Self-realization by identification with models would, in such cultures, excel self-realization by originality.

Cultures may thus manage to preserve constancy over long periods of time; yet some changes will always occur: unforeseen situations may arise, young individuals will replace old ones, external imports may introduce new gadgets or new ideas, or culture itself, by its constraints and limitations, will induce strivings for change. Society has to be able to cope with such changes, in other words, it must achieve stabilization under conditions of variation. Somehow, a balance between conservation and change has to be found, and such balances may differ between cultures.

Let us look at a modern example of stabilization and change. Our scientific community tries to stabilize information by storing it in libraries and obliging the individual to refer to it. Our compulsory (and often compulsive) quotations and bibliographical references bear witness to this cultural stabilization mechanism. In a sense, we have replaced the single teacher's authority by the collected testimonies of experts.

Yet, we know that it only partly works: quotations are torn out of their context, selected arbitrarily, and inserted into new contexts which sometimes may considerably alter their meanings. Change finds its way in spite of cultural barriers. Individuals, we have seen, select and transform information for furthering their action tendencies, in our case, for buttressing one's own theories or interpretations of phenomena. Should the scientist be a person of high prestige, power or influence, his subjective views tend to become common parlance. Yet, even in such cases, his readers or listeners would operate their selections and assimilations of the information received.

Considering the balance between conservation and change, we become aware of a quasi natural connivance between the individual and his or her cultural group. The individual too, strives at constancy. His orientation system requires a consistent and therefore constant world; yet, by the same token, the individual tendency at optimizing the action potential calls for variation, change, innovation, and therefore the individual will also have to establish his or her personal balances between the two tendencies. Doubt, we have seen, is antagonistic to conviction; however, conviction, although providing security, may constrain, may also be contradicted by events or new information, hence breeding doubt and stimulating curiosity, exploration and adventurism. There appears to be a rhythmic alternation between the movements away from and back to stability.

Since cultures, as we have seen, need this balance too, we might now assume that an individual striving for change would meet a different reception in moments of cultural openness for change than in more conservative times. We sometimes say that "Time is ripe for a revolutionary or an innovator," implying that a synchrony has arisen between individual and cultural tendencies for transformation. In other situations or times, the same innovator would be doomed to failure. In the 1920s Pierre Janet published (in the framework of his theory of emotions) what we would call today a "cybernetic action theory." It took more than fifty years before his approach was followed, although not tied up with his name. In 1936 Robert Dottrens wrote his seminal book "L'enseignement individualisé;" educators took no note of it. Today, over half a century later, his theses appear to be rediscovered. These are only two of many examples of "untimely" innovators.

What does "timely" mean? In a rational frame of mind we sometimes tend to believe that the group encourages originality and change because existing knowledge has proven to be insufficient and needs improving. Change then, would equal progress. Yet, knowledge may be logically wanting, practically inadequate, and still not considered to be deficient; but knowledge may also be perceived to be unsatisfactory in spite of no logical or practical failings. Magical beliefs and practices have persisted over the ages, and even scientific ideologies and techniques, although outdated, might enjoy a long life. On the other hand, a tool or a car which functions satisfactorily will often be "improved" and changed, even against the "felt needs" of their users (who however, as experience shows, tend to follow course). Deficiency is not a necessary condition for change. Cultures often remained conservative simply by learning to live with inadequacies, while others turn towards progress for reasons often far from rational.

Change may be sought for practical and economic reasons, yet let us not forget that it is also an actional and often, even an aesthetic phenomenon. Change provides action opportunities more numerous and varied than constancy, and while it reduces security, it enhances individual worth. But change also provides excitement, thrill, surprise, novelty, in other words, leads to enjoyable action experiences. Thus, what may be hailed to be progress is in many cases simply due to individual, or generational, needs of variation. Such would obviously apply to fashion, but I often suspect that it would also be true for much of what we call progress in the areas of social scientific theories or political ideology.

Let me summarize: Although the "cycle of knowledge" would vary according to culture, information offered will always be selected and assimilated by its individual members, and they will in turn feed it back, by praxis as well as by ideation, as a transformed message. The amount of transformation occurring will be dependent upon both the cultural grids of constancy or change, and the individual's specific situation and aspirations. However, this process makes cultural change inavoidable; it may only be slowed down or accelerated, suspended (for awhile) or fostered by historical circumstances. Thus, there would be good reasons for psychologists to be more interested in the transformation of knowledge in a cultural field. By studying the "cycle of knowledge," the destiny of information in its course from group to individual and back to the group, we would indeed gain important insights into the dynamics of action within a culture.

QUOTED LITERATURE

Bartlett, Sir F. (1954). *Remembering*. Cambridge: Cambridge University Press.
Boesch, E. E. (1976). *Psychopathologie des Alltags*. Bern: Huber.
Boesch, E. E. (1980). *Kultur und Handlung*. Bern: Huber.
Boesch E. E. (1983). *Das Magische und das Schöne*. Stuttgart: Frommann-Holzboog.
Boesch E. E. (1991). *Symbolic action theory and cultural psychology*. Heidelberg/New York: Springer.
Dottrens, R. (1936). *L'enseignement indivdualisé*. Neuchâtel: Delachaux et Niestlé.
Douglas, M. (1974). *Natural symbols*. London: Barrie and Jenkins.
Janet, P. (1926/1928). *De l'angoisse à l'extase*. Paris: Alcan, 2 vol.
Lang, A. (1990). *The "concrete mind" heuristic—human identity and social compound from things and buildings* (in print).
Lay, C. (1954). *The African child*. London: Collins.

INTRODUCTORY COMMENTS TO CHAPTER 10

"Reality as Metaphor"

The Authors

Originally published in French in 1994, this article was translated into English by Professor Boesch and Virginia Geck, an assistant hired specifically for this work. As is the case for most translations and for Professor Boesch's works particularly, the reader is advised to remain focused on the major issues and intent of the study. Boesch defined the term "reality" in this specific context as "lived reality," or the experiences one has when going about daily life. The particular meanings that may be assigned to one's reality as it is usually lived is what he called a "metaphor." In his observations and interpretations, all experiences are unique both realistically and metaphorically. No two people are the same in their physical or psychic characteristics and experiences. Therefore, experiences are metaphors for the reality each person encounters. When one describes her/his experiences, another layer of interpretation is added through the complex meaning of language. Boesch clari-

Discovering Cultural Psychology: A Profile and Selected Readings of
Ernest E. Boesch, pp. 213–216
213

fies his points through examples drawn from the psychological literature and his reflective experiences.

To illustrate his **main thesis**, that reality is always known both factually and symbolically, Boesch introduced a woman with whom he conversed about her daily chores as a wife, mother, and homemaker. She was carrying home the groceries she purchased for a meal she planned to serve her family. When asked the reason for selecting a particular cut of meat rather than sausages that would be easier to prepare, she indicated that she wanted assurance of high quality food, and sausage did not meet her standards because it could be too easily altered. With this example, Boesch introduced the crucial element of "polyvalence" which is a central component in his theory of human behavior, namely, symbolic action theory (SAT).

The title, "Reality as a Metaphor," also reflects Boesch's training and practice as a psychoanalytic therapist during part of his career. He has read and studied Freud's work with great attention to Freud's explanations for the levels of meaning that an individual might assign to objects and actions. Boesch emphasized that for Freud, everything can become symbolic as a result of repression when attempting free expression of inner meanings and desires. He used Freud's account of "The Woman at the Window" as an example of how one can be both attracted to and repulsed by multiple, hidden meanings assigned to everyday perceptions and experiences.

MEANING OF VALENCE AND POLYVALENCE

Employing terms introduced to psychology by Kurt Lewin, and using the example cited above, Boesch pointed out that one's work has symbolic value that is related to self-perceptions and the social and physical context in which one acts. When one works, the entire process is related to the goals or purposes that are sought through the completion of the work. For example, the homemaker chose her actions with the goal of demonstrating care and nurturing of her family to the best of her ability. The actions in themselves were a means to another level of value; that of exhibiting her dedication and love for her husband and children. Simultaneously, she felt pride and happiness about herself as a caring, loyal, and competent person.

Therefore, the most benign or mundane actions, such as preparing and serving a meal, when viewed by others usually have many levels of value based on various possible interpretations. From the "actor's" perspective, all behaviors are polyvalent and may closely influence or be derived from one's life goals. Actions are also dynamic in so far as they change the person and her/his social and physical environment. Values, deeply related to one's cultural context, are both unconscious and conscious with regard to levels of awareness and intention. They are both symbolic and factual given that they simultaneously arise from individual and collective meanings and include material objects.

Themes and Stories

Bosech dedicated a large section of this article to examining main themes he identified in Freud's writing. The theme of fear emerges from an account of a small boy who dreaded the loss of vision due to his persistent attempts to watch for and identify a woman who visited his father's study at night. The second theme is related to a young boy who feels compelled to look at a beautiful female figure who sits at a window located directly across from his own. In both stories, the symbolism of the actions and the motivations or values that support them is interpreted according to Freudian themes such as fear of castration and the Oedipus complex. The eye is considered a phallic symbol and the window is a symbol of human vulnerability given that windows both open and close, hide and uncover, the inner and outer world. Many variations on the meanings of these images are provided by Boesch in as much as the symbols can be found in many art forms.

Eyes also have great meaning of a factual and symbolic sense. Vision is a crucial means of perception and is part of developing relationships with people and things in one's environment. Vision is also a form of protection in as much as it gives information about possible dangers. Accounts of the importance of vision that Boesch presented indicate the universality of the symbolic meaning it has across cultures. As with other forms of experience, visual meanings are often constrained according to values one holds and the cultural guides one endorses.

In addition to the writings of Freud, the work of Levi-Strauss, also a scholar who had a major influence on Boesch's thinking, was referenced in the paper. The "hobbyist" was introduced as an important figure by Levi-Strauss. Such a person can find many uses for nearly everything, and therefore attaches values to many objects others discard as trash or valueless. Again, value is attached to materials individually as well as collectively. Picasso was referenced as a famous hobbyist who often used discarded materials in his highly acclaimed art work. Through his innovations, the artist moved beyond cultural constraints and thereby created new levels of artistic ingenuity.

Summary

The examples presented by Boesch were also applied to people and behavior more generally. Boesch stated that "we organize our reality in a way to feel capable of mastering the circumstances, whether they are desired or dreaded." In this interpretation of human behavior, there is no hard and fast "real world" that is commonly discovered when perceptions are accurate. Rather, perceptions and the meanings assigned to them are both individually and collectively determined. No one is immune to or devoid of social and cultural influences from the world of "the others." At the same time, each person relies on her/his perceptual capacities to learn about the world and what it may offer. In this respect, meanings are derived from symbolic interpretations of people and things that are encountered as real. A careful reading of this article reinforces the importance of respecting the unique ways a person perceives, interprets, and behaves. It also suggests the importance of thoughtful interpersonal communication if one desires to understand those encountered either at home, in the community, or in distant cultures.

CHAPTER 10

REALITY AS METAPHOR[1]

Ernest E. Boesch

THE POLYVALENCE OF MEAT

The subject is ambitious. Metaphors occupy the discussions of linguists, philosophers and other scientists, and the problem of reality is certainly—despite numbers of learned dissertations—as enigmatic as ever. All the same, I will not attempt to define these terms. I shall confine myself to the approximate pinpointing of their current usage. Thus I will not speak of reality in a philosophical sense, but simply of our experience of reality, of "lived reality," and I will use the term "metaphor," as being largely synonymous with "symbol." This is because even if one can, strictly speaking, distinguish the two terms in language, such a distinction would become artificial in concrete reality. However, in order to introduce these reflections, I will try to clarify a central term concerning our problem: that of polyvalence.

My main thesis will be that reality *is always lived both in a factual and in a symbolic way.* Let me illustrate this by a very commonplace daily example. I meet a woman whom I know, let me call her Jeanne, on her way home after shopping. A loaf of bread and some fruit can be seen in her shopping bag, but on chatting, I learn that she has also just bought a nice cut of meat. "Why," I ask her in the somewhat silly way of such encounters,

Discovering Cultural Psychology: A Profile and Selected Readings of Ernest E. Boesch, pp. 219–237
Copyright © 2007 by Information Age Publishing

"did you buy meat and not sausage? That at least makes less work, and with your children and big yard, you already have enough to do!" "Oh, you know," she answers, "I enjoy the work. I enjoy busying myself with plants and cooking, and the pleasure I give others is enough reward for me. As far as meat goes, at least you see what you have, whereas with sausages you never know what the butcher has stuffed into the intestines." This little exchange, which could easily be continued, puts us right in the middle of a metaphor of action and objects. Daily work, as Jeanne explains, has a symbolic value in connection with one's self-perception—physically, socially and subjectively; meat can relate to values of purity, honesty and certainly other qualities to which she has not referred.

Meat, obviously, was for her above all meat, a food essentially "prospective"—an exterior element destined to be incorporated, and thereby interiorised. Through this fact, its impurities risk contaminating us. Thus we must be protected from outside "intrusions." Meat, thus, represents an ambivalent "non-I": the exterior world, while nourishing us, threatens us at the same time. Therefore, to buy meat becomes an act both of laying in supplies and of vigilance, a concrete example of the fundamental relationship between the person of Jeanne and her world. It should be noted as well that the menaces implied in her thoughts were material as well as social—unhealthy fat, for instance, and a dishonest butcher.

Meat in effect participates in a more general manner in this ambivalent character of the exterior world: it represents living flesh with all of the taboos which are related to it. As a result, it can't be used directly as such, but must be transformed by cooking, which on the one hand makes it, as we believe, more digestible, but also on the other hand purifies it—materially as well as immaterially. Cooking, in other words, is a procedure—or a ritual—of categorical change: it transforms flesh into meat, and in doing this suppresses taboos or aversions and opens the way for "appetites."

Thus meat constitutes an object detached from its original reality and only becomes acceptable through this detachment. Our friend would firmly refuse to attend the butchering of the animal or to participate in its dismemberment. The sight of blood would awaken various subjective associations, usually unpleasant—extending from accidents and death to aggressiveness and sexuality. But the transformation of meat into a roast, of blood into a gravy ("from the raw to the cooked," as would say Lévi-Strauss, 1964) places it in a new context of conviviality, sensual and social pleasures, based on cultural rituals which carry their own connotations and functions—one of which, at any rate, will be to reinforce and to sanction the separation between the raw and the cooked. In buying her meat, Jeanne, of course, won't be thinking but of the future roast; but unconsciously or subconsciously, the other implications are present and even risk being felt—more or less amorphously—during the preparation of the raw meat. Such implications will obviously be coloured by the personal history of Jeanne; in part they will be cultural, in part private. We could without difficulty make similar observations on the other contents of her shopping bag—the bread, the vegetables, the milk, for instance; but what we have just seen will suffice to illustrate how much lived reality is enmeshed in a network of multiple implications; it is, briefly, always "polyvalent" (Boesch, 1991).

The concept of "valence" was borrowed by Kurt Lewin from chemistry, where it designates the attraction that one atom can exercise on another. Lewin uses it by analogy to show the attraction which a goal or an object possesses for an actor. Psychoanalysis has taught us that one can love an object and hate it at the same time; that one can feel oneself attracted, and simultaneously be afraid; thus one speaks of "ambivalence." But the example of the piece of meat suggests that the value attributed to an object tends to be determined in multiple ways, thus becoming "polyvalent"; in more psychoanalytic terminology, one would say "overdetermined." I prefer the term polyvalence, which avoids an overly deterministic implication.

The total valence of a thing being composed, one can therefore also speak of partial valences. However, our introductory example makes plausible the fact that the totality of these partial valences will never be conscious. Jeanne, at the moment of her purchases, certainly was not thinking of the diverse components directing her action. We can say that she might easily become aware of part of them during an interview, while another part of the "total variance of meaning" would remain unconscious for various reasons—the actual situation, momentary interests, repression. Therefore, lived reality will necessarily include an unconscious element, according to the nature of the action, of the situation or of the subject him-or-herself, as we will see below.

Let us summarize these considerations in saying that, on the one hand, the meaning of an object derives partially from its factuality in a context of action: meat as food. On the other hand, the meaning of the object will be constituted by the insertion of the object into a larger framework of experiences, of evaluations and of beliefs, a framework which reconnects the object of the action to situations other than the current one. Thus we can speak of partial "factual" valences of the meaning and of partial "symbolic" valences, understanding by that that the object or the situation reverts to related givens for various reasons. At the same time let us underline that "partial valences" doesn't at all mean that they are analytically separable: the factual and the symbolic often form inextricable combinations.

To conclude this introduction, let me point out that the metaphors of language possess similar characteristics. They have a factual, or denotative sense, whereby the generally accepted sense isn't at all the only one. Thus "to have bread on the shelf"[2] literally means to have bread in reserve, in other words something to eat; the currently accepted sense—although difficult to explain—is to have a lot of work to do (Duneton, 1978). But the terms "have," "bread," "shelf" possess in addition various connotations, public as well as private, giving a sort of "flavor" to the metaphor (rustic, craftsmanlike, nourishing, protecting, or anything else), and also to the one who uses it. At any rate, the language metaphor somehow signalises the non-validity of literal understanding; it points at its symbolism, while the real object hides it.

The omnipresence of the symbol has been demonstrated in a way which has become classic by Gaston Bachelard. More than others, I believe, he has drawn our attention to the hidden connotations of the home and its contents, of the earth, the water, the air or the fire (see for example Bachelard, 1949, 1957). Psychoanalysis has added to these the metaphors of the body and of the subject. Freud, however, would have been less inclined to say that everything is symbolic, than that everything *can become* symbolic: symbolism for him resulted from repression. Yet, repression somehow made use of pre-existent symbolic images, encountered above all in dreams, in which Freud found fixed meamngs—sexual, of course—which could be interpreted "on sight," as he said (Freud, 1940). Bachelard, I fear, erred similarly by a tendency towards phenomenological rigidity. Thus, for example, while for Freud a drawer would represent the feminine sex, for Bachelard, it would mean the experience of secrecy. However, since the polyvalence of symbolism results from relationships established among different domains of our experience, all contents of reality carry subjective meanings, demanding their individual analysis. In order to make these considerations concrete, I propose to look at two examples: one, more complex, but perhaps more familiar, concerns the symbolism of situations: the second, apparently more simple, will demonstrate the subtle metaphoric quality of objects. The first example will be taken from Sigmund Freud, the second, from Claude Lévi-Strauss.

"The Woman at the Window"

In 1919 Freud published an essay under the untranslatable German title: "Das Unheimliche," The article draws our attention on the fact that the symbolism of reality, while often remaining unconscious, manifests itself by emotional reactions difficult to rationalize, so to say by the "colour tone" of the situation. Taking as an example this sentiment of vague, profound and irrational disquiet which the German term calls forth (habitually translated as "disquieting strangeness"), Freud attempts to trace its origins and to unveil the pulsions which are unacknowledged, even repressed by the subject. He does so in having recourse to the novelette by E. T. A. Hoffmann, "The Sandman." This fiction as such will not interest us here, our preoccupation being the symbolism of the concrete reality. But it impressed Freud enough to incite him to relate an experience he made during one of his trips to Italy, and it is this which attracts our attention. I quote it here using the translation of Marie Bonaparte (Stirn, 1987).

Freud postulates first that one of the sources of his sentiment of anxious disquiet is the unexpected repetition of similar experiences. He bases this theory on the following examples: "One day on which during a scorching summer afternoon I was ambling through the empty and unknown streets of a small Italian town, I landed in a section about whose character I couldn't stay in doubt long. At the windows of the small houses, one saw only heavily made-up women, and I made haste to leave the narrow street at the first possible turnoff. But, after having erred around for some time without a guide, I suddenly found myself on the same street, where I was beginning to cause a sensation, and my haste to get away had no other result than to make me return there a third time by a different route. I felt an emotion which I cannot qualify other than that of disquieting strangeness, and I was very happy, when giving up other expeditions, I found myself back at the square from which I had set off."

And he continues: "Other situations, which have in common with the preceding an involuntary return to the same point, while otherwise differing radically, can still produce the same emotion of distress and disquieting strangeness. For instance, when one finds himself surprised in a high forest by fog, when one is lost and despite all efforts to find a marked or known trail, keeps coming back to a place recognizable by a certain characteristic. Or when one gropes through an unfamiliar and dark room looking for the door or the light switch and for the tenth time bumps into the same furniture" (Freud, 1947, pp. 249-250).

The example constitutes an experience of functional helplessness, the causes of which the actor cannot explain—which induces the particular emotion described by Freud. Proceeding from here, he attributes the unintended repetition to the "repetition compulsion"—which he connects, as one knows, to the threat of a reappearance of repressed and thus unconscious contents of mind. One would have liked to see how, in this light, Freud would understand his Italian experience; but he doesn't touch on it again.

My intention in this context is not to discuss Freud's theory of the emotion of disquieting strangeness, but to understand the significance of a real event which Freud places in relationship with the story by Hoffmann. This tale (of which Freud gives an excellent résumé, which I therefore need not repeat here) combines two main themes. The first is the childhood fear of a student, Nathaniel, of having his eyes torn out by the sandman. This fear, caused by the story of a female servant, is reinforced by a terrifying experience of the child, when, in hiding surreptitiously in his father's study, he tries to find out the identity of a mysterious nocturnal visitor. The second theme is the love of this same Nathaniel for the beautiful and enigmatic daughter of his professor. Her name is Olimpia, who finally turns out to be only a doll of deceptive human appearance. The themes of eyes and of love are connected by the intervention of a travelling optician—a kind of transformation of the sandman—from whom Nathaniel buys a lorgnette, which will permit him at his leisure to contemplate Olimpia seated at her window in the professor's apartment, which—as chance wills—is located directly across from Nathaniel's room.

The interpretation of this narrative follows the theorical tracks of Freud: The eye, as he says, being a phallic symbol, the fear of having one's eyes torn out would be tantamount to the fear of castration, which, as one knows, results from an Oedipian conflict. The sandman, the travelling optician and the professor would be the incarnations of the castrating father. Furthermore, the emotion of the "disquiet" produced by the narrative would betray by this very term an even deeper root: "Unheimlich" is the negation of "Heimlich," which has two meanings, "secret, hidden," but also equally "intimate," and this double meaning would thus indicate an object both desired and feared, namely the uterus of the mother. Let us mention in passing that it is often questionable to try to grasp the psychological meaning of a term by its etymology.

What Freud seems not to notice are the striking analogies between the Hoffmann narrative and his own Italian experience. In both it is a question of women seen at a window, and in both of the two cases, the women are "artificial," Olimpia through her fabricated beauty, the prostitutes through their makeup, which also constitutes a facticious beauty. In any case, in both instances the women are "forbidden"—for Nathaniel who is engaged; for Freud, married and of puritanical background. The theme of the two other examples mentioned by Freud is by the way not so different as he seems to believe: the fog as well as the darkness make it impossible to see, while in the prostitution section one has to see and to be seen; and just as the eyes of the unhappy Olimpia are finally literally cast on Nathaniel, so Freud feels himself bothered that these women cast their eyes on him. Nathaniel for his part vacillates constantly between the desire to look at Olimpia and the fear of losing his eyes, and thus his sight.

Let us regard more closely two of the central themes of the two stories: on the one hand, that of the "woman at the window" and on the other hand, the "phallic symbolism of the eye." In trying to specify the meanings, I will beware of proclaiming that "this means that"; the significances of the real are polyvalent, as we have seen, and each perceived significance can thus only be one among others which are equally possible; even if common cultural references make it plausible, it will, on principle, still remain no more than a hypothesis, which requires a verification through individual analysis. For the same reason, the essentially private meanings —in general of the kind which I had called "situational" and "functional" (Boesch, 1983, 1991)—cannot be exempt either from this attempt at analysis.

The window is already an object of complex significance. It closes at the same time as it opens; it allows looking and being seen, at the same time retaining distance; it even permits to watch hidden behind a curtain, or—as in Islamic architecture—from behind an elegant grille. It offers access, and by this fact constitutes a point of vulnerability; it protects from storms, but not from violence. Protection as well as vulnerability thus represent essential connotations of the window, not merely in a material sense: from the fact that it closes off, a window suggests secrets, but its transparency allows also to spy on them (hence curtains—or, to show that there is nothing to hide, the absence of curtains). Closing in at the same time as allowing to look out, a window can in a sense become a place of longing, of an unfulfilled wish for escape, or of an impatient and helpless waiting. A child confined to the house presses his nose against the pane to longingly watch his playing comrades. Thus a window separates the inside from the outside and joins them at the same time, creating two adverse elements: on the one hand, the one of being at home, of an intimacy protecting against a barren and threatening exterior; and, on the other hand, the one of an imprisoning interior, restraining and opposed to the outside promises of freedom and adventure.

The interior which the window separates from the outside corresponds thus to an intimacy denied the public domain. This intimacy, of course, will include first the material possessions of the inhabitant with their multiple significances, from trinkets to the washing machine, from pictures to fashion articles, from travel souvenirs to diaries, or from the kitchen knife to the hidden revolver. These examples already signalise a different, deeper dimension of intimacy: Collecting objects which serve our activities as well as those which symbolize our hopes and fears makes one's home represent both the I we feel to be and the one to which we aspire.

The window thus becomes in a sense the osmotic membrane between the I and the non-I.

Looking from the outside into a house would consequently correspond not only to an indiscretion, to a violation of a private sphere, but more symbolically still to taking possession of it; to know an interior—in the concrete as well as the figurative sense—holds the promise of power over the resident. The house symbolizing the individual who lives there acquires thereby a corporeal significance, and, as Freud had underlined, it can then through its forms and openings represent parts of the body. All the same, these physical analogies remain partial. A house represents its inhabitant in a more complete manner—his status, his taste, his ambitions, even his dreams—as Gaston Bachelard has so subtly shown (1957). It is not without reason then that one encases windows in frames, almost like paintings, and that those who cannot afford this at least decorate them with curtains, with plants or with pretty—although not valuable—objects. One expects curious looks, one may even desire them, while at the same time calling them intrusive. One begins to understand thus that the modern "sport" of breaking windowpanes means more than simple material aggression. It unveils symbolically that which is hidden, eliminates the separation between the private and the public and denies thereby the inhabitant not only his private sphere, but equally his social status; it may symbolize sexual violation or even a threat to one's life.

Nevertheless, looking through a window becomes equally an act of participation or even of compassion. We should not mistake the importance of this curiosity for an interior. Of course, we possess a kind of "heliotropism" which urges us to look for clearness in the physical as well as the cognitive sense; yet, at the same time we possess what might be called a "claustrotropism," an attraction for things that are hidden, closed off, banned from our investigation. Fairytales speak to us of the generally nefarious attraction for closed off doors or cabinets, and many parents complain about the often irresistible curiosity that infants have for drawers and cupboards—infants, for whom, after many unsuccessful attempts, the opening of such furniture is an important experience of triumph. But it is not just for an infant that the hidden possesses a particular interest: it can contain what we may be deprived of, that which we desire, but also what could threaten us. More fundamentally, it can constitute a "blank space" in our field of action and thus obscure the transparency of our world and hinder our potential to act. Looking inside is an attempt to increase order in our experience.

Consequently, the theme of the woman at the window can carry various significances. By the way, it is an almost archetypical theme, which we encounter from the time of the troubadours to "Don Giovanni" by Mozart or the "Minnesänger" by Wagner; but also in the traditions still widespread in certain regions of nocturnal visits through the window to one's lover—or sometimes even an abduction in this way. The theme seems similar to that of the woman watching from a balcony the tournament of knights, a bullfight or a parade. In these instances, a woman participates in a spectacle while at the same time staying above and distant, and it is often a noble or otherwise superior women. Thus, the woman at the window seems to possess a special kind of erotic attraction; although facing the spectator, she remains confined in her intimate femininity; she can be desired and idealized—withdrawn from immediate interaction, she stimulates nostalgic projections as in the case of Olimpia. In other cases, on the contrary, she may be invested with a superego quality—like the woman in Picasso's "Guernica" holding a lamp out of a window (Boesch, 1991).

However, the woman at the window may just as well be a gossip on the alert for new material. In contrast to the woman who inspires serenades, she would rather be on the old side, have her hair in curlers or be wearing a bathrobe and will represent a social control of the type, "what will people say." She will thus constitute an antithesis to the young and pretty woman at the window. One will notice that the prostitute tends to be viewed as belonging to both, the woman of erotic attraction and the gossip. On occasion the woman at the window will even be transformed into a threatening witch—in a painting by the German Hans Baldung Grien for example, or more recently, by Picasso. Indeed, the woman leaning out of a hidden, inscrutable interior may easily be taken for the mistress of obscure forces—as perhaps the Italian prostitutes, unconsciously, were by Freud. In the tale by E. T. A. Hoffmann, on the other hand, the woman seen by Nathaniel is nearer to the plot popular in fairytales of a bewitched woman kept captive by a monster or sorcerer. Thus the woman at the window, placed between the interior and the exterior, between the private sphere of her secrets and the one of the viewer, will appear according to the circumstances alluring, nostalgic, menacing or menaced and in some cases may be idealized, in others, vilified.

Indeed in many places young girls have been taught that "a well-bred young lady doesn't stare out of windows"; this would be a gesture of invitation contrary to good breeding—whence grills and curtains. This was obviously a way of withdrawing young women from the cupidity of the world, but also of keeping them under control. Thereby, looking through the window acquired a connotation of longing, of dreamy waiting, even of an invitation to abduction, and if this were carried out through the window, its symbolism would converge on violation. C. G. Jung, on the other hand, would have seen in the woman at the window rather an image of the "anima," symbolizing the not real, but aspired self. Olimpia, of whom the student Nathaniel is enamoured, would thus become an ambivalent metaphor, signifying a split between the real and the fantasmic woman, as well as between a lived and a wished for self.

In all of this the act of looking is important: it clears distances at the same time as it marks them. The subject of the eye is therefore intimately connected to what we have just discussed. For Freud the eye was a phallic symbol; the window, being an opening of a house, carried a vaginal significance; to watch a woman through a window would thus be equivalent to violating her, more precisely, in Nathaniel's case, it meant Oedipean incest. But is the eye really phallic? Can one through a doctrinal gesture sweep away the generally much more vast symbolism of the eye?

The strengthening of the functional potential is the most important motive of human activity (Boesch, 1976, 1991). It is therefore not redundant to remember that vision constitutes above all a functional capability. It is through our eyes that we can get our bearings, take note of our surroundings; they warn us of dangers and allow us to ward them off. The cruel joke of an African boy yelling at a blind man: "Watch out, a snake!" (Smith Bowen, 1964) tells a lot about this protective power of vision. But at the same time our eyes are the principle source of a multitude of pleasures and joys, of information, of excitement, of beauty, but also of creativeness—the painter, the sculptor, the gardener, the architect, are only the most striking instances. The fear of going blind is widespread, as Freud already mentioned; yet, this loss, by fundamentally reducing our capacity for experiencing and controlling reality, means much more than castration: it means the elimination of an essential part of our functional potential—and thus of our self.

At the same time this functional capability implies human interaction. To "cast one's eyes on someone" expresses interest for the person, and thus even the fact of being looked at signalises being noticed, being seen, and thus strengthens in one way or another our self. We speak of the "evil eye" which threatens, but also of "kind eyes" which smile at us, or of the amorous look, which allures. The "depth of the eyes" implies the secret which the other person hides from us. A severe and reproachful look shows authority with the power to punish. God is often represented by a large eye watching over the world, and sculptures or masks portraying certain gods and goddesses in different parts of the world are often distinguished by exaggeratedly large eyes. These same large eyes, by the way, can be found in Picasso's works—especially noticeable since the "Demoiselles d'Avignon" (1907); they seem to reveal terror, aggressiveness or depressive emptiness, but the watchful, "superego" eye is not absent from his work. In passing, let it be said, the representation of eyes by Picasso—from their large size to their duplication in profiles—would deserve a study of their own.

Let us go back to Freud's Italian episode. The student Nathaniel suc-
cumbs to the seduction of a "woman at a window" with disastrous results.
Would this seduction not also be the central theme of Freud's experience?
Freud doesn't at any time reveal the meaning for him of his involuntary
returns, but it seems legitimate to suspect that the theme "a woman at a
window"—looked at as much as looking—possessed its particular connotations for him as well. These connotations, encompassing enough by
themselves, as we have just seen, were circumscribed the minute Freud
identified these women as prostitutes—an act of classification, social as
much as "ideological." Indeed, the term "prostitute" connects such
women to the type of ideology which I have become accustomed to call
"myths"—meaning collective systems of evaluation and explanation
underlying cultural behaviour (Boesch, 1980, 1991). In this terminology,
the prostitute would constitute a "mytheme," i.e., a single theme belonging to the encompassing "myth" of the woman as well as the one of the
man. These prostitutes must have disturbed Freud for two reasons: on the
one hand, the evaluation of prostitutes according to the myth of his age
and society made them "taboo" for a scholar and respectable bourgeois;
on the other hand, the "fantasm" (Boesch, 1976, 1991) connected with
the "woman at the window" unconsciously made them attractive. His
hasty flights and his "surprising" returns seem to explain themselves by
the dynamic play between myth and fantasm: in the "quarter," namely,
the concrete presence of these women, their cultural value, negative and
thus menacing, must have predominated; but the minute they were withdrawn from definite confrontation, their deluding qualities gained the
upper hand—whence his returns. At the end his flight became definitive,
because, as we may suppose, to the confrontation with the reality of the
prostitutes was joined the feeling of a weakness of control threatening the
self of the actor. The "compulsion of repetition" thus asserted itself like a
dynamic game between the valences of attraction and repulsion. Is it too
daring, finally, to suppose that the history of Nathaniel allowed Freud to
displace a personal unrest in order better to objectivize and rationalize it?
The lived metaphor would launch a process of assimilation.

In doing this, Freud attempted to reduce the complex polyvalence of
the experience—inaccessible to conscious awareness—to his rational
structures of "plausible" dimensions. In fact, this is what we are constantly
doing: we reduce, as much as possible, the polyvalent significances of our
lived reality to fit the denotations of our current concepts. A knife is
meant to cut, we say, and we easily forget the slightly anxious respect with
which we handle it or the aggressive images which we suppress. Thus we
simplify lived reality and facilitate our orientation—at the price, all the
same, of ignoring the rich context of our actions. The connotation of the

"lived" constitutes a fabric, in which one cannot picture the design in isolating a single thread.

The Hobbyist[3]

The example which I have just discussed suggests that a lived situation draws its significance from two sources: on the one hand, the past of the subject, and on the other, the valence which the situation presents for the actions in course. Freud, at least in his understanding of neuroses, attaches primary importance to the first, the history of the subject determining the significance of the present. An opposite position remains nevertheless conceivable, namely that the individual constantly reinterprets and re-evaluates his history in connection with actually projected actions. In fact these two concepts contradict less than they complement each other; an interaction of the two determinants of meaning—memory and anticipation—is what currently takes place. All the same, let us consider yet a further example in which action *projects* are of predominant importance. The example, by the way, seems particularly fascinating to me, since it offers us no less than a metaphor of human existence.

Claude Lévi-Strauss made famous a personage, who in himself is unassuming and not at all spectacular; the hobbyist. All of us know some, it might even be that we are that ourselves. One of the most famous "bricoleur" was Picasso—remember his "bull's head" (1942) made in combining in a most unusual fashion a dismantled handlebar and a saddle from a bicycle, found on one of these piles of trash which he loved to go through. The hobbyist is deeply loath to throw away anything which he thinks "might still be of use." Of use for what? Usually he doesn't know, but he fills his cellar or his studio with old pieces of wood, parts of furniture, wires, screws and nails, parts of dismantled appliances, and if his name is Tinguely or Picasso, he will combine them into objects of art; if his name is simply Dupont or Dubois, he will use them for most ingenious repairs or for making some furniture needed—or even—like the mailman Ferdinand Cheval, to construct a fantasy villa. In any case, be he Picasso or Dupont, the hobbyist lays aside or looks for heterogeneous items with a potential significance not necessarily connected to their material or conventional nature. A potential and unknown significance, has to be emphasized. It was certainly not with the intention of composing a bull's head that Picasso would have looked for a handlebar and a saddle: these were, on the contrary, objects which at the time of an accidental encounter, gave him the idea. The object of the hobbyist is a sign on the lookout for its meaning. We might call it a "projective object."

The possible use of these objects is, of course, limited by their material quality, but not less by the mentality of the "bricoleur." Picasso sees a bull's head in the handlebar and the bicycle saddle precisely because the image or the idea of the bullfight fascinated him in an almost obsessive way; even the woman, perhaps his principal obsession, was constantly associated to this theme. His creativity, of course, rejected and exceeded the limitations of custom, freed him from the constraint of seeing nothing but a bicycle in a bicycle; but these conventional constraints were replaced by those of his fantasms. Indetermination or specification of an object would thus reflect the open-mindedness or the closed-mindedness of the hobbyist.

What remains fascinating however is this character of an "indeterminate future" of the hobbyist's objects. He gives them a future, but refuses to attribute them a significance. In refusing to specify the nature of their future, he preserves his liberty, while providing himself with the means of a possible success. To put it in other words: the material and the utensils collected in the studio of the hobbyist symbolize his action potential. An action potential consisting on the one hand of his savoir-faire, his mastery, and on the other hand, his acceptance of the non-specific, his "tolerance of indetermination," implying confidence in his creativity.

The two phrases, "that might still be useful" and "I will be able to use it" risk calling forth the habitual double roles between a subject and an object, between the actor and his world. Yet, are objects real by themselves? Picasso certainly didn't believe that he had created a real bull's head; he knew that what he had transformed into an appearance of horns was in reality a handlebar and that what seemed a head was still actually a saddle, but his imagination substituted a different meaning on this real one. The aesthetic emotion which this object of art awakens in us is, of course, inside of us; it is not a quality of the object itself, or rather, it is due to this incongruity between the "real" nature of the object and its significance.

Our reality is "objective" in the sense that it permits a consensus and a coordination of experiences and interpretations; which implies that this objectivity will always be temporary—as proven not only by the history of science, but also by the cultural changes in the meanings of objects. However, all objective reality always carries an element of subjectivity upon which it will remain difficult or impossible to establish a consensus. The hobbyist will readily agree on the material qualities of a block of wood, but these will only partly determine his relationship with the wood. On the contrary, this relationship has a history and a context; it is imbued by the significance for him of trees, the cosiness of a cottage, wood fires; and it has been strongly coloured by his functional experiences of sawing, planing, filing, glueing, joining, screwing or nailing. Without this subjective-functional component leading to a private symbolism, the piece of wood would have constituted a different reality, most likely to be simply burned up in the fireplace; and without these subjective components, the individual would not be a hobbyist. Together with his object, he forms a "mutually constitutive unity": through his action, he creates the significance of his object, just as, inversely, his object forms his action, and thereby equally his personality. In the last analysis, it is this interaction which constitutes the lived individual reality. Through this subjective variance, a given level of reality, even though of the same denotation, will differ from one individual to the next—between a wood sculptor for instance, a violin maker or an architect.

In a sense, our world is closed, confined by material, social and ideational constraints, encountered or created by our own actions. It is obvious that these given structures can constitute boundaries, but quite often we cling to the certitudes and facilitations which they offer us. We fear that to abandon them would jeopardize our functional potential. Nevertheless, we reduce through this our capacity of facing the unexpected and risk being helpless in confronting eventualities. Our certainties constitute at the same time our limitations. For the hobbyist, however, the unexpected can be a promise.

The unexpected will always be unreal, yet, its importance for our experience can hardly be overestimated. Its promises sustain us, perhaps more than its threats frighten us. A good number of us define our "real self" through what we aspire to be more than what we really are; and in what we are we sometimes appreciate most the feeling of being capable of profiting through the unexpected or fortifying ourselves against it. Therefore, our actual reality will necessarily be coloured by its future potential—one will see in it expectations, warnings or threats; according to current situations and actions, this "future variance" of the present can of course vary, but it will always carry with it an indetermination which will make it sometimes attractive, even exciting, sometimes threatening. Here we discover the analogy with the hobbyist, who thus sees himself promoted to the role of a metaphor. Despite our "tempocentrism" (Textor, 1980) which binds us to the present, we perceive ourselves, like the hobbyist, confronted by an open future; like him we dispose of handy resources of which we will not know the specific use except at the given moment, and like him we organise our reality in a way to feel capable of mastering the circumstances, whether they are desired or dreaded.

The partial indetermination of our world is thus just as important in forming our self as are the contents of which we feel sure.

The Metaphoric Reality

The examples discussed enable us to surmise that in lived reality there is no pure factuality. A cup of tea is a cup of tea because we classify it as such, and this classification implies material properties which already in themselves go beyond the simple object: the cup, being fragile, calls for care in handling it; its whiteness needs to be kept clean; its decoration is related to a life style with which other objects have to match. But the connotative network branches out much farther: the tea as a beverage, the tea hour as a social institution imply customs and values tied into a complex of varied actions, collective as well as individual.

The meaning of an object thus contains what it implies and to what it refers. But we forget too easily that an object equally implies what *it is not*. Although we consider this very seldom, in principle every situation A implies non-A. The circle, the exemplary round object, obviously represents other round and curved objects; but as a circle, it must be able to be contrasted with forms which are angular, and thus on principle it will symbolize also the square or the cube. The flag of our country draws its value from those of other countries—in the last analysis, each given of experience has become what it is in differing from other givens, which, therefore, it implies too. Freud understood this very well, when in "The Interpretation of Dreams," he showed that the contents of a dream can always signify both itself and its opposite; but what is true for a dream is valid for lived reality in general. Because of this fact, the "alterity," these various alternatives to lived reality, constantly affect our subjective reality—from the menu not chosen at a restaurant or from unfulfilled dreams to a dreaded failure which even taints our triumphs of success.

The example of the hobbyist has taught us another aspect. Action envisages aims, which are events of the future, and thus carry uncertainties. Consequently, succeeding in an action not only constitutes a factual success, but also a functional triumph. In a world where every thing would have its place and its significance clearly established, man might feel himself secure. But for the hobbyist, the significance of an object is not fixed, and this indetermination makes his reality more interesting, more stimulating, sometimes even constituting a challenge. To the indetermination of the future he opposes his functional potential, and thereby he gains not only a measure of freedom, but also a reduction of anxiety. For other individuals, as we have seen, indetermination threatens established order. It renders insecure, hence the temptation of firm and precise structures, the tendency to transform indetermination into a specific project; scholars with their methodical or theoretical inflexibility are only too often inclined to do this. Thus indetermination implies its own symbolism: freedom and threat versus order and protection; it therefore relates to a particular functional skill.

Freud's Italian experience reveals various aspects of the symbolism of reality. It surprises him as an unintended result of an ongoing action. Thus the event signified first of all a discrepancy between his intentions and the reality encountered; it signalises therefore, as we have seen, an inadequacy of his action potential. Freud's reaction, spontaneous and unreflective, is to flee the disagreeable situation. We all appraise syncretically the valences of a situation, and we react to it impulsively, without a rational analysis. We have tried to understand the dynamics of Freud's behaviour, and we find it plausible that a person engaged in an action of complex and progressively changing connotations, can be conscious of them only incompletely. The frequent unconsciousness of symbolism thus results from the fact that consciousness necessarily has to orient itself towards the reality of the action situation (Boesch, 1980, 1991)

Indeed, the function of consciousness is principally to structure and control the aspects important for the ongoing or projected actions. Furthermore—we forget this too easily—consciousness of components of action reality is often limited to the mood induced by the situation (remember the "levels of consciousness" described by Pierre Janet). In his Italian episode, Freud experienced it as a "disquieting strangeness"; I have suggested that he did come closer to a more rational comprehension of its polyvalent significance only through the analysis of Hoffmann's tale —thus sheltered, one may say, from the concrete situation. This obviously is not the rule: except for special reasons, we hardly dwell on the meaning of past actions.

One last point of rather practical importance. Freud, as we have just seen, tied his Italian experience in with a story to which he applied his concepts of "compulsion of repetition," "Oedipus complex," "fear of castration." This is a "reductive" interpretation: it reduces, in effect, the experience of a new situation to a past dynamism. Our own reflections would tend to show, however, that such an interpretation would be neither complete nor sufficient for understanding a behaviour. Our perception of reality operates by continuous structure formations, which, dependent upon our action projects, also transform the memory and the significance of past experience. The symbolism of "lived reality" should therefore be understood as implicating an individual oriented towards his aims. It will certainly remain important to understand the origin of a behaviour in early childhood; to understand its prospective function in relation with— current as well as anticipated—realities is not less important.

Let us accept therefore in general that lived reality always contains both denotative, or "objective" valences, and connotative, or "subjective" ones (there exist, of course, also collective connotations, but in this context, we can ignore them; see Boesch, 1991). Denotations as well as connotations always refer to other realities by analogy or contrast, realities which, be they situational or imaginary, always have a double, material and functional, aspect. These multiple implications constitute the metaphoric dimension of lived reality. What then, it remains for us to ask, is the function of these symbolizations?

The metaphor of language signifies something different from what has been said; the metaphor of reality refers beyond of what is actually experienced. The polyvalence of a symbol thus establishes relationships: It fulfils the function of integrating different domains of experience. These relationships will always be both cognitive and metaphoric. The cognitive structures are analytical; they divide reality into specific categories and regroup them into rational systems at the expense of subjective experience; the metaphoric structuring on the other hand ties together, establishes relationships among subjective experiences, sometimes going so far as to contaminate them. If, in contemplating the play of light on a calm surface of water, I suddenly think of the springtime song of blackbirds, my emotional sensibility unites both in a connection which, far from being denotative, links qualities which affect me in an analogue fashion. Such processes, as we guess, are of primordial importance for the formation of symbols, but at the same time they blur the essential differences between distinct realities. Analysis and integration are therefore both indispensable, they have to complement and control each other in order to understand our world—and ourselves.

I had emphasized at the beginning of this expose that our experience of reality is always at the same time factual and symbolic. Nonetheless, the proposition of an omnipresent symbolism tends to raise objections. Certainly, one will say, we can associate everything to everything, and in doing this discover that everything is linked. This is by no means revolutionary—nothing in our world is independent. But this is only a question of systemic interdependences, rationally definable and accessible to empiric control. The concepts of symbol or metaphor will tend to confuse rather than to clarify.

I fear that literature on the symbol, for example in psychoanalysis, in ethnology and in linguistics, has spread an opinion difficult to erase: that there exist objects which have the special quality of being symbols, in contrast to the "objective," non-symbolic reality. What one is calling "symbols" there corresponds in general instead to "signs" with a socially shared meaning; these would be more correctly designated by terms such as emblems, icons or allegories. In our context, on the other hand, the term symbol is essentially applied to the subjective polyvalence of experience, distinct from rational relationships by the fact that it creates "amalgams" of valences which orient and regulate action. If a rose were nothing but a rose, as some sceptics like to say, and the dog in a dream nothing but a dog, as Medard Boss (1971) believed, our reality would not only be impoverished but we would get lost in it. The rose is a rose only in relation to realities which are analoguous and different at the same time; and it becomes "my" rose, the one which delights me or pricks me, through the place that it occupies in a personal network of actions. Certainly, we group together the contents of our world in conceptual systems of classification and of causality; the symbolic quality of objects, of persons and of situations, on the other hand, links them in constellations of attachments and aversions which regulate the direction and the intensity of our actions. Conceptual systems remain sterile—men die for ideas, not for theories. It is the metaphors incorporated in our reality that "affect" us, that stimulate us, and that, in the last analysis, form the basis of our personal identity.

NOTES

1. Translated from, La réalité comme métaphore » in *Métaphore et représentation*, Journal de la psychanalyse de l'enfant 15, 1994. Edition Bayard, Paris.
2. "avoir du pain sur la plache"—a French saying.
3. the French term "bricoleur"—corresponding to the German "Bastler"—seems to have no equivalent in English. The term "hobbyist" appears to be the closest we could find. But we will occasionally also use the French term "bricoleur."

BIBLIOGRAPHIE

Bachelard, G. (1949). *La psychanalyse du feu,* Paris: Gallimard.

Bachelard G. (1957). *La poétique de l'espace,* Paris: Presses Universitaires de France.

Boesch, E. E. (1976). *Psychopathologie des Alltags,* Bern: Huber.

Boesch, E. E. (1980). *Kultur und Handlung,* Bern: Huber.

Boesch, E. E. (1981). Möglichkeiten und Grenzen psychotherapeutischen Handelns. In: Minsel + Scheller (Ed.), *Brennpunkte der klinischen Psychologie,* München: Kösel.

Boesch, E. E. (1983). *Das Magische und das Schöne,* Stuttgart: Fromann-Holzboog.

Boesch, E. E. (1991). *Symbolic action theory and cultural psychology,* Heidelberg: Springer.

Boss, M. (1971), *Grundriss der Medizin.* Bern: Huber.

Douglas, M. (1966). *Purity and danger An analysis of the concepts of pollution and taboo,* London: ARK Paperbacks.

Douglas, M. (1970). *Natural symbols. Explorations in* cosmology, London, Barrie and Jenkins.

Duneton, C. (1978). *La puce à l'oreille.* Paris: Stock.

Filipetti, H., et Trotereau, J. (1978). *Symboles et pratiques rituelles dans la maison paysanne traditionnelle.* Paris: Berger-Levrault.

Firth, R. (1973). *Symbols, public and private,* London: Allen and Unwin.

Freud, S. (1900/1942). *Die Traumdeutung,* London: Imago Publishing.

Freud, S. (1917/1940). *Vorlesungen zur Einführung in die Psychoanalyse,* Gesammelte Werke XI, London: Imago Publishing.

Freud, S. (1919/1947). «Das Unheimlich ». In: Gesammelte Werke XII. London: Imago Publishing.

Hoffmann, E. T. A. (1817/1991). *Der Sandmann.* Stuttgart: Reclam.

Lévi-Strauss, C. (1962). *La pensge sauvage.* Paris: Plon.

Lévi-Strauss, C. (1964). *Le cru et le cuit.* Paris: Plon.

Rubin, W. (Ed.). (1984). *«Primitivism» in 20th century art,* New York: Museum of Modem Art.

Stirn F. (1987). *L'inquiétante étrangeté.* Paris: Hatier.

Textor, R. B. (1980). *A handbook an ethnographic futures research,* Stanford: Stanford University.

Weber, U. (1984). *Fenster. Zu ihrer kulturspezifischen Funktion und Bedeutung.* Diploma Thesis. Frankfurt a.M.: Institut für Kulturanthropologie.

C. THE MESSAGE THROUGH THE OTHER

INTRODUCTORY COMMENTS TO CHAPTER 11

"The Seven Flaws of Cross-Cultural Psychology: The Story of a Conversion"

The Authors

The "Seven Flaws" essay presents a case example of a "fictional" cross-cultural study that Professor Boesch used primarily to illustrate some of the major difficulties implicit in conducting cross-cultural research. Its original intent was pedagogical. However, the difficulties identified in the illustration are not fictional. They reflect the challenges Professor Boesch experienced during his career as a cross-cultural and cultural researcher. Such recognized and unrecognized barriers are often faced when psychologists are planning or engaging in research about cultures other than their own. Often, the less familiar the researcher is with the host culture, the more difficult it may be to conduct meaningful and valid research.

Taking the perspective of the research director who is a clinical psychologist, the study is described as strategically planned and supported by

Discovering Cultural Psychology: A Profile and Selected Readings of
Ernest E. Boesch, pp. 241–245
Copyright © 2007 by Information Age Publishing
241

grant funds. The investigator who directed the study wanted to learn more about possible interactions between the occurrence of depressive symptoms and the level and kind of social support available to those who experience depressive symptoms. Like most well constructed cross-cultural research, the investigators hoped that the results would make a significant contribution to the literature. Social support was identified as the independent variable and was studied in three cultures where the levels of support ranged from low, to medium, and high. The three cultures were carefully selected after the researcher carefully reviewed anthropological reports. The survey, selected as a measure depressive symptoms, was one that had been validated through previous usage. The researcher adapted the instrument to render it "culture free" or at least as "culturally-sensitive" as possible. This included the careful use of translations and back-translations that were completed by university students who were native speakers of the three languages commonly used in each of the three cultures studied.

RESEARCH METHODOLOGY

The research director collaborated with psychology faculties at universities in the host cultures to identify advanced graduate students who could understand the nature of the project and could be trained to effectively administer the surveys. After the research assistants were selected, they traveled to the director's university and participated in a training session to prepare them for the many challenges of conducting field-based research. All who reviewed the research plan agreed that it was carefully constructed and deserving of support. Indications that there were problems with the study arose only when the research director began examining results from one of the three cultures studied. There were inconsistencies in the data that indicated something had gone wrong. The principle director called for a complete review of the data collection and reporting methods used by the two research assistants.

When the graduate students' methods were reviewed in detail, the director discovered one assistant deviated from the sampling procedures that were specified in the training session. Rather than taking the extra time and trouble needed to reach remote villages and towns to gather data from the residents, one assistant chose to sample a population that was easier to reach and where the education level of the subjects was higher than that of the remote villagers. In contrast, the other research assistant had followed procedures and sampling methods exactly as specified by the project director. This variation led to the discovery of other complications.

When the research assistants were asked to discuss in detail the methods used to carry out the study, more questionable practices became evident. This raised questions about the reliability and validity of all the data reported. The innovative assistant who used impromptu techniques had a manner of interacting with the director and colleague that resulted in concerns about how the subjects who were interviewed in the field felt about answering many personal questions included in the study. The temperament and personality of the two graduate assistants were strikingly different, one being very respectful and patient, the other being rather aggressive and curt. These differences in communication styles and interpersonal traits were obvious. How could this not have influenced the responses of subjects included in the study? The more the director probed into the field experiences of the two assistants, the more obvious it became that previously undetected problems existed with the translation and interpretation of the instrument. There were clear variations in the word usage of the "subjects" in their typical speech and that of the researchers when asking questions. The director was concerned about subjects' willingness to respond honestly or fully to the researcher's questions about personal behavior when experiencing emotionally charged situations. Furthermore, greater differences emerged within the cultures as more pertinent factors were uncovered.

Defining Terms: Depression

When reevaluating the research questions, the director was forced to wonder to what degree the concept of "depression" was commonly defined between and within the cultures. Could family relationships and communication patterns influence whether certain behaviors were considered "depressed" or "normal emotional coping?" Could different emotional states of an individual person vary in response to life changes such as: sources of enjoyment in daily social interactions; sources of discomfort due to fluctuations in health conditions; sources of concern due to difficult economic conditions; sources of self-satisfaction or dissatisfaction due to various levels of self-efficacy? The more carefully the researcher thought about how subjects' language interpretation might vary, the more caution was used about the validity of the data.

Selecting Samples Across Cultures

In essence, rather than accepting the original research question and design as workable for a cross-cultural study, the research director found that identifying representative samples was extremely complicated. As cultures were studied, it became evident that they were constantly evolving. Those who "belong to a culture" usually have many unique and distinctive values and beliefs that are not widely shared with others in the same cultural group. When research personnel were sought to interview subjects, their personality traits and communication skills interacted strikingly with the statements or responses of the persons being studied. Whether a particular researcher might be perceived as non-intrusive or non-threatening is difficult to assess. However, subjects' reactions to the researcher influenced the quality and quantity of information they conveyed. In fact, in every respect, research projects that are cross-cultural or cultural in nature are very complex and require great care in planning and execution.

Summary

In summary, the main cautions Professor Boesch offered were: culture(s) cannot be considered as an "independent variable"; representative and comparable samples are difficult if not impossible to obtain; the language used and meanings assigned to research instruments is not equivalent; no two researchers behave in the same ways with subjects, nor are they regarded alike by all the subjects. No research problems or questions are interpreted in the same way by people from different cultures. When participating in psychological studies, research subjects are not able to respond as though they are held constant or are isolated from many of the influences and conditions in their lives. Before conducting a study cross-culturally, Professor Boesch recommended that the study first be conducted within one identified culture as a test of its workability.

Professor Boesch also identified philosophical concerns about the right of psychologists to enter into the personal lives of their subjects. Respect for and awareness of the feelings and needs of others requires that the psychologist honor the integrity of their subjects rather than merely gathering and manipulating information as if it were impersonal data. In Professor Boesch's words, a summary caution was offered: "We (researchers) may claim the right to treat human beings simply as units for our measurements by pretending that our research serves the good of mankind in general- but is this honest and true? Or do we delude ourselves believing wrongly in the cultural validity of our findings, and even worse—refusing to be aware of the conceit, or voyeurism, or power lust, or egocentric intellectual ambition in what we do?" (Boesch, 1996, p. 9). Given that all people are members of at least one cultural group, all human psychological investigations are necessarily affected by the cultures of the researcher and their subjects. Note that Professor Boesch said this story "might appear to be a plea for cultural and against cross-cultural psychology." He asserted that this is only partly the case. Each of these traditions is needed. However, Boesch argued that a good cross-cultural study has to be complemented, and we (Lonner & Hayes) suggest preceded by cultural investigation.

CHAPTER 11

THE SEVEN FLAWS OF CROSS-CULTURAL PSYCHOLOLOGY

The Story of a Conversion

Ernest E. Boesch

The following expands on an example that W. J. Lonner, in the not yet published draft of a chapter, used for illustrating the method of cross-cultural psychology, and which I take the freedom to elaborate here. It is therefore an entirely fictional story, but all it says is based on personal experience. One could call it, then, a true fiction.

This is the story of a clinical psychologist who got interested in the relation between depression and social support and decided to study it cross-culturally. Let me call her Jane. Her idea was to take social support as an independent variable, and to operationalize it by three cultures, one highly supportive, the second with moderate social support, and the third with low support structures. She took care to select these cultures conscientiously on the basis of anthropological reports, and she adapted an already proven questionnaire on depressive tendencies in order to make it "culture-free." She then had it translated and back-translated by students

Discovering Cultural Psychology: A Profile and Selected Readings of
Ernest E. Boesch, pp. 247–258

in her university who were natives of the chosen cultures, and with the help of psychology departments in those countries she found local researchers who appeared to be competent enough for her project. She had them come to her university in order to instruct them in the use of the questionnaire and the rationale of her project. It looked to her a neat and carefully prepared research design, and so it did to others, because she had no trouble finding the required funds. Yet, when the results came in, she found the data sent by the two researchers from Culture 3 to be inconsistent, and, her sabbatical year approaching, she decided to go and look for herself.

She was met at the airport by a young, apparently shy woman and a freely talking man who visibly tried to impress her. Both seemed to be in or close to their early thirties. The woman introduced herself as Sarah, the man as Arun. He had, as she learned quickly, studied at Stanford, while Sarah was a graduate of the local university at which they both worked. They drove her to the university to meet their boss, the head of the department, a graying and jovial man, who declared himself glad to help by "lending" his two assistants to her project, but seemed not very much interested in it's details.

After quickly refreshing herself at the hotel, Jane was eager to set down to work and asked her young colleagues about their experiences so far. Arun said that all had gone according to plan, and he had not encountered any problems; his subjects were willing to respond and had apparently had no difficulty in answering the questionnaire. Sarah seemed to feel less confident, saying that she was probably not as experienced as her colleague, but, besides problems in reaching the villages that were included in her sample, she had found the subjects often unwilling or embarrassed by the questions. Jane, wondering about this difference, asked them how they had established their samples. It appeared that, as had been initially agreed, they had constituted a representative sample by applying a space sampling technique, both for the different quarters of the capital and for villages in the country. Sarah had adhered to it conscientiously, in spite of the almost unpassable roads in the rainy season that had made it difficult to reach some of the villages. Furthermore, the subjects included in the random sample of the village populations were often difficult to locate or unwilling to respond. Arun, questioned again, admitted a bit too confidently that, anticipating this problem, he had allowed himself to "correct" his sample and had excluded villages of difficult access. In the capital, he had similarly avoided the ill-famed quarters. And finally, it also turned out that, since the farmers in the villages were often illiterate and away in their fields during the day time, he had also concentrated his interviews more heavily on teachers, local officials, and merchants.

Jane despaired. Here were two incomparable sets of data and she said so. Sarah seemed quite contrite, although she had done nothing wrong, while Arun volubly explained that the social structure of the villages and town areas he had visited was quite comparable to the ones he had excluded; and after all, he added, the propensity towards depression that Jane wanted to study was more likely to occur among his interviewees than among the farmers who were too busy and too uneducated anyway to feel depressed. Jane began to sense that this man, besides being somewhat lighthanded in his methodology, also had a way of dealing with people quite different from that of the woman. She remembered a basic requirement of scientific measurement: the way of applying instruments of measurement had to be strictly constant. But how to control that? Here were two different personalities and temperaments, perhaps also different conceptions of psychology—what should she do?

She tried to insist: The sampling procedure selected, she said, had to be obligatory, and the research steps should adhere to it, in spite of difficulties. Sarah looked embarrassed, and Arun remained silent for a moment. Then he asked, hesitatingly but also a bit rebellious: "You want to draw a representative sample—representative of whom? Of the women, the men, the different ages, the different levels of education or of income, of the different regions of the country, the different occupations and religions? A truly representative sample should be stratified, and how could we two manage that?" Jane countered: "I want to know the average incidence of depression, and not the one among fishermen or taxi-drivers." But Arun did not give up; "This would only weaken your correlations." Jane looked puzzled:

"Why?" "Because," he answered, "there are high and low risk groups in our country, people more prone to depression than others, but if the sample includes them all, trends will be masked." Jane countered: "All anthropological reports agree that your society is loosely structured throughout, meaning that social coercion as well as support are generally low; therefore, the relationship between depression and social support should materialize in a representative sample." Arun laughed: "Loosely structured"— the term was coined by Myer-Johnes some 40 years ago, who had stayed here for about three to four months, and didn't even know the language. But, he was an influential professor, so every following anthropologist quoted him approvingly. Probably, they were even being honest—the views of an influential man are likely to influence your own perception. But this is just one of these anthropological myths: we may be loose where you expect stringent structures, and stringent where you don't suppose it. Look at the school children kneeling in front of their teacher, to the students who would never dare to contradict a professor, or to the power of the elders over their juniors. No, unequal support structures exist here as elsewhere, but perhaps they are different," "And by the way," he added, "if our society were as homogeneous as you seem to believe, any sample would do; it would not need to be representative."

Jane, a bit shaken, changed the topic. Turning to Sarah, she asked her to explain what kind of difficulties her subjects had in understanding the questionnaire. "Well," Sarah said hesitatingly, "the wording of the questionnaires was, of course, correct, but it was the language of educated town people rather than of the villagers. And, the phrasing sounded stiff, a bit like the language of forms the villagers occasionally had to fill out at the local administration, which tended to make them apprehensive." Often, too, she continued, "they were suspicious of her intentions in other ways. Although she tried her best at being friendly, she, of course, remained a stranger to the village, unmistakably a town person, and so they either associated her with some government institution or suspected some other hidden purpose. She gave examples, which Jane, being unfamiliar with the world of these villages, could of course not appreciate. Arun, however, contradicted: his subjects had understood quite well and cooperated willingly. There ensued a discussion in their native tongue between the two, and from occasional English terms Jane guessed that it was about the translation—they seemed to disagree quite strongly. She asked for an explanation.

The discussion seemed to turn around two linguistic formulations: One, Sarah contended, she could not, as a younger female, use with older people, not even in the village; the other, about feeling tired in the morning—a depressive symptom in Jane's mind—in some regions had an awkward double meaning. Jane did not pursue the question, feeling entirely incompetent, but again she thought of a basic tenet in her science: that tools for measuring had to be adequate to the reality measured. In this short discussion, she had already encountered four problems that could all explain the oddness of the data sent to her: The personal style of the interviewers, the inadequacy of representative sampling, the quality of the questionnaire, and the fact that the assumed low intensity of the independent variable appeared to apply unevenly to this culture. This was not to mention the practical difficulties in trying to adhere to the established sample. She would have to reconsider all that carefully.

At the end of the afternoon Arun wanted to go back to his family. Jane asked Sarah, who was single, to show her to a restaurant and invited her to join her for dinner. Being alone with the young woman, who had remained rather shy during the earlier discussion, Jane raised again the question of the interview problems Sarah had mentioned, wondering again how to explain that Arun had apparently encountered none of them. Sarah seemed to hesitate. "Well," she said somewhat reluctantly, "he is a very competent and well trained psychologist, but a bit too academic. He is a town man, not used to dealing with the simple village folks, and easily intimidates them by his manner. Furthermore, as he had told you, he has avoided all the difficult sections included in the sample and interviewed mostly persons with some education—while a considerable proportion of the villagers are illiterate. Even for many of those who had some years of primary school; irregular school attendance, and subsequent lack of practice, made them forget most of the acquired skills." "And, of course," she continued, "after long and difficult journeys to the outlying villages, where in addition I often had to spend much time locating the houses of my subjects, I, myself, was tired and might not always have been a stimulating guest to the farmers after their hard day."

"I really do sympathize with your troubles and am grateful for your efforts," said Jane. "But as to the questionnaires, I still do not understand the difficulties. They are worded very simply, and the questions relate to easy experiences, like sleeping, feeling tired, having bad dreams, or being afraid of the future," "It is not simply that," replied Sarah. "You see, when they come back from their fields, they are tired and yet still have to attend to household affairs. They accept reluctantly, out of politeness and also partly fear, to be interviewed, but I am a stranger and they don't understand what my curiosity means. I tried of course to explain my purpose, but it relates to problems which either are not their concern, or on the contrary, worry them too much to talk about; because in our culture, voicing your worries openly threatens to awake malevolent spirits. In this situation, I had only two options: either to apply your questionnaire faithfully, or try to make them talk freely about the problems it addresses. The first is anti-cultural: only government censors would approach them with such a request, and since it probes into very personal experiences, it makes the respondents the more suspicious. The second is unusual, too, but once I have overcome their reticence, it is difficult to keep them on track. Furthermore, you can gain the confidence of the interviewee only by also telling about yourself, your background, your life-situation. In our culture, a relationship between two persons can be established only by showing trust, and that implies being open about oneself—at least to some extent. In doing so, however, I cannot avoid the risk of steering the responses of the interviewee, and if he or she trusts you, the interview may indeed wander far astray; if not, the answers will remain cautious, monosyllabic, and in all likelihood will not be honest.

There is another problem: The items in your questionnaire. You tried, of course, to operationalize them: Do you sleep well? Do you often wake up tired? Do you have bad dreams? Do you often worry? About what? and so on. The villagers, of course, soon start wondering—why should a stranger want to know such private things? Speaking about them abstractly is not without problems: villagers do not tend towards abstract self-scrutiny. If they are worried, it is about something. One is tired for a reason. One is not afraid unless of a thing or an event that has to be feared. And, as I just said, speaking about it may increase the danger of the threat becoming real. And don't forget, that the answers you collect may depend upon circumstances: of course, one often sleeps badly—during the hot season or during thunderstorms. Of course, one wakes up tired in the morning, because the day before one worked hard in the fields. One is of course worried when the rains fail to come, or when the rice in the barn will not last until the new harvest. Thus, you will get different answers in different seasons, and they will always sound reasonable. You will have to decide when a fear of snakes is justified, when it turns to over-caution, and when it becomes phobic. How will you decide that without knowing the specific circumstances of the respondent? People in town will only rarely be afraid of a fire in the house, so such a fear might have a symptomatic value; but for many villagers this is a constant and real concern—use, and on the help they could expect if needed. How then would you rate the answer? I talked to a psychiatrist in the university clinic. He told me that depression in your sense is rare here; most cases of depression are what you would call "somatized." So you would need a different diagnosis, you would have to know about the forms of somatization and to be able to ask about the corresponding worries, but nobody would answer honestly unless they believed you to be a doctor. All these are difficulties I have encountered. If the respondents were well acquainted with me, I might perhaps obtain, valid answers, but scarcely as a stranger, or as a young woman. And without more intimate knowledge, it remains often impossible to tell an honest answer from one intending to please me or to get rid of me."

Sarah had become quite involved and loquacious. Jane felt bewildered. Her careful structure of an independent variable, of a representative sample, of a well constructed questionnaire, and faithful data gathering by her researchers tumbled down. She could not console herself by invoking the error variance to be separated from the true one: the errors appeared too manifold—and could even hide important information. The thought struck her, that the data from the two other cultures might simply look more consistent because in each of them she had employed only one researcher—and what, if in one culture there worked another Sarah, and in the second another Arun? How could she possibly check that?

How, with all these obstacles, could her project be saved? If Sarah was right, she would, at any rate, have to abandon the idea of culture being an independent variable of sufficient homogeneity. But, could she not then use the variations within the culture for a new design, still pursuing the same question? Of course, she would not have needed to come here for studying that, studying variations within one culture could as easily have been done at home; yet, the support structures in this country might be different, and so it would still be worth the attempt.

So when she met the two again, she said to Arun: "I think that what you told me yesterday makes a lot of sense. If the society in your country is not homogeneously loose, so that we would have to accept the existence of different supportive structures, could we then specify groups with high, moderate, and low support and study the incidence of depression within their areas of influence? How would you define them?" He looked at her quizzically and said, "Well, it depends on what you want. There are, for instance, the royals and the nobles who stick together and the political parties who support their adherents. In the up-country market places there are the merchants, the administrative officials and the farmers who constitute groups of mutual support. The monks in the temples and the lay community form other ones. In the clustered villages you often find close neighborhood ties, less so in scattered settlements. But the kinds of support are different. Farmers support each other in harvesting and house building, the laymen support the monks through food and offerings, while these give them spiritual and ritual support. Each person of standing has a "clientele," a circle of followers who provide as well as receive support, although in various ways. In a family, the eldest daughter has to support her younger siblings, while the youngest daughter will, once grown up, have to support her aging parents. Most of this may be predominantly material assistance; psychological support is much more difficult to assess. It may come from different groups, like age groups, both for boys and girls, while the older ones find it in ritual and the temple. It may be offered very subtly, just by tightening a bit the circle of friends around a distressed person, or by providing distraction from worries."

"I know," Arun went on, "that you are interested in the kind of support which helps a person not to fall into depression. I understand depression to be a state of extreme self-depreciation. So, in fact, everything which improves self-valuation can have an antidepressive effect. It can be falling in love, bragging to friends, common drinking, gambling or whoring— the many ways of escaping into various enjoyments, which our culture looks down upon less than yours. You see, doctors find depressive syndromes to be relatively frequent among monks, in spite of their tightly knit mutual social support. I think that this is so because they have to abandon all these self-supporting escape behaviors. So, which kind of support do you want to study?"

Jane felt bewildered. She tried to grope for firm ground, and so said: "What about taking a couple of clustered and scattered villages for comparison, and some temple groups, and contrasting them with non-temple-goers?" "That," Arun answered, "would, at any rate, be better than a representative sample. But you would have to consider co-variances. The non-temple-goers would tend to be younger and better educated than the temple folks and would probably also be engaged in other kinds of work. Furthermore, people belong to temple groups for very different reasons, by far not always spiritual. The scattered villages tend to be predominantly rice-growing, while the clustered ones have not only a high proportion of political, military, clerical, and commercial inhabitants, but would also have better roads, which means more goods, television, newspapers, occasions for having fun, more money and better medical services. So support structures would have to be considered within those frameworks, and these, furthermore, would not necessarily be internally homogeneous. For instance, within the same clustered settlement, in the areas where the farmers live you would find close neighborship with mutual help in child care and household chores. This would be much less so in the merchants' and government officials' quarters. So you would have to look closely and with discrimination at the diverse social and material constellations."

Jane turned to Sarah, who had remained silent: 'What do you think?" She answered: "Well, of course I agree. But it brings up many problems. First, a problem of sampling: We could not simply go into the villages and pick out randomly selected subjects, because the interaction of one person with others would force us to include informants who were not on our sampling list—you would necessarily have to consider person clusters. Second, a problem of measurement: You cannot find out about the various forms of social support a person receives or gives by applying a standardized questionnaire—I have already told you why. If you want to collect valid and sufficiently significant information, you would have to understand the network of a person's life, which would imply participating to some extent in his or her everyday affairs, as well as knowing about his or her biography. Third, a problem of design: to proceed in this way would make it impossible to compare our findings with those in the two other cultures you have selected. And, fourth, a problem of personnel: it is difficult to find qualified researchers willing to stay in the villages for a sufficiently long time to obtain valid information. For instance, even if I were willing, I would not be able to free myself from the work of this institute. So, I feel a bit at a loss."

And so did Jane. But she decided at least to explore the option. So they discussed ways of sampling clustered and scattered villages and decided that it would be advisable to omit outlying parts of the country because of different dialects and customs. Not wanting to exclude the urban population from the project, they pondered how to establish an analogous distinction between clustered and scattered groups in the town. Arun suggested contrasting members of associations, clubs and political circles with non-organized people, or, as even closer analogies, suburban street neighborhoods to city blocks, or temple congregations to non-temple-goers. Although this remained no more than brainstorming, it looked as if a way could be found. But as to organizing the investigation itself, the data gathering, they groped in the dark. It would be hard to find researchers to live in the villages, and if one did, they would be much more familiar with their samples than would be possible in the town—how then to maintain comparability? So the discussion remained inconclusive, producing interesting yet not sufficiently convincing ideas.

Going back to her hotel, Jane felt uneasy. She dined alone and for companionship she picked up a book that an anthropologist friend had recommended. She remembered his promise that it would "help her find the right questions." It was about action symbolism, and the author seemed quite obsessed with the idea of considering everything as an action. Even dreams, he said, could, and in psychotherapy, should be looked at as actions. She thought, could depression, too, be considered as an action? In fact depression was rather a refusal to act; in the extreme, an absolute, unconditional and general refusal. An action against action, she thought with some amusement. What could that mean? People renounce action when either the goal seems inaccessible, or when they lack the means to reach it—which, after all, amounts to the same. This occurs all the time, and is, of course, not yet depression—irritation, yes, perhaps anger or sadness, but not more. It is the *generalized* refusal to act that constitutes depression—but what explains this generalization? Most people lead hard lives, are continuously unable to reach their goals, and yet, most of the time are not pathologically depressed. Depression, she felt, must relate to the basic goals of an individual, those that constitute his self-worth or the sense of his life. What could those be? She found no answer, but felt that she had touched upon an important problem. And, it shed a new light on her initial hypothesis of support. There were, she knew, wives of caring husbands, children of loving parents who fell into depression, while many sufferers and deprived people did not. Support, she thought, may be a factor, but not the determining one—even more, she suddenly thought, what counted was not the objective, the observable support, but the support perceived by the subject. Stress (she remembered a famous psychologist of her country) is in the eye of the beholder. So would be consolation and support. Thus, instead of specifying in advance a causal link between two amorphous variables, it would be more important to find out what kinds of experiences induced an individual to "strip" his relevant goals of their valences. Of their positive valences, she added in thought, Could it perhaps be that in depression all goal representations of an individual became negatively loaded, replacing hope with apprehension? This, of course, would have to be researched.

But then, would it still make sense to sample villages according to pre-sumed support structures and correlate them with a construct of "depres-sive tendencies"—whatever, in fact, that might be? It appeared to be much more rational to study depressive and non-depressive individuals in their daily environment and find out reasons that might have led to gen-eralized goal devaluation.

How to do it? She thought of asking doctors about where to find patients, but, even if they would provide such information, she could not simply go to the homes of these persons and start interviewing them. Moreover, there were depressive individuals who did not consult a doctor, or who consulted him for apparently physical complaints. Thus, the patients a doctor declared to be depressive represented a potentially biased selection of persons. Priests might be another source of informa-tion, but they would probably be even less willing to divulge names than doctors. To select depressive and nondepressive individuals by question-naires appeared to be unfeasible, not only because of the language prob-lems Sarah had pointed out, but because the validity of the results would first have to be established for this culture, which would have implied finding depressive people by other means—but which ones?

Then came the thought that depressive persons would betray their state of mind by the range of their actions. They would move around less, engage in less activities, show less interest in events around them, avoid situations which might be too loud, or too animated, require initiative, or appear threatening. Looking at that, she might of course miss those who covered a latent depression by "escape-actions," but that problem might be faced at a later stage. Yes, she thought, it could be done: station a researcher in a village, let him become familiar with its inhabitants, learn about their ways of life, observe the activities of the individuals, get acquainted with some two or three knowledgeable informants, pick out some individuals on the active and on the passive side of behavior, and start taking their life histories, draw their circle of activities, of interests, of fears and of future expectations. Particular supporting and discourag-ing events and circumstances should certainly emerge in this way, and she would ultimately be able to pinpoint cultural factors contributing to depression, or helping to avoid it. Which, she began to feel now, would be much more meaningful than what she could gather with a conventional experimental design.

But how to proceed? For a moment she felt tempted to try it herself, to learn the language and then stay in a village herself. But, of course, her sabbatical leave would be too short for that, and she suddenly got struck by the presumption hidden in the idea: Is it a colonial left-over that makes us think we can go any place in the world, and, as strangers, ask unknown individuals about their private affairs? How would she react to a psychologist from Zaire who in halting English would request an interview and ask her about her sleep and dreams and future anticipations?

No, she decided, she would stay here during her leave and intensively train some two or four people in observing, interviewing and theoretical understanding, and then assign them to a village; she would at the same time do her best to learn the language, and she would later try to stay with each of them for one or two months, a guest and quiet observer, and as an alien she might be struck with aspects the native world would overlook, and thus she would be helpful to her helpers.

She realized that in a few days she had gone a long way, leaving behind the illusionary belief in representative samples, in culture as an independent variable, in culture-free interview techniques and irrelevance of the personality of the interviewers. She would, of course, have to face resistance in her academic community, and she might have to try hard to gather the research money. But, she felt confident that somehow she could find a way.

Well, so far goes the story. It might appear to be a plea for cultural and against cross-cultural psychology. This is only partly so. The relationship between cultural and cross-cultural psychology is not one of either-or, one of simply choosing to be the one or the other, because, at their appropriate place, each is needed. But, we should be aware of their respective functions and qualities. And in this sense, our Jane experienced some basic flaws of the cross-cultural approach. The main one she discovered, is the status of culture as an independent variable. The second is the implausibility of finding representative or simply strictly comparable samples. The third is the problem of equivalent meanings in our measurement instruments. The fourth is the idiosyncrasy—personal and cultural—of investigators. The fifth is the culture-specificity of our research problems. And, the sixth is the assumption that persons can be considered simply as subjects, i.e., as providers of the type of information required by our "design." Having become aware of these flaws, she concluded that cross cultural psychology had to be complemented by cultural investigation. In other words, the validity of findings in the first has to be established by intra-cultural research. The inverse is true, too, but to a lesser extent; cross-cultural psychology cannot establish, validity, but can control the generality of cultural findings. And so Jane decided that the cultural investigation had, of necessity, to precede the comparative one.

Jane also felt rather intuitively that there was a more basic flaw of an almost philosophical nature—or should she call it a sin? It had come to her in the words "left-over from the colonial past" and "presumption." She sensed that psychological research—and particularly psychological research in a foreign culture—is not a matter of "measurement," but of personal interactions, which requires much sensitivity and modesty, an honest effort to enter the world of experience of other "subjects"—a term which she began to dislike. Were they "subjects"? Did they not have the right to as much dignity as we expect for ourselves? We may claim the right to treat human beings simply as units for our measurements by pretending that our research serves the good of mankind in general—but is this honest and true? Or do we delude ourselves, believing wrongly in the cultural validity of our findings, and—even worse—refusing to be aware of the conceit, or voyeurism, or power lust, or egocentric intellectual ambition in what we do?

Jane remembered the belief of the philosopher Kant, who argued that "man should always be a goal, and not a means." We tend to demonstrate that people can be considered mainly as matter to be measured. They are means, but for what? For rituals required in our professional world that we cloak in an ideology of scientific progress? Without ever checking that ideology's own cultural validity? Jane, in a sense, was converted from an experimental to a "humane" psychologist.

INTRODUCTORY COMMENTS TO CHAPTER 12

"A Psychology of Concern"

The Authors

The essay offers readers Professor Boesch's reflections on the psychological study of disruptions in human life, particularly when tragedy results from human causes. Europe was torn apart by military, economic, and philosophical forces. Recalling his studies at the University of Geneva, Professor Boesch and his fellow students were intensely concerned about the atrocities of World War II. They wondered how the study of psychology might help them "save humanity" from such destruction. However, within their psychology lectures there were no discussions about war. Students and faculty examined human learning and carried out detailed research on various stages and aspects of child development.

Professor Boesch observed that when the war ended, rather than attempting to understand what caused such widespread horror, leaders and community members focused their efforts on a return to prewar normalcy. The challenges were daunting, and there was no time for reflection

Discovering Cultural Psychology: A Profile and Selected Readings of Ernest E. Boesch, pp. 259–261

when mountains of rubble stood where large cities had once thrived. Psychologists of the time became even more deeply concerned about scientific studies of human behavior. In their attempts to be methodologically precise and exact, they lost site of human life as a dynamic function of people acting in culturally shaped contexts. In effect, Professor Boesch wondered what psychologists had learned from the agonies suffered by millions.

He also raised questions as to how psychologists are currently responding to early twenty-first century human tragedies. He wondered if efforts to be scientific were adding to human insight.

PURPOSE OF PSYCHOLOGICAL STUDIES

As he approached the completion of his studies at Geneva, Jean Piaget acknowledged Ernest's promise as a researcher by offering him a position as his research assistant. This may well have led to early distinction for the young scholar who had so impressed his highly regarded and famous teacher. Somewhat surprisingly, Ernest chose to take a position as a school psychologist where he would be immersed in helping teachers, parents, and students improve their educational experiences. He wanted to learn how psychology might be applied to human concerns. This pursuit was consistent with his early motivation for choosing to study psychology.

Over his long and enriched career, Professor Boesch came to realize that the study of humankind required a cultural psychology with culture being described as: "an interwoven system within which we experience and act, which permeates in many ways our development and view of the world." Therefore, Professor Boesch considered the study of human culture to be indisputably crucial to understanding human intelligence, motivation, and action.

Parallels of Past and Present

Just as the world stood aghast over the destruction of previous wars, Professor Boesch recognized the shock and violent consequences of the 9-11 events. Those who were labeled "terrorists" after 9-11 were known to be educated, intelligent, normal people. How did these men transform? What undetected factors existed beneath the surface of their public lives? Professor Boesch focused on an aspect of their lives that most contemporary psychologists completely ignore: the meaning and depth of their faith.

The men knowingly and willingly sacrificed their lives for goals and ideals that were directly linked to their faith in the Muslim religion. In the contemporary world, few realize how or why faith can be so compelling and have such all encompassing influence. Yet, it needs to be examined with great thoughtfulness and immediacy.

Summary

While Professor Boesch did not intend to identify the meaning of faith in this essay, he did raise many important questions that are pertinent to the contemporary world. He recognized two dimensions of faith that psychologists and others may ponder. Faith implies a vision of the future that is shaped by the beliefs a person internalizes and integrates into their values and judgments. Second, faith is woven into one's culture through legends, myths, art, architecture, music. While each person experiences faith uniquely, faith is also shared through cultural rites and rituals. Finally, Professor Boesch advises that to clearly understand human behavior, no aspect of human life, such as faith, can be overlooked even though it is difficult or impossible to accurately measure.

CHAPTER 12

PSYCHOLOGY OF CONCERN

Ernest E. Boesch

When studying in Geneva, one day I met a fellow student on the way to the Institute. While walking together, I asked her why she studied psychology. She replied: To help save humanity. To our modern ears, that sounds trite and pathetic, and nowadays such an answer would, of course, be most unlikely. Yet, at that time the world around Switzerland stood in flames, young Europeans were busy killing each other and the civilization in which we had trusted lay in shambles. Therefore, the desire to help end the surrounding madness which ominously threatened our country day after day was by no means ridiculous. The naïve ardour of my companion expressed despair as much as hope, a kind of bitter obstinacy.

The psychology we looked for at that time was one of concern—you might also call it one of compassion, of involvement with real life. Yet, sitting in the fascinating lectures of Jean Piaget, we heard nothing of war and barbarity. Instead we learned about how children dealt with objects, solved problems or how, in the course of development, our emotions were transformed. For my diploma thesis I carried out painstaking experiments with children on the size of their perceptual illusions. All that was pure science—no psychology of concern.

I felt tempted, of course, when Piaget offered me a post as one of his assistants, yet I refused, choosing instead to succeed Bärbel Inhelder as a

Discovering Cultural Psychology: A Profile and Selected Readings of
Ernest E. Boesch, pp. 263–267
Copyright © 2007 by Information Age Publishing
All rights of reproduction in any form reserved.

school psychologist in my home town of St. Gall. I wanted to do practical work rather than academic research. The war still raged on, suffering and death surrounded our country. We remained concerned, helpless and yet wanting to act usefully.

But feeling concerned during the war was, in a sense, easy. It arose from the spontaneous feelings of pity and horror, as well as the continuous threat one had to face. But once this immediate threat had dissipated, concern became more difficult. It would have implied a careful scrutiny of the reasons and forms of the disaster. And so, in the chaos of post-war Europe, people felt less of an urge to understand what had happened than a desire to return to normalcy as quickly as possible, to re-establish a reasonably comfortable everyday life, to restart business, while the universities reverted to the emotional security of pure science. Psychology eagerly turned towards behaviorism as its leading ideology and the accompanying formalistic methodology—which, in a continent ravaged by probably the worst years in its history, should in fact have given rise for deep concern. But all this seemed to work well; progressively we refined our theories and methods, invented even computer programs so sophisticated that most users no longer really understand them. Yet, psychology developed and expanded to an unexpected degree, although as a pure, "aseptic" rather than a concerned science. For the considerable price, however, that psychologists tended increasingly to know their fellow humans as respondents to experiments and questionnaires rather than as real actors in a real world.

Then came the long years of apparent peace, when even wars in Korea, Vietnam or racial and religious conflicts did not disturb our more and more reassuring view of the world. Psychology became accustomed to considering human beings as basically determined and determinable, an ideology which it tended to justify either by combining behavioristic and psychoanalytic pieces of theory or by reducing human behavior to neurophysiological factors. Man as a pliant and manipulable object progressively replaced the responsible subject of action.

Voices of warning then arose, faintly at first, easy to overhear. They struck me in two newspaper items, reporting the opinion of the British physicist Stephen Hawking. Namely he said that the human genotype would need to be changed, both, on the one hand for retaining control over the advancing technical systems, and, on the other hand, in order to prepare the human species for survival in other parts of the universe, should—as he seemed to believe—our Earth turn uninhabitable.

These, as I say, were notes in a local newspaper, and I have not seen the original articles. Yet, their message appeared to me unmistakably clear: That our human intelligence ceased to be adequate for the complexities of our continually expanding world. This inadequacy, research like the one by Stanley Milgram seemed to suggest, is not simply one of cognition, but is more deeply grounded in human nature, its syncretic perception and evaluation of situations and its suggestibility. Therefore, intelligence should not be considered as an isolated function, but within the contexts—functional as well as environmental—in which it has to operate. Thus, implicitly, Hawking's thesis calls for a cultural psychology of intelligence and action. I have elsewhere explained extensively what this means, so let me stress here only that this in no way implies to add simply "culture" as an additional "independent variable" to the study of problem solving actions. "Culture" is not a single variable, but an interwoven system within which we experience and act, which permeates in many ways our development and view of the world. Should psychology (at last) realize this, it would have to reorient both its theoretical and methodological thinking quite considerably.

Hawking, as a physicist, did of course not think in this direction. But the fearsome blasts of September 11, 2001 resounded throughout the world as an unexpected demonstration of his thesis: It lay open our inadequacy to cope with an increasingly complex reality. And psychology had to face—once again—its oversimplified concept of human nature. The preceding suicide attacks in Israel had not disturbed it. Psychology was satisfied to explain them along its habitual categories, as acts performed by uneducated and economically frustrated young people, influenced by a fanatical environment. Our usual schemas of explanation—such as social modelling, role learning, discharge and displacement of aggression—seemed to fit adequately.

However, no longer. Here were people who sacrificed their lives for goals we could not understand, and who seemed to contradict our schemas of explanation. They were students, engineers, businessmen, young, intelligent people, living quite normally within Western social groups, where they had formed friendships, even love relationships. Far from any fanatical social pressure, they yet had lived for years with the silent knowledge of having, one day, to sacrifice their lives for a goal which they did not know concretely until close to the actual performance. Inconspicuously and serenely they lived in the queue for death. In a way they were like the soldier in war, yet more voluntarily and more certain of the end. They did not act in a drunken state or in a trance, nor were they drugged or hypnotized. They rather, we have to assume, strove consciously towards a goal beyond their own lives. It was not worldly happiness or success they wanted, for their lives were to them just a means to reach a goal beyond any of their experiences.

Actions are over-determined, as we should know since Freud and Lewin, although psychology never really took notice of it. Thus, the suicide attackers certainly acted from complex motives. We cannot know which different strains of motives concurred in each of those individuals. But one thing united them all: A FAITH. I hesitate to use this word, since "faith" does not exist in standard psychological lists of motives.

This, actually, should be surprising, since faith is one of the strongest human motives, driving people to most noble as well as to most evil actions. Martyrs no less than torturers and hangmen, saints, healers as well as tempters, visionaries as well as illusionaries, artists, cathedral builders as well as iconoclasts, they all acted or suffered out of their own unshakable faith. But faith can neither be observed nor, even less, measured. It is a conviction, yet irrational, an emotion, yet not mere feeling, and as such it remains inaccessible to our rigid methodology. But September 11th should have sounded an alarm for our scientific purity.

I don't intend to expand here upon the psychology of faith. Let me only point at two dimensions of it. One is that faith implies a vision of a future, be it an innerwordly utopia, be it a bliss in afterlife. The second is that faith reposes on beliefs and images of a culture, such as legends, myths, tales of salvation, as well as values and meanings applied to our community, our selves and actions. We do not know, however, how these two dimensions merge or coalesce, how they can give birth to those passionate convictions which even transcend the power of material and social rules. Our knowledge of these phenomena remains scarce because they command only marginal interest in our science. We may assume, of course, that private mystical experience is nourished and supported by a cultural net of customs and beliefs, but this does not yet constitute faith; faith emerges only from personal elaborations of external and inner experience. Culture may stimulate and confirm a faith, yet its models need to be selected, evaluated and given personal meaning in order to create, in the individual, the specific vision of himself and the world, which we call faith. In short, private and public meanings amalgamate in faith.

But all faith has to encounter the resistance of non-believers, and it will react defensively—tolerance is no natural reaction. To admit a different belief always threatens to weaken one's own. Therefore, faith proves its strength in resistance, and only active opposition against wrong beliefs will truly provide the promised salvation. Thus, self-sacrifice in fighting the faithless is, for the believer, the ultimate confirmation of his worth and dignity. Death is a door to paradise—whatever that be.

There are also martyrs who sacrifice themselves for worldly paradises, but even those have scarcely caught our attention. Of course, to study them would be difficult or even impossible—how would you interview a dead martyr? Yet, to study the culture of belief, its myths and images, its promises and pressures, the fantasies, fantasms and self-views of its adherents, their empathy and other-conceptions—all that would be possible and would provide a framework for understanding their actions. Faith or other passionate convictions—I repeat—often had and still can have a dramatic impact on our lives. But as long as we refuse to consider human beings in their cultural embeddedness, we will remain unable to control or prevent such events.

Our actions are shaped by multiple, often subterranean influences. Individuals transform them into their own, idiosyncratic visions of the world, themselves, and their future. Theirs is a creative potential which may be modest, but never absent—and in some cases it may transform the world. Refusing to consider it, we fail to fulfil the aspirations of our science. The German Society of Psychology once chose the following caption for their New Year's greetings: "PSYCHOLOGY DELIVERS THE WORLD"—a claim no less bombastic than the one of my fellow student in Geneva, and as questionable whether it will ever be satisfied. Yet, it somehow calls to mind the maxim of Paracelsus "NIHIL HUMANUM MIHI ALIENUM ESSE POTEST"—nothing human should remain alien to me. This is meant as an exhortation rather than as a pretension, and by the term "human" it does of course not imply experimental subjects, but people as both creations and creators of culture. Without which they remain as difficult to understand as animals outside their biotope.

INTRODUCTORY COMMENTS TO CHAPTER 13

"Why Does Sally Never Call Bobby 'I' "?

The Authors

In this article Professor Boesch addressed his deep and lasting interest into I-Other relationships that are crucial to the definition of the self. The "I" is considered central to one's locus of control of action. This begs the question regarding ways that society, a heterogeneous collection of "others," influences the formation of "I" for any and all individuals. In this article, Professor Boesch addressed the process of self-identity on the part of very young children.

HOW YOUNG CHILDREN LEARN ABOUT 'I'

As a child psychologist with extensive field experience since 1942, Professor Boesch has had many opportunities to observe how children learn to refer to themselves in social contexts. He cited the fact that at an early

Discovering Cultural Psychology: A Profile and Selected Readings of
Ernest E. Boesch, pp. 269–272
Copyright © 2007 by Information Age Publishing

age, children learn the given names of themselves and others. They also hear others use the pronoun I rather than a proper name when referring to themselves. They are also able to use I as a self reference but do not become confused about the common use of the pronoun and the distinct and unique use of proper names. The question is raised, how does a child come to realize that "I" is not a name but is used by everyone when referring to her/himself?

While social modeling may influence a child's ability to effectively make distinctions, the most convincing basis of a child's correct use of "I" comes with awareness of her/his inner experience, an interior process of self-discovery that is not taught to the child by others but is learned nonetheless. Within Professor Boesch's theory of development, self realization of children occurs with consciousness of inner life.

How might it occur to a child that she/he has an internal life? It may start with a want or desire that a child experiences and then takes action so the wish or motivational prompt becomes real. However, experientially, others may oppose the child's intent and prevent fulfillment of the wish. In Boesch's view: "striving for something against opposition induces the realization of oneself being an agent, a source of action, differing from others" (p. 277, chapter 13). In addition to the learning effect of being thwarted by others, failed efforts to achieve a goal leads to self-awareness that a more disciplined or concerted effort needs to be made to achieve a desired result.

Learning About One's Action Potential

Through repeated attempts, success, and failure, a child eventually learns how to set achievable goals and to apportion her/his efforts so that goals can be fulfilled. Professor Boesch presented the example of how a very young toddler who is placed in a playpen with many toys discovers her/his action potential. It is common for the toddler to grasp the toys and then toss them around in the playpen. Before long, the tossing behavior expands to gleeful throwing of the toys with such force that they land all about the room. The toddler learns that not only can her/his immediate environment be rearranged, but the whole room can be changed. Furthermore, he she may attract the attention of a nearby adult. If the adult returns the toys to the playpen, there is a very high likelihood that they'll again be pitched out with glee. The toddler now knows she/he can use the toys in very rewarding ways that are the result of individually initiated action. Professor Boesch indicated that he first realized how very young children fulfill their action potential when he was a student of Pierre Janet at Geneva. By trial and error learning even an infant is able to realize the power of action potential to achieve a range of goals that are self-initiated.

The realization of one's action potential builds over a lifetime. One strives to optimize "I-World" interactions that maximize self-efficacy and minimize limitations to self-awareness and power. With increased power of I, the normal developmental process is to find ways to expand the range and nature of one's action potential. Thus, the child who learns to walk is not content with confinement but wishes to expand the range and speed of mobility. It doesn't take much time running replaces walking as the toddler's mode of self-propulsion. The interior motivation to explore and venture beyond previous limits is all part of self-development and growth.

Developing Empathy by Distinguishing "Self" From "Others"

Professor Boesch presented another classic mode of psychological investigation into infants' development of self-awareness by examining their responses to mirror image reflections of themselves. Initially, the child may turn away from the image or find it disturbing and avoid looking at it. However, it has been found that infants as young as four months eventually relate to the figure reflected in the mirror as "self" when the figure complies with self-initiated actions such as smiling, leaning, reaching. The infant sees and recognizes familiar images and objects in the reflection and attempts to enter that space. When she/he realizes that the mirror prevents entering a shared space, the awareness of self is confirmed when the child realizes the image is her/himself rather than another person. Initially, the child reacts to the reflected image as "other" in part due to lack of experience with mirror images. Then gaining awareness that "other" is "I", the child begins to move toward her/his ability to sense empathy with "others." She/he realizes that "I" and "Other" do have much in common even though the two are distinctly different beings. In some respects, the more "I"—"Other" encounters the child has the more capable he/she is of experiencing empathy due to multiple affirmations of similarities shared with multiple others.

Summary

As a Piagetian constructivist psychologist, Professor Boesch considers early experiences as essential to the development of the person. By examining how language use reflects awareness of self and others, the interior life of children was examined to discover how and when it is possible for a child to realize her/his action potential as an independent agent. Several examples are presented as indicative that a child has reached awareness of agency: rearranging his or her physical environment by throwing or placing toys around a room; or by examining a mirror that reflects her/his image and reaching apparent recognition that the reflection is her/himself. Such experiences are presented as elements that contribute to what becomes an expansive level of self and other awareness, the two dimensions of growth being simultaneous.

CHAPTER 13

WHY DOES SALLY NEVER CALL BOBBY 'I'?

Ernest E. Boesch

ABSTRACT

Coelho and Figueiredo (2003) raise the issue of intersubjectivity. I propose to consider the problem from an action-theoretical and constructivist perspective that in some ways agrees, in others contradicts, the theses of the authors. The view I present is based on various publications on the 'I'-Other problem since 1975. The centrality of the person's 'I', as the overarching locus of action control and regulation, is re-claimed. By the same token, the role of society is re-defined, society being too heterogeneous, too contradictory, to influence directly the formation of the 'I'; social impacts have to be filtered, selected, evaluated and assimilated by individual 'I's, and thus the 'social other' is itself personally constructed.

Key Words empathy development, I differentiation, self- and other-construction, self-recognition in the mirror, subjective action perception.

Discovering Cultural Psychology: A Profile and Selected Readings of Ernest E. Boesch, pp. 275–285

THE 'I'

"Why does Sally never call Bobby 'I'?" A queer question, indeed. But consider it for a while. Very early a child starts referring to itself by the name it is called by others. The child would not say 'I am hungry' but 'Sally hungry' or 'Bobby tired'. And it will also call others by the names they are given or give themselves—if the mother, baby-talking, will say, 'Don't cry, Mommy will help you,' the child will call her 'Mommy', too. And if she hears that others call the boy with whom she plays 'Bobby', she will call him so. Yet, while other persons continuously refer to themselves as 'I', the child will never call them 'I'. Strange, isn't it?

It will take some time before Sally discovers that the pronoun 'I' also applies to herself and not only to others. Why, after all, should it? 'Sally' is not only sufficient for distinguishing her from others, but, even better, calling herself 'I' like everybody else would make her less of a person. Why, then, use such an ubiquitous pronoun? Might it be because of its undiscerning quality that Sally does not use it for calling Bobby? There are in fact cultures – e.g. Thailand – that do not know an all-pervading 'I'; there a person will refer to him or herself either by the personal name or by a pronoun varying according to partner and situation. It has been thought that people in such cultures did not develop individual selves—the contrary might be said as well: "I" is so pervasive, used similarly by everybody, that it scarcely hints at a distinguishing identity. But I shall have to come back to this problem later.

Sally, of course, knows very early that she is Sally and not Bobby or Jimmy; she discovers early that names of persons as well as of objects are labels indication differences in kind. However, the differences she perceives tend at first to be mainly external: Bobby wears other clothes, or plays different games; he also behaves differently, laughs, for instance, when she cries, handles spiders, which she abhors. So she considers him to be a different person, although probably without introspective discrimination. But why then should she call herself 'I' the same way as he does? How does she come to realize that 'I' is not a name but applies to all, including herself? When mother speaks to Sally, she might say 'Mommy will help you', but to Bobby, she would say "I" will help you'; to Sally she will say: 'Mommy is tired', to Bobby, however, 'I am tired.' What is the difference?

Semantically it appears to be a simple problem of switching synonyms: Sally will of course, at some time, discover the identical reference function of her name and the 'I'. yet, subtly, the two carry different connotations. When mother says: 'Mommy goes out to buy bread,' this is a simple descriptive statement, similar to 'Mrs. Miller crosses the street' or 'The cat climbs the tree.' In other words, she refers to herself as to an object. But when saying 'I go to buy bread', she implicitly expresses also an intention and decision; in other words, internal operations: she states herself to be a subject. Referring to herself as 'I' implies a different relationship towards Sally and a different representation of the world. 'Mommy goes to buy bread' refers to a world where physical objects move around and to a Sally who, mother believes, is not yet aware of her inner processes; 'I go to buy bread,' to the contrary, addresses a child thought to be reflecting and implies a world of psychological agents. Of course, neither Sally nor her mother will realize this in a reflective way; it is a simple change of connotation, yet significant.

But could Sally realize the meaning of this pronominal change? Could she realize the 'I' is not a name but refers to an individual person with an own inner world of intentions and feelings: I don't think that the question can find an answer in conceptions of social transmission, be it of a conditioning or of a modeling kind: Sally has of course heard the 'I' over and over again, but *she will understand its meaning only once she starts becoming aware of her own inner experiences;* and, of course, such awareness can be neither demonstrated nor taught. In other words, self-realization does not follow, but has to precede, the adoption of the pronoun 'I'. The origin of the self is not social induction, internalization, imitation or what you would call it, but a 'budding consciousness' of inner life.

Let us, then, concentrate not on the 'semantic I', the pronoun, but on the 'I' as a genuine inner experience. What I just called 'a budding consciousness of inner life' starts, probably, with two kinds of realizations. The one is the awareness of 'I want' against outside resistance; indeed, striving for something *against* opposition induces the realization of oneself being an agent, a source of action, differing from others. Connected with this would be the experience of failure; missing a desired goal may reinforce not only the 'non-I' quality of the outside, but also the realization of the inadequacy of one's anticipation or ways of action and thereby lead to increased self-control—however unreflected.

The I-experience thus begins as an awareness of action-impulses. It is anticipatory, goal-oriented, and it is reinforced and differentiated by outside resistance and the experience of failure; both contribute to the double quality of the I-experience: to be, on the one hand, the source and motor of action, and, on the other, the locus of its control and regulation. In other words, all actions have the quality of 'I-ness', a necessarily inner quality, be it active-like 'I-writing', 'I-walking', 'I-speaking', 'I-listening'— or passive-like 'I-joyous', 'I-in-pain', 'I-tired' (where the adjective form hides the fact that these are not 'states' but actions in their own right, as Pierre Janet showed long ago-Janet, 1928).

All this, however, can be experienced only by inner awareness; there is no way of observing it in others or for others to describe it-it remains genuinely private, as refractory to verbal description as, for instance, the sensory quality of a particular blue or of a musical minor chord. Therefore it seems to me that it makes little sense to assume-as the concept of 'intersubjectivity' already might suggest-that a child needs the social induction of it by examples or verbal learning.

It is likely that the child makes such inner experience very early. Look at a toddler in his playpen, where the mother has left him with all kinds of toys. Suddenly he starts throwing them one after the other joyfully over the fence, each time shouting with delight. We may reasonably assume that in doing so the child experiences, however dimly, his 'I-throwing' as a power to act, as a pleasing quality of doing. Thus, the conscious awareness of private I-ness is likely to start from obtuse early action impressions; meeting resistance and failure, they will, as I said, further self- and object-consciousness, thereby improving action control. On the other hand, however, successful, joyous actions will have their own kind of impact: they enhance the feeling of 'action power' or, as I call it, of 'action potential'. The development of the 'I', a year-long process of expansion and differentiation, thus starts with such early obtuse experiences. But at some early point of this development, the 'budding awareness' will make the child receptive to the use of the pronoun 'I'.

An important landmark in this development must be what German child psychologists called the *Trotzphase*, the age of obstinacy, generally located between two and three years. This is the stage when a child for the first time systematically tries to oppose her will against others, when the word 'no' begins to have much importance. The use of the 'I' soon follows this period, although not as a clear-cut shift, but for a time marked rather by the use of the child's proper name combined with the possessive pronoun 'me', which seems to precede the 'I'. It is difficult to assert to what extent the child at that time is introspectively conscious of her 'I-ness', but it is at any rate likely that her stubborn insistence on having her own way will contribute, by many singular incidents, to strengthen the awareness of her subjectivity. The *Trotzphase* must be a period of increased self-realization.

Let me return to what I called, a moment ago, the *'action potential'*, in connection with the child's experience of 'I-throwing as a power to act'. Indeed, during the ongoing development, the child meets success and failure of various kinds in many situations; thereby he will progressively build up an intuitive assessment of his own action possibilities and limitations. I spoke of 'specific' and 'general subjective action potentials', the first relating to specific skills the individual attributes to him/herself, the second to a general trust or distrust in one's strength and capacities. I stressed the quality of self-attribution in contrast to 'objective action potentials', that is, factual abilities and skills; indeed, subjectively felt action possibilities may over- or under-estimate objective competence (e.g., Boesch, 1991). Of course, subjective action potentials also expand and differentiate with increasing experience, yet they are influenced as much by wishes and anxieties, social models, incentives or threats. In other words, action experiences are subjectively perceived, and evaluated according to their meaning for other projected actions and life anticipations (see also the chapters on 'fantasms' in Boesch, 1976, 1991).

Thus, the term 'action potential' should be understood, altogether, as *the power the individual attributes to him/herself*. It may be sheer physical power, as is often manifested in the senseless destruction by wanton youths or by quarrelsome individuals. But it need not be destructive: a friend of mine dreamt that a locomotive ran over him, and he lifted it into the air by raising his belly—that is action potential in its double physical form: as the power to act and the power to resist. Being able to jump over fences, to flit pebbles dancing over the water, to lift heavy stones, to open a beer bottle with one's teeth, but also to stand pressure or even pain—all this is action requiring less skill than mere power.

Yet the action potential can be much more subtle—and also less easy to describe. Why, for instance, does a violinist spend long exercise hours in trying to produce what he or she considers a perfect sound? Why did I spend years searching for hi-fi equipment whose tone satisfied my ear? Why do we contemplate with fascination a combination of colours in, let's say, a painting by Mondrian—or even simply the reflection of a bluish sky in the water? Or why the irritation by the cutting voice of a bad singer or speaker? Or why does a dish with not enough or too much salt displease the eater? All these instances point to what could be called a 'sensorial action potential' that we try to optimize; in making full use of our sensorial possibilities, we somehow assure ourselves of an optimal receptivity, vigilance and enjoyment potential. The same is true for the enjoyment of imaginations, the pleasure in solving riddles and other tests of cognitive performance. Thus, 'action potential' stretches from mere bodily power to the most subtle exercise of one's senses and intellect, from the refinement of a skill to the general trust in one's readiness to face adversities.

What has all this to do with the 'I'? Very basically this: the main function of the 'I' is to ascertain and control the individual's power, that is, his or her readiness to act on reality. This stretches from regulating degrees of consciousness to focusing on action-relevant aspects of situations, from evaluating experience to structuring of anticipations; in short, the 'I' strives at optimizing the 'I-world relationship'—which of course, closely relates to the subject's action potential. More specifically: the vagaries of life may confront us with very different living conditions, yet in each of them the 'I' would strive at making optimal use of opportunities, at minimizing the impact of limitations; even in very constricting situations the 'I' will try to maintain and optimize as far as possible an action potential.

This general function of the 'I', however, operates in two directions. In growing up, the child encounters gratifications and disappointments, promises and threats; models as well as anti-models. All these allow the 'I' to refine its criteria for regulating and steering action, to differentiate its means of control. Experience, thus, increases the power of the 'I'. Yet, by the same token, the individual builds up his or her appearance in the world, the forms and possibilities of outward action, in other words, his or her material and social 'identity'. I tend to call this 'self-development'. The distinction between the two processes, of 'I' and 'self-structuring', may at times appear difficult, yet it has some importance, the 'self' being much more dependent on the contingencies of life than the 'I'. Thus, I tend to believe that the 'I', although differentiating with experience, will basically remain a constant locus of control and regulation throughout development; somehow like a plant, which both changes and remains the same during growth, while the self will vary according to concrete living conditions. This—admittedly very personal—assumption will of course remain without empirical corroboration, but it corresponds to some philosophical beliefs, particularly in Asia, on the impermanence of the self (for a more detailed treatment of the I-self problem, see Boesch, 1975a, 1975b, 1976, 1980, 1991, 1995).

The 'I' and the Other

Of course, in all this, social impacts are never lacking, and in order to look at them, I propose to turn back to an early developmental phenomenon: the reaction of the small child in front of the mirror. The child's recognizing his reflection in the mirror as the image of himself is usually considered to indicate the presence of 'I-consciousness' or even, more ambitiously, an 'I-concept'. The ages of this recognition mentioned in the literature vary greatly, from a rather speculative six months (Lacan) to over two years (Zazzo) with, probably, considerable individual—and cultural—variation. While this question of age remains, for our problem, rather peripheral, an observation with chimpanzees made by Gallup seems to be highly relevant. His four-year-old monkeys showed various reactions of curiosity and experimentation in front of the mirror, but after ten days they recognized themselves unequivocally (according to the 'dot on the face', a test Gallup had invented). However, chimpanzees raised in isolation remained unable to recognize themselves in the mirror:

But after three months of social experience and of physical contact with another chimpanzee they presented the behavior of self-identification with their mirror image. Is this not the first experimental demonstration of the role of others in the self-consciousness? (Zazzo, 1975, p. 185)

But what, more exactly, is this 'role of others'? The experiment shows, of course, that self-consciousness develops through comparison with others. To say 'This is me' can become a meaningful statement only when it implies 'This is not s/he'; it supposes a 's/he-experience'. But how can a 's/he-experience' foster I-consciousness? Does it really? Might it not be that some kind of I-consciousness—however flimsy—pre-exists the recognition of one's image in the mirror? Which would then suggest a different relationship between I- and he-experience. The term of 'recognition' already may hint at this, because we can re-cognize only what is already somewhat known, but let us not rely on such merely semantic evidence. In fact, the mirror recognition is a rather complex phenomenon.

The child experiences the other as a physical form, moving around, speaking and doing things. Quite different is the child's self-experience: it consists in proprioceptive sensations, intentions and feelings; the child has only a very fragmentary, incomplete picture of his or her body, which, furthermore, is rarely considered as such, but experienced mainly as acting towards goals, thereby intimately confounded with inner correlates—the subjective components of what I called 'I-doing'. Of course, such inner awareness of others will always remain hidden to the observing child.

This makes the mirror image strange. The mirror presents the child with the picture of an entire person, similar to the perception of others, but whose every movement is intimately correlated with the inner concomitants of the child, his or her own 'I-doing'. This strangeness, at first, is unsettling, which enables us to understand the frequent reaction of avoidance, of turning away from the image, that precedes the reaction of recognition (observed by B. Amsterdam in 94% of 21 4-month-olds; see Zazzo, 1975, p. 158). Thus the child is confronted with the cognitive problem of integrating two different realms of experience: what can this person be whose moving, unlike the one of others, is consistently consonant with my 'I-doing'? The child solves this problem through experimenting behaviors—knocking or tapping on the mirror, smiling at the image as if to another child, looking around, grimacing, etc.—which usually (often for quite a while) precede self-recognition. The problem is made the more difficult since—as Zazzo points out—this perceived other moves in a strange space, which, although appearing real, is not able to be entered; it contain objects and persons looking and acting normally but whom the child is unable to touch.

When the child, finally, recognizes himself in the mirror, does this really announce—as is often said—the discovery of his 'I'? Self-awareness, however dim, starts early, as we have seen, and identification in the mirror could not occur unless some degree of it was already present. Our preceding discussion suggests that the 'self-discovery' in the mirror would in fact less concern the 'I' of the child than the one of the other: By saying 'What I see in this glass looks like another, but it is me', the child implies—and this, in fact, is the real discovery—that others may experience similar 'I-doings'; in other words, he realizes that the objective other also has an inner dimension similar to his own. We might say that the mirror reaction somehow starts bridging the gap between hitherto incompatible realities.

I shall not go into the question of to what extent the recognition in the mirror announces increased I-consciousness (of course, as again Zazzo has already pointed out, recognizing does not necessarily imply more than superficial identification); let me rather insist on what it means for the development of *empathy*. Doris Bischof-Köhler (1991) has demonstrated that children, once able to recognize their mirror image, also show increased 'empathic' reactions, such as trying to console a weeping playmate. We may, in the light of the foregoing discussion, look at it in a slightly different way. If, in solving the mirror problem, the child starts identifying the other with him/herself, then a playmate's manifest sadness will evoke his/her own inner experiences plus the recollection of having been consoled; the child will then apply the same to her/his playmate. In other words, the mirror experience initiates identification; which, of course, is not yet empathy, but marks the beginning of its development.

In fact, empathy is a complex—and costly—form of acting towards others, the development of which takes years, or accompanies even the whole of one's life; in not a few persons it never reaches more than modest levels, just sufficient for usual everyday interactions. What makes empathy difficult? Of course, to some extent it always identifies the other with oneself; but the difficulty starts with the insight into his or her also being different. However, let us distrust simple statements about 'the other'. Who in fact is this other whom we identify with ourselves? Which is the self to be identified with? What does it mean to concede differences? There exists, obviously, no 'other', but only a multitude of 'others', different among themselves according to age, personality, status, sex, glamour, culture and other criteria. Even the 'I', or more so the 'self', tends to differ according to situations and life-stages. And as to allowing others to be different, this depends again upon the kinds of persons and situations, of social values and rules, up to cultural as well as individual preferences—without forgetting the multiple 'fantasma' and 'myths' shaping our perception and expectations towards others and ourselves. Empathy, thus, requires multiple experiences, of others as well as of oneself. It requires differentiating insight and evaluation, and, therefore, its development will go on through life.

Empathy is costly, furthermore, because it implies transformation of the child's (and many adults') egocentric behavior into what Piaget called the 'respect mutuel'. Look at those chatting men and women who never listen to what the other says but always only rattle on about themselves— 'mutual respect', a concomitant of empathy, demands that one listens, inhibiting one's own propulsion to speak. In other words, empathy imposes limits on one's own action—while, however, also offering new action orientations: the other, from a mere source of gratification, is transformed into an addressee, a goal or even a model (e.g., see Boesch, 1976, 1991, 1995, 2003).

Two things, however, have to be stressed for our context. The first is that the development of empathy is a process of jointly structuring the 'I', the self and the other; the second is that in this I-other construction the contributions by the 'I' and the other fulfil different functions. Let me stress again that the social influences, important as they are, cannot convey I-ness by any kind of direct impact; it is rather by multiplying various action experiences—'I-doing-with-others' and 'others-doing-with-me'—that they contribute to differentiating the action potential and thereby the I-consciousness of the individual; yet, of course, by the same token they multiply and differentiate knowledge about and insight into others. Language starts playing a role here which it did not yet possess at the mirror stage; it opens new ways for gauging the other's inner world; it somehow offers the child various clues for imagining the inner concomitants of his or her actions. But it also presents the subject with social conceptions concerning his or her own inner qualities, about what one should not only do, but also think and feel in a given situation. It is both by action experience and by those ideational 'should values' that the social and cultural world influence the self-formation—maybe also (to a minor extent, I would guess) the differentiation of the 'I'. In this complex and continuous double process, empathy and self develop their similarities and differences; indeed, empathy concedes not only the other to be different, but also oneself.

Language transforms a living reality in to an artificially fixed system of signs. All that I have tried to describe here—the formation of 'I', self, other and their interaction—are intermingled processes. So I would not cling to details of my presentation, all the less since much of it remains outside possible empirical proof. Just one aspect appears to me to be essential: the active constructive role of the 'I'. Although I plainly see the importance of social impacts, I never felt at ease with socio-genetic theories of the 'I' that bluntly claim the centrality of 'social experience'. Society is too heterogeneous, too contradictory in its influences to allow it to have a direct forming influence: social impacts have to be filtered, selected, evaluated, assimilated by individual 'I's, and thus the social other is certainly no less a construct by the individual than the individual is one of society.

But my 'I'-constructionist insistence has another, more important, although less scientific, reason: socio-genetic theories minimize the autonomy of the individual and therefore his or her social responsibility. Present events as well as past history clearly demonstrate that a democratic society cannot flourish without individuals who are conscious of their autonomous responsibility.

A 'Mouse' Instead of the 'I'?

Let me, to finish, come back to my initial question: Why does Sally never call Bobby 'I'? Would she not, in some cultures, do just that? A Thai Sally, seven years old, will refer to herself as 'noo' when speaking to her teacher or any other older person she has to respect; but she may also call 'noo' the neighbour's Bobby, three years her younger; her teacher will refer to herself as 'noo' when talking to her headmistress, but in front of her class she will call the students 'noo' and herself 'khroo' (teacher). Thus, 'noo' (literally 'mouse'), like our word 'I', serves for calling oneself, but also others, provided they are younger and required to respect the caller. Such a system, instead of a general first-person pronoun, uses varying pronouns indicating the social relationship, may it be super- or subordination, respect, affection, or even, according to situation and person, disdain or rejection. By marking, through the addressing pronouns, the relative personal standings and roles, the Thais will certainly differentiate —sometimes also complicate—social interactions, regulating them more finely than our language does; this may influence, perhaps even contribute to some fragmentation of the self-formation, but will not affect the unity of the 'I'. The 'I', we have seen, differentiates in the course of action-experience, sharpens and multiplies its criteria for action control, but as the general locus of this control, it remains above action; it embraces actions in their variety, but remains the over-arching, unifying instance. Although the pervading experience of our being, ultimately no psychologist or philosopher can really grasp its nature. And so our 'I' will certainly not be affected by different semantics.

REFERENCES

Bischof-Köhler, D. (1991). Jenseits des Rubikon. In E. P. Fischer (Ed.), *Mannheimer Form 90-91*. Munich: Piper.

Boesch, E. E. (1975a). *Zwischen Angst und Triumph: Über das Ich und seine Bestätigung*. Bern: Huber.

Boesch, E. E. (1975b). La determination culturelle du soi. In Association de psychologie scientifique de langue française (Ed.), *Psychologie de la connaissance de soi*. Paris: Presses Universitaires de France.

Boesch, E. E. (1976). *Psychopathologie des Alltagslebens: Zur Ökopsychologie des Handelns und seiner Störungen*. Bern: Huber.

Boesch, E. E. (1980). Action et objet: Deux sources de l'identité du Moi. In P. Tap (Ed.), *Identité individuelle et personnalisation*. Toulouse: Privat.

Boesch, E. E. (1991). *Symbolic action theory and cultural psychology*. Heidelberg: Springer.

Boesch, E. E. (1995). *L'action symbolique. Fondements de psychologie culturelle*. Paris: L'Harmattan (translation and revision of 1991).

Boesch, E. E. (2003). *Kunst, Glaube, Terror*. Unpublished manuscript.

Coehlo, N. E., Jr., & Figueiredo, L. C. (2003). Patterns of intersubjectivity in the constitution of subjectivity: Dimension of otherness. *Culture & Psychology, 9*(3), 193-208.

Holland, N. N. (1985). *The I*. New Haven, CT: Yale University Press.

Janet, P. (1928). *De l'angoisse à l'exstase* (Vol. 2). Paris: Alcan.

Zazzo, R. (1975). La genèse de la conscience de soi. In Association de psychologie scientifique de langue française (Ed.), *Psychologie de la connaissance de soi*. Paris: Presses Universitaires de France.

INTRODUCTORY COMMENTS TO CHAPTER 14

"The Enigmatic Other"

The Authors

The relatively brief and deeply reflective essay is Professor Boesch's response to a request that he write about "the other." Despite his many years of intense involvement in the study of individuals and groups as a clinical and cultural psychologist Professor Boesch wrote, "I do not feel competent to deal reasonably, in rational scientific terms, with the problem of the other." This is a disarmingly frank statement from a trained psychoanalyst who practiced professionally for several years. Furthermore, if Professor Boesch does not feel competent to address the question of "the other," who is able to do so with greater insight and clarity?

THE SEARCH FOR INTERPERSONAL UNDERSTANDING

The age-old search for understanding "the other" can be found in ancient historical records. Examples abound in the great art of the ancients, their

Discovering Cultural Psychology: A Profile and Selected Readings of Ernest E. Boesch, pp. 287–291

statues, portraits, prose, poetry, plays, operas, and scientific investigations. Questions about the meaning and essence of life as others lived it abound in human historical records. Over time, new ways of exploring the reality of "the other" have been devised with great ingenuity and persistence. Despite all the attempts of psychologists to reach insight and understanding through naturalistic observations, diagnostic interviews, dream analysis, inkblot interpretations, story completions, or data collected by electronic scanners, the seal of secrecy that envelops "the other" remains unbroken.

Professor Boesch reflected on his experiences as a student of Edouard Claparede who experimented with "reflection parlee," a method he developed at Geneva. Subjects were directed to verbalize their thought processes while attempting to solve a specific problem they were given. The spoken communication between subjects and investigator was intended to be the bridge of understanding. Yet there remained the challenge of the subjects to translate their ideas and feelings into words. In turn, the investigator had to accurately interpret the spoken words and compare them with her/his impressions of the experiences the subjects described. As direct and open as this and the many other techniques that Claparede used appeared to be, Professor Boesch believed that knowledge of the other remained scant at best.

Based on over 60 years of experience as a psychologist, Professor Boesch concluded that no one could ever perceive or know "the other" as she/he perceives and knows her/himself. Reciprocally, "the other" cannot perceive or know the "I" as that person perceives and knows her/himself. Each person is always somewhat encapsulated in a unique world of their thoughts, feelings, and behaviors. Individual identity includes at least some elements that remain unknown to the self as well as others (Luft, 1970).

Is In-Depth Understanding Achievable?

Reflecting on the difficulty most people encounter when trying to know and express their thoughts and feelings, Professor Boesch stated that there are many indicators that one's efforts are somewhat flawed. Even when trying to understand why or what one was thinking or feeling when interacting with another person, many interpretations and explanations are possible. However, no answers can be proven to be completely correct or erroneous. A pivotal question remains. If one cannot understand one's self, how then can one understand "the other" who exists within a unique sphere and interacts in a unique experiential context? Simply put, Professor Boesch concluded it is impossible.

Even when attempting to understand family and close friends, perceptions of others are often seriously flawed. Most people have had experiences where an individual whom they thought they knew well, even a spouse or partner, behaved in ways that were completely unanticipated. In a state of disillusionment, many have had to admit that the person whom they thought they knew and understood well has proven to be mysterious, perhaps even shockingly so.

Cultural Models of Expression and Relationship

Professor Boesch pointed out that cultures provide models for expressing all kinds of emotions especially these that are strongly felt and have great influence on others, particularly feelings of sadness and happiness. Cultural modeling and shaping that begins at birth and persists throughout life provides instructions on managing one's feelings interiorly and expressing them appropriately to others. Even if people wish to break with cultural norms and the influences of their social group, the collective "others" still affect their behavior. Therefore, when one conveys emotions to others, gestures and language are chosen based on what one considers to be suitable for the individuals and circumstances involved. As carefully selective and thoughtful as one may be in complex communication processes, there never can be complete assurance that the intended message is successfully conveyed. Realization of this profound separateness of "I" from "Other" may lead one to withhold feelings and ideas, or to use words or expressions that seem "safe." Some may wish to avoid the risk of misunderstandings within or between members of similar or different cultures by remaining relatively incommunicative. The feelings of an individual may seem to merge into the norms of the society. Furthermore, true feelings may never be completely known or understood by either "I" or "Other."

Expanding on this point, Professor Boesch stated that the meaning of "I" and "Others" is dynamic and interdependent. Within changing social and physical contexts, each person is unconsciously and consciously alerted to the emotional and behavioral input and reactions of others. Gaining knowledge of self and others may occur simultaneously. As contexts change, new elements of awareness and insight can emerge, thereby confirming the importance of experiential learning.

An Example: Opposing Soldiers Celebrate Christmas

To exemplify this point, Professor Boesch cited an account of some unique exchanges between German and English soldiers who were on the battlefield at Christmas time during World War I. Men who had just been shooting at each other chose, on that mutually observed holiday, to put down their arms, share food, exchange presents, and even play soccer. On that day, the men acted as though they were friends. They expressed empathy, realizing they had much in common despite the war that forced them to do battle. When Christmas day ended, the men returned to their opposing sides and resumed their roles as enemies.

Many examples of radical shifts in relationships abound. Recently married couples may seek a divorce after discovering some previously hidden and unacceptable aspect of the other's life. Dedicated public servants or trusted corporate leaders may behave as thieves and liars. Attentive parents may also harshly punish their children. Volumes of literature and music document laments of unrequited love and broken promises. There are also examples of great faithfulness, tenderness, and delight in the fulfillment that positive relationships offer. These phenomena are not restricted to any specific culture; rather they seem somewhat universal.

Knowledge of "I"

Reflecting on self knowledge, Professor Boesch stated that "I" can be known from the perspective of the person inside looking outward. Or one can try to know "I" from the perspective of an observant "other." These two views may be discrepant and can be brought into focus through such fleeting events as unexpectedly viewing one's self in a mirror or seeing a recent photo that reveals an image of the self that seems unfamiliar. Professor Boesch stated that he often would direct students to imagine themselves in front of a mirror and then asked that they describe what they see to their peers. Often, responses included statements of approval, embarrassment, anxiousness, and destructiveness depending on self image and perceived public image.

As perceptions of "I" and "Other" vary, so can feelings of empathy and antipathy. A military officer may have great love and respect for his troops yet send them into combat so they can fight the enemy and possibly be killed in the process. Teachers may love their students yet engage them in challenging exercises that might result in disappointment or humiliation. Even professional helpers such as psychotherapists may without empathy between "I" and "Other." Parents may feel great love for their children yet not express their emotions. However, if the children behave unacceptably, the parents may express disapproval or anger. Might the child conclude that her/his parents feel more anger than love? Undoubtedly, the complexity of interpersonal communication influences perceptions of self and others.

Professor Beosch stated: "Empathy is costly behavior." It necessitates that a person takes into consideration the needs and wants of others, and consequently limits her/his own range of emotional expression. The more readily one can put her/himself in the position of the other, the more readily empathy develops and enriches relationships. In Professor Boesch's view, empathizing with another not only stabilizes relationships, it may optimize one's self-image, "empathizing with persons we value positively creates a feeling of identification as well as—quite unconsciously—a feeling of superiority." One may gain a sense of personal confidence by demonstrating emotional understanding of others.

Summary

Finally, Professor Boesch stated that when empathy is extended beyond family and close friends, the confidence that an empathic relationship is sustainable may be tentative. As he stated (see chapter 14, p. 298), "*Homo homini lupus*— 'The Other' as prey, openly or concealed, is more common than we like to admit. The distrust may be hidden under politeness and smiles, but is made obvious in the many laws trying to regulate human relationships." Historically, in all sectors of society and across cultures there are abundant examples of collective and individual aggression. Both empathy and aggression are culturally learned and reinforced.

Being true to one's self may be a useful rule to follow. However, as Boesch pointed out, knowing one's true beliefs and feelings is not automatic or certain. A person may be quite blind to her/his true feelings and may also have unconscious reasons for negating or disregarding true feelings for others. Some human relationships may never become deeply meaningful or trusting no matter how long people know each other. There are multiple factors from within the person, between the persons, and within specific contexts that influence how and why people feel and behave as they do in relationships.

REFERENCE

Luft, J. (1970). *Group process: An introduction to group dynamics*. Palo Alto, CA: National Press Books.

CHAPTER 14

THE ENIGMATIC OTHER

Ernest E. Boesch

I am invited to write about "The Other," yet, I hesitate. Why? I have dealt with others all my life, privately, of course, but also professionally. I have tested them, analyzed them, diagnosed them, advised them—why then do I not feel competent to deal reasonably, in rational scientific terms with the problem of "The Other?"

The reason may be that I more and more tend to conclude that "The Other," ultimately, remains a tightly sealed secret. After all, this is why we design various subterfuges for gaining insight into this enigmatic companion of ours. We observe his and her gestures, facial expressions, tone of voice, the reactions toward pleasing or frustrating events, we ask them to complete stories, interpret inkblots, tell dreams, we put electrodes on their heads and skin, push them into electronic scanners—all to break open the seal. But still, the secret remains.

One of my teachers, Edouard Claparède, invented the method of *"reflection parlée,"* of "spoken thinking." His subjects had, while solving a problem, continuously to tell what went on in their minds, thereby—so was the expectation—revealing the trace of their reflections. Yet, what the experimenter collected was not a private, but a communicative, somehow socialized thinking. Comparably, the dream a patient tells his analyst is different from the nightly dream—even the dreamer himself will be dis-

Discovering Cultural Psychology: A Profile and Selected Readings of Ernest E. Boesch, pp. 293–299
Copyright © 2007 by Information Age Publishing

mayed by his inability to reproduce faithfully his inner experience. Telling a thought or a dream requires structuring what in one's mind was present only as fleeting images and vague bits of sentences, giving it rational cohesion and translating it into language, which implies all the limitations and transformations of that medium. The secret remains.

Does it matter? Of course, it does! How often do we not feel irritated by what we said ourselves, having the impression that it did not really express "what we meant," but still feel at a loss to correct it. And a listener may believe to have understood the meaning of our words and then be baffled by a contradiction between our action and our statement. We may be certain to "know" intimately our spouse, children, friends, and suddenly be surprised by some apparently "out of the way" saying or doing. And so I have to confess that when, as a psychologist, I formulated careful conclusions based on tests and analyses, I all my life often felt somehow guilty of pretending expert knowledge in spite of still remaining ignorance.

Society is, of course, conscious of the continuous uncertainty relating to "The Other," and has devised its ways for dealing with it. We hand a person a lovingly chosen gift, yet always somehow doubting whether she or he would like it. But there is no need to worry—liking it or not, the receiver will express delight. Displeasing news—unless too serious—will not provoke open despair or anger, but will be received with an appearance of objective rationality. We have learned to present socially adequate responses to all kinds of situations. Even the open expression of violent emotions—in grief or joy—may in some cultures be socially modeled and may hide the inside reactions as much as does the emotional restraint elsewhere. Society wants us to standardize how we express emotions and speak about ourselves, and it does so in an all encompassing way. We learn to speak like others, up to the minute intonations of dialect, we seem (and even believe) to share their tastes in food, fashion, art, music, and politics. This cultural modeling makes us oblivious of the basically enigmatic nature of "The Other." We are convinced to know him or her, can anticipate how he or she will react, even imagine how they feel and think. In this respect, psychoanalysis is an eye-opener. It may have its snags and drawbacks, but it leads to penetrating the social standardizations, to take words not for what they seem to mean, but as carriers of often complex private connotations—which to unravel may even take a very long time. Yet, cultural modeling has its undoubted use in social interaction. The standardization of behavior and expression which it generates has even led some thinkers to state that our "I" is but an introjection of "The Other."

Let us, then, raise a second problem. Indeed, what would we introject? In fact, "The Other" is a fiction. There exist only others, but no Other.

And these others are a multiple variety. The shouting politician, the glib banker, the dreaming poet, the harsh policeman, the cruel torturer, the compassionate healer, the Mother Theresa, Hitler and Stalin, the Eskimo in his snow igloo, the bushman in his cave, the insane in the asylum, the beggar in the slum—those and many more are "others." A pet animal may be an other to its master, while, at the opposite end of the scale, God is "The Other" to whom we address our prayers—God, although possessing no human qualities, is even the prototype of "otherness." In fact, "other" simply means "not like I." What of all this should I introject? Even looking only at the ones close to us, the members of one's family and friends, even those are often such different that introjection would threaten to be rather chaotic. And remaining ignorant of much of their inner being, we could in fact at most imitate their speech and action, but certainly not their dreams, feelings or private thoughts. Of course, in the process of constructing our self all we experience around us has its impact, but the process implies selections, evaluations, transformations— in short, what Piaget called a dynamic interplay between assimilations and accommodations. Terms which are certainly more appropriate to the psychological nature of development than "introjection."

This leads to the probably central problem concerning "The Other." Otherness is a relating term. There is no other without an "I." Therefore, "The Other" is seen in the perspective of an individual, and this perspective changes, of course, with the individual's action situation—and accordingly, then, the image of "The Other" changes, too. I have read that in World War I German and English soldiers, dug in their opposite trenches, at Christmas climbed out of their hideouts and congregated in the no-man's-land, fraternized by eating together, exchanging presents, playing soccer against each other, and promised to shoot not at each other but over the heads. But in the days to come, of course, friendship turned into hostility again, first on command, then by accidental hits, then by a change of perception. That sums up the problem of "The Other." Lovers who craved for one another, may change to indifference and even to hatred, and will in the course progressively alter their mutual perception. In other words, our image of "The Other" is not constant. Of course, social role stereotypes may reduce this inconstancy, but they do so only in appearance. A student's view of her professor may vary considerably, although her manifest behavior might not show it.

Let us look at it more systematically. I do never see "The Other" as he sees himself, and he never sees me as I see myself. Our proprioception and heteroception differ in essence. Bringing the two visions together may appear to be quite natural in self-perception. I feel my movements and gestures to be in exact synchrony with my intentions and feelings, and I have no choice than to assume the same for "The Other." This leads me to construct a kind of relationship between external appearance and the hidden inside. Somebody looking like that, I might then feel, is kind or brutal, warm-hearted, or egoistic—a sort of personal, "intuitive" taxonomy born out of a mixture of projections and experiences. But then it may happen that we feel dismayed by our own mirror image—our image may somehow appear different from how we imagine ourselves to be, and we may ask with some feeling of unease or astonishment, "Is this really me !?" Suddenly, our taxonomy of appearances clashes with our inside experience. We see ourselves like an Other, but it does not fit with our inside-perception. In our mirror-rich cultures such may occur only exceptionally, having become accustomed to our daily mirror image. Yet, in situations of fatigue or depression, the discrepancy between inside experience and outside appearance can become felt, even painfully. In seminars on day-dreaming therapies I often asked students to imagine themselves in front of a mirror, and they not rarely produced embarrassed, anxious, or even destructive fantasies.

In fact, in front of the mirror we evoke the discrepancy between a private and a social self. This is why many persons, women probably more than men, spend much time in front of the mirror in order to create an image of themselves they believe to be socially pleasant. And in doing so they may even be quite conscious of the fact that the appearance they create is not how they "are really." Thus, we become aware, too, of the fact that "The Other" may also try to hide his inner reality. However, whether he tries or not, his appearance remains intransparent. And yet, it may be vitally important to know what it conceals. Because the attitude and intentions of "The Other," his or her appreciation of ourselves, may seriously affect our own action and being.

Of course, we can talk with her or him, trying to understand their attitude, but words, we know it, can deceive, even unintentionally. Therefore, our perception of others is always fraught with speculation, guessing—in short, it is projective. While, in the I-other relationship, introjection is a questionable term, projection remains of central importance. In fact, to be more exact, I should say "projection and transference." Because our evaluations of "The Other" draw from two sources: The own inner experience, the proprioception, and the previous experience with other "others." As we have to assume—and do so intuitively—that "The Other" feels and thinks as we do, we inevitably encounter experiences which contradict our projections. Thus, our perception of "The Other" is influenced by projections modified by previous other-experiences, or transferences. To these two basic sources are added, of course, the influences by the actual interaction, our present action tendencies, and the particular reactions of "The Other."

This rather complex process operates throughout the course of development, and the increasing amount of self-and-other-experience will refine "The Other"—perception. It results in continuously differentiating, with age, the capacity for empathy. There are psychologists who believe empathy being present already at a very early age of about 3 years. This confounds empathy with a kind of spontaneous mimic induction, as can be observed in a child that starts being sad when it sees another weeping. I call this the manifestation of a "functional disposition," similar, for instance, to the capacity for various vocalizations which initiate the development of language but is certainly not yet language, as little as the mimic induction can already be considered to be empathy. Thus, empathy implies a complex construction of "The Other," integrating, as its essential basic elements, our proprioceptive experiences, modified and enriched by the various experiences made in social contacts, and, finally, strongly influenced by the personality myths of the cultural group—which tend to define how individuals should act, think, feel, behave, according to their kind and status. Of course, this other images are somehow flexible, in as far as they adapt to individual persons and situations.

Considering all this, empathy appears to be a functional potential which is limited, action related and therefore unstable. It is limited, of course, by the extent of our self and other experiences as well as the cultural myths. Therefore it may function adequately with regard to known persons in familiar situations, but may fail us with strangers, especially in foreign cultures. It is, second, action related because "The Other" can be of varying relevance for our actions. Remember that he or she can be a source of gratification as well as threat, may frustrate or reward, help or obstruct. Whether he or she will be a friend or an adversary is often uncertain, and thus we look out for signs helping our empathy to see through the outer appearance. Which, of course, will depend upon our familiarity with the cultural context. This causes some instability of the empathic process, since situations change, action motivations vary. Frequent are the vacillations in the self-other relationship to be observed in the interaction between a child and his or her mother or father, but, more extreme are the radical transformations of empathy in the course of conflicts between previously loving partners, or when friends suddenly turn to enemies in a situation of war.

There exists no Other, I said, only others. Their multitude makes empathy selective. Not only does it, as I just pointed out, function more or less adequately according to different individuals, but there are others with whom we refuse to empathize. In other words, we can activate or de-activate empathy. Soldiers are systematically trained to de-empathize, but to a minor extent this is even true for certain professions, such as surgeons, dentists, policemen, debt collectors. For those, de-activating empathy is needed for the efficient exercise of their activities and for protecting their own personal stability. Yet, more generally, we can observe that we all tend to refuse empathy to persons we despise, dislike, fear, or hate. Our empathic openness diminishes, too, with anonymity or distance of "The Other"—as demonstrates the bomber pilot who coolly drops his lethal charge, or the daily examples of exploitation, profiteering, cheating, mistreatment in commerce, industry, politics, or crime. Empathy, it thus appears, is no general, quasi automatic reaction; it can be activated to different degrees, can be refused to some, directed particularly toward others.

This, then, seems to point at a final funtion of empathy. Of course, it serves to stabilize interactions, to increase the—apparent—transparency of our social environment. Yet, we appear to use it, too, for stabilizing or even optimizing our self-image. On the one hand, empathizing with persons we value positively creates a feeling of identification as well as—quite unconsciously—a feeling of superiority: Understanding "The Other's" inner thoughts and emotions provides an impression of power. To derive self-enhancement from one's belief to understand the secret longings and fears of others is not limited to psychologists or psychoanalysts, but also nonprofessionals may profit in their self-esteem by sympathyzing with others. On the other hand, refusing to empathize is self-rewarding, too, although in quite a different way. Empathy is a costly behavior. It may facilitate social intercourse, but for a price: it limits one's freedom to pursue personal goals. It forces us to take into account the intentions, wishes, tastes or aversions of "The Other" and constrain our action accordingly. Being unconcerned by such considerations, one may of course gain a feeling of unhampered action potential.

Thus, who is "The Other?" We may feel safe in the warmth of our family and friendships, we may trust each other, be confident to know their opinions, their attitude toward ourselves, but it may all too often appear to be a fragile confidence, betrayed by many smaller or more serious conflicts. Thus, "The Other" remains an enigma, and we feel inclined to distrust him or her the farther we venture out of our familiar world. *Homo homini lupus*—"The Other" as a prey, openly or concealed, is more common than we like to admit. The distrust may be hidden under politeness and smiles, but is made obvious in the many laws trying to regulate human relationships, in the law insurances to which a great number of people subscribe. History shows even that to be insufficient. We have— only a lifetime ago—experienced the breakdown of empathy in a considerable part of the German population, where families, friendships, marriages split into hostile sections; we have witnessed similar splits among before friendly parts of the Serbian population; we look with dismay at the hatred between North-Irish Protestants and Catholics, and register impotently the wanton killings between religious, ideological, economical, or racial factions in many parts of the world. Psychology has apparently found ways to desensitize soldiers for the pains they would have to inflict. It would be a better use of our science to find methods for sharpening empathic sensibility. This is by far not yet done enough, mostly, I surmise, because we think empathy to be a natural endowment of mankind. It is not, as I tried to show in these sketchy pages. Our image of "The Other" is culturally molded, and so are our attitudes toward him or her. But, as I tried to show, too, it is also related to our self-image. Thus, empathy education would have to intimately relate the image of "The Other" and the ways of dealing with ourselves. An enormous task which, I fear, psychology is still far from mastering.

INTRODUCTORY COMMENTS TO CHAPTER 15

"A Meditation on Message and Meaning"

The Authors

The final essay addresses several philosophical questions. How does one make or find meaning in events, expected and unexpected, that constantly happen in daily life? Do some people shrug off chance events without questioning their purpose or meaning? Do some expect that meanings are obvious, and if not obvious then they disregard the events? Do some people assign meaning to all events whether they search for the meanings or not?

Ernest Boesch stated that much like Joseph Campbell's reflections on events in his life, he too has wondered how and why things occurred as they did, and what meanings they held individually and collectively when tracing through his past. As a young man, Ernest assiduously searched for meaning particularly given the social, economic, and political challenges that confronted him. From a retrospective point of view, he identified a flow of meaning as if there had been a master plan. However, in day to day life, he definitely experienced situations that felt distressingly chaotic.

Discovering Cultural Psychology: A Profile and Selected Readings of
Ernest E. Boesch, pp. 301–307
Copyright © 2007 by Information Age Publishing
All rights of reproduction in any form reserved.

SEARCHING FOR MEANING

In terms of the practice of searching for meaning in one's experiences and observations of self and others, Ernest considered the process to be rooted in cultural heritage and practices. He stated that even common functions encountered within a new cultural context can leave a person feeling confused and struggling to cope. In contrast to one who experiences depression and lack of meaning in life events regardless of cultural context, most people who venture into a different cultural context realize they can seek advice and instruction from members of the host culture. Feelings of estrangement are temporary and a factor of limited information that can be corrected. Sojourners can successfully adapt even if the cultural context appears alien. Professor Boesch stated that the various ways of discovering meaning within any culture could be classified according to a taxonomy including structure, function, and emotion.

Structural and Functional Meaning

Professor Boesch presented examples of structural and functional meaning by offering a detailed explanation of how his home, particularly his study, was designed and furnished to suit his needs. His immediate neighborhood is a small, quiet suburb of Saarbrucken. His home was designed to suit himself and his wife Supanee, originally from Thailand and deeply influenced by Buddhist beliefs and practices. Professor Boesch's study is situated somewhat apart from the main living area allowing privacy and quietness. In the study is a wide doorway that opens to a peaceful garden and patio. Based on his desire to continue as an active scholar after retirement from university life, he remains dedicated to ongoing writing and correspondence, addressing psychological and philosophical questions that require much thought and reflection.

When arranging his personal library, Professor Boesch included the publications of his intellectual mentors Piaget, Freud, and Levi Strauss all having great influence on his thinking and writing. Other frequently used texts such as dictionaries in English, French, and German were critical to his writing and understanding of books published in those languages. Reflecting his wide interests, the topics of his books included art and artists, ethnology, philosophy, and religion. There are also many books about Thailand where he lived in the late 1950s and conducted studies for UNESCO. He stated emphatically: "Books are potentials, they promise information, insight, broadening outlooks, all the more so when a library is multilingual" (p. 316, chapter 15). Over his career, books have offered and held great meaning for Professor Boesch.

Researching for Meaning

In addition to the books Professor Boesch uses regularly, he also has collected texts that contain information related to his writing and research interests. Some of the collection has yet to be read. When Professor Boesch hears about new works that peek his curiosity, he will purchase them and read as time allows. For Professor Boesch, his books are like a reserve of energy and are always available as needed. His library is a manageable size rather than overwhelmingly large as are public libraries with massive collections that can be difficult to search. He has organized his study as a convenient, comfortable room with many excellent resources. Every book on his shelves is inbued with a collage of memories, meanings, and messages.

Music and Meaning

In addition to his books, Professor Boesch described the meaning he attached to his extensive music collection including favorite works of Bach, Chopin, Brahms, Schubert and other favorites. Like his books, music bridges the distance between himself and the wider world. Specifically, playing a particular piece takes him away to the great concert halls he no longer visits. Music also connects him to his earlier life when he heard music at home and when he performed with school bands and orchestras. Through music, Professor Boesch bonded with his school mates and friends. As an adult, he bought his own piano and often accompanied his first wife, Claire, on the violin. Music has allowed him to give and receive messages of great meaning and happiness all through his life. His current collection of compact disks affords him memorable associations with the past as well as continued forays into imagined realms.

Art and Meaning

Various works of graphic and sculptural art that Professor Boesch found while he studied and traveled around the world have been carefully selected for his study. Like his music collection, they contribute to the structural and functional meaningfulness of his environment. Various statues of Buddha remind him of the wisdom at the core of Buddhist teachings and practices. The statues are readily visible when entering the study or when looking up from the computer screen. Professor Boesch can rest his failing eyes or reflect on many messages that his statues silently invoke. They bring to mind the spiritual tradition of Supanee, her family, and the people of Thailand whom Professor Boesch came to know, respect, and love for their wisdom and peacefulness.

Another art form of great meaning that Professor Boesch has selected for his office is a simple wine carafe. It stands on a bookshelf as a symbol of his beloved cousin, Dora, a joyful person who led an uncomplicated life as a pub owner. She lived in a small community in an area of Switzerland that Professor Boesch dearly loves. The carafe itself has no exceptional characteristics or beauty for someone who is unaware of its symbolic meaning. However, it is a sentimental reminder of happy times with a beloved person.

Indicative of the meaning that guided his selection of books and art work for his study, Professor Boesch stated that he recognizes simple, direct language as far more meaningful and appropriate for intelligent discourse than the style of writing often found in texts he has reviewed. The "fluttering words, the puffed up phrasing" in some philosophy and social science publications seem to be a cover-up or façade for careless writing and maybe even empty thoughts (p. 317, chapter 15). Limitations of highly stylized writing come to light under the scrutiny of translation. Professor Boesch selects books that help him think more deeply about topics related to the current conditions and future directions of people around the world. He stated that some of his childhood reading interests included Karl May's popular stories about American Indians. As a very curious child, these accounts of Native life styles and rituals were fascinating and sparked an interest in different cultures. When Professor Boesch participated in local children's carnivals he dressed himself as an 'Indian' described in May's books.

Ernest's study is a space that affords rich opportunities for continued examination of past scholarly endeavors and for the review of new scholarly works. It is a kind of sanctuary for concentration, reflection, and dreams about all that has been and might be in life. The study is a workshop for an active scholar.

Time and Meaning

Being born into a "century of terror," Professor Boesch stated that he has felt compelled to search for deeper meanings when confronted with such profoundly destructive behavior. As he reflected in his essay titled "The Enigmatic Other," people choose either destructive or constructive behavior depending on their emotions and beliefs. Professor Boesch has questioned why humans so frequently choose to use their power for injury and death rather than find constructive outlets for energy and abilities. As a young adult he knew of the violent forces directed by military forces around the world. Even though he protested against war as a conscientious objector, he could not escape its ravages.

Now, as an esteemed scholar, Professor Boesch continues to search for meaning through dialog, reflection, and writing. His correspondence has become a source of balance between the interior energy and the exterior messages that are encountered when sharing thoughts and feelings with family, friends, and colleagues. He has surrounded himself with art, music, books. His work is to search for and create messages that convey human meaning. Since his participation in academic conferences is now limited, his letters, articles and books are his primary forms of outreach to the wider community.

Age and Meaning

When he compared writing books to writing letters, Professor Boesch stated that books have multiple addressees while letters are usually written to individuals. When he writes about psychological questions and issues, he is mindful of his readers' frame of mind, and attempts to balance theoretical and scientific concerns with public concerns. Professor Boesch holds himself and other writers responsible for creating messages that are both functional and beautiful in a manner that to the reader are agreeable and understandable. Furthermore, he stated that he wrote more to find knowledge, to organize that which may appear amorphous, than to convey what he already knew. In essence, writing is a way to improve and clarify his thinking so it can be shared with his audiences. At the same time, Professor Boesch finds that who has reached the ninth decade of his life, writing can be a kind of dialogue with himself, asking questions and seeking answers that may exceed his original purpose for writing. As a scholar, the range of information he knows from observation and experience far exceeds that of most psychologists today.

Constancy of Meaning

When Supanee saw a small twig on the tree in front of the kitchen window unexpectedly snap and break, she said it was "a message." In Professor Boesch's thinking, the meaning of such messages clearly depends on one's perspective and values regarding the connectedness of natural and human life. Supanee, as a devout Buddhist, believes the connectedness is constant. If the meaning of a message remains elusive, the event can be examined in light of one's memories and personal history. From this point of view, no event is without meaning. However, the discovery of meaning usually requires meditation and probing.

For those who search for meaning in all they perceive, meditation may result in the integration of daily events into a harmonious stream of life. Professor Boesch stated that the words anyone chooses to express thoughts and feelings, regardless of purpose or discipline, are symbols of meaning. Given the imprecise nature of language and the ease with which misinterpretations happen, all people need to be careful when seeking meaning embedded in words. Paralleling his life-long interest in music, Boesch said that he "could never write without paying close attention to the rhythm and sound of the words and phrases" (p. 317, chapter 15).

The search for meaning is necessarily a constant challenge. Often language is used to express feelings that influence or regulate actions as Pierre Janet pointed out. All emotions signal an "I-World" relationship. The ease or difficulty of expression is closely related to how one feels about her/himself in the world. In Professor Boesch's view, feelings about the self have their origin in "pre-cultural messages" (p. 325, chapter 15) that come from one's inner experiences and dialogues with the "Self."

Messages may also carry threats or promises about experiences that will happen in the future. Tapping into the worlds of the self ("I") and "others" needs to be balanced so that meanings are interpreted with a focus on both inside and outside realities. Material objects, like those Professor Boesch has in his study, reflect aspects of imposed structure. Imagine if the only space Professor Boesch had for his study was a dark, oppressive room devoid of music or art work. Would he even want to engage in writing and correspondence in such an atmosphere? In his own words: "The meaningfulness of my world depends on my personal action, experience, and outlook. There are large overlaps of meaning between persons, but also persistent differences" (p. 328, chapter 15).

Within his study are objects from cultures that represent a vast world, very different from his native Switzerland. The statues, prints, silver bowls, and books bring the distant world into the immediate one. Professor Boesch finds that these reminders of human diversity enliven his curiosity and desire to learn. Through selected art works, his home contains representations or symbols from a enormously expensive world of people, places, and ideas.

The Picasso numbered lithograph that hangs on the wall near his music collection represents a chaotic and threatening world where destructive and creative forces engage in constant conflict. Professor Boesch has made a careful study of Picasso's life and works to gain insight into the complex psychological and emotional life of an acclaimed genius. Because Picasso has so deeply influenced modern art, a study of his works opens doors into understanding those who create in that genre as well as those who cherish it. Barriers between the known and unknown are removed through diverse searches for meaning. The messages exist in time and space, and are multi dimensional and varied in meaning.

Summary

In the following, and last chapter, one encounters the depth and range of Professor Boesch's efforts to understand how humans constantly search for meaning. While some of our experiences and reactions are similar to those of our neighbors, and we describe them in relatively common terms, every person's experience is unique to her or himself. Furthermore, even though one may behave in similar patterns from day to day, using routines that provide stability, no two days are alike. Human life is a composite of dynamic forces influenced by time, past, present, and future as well as space. Matter constantly changes, emotions change, thoughts change. The search for meaning is as Professor Boesch has called it, a journey of discovery. For some, that journey is within the walls of a study at home. For others it may involve travels across vast stretches of land and sea. Living beings are in perpetual motion at multiple levels within ever-changing cultures. Ernest's meditation on message and meaning, beautifully written and deeply written, is a fitting conclusion to this collection of his writing.

CHAPTER 15

A MEDITATION ON MESSAGE AND MEANING

Ernest E. Boesch

I. Unexpectedly a twig breaks in a garden tree, a bird sings in front of the kitchen window, a nut tree sapling sprouts up from nowhere, or my computer strikes—as in so many other insignificant small events Supanee, my wife, will say: "A message." A message of what? She won't tell. Of nothing specific, probably. It may be felt simply as an invitation to be open to life, to the wonders of nature, to the gift of being, to let nothing go by as insignificant. It may awaken her awareness of ever present, all pervading meanings.

This is indeed strange: Message without a content one could spell out. Nothing else than a feeling of meaningfulness, somehow the opposite of what depressive patients complain about: That nothing makes sense, that all is meaningless. A real puzzle to a psychologist who wants to define meaning in terms of structure or information.

Such a feeling of meaningfulness may be experienced in other, yet equally puzzling ways. Joseph Campbell writes: *"When you reach an advanced age and look back over your lifetime, it can seem to have had consistent order and plan, as though composed by some novelist. Events that when they occurred had seemed accidental and of little moment turn out to have been indis-*

Discovering Cultural Psychology: A Profile and Selected Readings of
Ernest E. Boesch, pp. 309–330
Copyright © 2007 by Information Age Publishing
All rights of reproduction in any form reserved.

pensable factors in the composition of a consistent plot. So who composed that plot
?... And he goes on: "It is even as though there were a single intention behind it
all, which always makes some kind of sense, though none of us knows what the
sense might be, or has lived the life that he quite intended."[1] I confess having
often felt exactly what Campbell describes. To recognize meaning in one's
life or in some event, although unable to tell what this meaning is, seems
to occur frequently. To experience such meaningfulness, even if scarcely
articulate, is profoundly satisfying, reassuring. Should it be lacking, it
seems, as mentioned, to qualify depression. What then can it be?

A first understanding might be that the feeling of meaningfulness
marks the difference between familiarity and strangeness. I walk along a
shopping street—windows full of all kinds of goods, clothes hanging on
outside stalls, bargain priced books on sidewalk tables, a noisy saxophon-
ist at a corner, women with shopping bags, others with a pram or an
unruly child, lovers, old people, bar tables in the pedestrian area and so
on—all of it means something, although what exactly I may ignore, but it
belongs to a society whose habits, customs, rules and language are familiar. However, should I walk in an Arabian Suk, even the smell there would
be strange, the goods displayed in narrow shops unknown, the sounds
reaching my ear cryptic, and soon, without a guide, I would feel lost. All
that, of course, means something to those living here, but to me it is
meaningless—or rather, it signifies threat, loss of self confidence, helplessness.

The meaning of things and situations, thus, relates them to my cadres
of orientation, it would qualify my world view and my action potential.
Yet, should we not distinguish degrees as well as kinds of meaning? Is the
Arabian Suk really "meaningless?" It may appear so at the moment, but it
also promises meanings, otherwise I would not have gone there. Thus,
meanings may be anticipated, hoped for or feared, although not yet specified. This prospective quality makes the meaninglessness in the Suk very
different from the one in depression. For the depressive patient, the world
is entirely void of meaning, he despairs even of his own meaningless self;
while I still feel myself to exist in a meaningful world, the Suk being simply an island of provisional "un-meaning," a "not-yet-meaning" promising to become meaningful as far as I trust my action potential.

Yet, is this exact? The depressive patient knows of course that a knife
serves to cut, a pen serves to write and so on: The meaning of things, in
the sense of their function and relationships, have not disappeared from
his mind. Thus, although remaining conscious of the structural and functional meanings of his world, it is bare of sense.

Could it be that his meanings have lost their emotional quality? We
might feel tempted here to establish a taxonomy of meanings, such as
structural, functional, emotional, and search for examples to illustrate

each of them. I fear that this would take the second step before the first. Therefore, instead of hastening to classify what we not yet know enough, I would rather look first at a real situation and try to disentangle its meanings. Since this can be done only with a situation intimately known, I may be allowed to reflect on the nearest situation at hand, namely the study in which I work just now.

II.   This study is a room in the house jointly owned by my wife Supanee and myself. It was built some 25 years ago, after long looking around for a suitable location and assembling the finances needed. Today, the debts are paid, no limiting liabilities anymore. A garden with a large lotus pond, some bamboo and other bushes, surrounded by big trees—all planted by ourselves—guarantees much privacy. Protected by a big pine tree, a slightly rising, decoratively paved walk leads up to the entrance—a bamboo bush near a big natural stone give it a rather Asian look. The flat roof carries a sun collector and a parabellum antenna. The neighbourhood is quiet, modestly upper middle class, with agreeable relationships, helpful if needed, friendly, but not intrusive.

At about a hundred meters from the house begins the big wood, a year-long area of recreation, covering a hilly area which separates us from the town of Saarbruecken on the West, and the University on the North, the first at about one hour walking distance, the second half of that, so that, during my active years, I frequently walked through the wood to my Institute. The small village in which we live is a relatively newly built, quiet part of an otherwise rather drab suburb. Let me add that Saarbruecken lies at abour 15 kms from the French border—which to me greatly increased its attraction. And its 270 km. distance from Switzerland still allowed relatively easy visits to my home country.

Our house lies in Germany, and I not only closely witnessed, after 1958, its turbulent social developments, but remained also painfully conscious of pre-war and war German history. Having grown up in war-torn Europe, although in the relatively protected Switzerland, made me indeed very sensitive to this side of our domicile.

The house, built according to my plans, conserved of course its basic structure, but in details it changed progressively, adapted more intimately to our needs and tastes, so that today it offers all the amenities corresponding to our age and inclinations. Its large windows open on the garden, there are inside spaces for privacy as well as communality, a health area containing sauna and fitness room, comfort for relaxing, pictures and art objects for enjoyment.

All that, of course, is not yet my study, but the meaning of an object never derives from the object alone, but also from its imbeddedness in larger contexts. My office at the University, although in part serving similar activities, carried different connotations and meanings. And while that office lay at the end of a dark corridor lined by rooms of other members of the Institute, with all doors closed, my home study connects openly with areas of our private life, allowing an easy come and go between the two.

So let me now present the study itself. It is a moderately sized room, yet large enough for working as well as occasional resting. My working place, at an L-shaped desk, faces the view on the garden. On the side a large glass door opens on a small terrace, enclosed on three sides, paved in a yin-yang design, over which watches the iron sculpture of a mythical Thai-Burmese swan. A book case plus two cupboards filled mainly with books line two walls, while a third is taken by a shelf holding amplifiers, recorders and the rather voluminous collection of CDs, flanked by two high quality loudspeakers. Two easy chairs complete the furniture, one of which can be extended for my siestas and formerly for psychoanalyses.

On the walls hang Thai paintings, two traditional, one modern in style. a gilded wooden Thai relief representing two intertwined Nagas, an African mask of a mythical animal, a lithography by Picasso, signed, numbered but not dated, an etching by the British painter Ben Nicholson, an engraved African calabash and a Matakam hand harp from the North of Cameroun. Two Thai hand drums stand in a corner. On the music shelf a Sihing Buddha statue sits on the traditional lotus bed, while over my working desk presides a smaller sized sitting Buddha, delicately sculptured and dated B.A. 2517—the year (AD 1974) when it was cast and also "entrusted" to me in response to a donation to the Sirirath-Hospital in Bangkok (Buddha images do not belong to anybody, so they cannot be bought, sold or given away). On top of the bookcases are, on one side, examples of artful Thai potery, on the others a wooden statue of "Mae Phra Thoranee," the Earth Goddess and protectoress of the Buddha in Thai mythology, and some of the silver bowls embossed with mythological or religious figures, which are a speciality of Northern Thailand and adjoining Burma. Also probably Northern Thai is a carved lintel over the door which, traditionally, is believed to protect the house. Be it added that all the furniture, except the chairs, was made according to my designs —a half exception is the music shelf which, originally, was a styled book case bought in Switzerland during my first marriage; later I had it transformed in order to contain the Hi-Fi equipment and the collection of CDs.

This is a very dry, merely physical description of my study and its situation. Yet, it already hints at the complexity of enclosed meanings—the working desk with computer, telephone and a lot of paper disorder, books, a musical installation, Thai artistic, religious and mythological objects, and, of course, much I have not mentioned, like the flute I played until a few years ago, the Thai opium weights arranged around the Buddha on my desk, the kinds of books kept here (while others are stored at different places in the house), the uncounted photographs kept in a cupboard, to mention only a few. This constitutes a heterogeneous collection of things likely to have very different meanings. Let us therefore look more closely at some of them.

To begin with perhaps a very inconspicuous one, a glass wine carafe which incongruously stands in one of my bookcases. It is a plain vessel used all over in Switzerland in the more popular restaurants and pubs. Its shape, although elegant, easily comparable with the artful Thai pottery in the study, is too common for attracting aesthetic appreciation. This particular carafe belonged to my cousin Dora who had spent a year in Japan and later married a Swiss painter of some renown. They settled in the Tessin, the southern part of Switzerland where, after the death of her husband, Dora kept a small pub in a rather remote village which clings to one of the steep slopes of a Tessin valley. We often went to see her in her big, yet simple, even uncomfortable country house, high over the canyon, with a small garden and a cool pergola, a pub room with large, old, shiningly polished wooden tables. She liked Supanee in a sometimes friendly teasing and protective way, and we sampled with her the country restaurants where she knew to get delicious roasted chicken. She liked white wine, was good friend with her village folk who regularly came to play cards in her pub, and she spread around her a healthy, cheerful outlook and wisdom. I was, of course, in a way jealous of her living in a part of Switzerland where all my life I had dreamed to settle one day, of her simple, undemanding and still deeply satisfying life. When she came to die, I could arrange to find a private hospital with kind care. My grandmother, too, died in her house of a stroke at the tea table, and was buried at a beautiful spot high above the village.

Thus, the carafe represents Dora, my only close cousin, the Tessin with its attraction, and even my grandmother who was important in my childhood and adolescence. But it is of course also a wine recipient. Slender, with the elegant curve of a young girl's narrow waist, it is much more friendly hospitable than a wine bottle. A wine bottle with its dark glass and rigid form is severe, it hides its content, while in the carafe the wine shines in a warm glowing red. Its large mouth and the unassuming simplicity of its form create an impression of spontaneous, informal generosity. I am, I confess, an amateur of good red wine (although in moderate quantities), and thus the carafe not only reminds me of Dora and her house on the mountain slope, but also of other festive moments. Let me add that Ben Nicholson, the artist I mentioned, seems to have understood the aesthetic attraction of these carafes—the etching of his which hangs in my study represents a combination of three of them. So this unassuming glass vessel is in reality a symbol full of recollections, cheerful, but also sad ones; it associates, in addition, images of a simple, good and hospitable life. I might say that it condensates part of my history, but also some of my dreams.

The Buddha Sihing on top of my music chest faces me each time when I sit listening to music. It is a sculpture of perfect beauty, sitting in a pose of relaxed and yet concentrated absorbtion, each time making me wish somehow to assimilate, to interiorize such perfect serenity. Imperceptibly, it seems even to influence my musical orientation—noisy, chaotic music just does not harmonize with it. The Buddha Sihing is the type of image which the Thais deeply venerate – it demonstrates, I would say, how intimately aesthetic beauty relates with religious sentiments. We met this statue accidentally in the display window of an antiquity dealer in Saarbruecken. Supanee attracted my attention to it, and I spontaneously went into the shop to "rent" it (since, as I mentioned above, Buddha images cannot be bought or sold). This is one of perhaps three Buddha images of which my Thai wife and friends tended to say: "It waited for you." One of them "met me" at the night market in Chiengmai, another in a backstreet of Paris, a third one in a shop window of a noisy business street in downtown Bangkok, and each one of them came or stayed in my possession in an improbable way. The Thais' saying that a Buddha statue "waited for me" might have been only half serious, but involuntarily it expressed the belief in an intimate relationship between things and man. Quite differently, the small Buddha on my desk was "entrusted" to me by a friend, Ouay Ketusinh, who at that time was professor of physiology at the Sirirath Faculty of Medicine. While this Buddha did not "wait for me," I would surmise that, knowing the Thais' attitude towards those objects of their faith, my friend must have considered me worthy of receiving it. And, of course, this Buddha reminds me also of a very impressive person I was lucky to know.

I knew very little of Buddhism before UNESCO sent me, quite unprepared, to Thailand. And my wish to acquire a Buddha image did not stem from any religious interest. In the house of a Swiss friend, then already a Bangkok resident, I was struck by the beauty of a Khmer Buddha head. Now, although my father was an industrial artist and partly painter, we did not possess any sculpture—during the economic depression in which I grew up, the idea of acquiring something like that would have been unthinkable. So the Buddha head in Kurt's house struck me not only by its beauty, the serenity of its expression, but also as a token of luxury and wealth. Such was the origin of my wish for a Buddha statue—soon fulfilled when a member of my Institute led me to one of his friends who agreed to "lend" me one of his Buddhas.

In the meantime, of course, my interest had deepened. I had visited the beautiful temples of Bangkok, observed the quiet devotion of the faithful, had read about Thai mythology and Buddhism. I was impressed by the airy, colourful luminosity of temples in contrast to our dark and stale smelling churches, by the tolerance of the Thai Buddhists contrasting with the narrow sectarianism of Christianity. And, indeed, my sense for the aesthetic qualities of Thai Buddhist statues—which are among the most beautiful of their kind—had been sharpened. Bob Textor, an American anthropologist, who became a real friend during my stay in Bangkok and who, for a while even as a monk, studied Buddhism intensively, had also helped me deepen my understanding for so-called superstitious practices, and I looked with sympathy on the Thai women in temple compounds shaking the bowl with oracle sticks, reading eagerly the message it conveyed, and then, after having thanked the Buddha, walking away—consoled some, worried others. It was all so simple: lightening candles and incence sticks at the right place, prostrating oneself in front of the serenely watching Buddha image, was sufficient for creating hope. There were, of course, other places with Brahmanic shrines one went to in order to beg for success in business, examinations or love, where all kinds of offerings were deposited—food, elephants and other wooden figures, flower garlands—, but no Buddhist would consider that to be heresy; their faith included tolerance even for "paganism."

So in the course of time quite a number of Buddha statues "congregated" in our home, and their meaning had become quite different from the one I initially attributed them in the house of my friend Kurt. They, of course, still impress me by their aesthetic beauty, but they became, too, symbols of a relaxed, brighter faith. Of something which Buddhists tend to call "power of mindfulness" and, though against all rationality, they seem to emanate a message of peace, or at least remind us that peace has to start as peace of mind, which must be sought before all within ourselves, that wisdom is the ultimate goal of life. Whatever that means. I am of course still far from that wisdom, but the two Buddha statues in my study somehow continuously present their messages—yet varying according to mood and day.

Let me turn to another content of the study, the books. I don't intend to mention any particular book, as an answer to the ubiquitous interview question: "*Should you be allowed to take only one book with you on an island....*" No, I could not name any particular book as being of special and permanent value to me. Yet books, as a plural, are. There are books kept all over the house, many of them even not yet read. The ones in the study are partly needed for my work—a host of dictionaries and reference works; then the publications by Piaget, Freud, Lévi-Strauss—my intellectual "mentors." The rest is a relatively heterogeneous collection, books which for various reasons are of particular interest to me—art volumes, publications on Thailand, on philosophy, mythology, ethnology, religion for instance. They are in German, English or French, a few even in Thai (two of which I had hoped to translate, but I soon discovered that my knowledge of Thai did by far not allow me to understand all its intricate connotations. My claim to include also literary documents in studies of cultural psychology thus met its obstacle).

To be surrounded by books may give an agreeable feeling of intellectuality, but more precisely, what is their function? Books are potentials, they promise information, insight, broadening outlooks, all the more so when a library is multilingual. Each book I buy is a project, it stays on my shelves as a potential for action. Thus my daily activities are somehow lined by multiple taps which I can open according to need or wish, and in reading a book, the potential turns real, it strengthens my action or perhaps also changes it. Therefore, even the non-read books have their function—they contain the rescues needed in case of difficulties in m work. Our action always risks encountering unforeseen obstacles, and the reserve of books provides the potential to deal with them. For this reason I only rarely resort to our university libraries—books have to be available whenever needed, and moments of need may arise unexpectedly. But the availability of too many books may also worry—somehow, each unread book hints at a waiting project, at my limited action potential.

My associative links with books range wide and far. Very early they have provided me with vicarious experiences—first, as far as I remember, the Karl May stories of American Indians which I read as a boy, with hot cheeks until late in the night. Then came, as a potent source of adolescent identification, the jungle adventures of Tarzan, later, more sophisticated, Hans Carossa, Rainer Maria Rilke, Hermann Hesse, plus of course writings by many other authors, influencing me perhaps less. Among them were, of course, the classics we read in high school – some of which, I confess, impressed me at that time, but did not stick in my memory as intimately as Rilke or Hesse. I wrote poetry, wanted to become a writer already at 18 or 19 years, but after the war, when the extension and depth of Nazi German depravity became known, I began to suspect that evil could have its roots also in works of art, as for instance, I found, in the ruthless self-centredness of Goethe's Faust, and my admiration of German poets turned to deep distrust. For years to come I would stop reading German literature. It was probably at that time, too, that I began to realize that writers, even the ones of fiction, did bear a humane responsibility. Of course, writing, among other functions, helps to control and to construct one's self- and world-view; but as soon as it is published, this private function turns into a public one, the written text becomes model, appeal, warning, seduction, and thus no writer can evade responsibility towards his reader. Goethe's "Werther" is reported to have caused many suicides – should he not have been blamed for it? Questions, a writer should face.

Justified or not as these thoughts were, they made me sensitive to the germs of evil hidden even in high culture. Freud would of course agree – there is much repression behind art and philosophy. Which does not deny their value and function, but warns the creator of culture to remain wary. However, all that did not stop my wish to be a writer. I continued writing stories and poems, but practical psychological and psychoanalytic experience strengthened those doubts and slowly pushed my literary ambitions into the background.

Not, however, by reducing the attraction of books. The volumes around me still sample the possible dimensions of writing—fiction, philosophy, science—, including, too, the aesthetic quality of the written word. Beautiful page setting, beautiful letters always impress me, not least alien calligraphy, be they Chinese, Arabic, Sanskrit or Thai—which I struggled hard to learn. Thus, the aesthetic combined itself with the stylistic. Books, of course, contain language, and language, independently of its content, has an appeal of its own, by its sound, its rhythm, the elegance of its wording —which, perhaps, should rather be called its honesty. I myself could never write without paying close attention to the rhythm and sound of the words and phrases, and I progressively discovered that these aesthetic aspects somehow connected with the honesty, or frankness, of content. The fluttering words, the puffed up phrasing one encounters in so many texts of social science or philosophy, frequently only hide carelessness— maybe even emptiness—of thought. It is surprising, by the way, that opaque language impresses many readers as deep thinking, and so intransparent texts in a repulsive jargon of "learned science" often receive highest praise. Should one attempt to translate them into simple language, their message tends to loose its glamour. For this reason such authors, as famous as they may be, are almost totally lacking in my library. I am convinced, by the way, that a renewed discipline of honest and responsible writing would also greatly profit our public discussions.

So much for the books. A last look perhaps at the music shelf. Music, too, has a long past in my life. My first recollection was sitting under the piano while my father accompanied my mother's singing. That was, of course, before their divorce and the economic depression which made us poor—as almost the whole town of St. Gall. Later I learned by myself to play my grandfather's harmonium, and my father taught me to play the flute. In fact, music was important at home, although more as a kind of mastering instruments than of higher musical culture. My father played the piano as long as he had one, plus the flute and the bassoon, I myself, in high school, played first the piccolo then the trumpet in our cadet band and school orchestra, in addition, later, the guitar for accompanying the songs I liked, and finally also the piano. The flute, however, remained the only instrument for which I had got some lessons, with the reputed flutist André Jaunet.

Most important for my musical experience was the friendship with Andreas Juon, an organist, pianist, conductor of a Bach choir and composer himself. I think that I owe to him my introduction into "serious" musical culture, mainly to Johann Sebastian Bach. I sang in his choir, played the flute to his piano, or to his recorder on New Year's nights in front of the houses of some friends. In addition I joined our local lay orchestra as a flutist, while my first wife sat among the violins. Towards the end of our marriage, accompanying her on the piano remained almost our main medium of communication. Later, after having bought an own piano, I preferred it to the flute for many years.

All this, of course, somehow enters the connotations of the music shelf, but it has also a history of its own. The first record player I heard was, if I remember well, in the room of Paul Osterrieth, a student friend in Geneva who later became a well known professor in Brussels (and who, once I was in Saarbruecken myself, offered me a chair at his University—which I declined, Brussels being for my taste too distant from Switzerland). I seem to remember that it played one of Bach's Brandenburg Concertos and impressed me much—as did Paul's and his friend and later wife's Catherine cultivated life style anyhow. Later, in St. Gallen, we owned ourselves one of those early boxes which for each record had to be wound up by hand. But the real "revelation" came in Thailand. There, my friend Kurt (already mentioned) possessed a house at the seaside. One night we sat on its terrace, over us the dark tropical sky with its bright stars, enjoying the mild breeze after the heat of the day, and while we sat and chatted, from two loudspeakers sounded Smetana's "Moldau." That was the first time I heard stereophonic music, and, of course, in a particularly attractive setting.

At that time, the Saarland still being separated from Germany, it was impossible to buy such a stereo equipment there. So I drove to Mannheim, bought two loudspeakers, smuggled them back to Saarbruecken, where I had found a two way amplifier and connected the necessary elements for my first Hi-Fi installation. Which, of course, was progressively improved over the years, with the help of a friendly engineer-shop owner, and finally I decided to acquire the very expensive loudspeakers I own now (they work not on a membrane, but an electrode system). Because my deteriorating eyesight made it less and less possible to attend concerts, I wanted to compensate this loss by an optimal musical installation. I had, however, to locate it in my study—Supanee, with her Thai background, doesn't share my musical tastes, so she has her televison area, I my Hi-Fi study. Yet, with time I acquired at least some understanding for Thai and Indian music—wondering, however, what makes cultures elaborate such different musical forms, listening habits and tastes; I still lack an answer.

All this, plus many other smaller objects, surround my working table, and they all, of course, comprise more associations, memories, connotations, values. And they relate all, although in complex ways, to the main function of my study, which is writing. In former times, writing the texts for my courses and lectures, but also articles, letters, and books; nowadays, the last three are my main occupation. Thus, at last I have become a writer, less of fiction, yet more personal than "scientific" writings usually are. Let that remain undiscussed, and let me rather consider, how all these peripheral contents or even the outlay of my study would relate to the meaning of my writing.

III.   In a book published some four years ago a chapter carries the title "The myth of the lurking chaos." It tries to show our frequent penchant to anticipate disasters or catastrophes, be they real, like thefts, accidents, earth quakes or other misfortunes, be they imaginary, like evil spirits, witches, the wrath of God, the end of times or the Ultimate Judgement. In a new book there are two chapters entitled "Art, faith and terror", respectively "Welcome enemies—lost community." The worried look on our cultures expressed in these chapters is of course amply justified by the events of our times. Yet, my thesis might have been irritating all the same: Namely, that evil, like terror, undoubtedly has many roots, some in defects of the social system, others in human nature, but, unsuspected, some also in positive domains of culture; I tried to substantiate this concerning art and religion, leaving aside philosophy and science, where similar demonstrations might have been possible. In addition, I held that enemies are not always unwelcome threats, but that we often seem to need and even seek them for our self-confirmation. Of course, this is too short a summary of my theses, but it may suffice here for our problem.

Now, the contents of my study seem not at all to correspond with the ideas exposed in those writings. I am even surprised too, that, except perhaps a few books, nothing in my study relates to the many anxieties which accompanied me throughout life. Real ones, since I lived in a century of war, horror and economic hardship, imagined ones concerning many irrational worries. On the contrary, my study seems to surround me with symbols of a safe world and a happy or at least fortunate past. Why then do I, over and over, conjure in my books what is threatening in the world? It looks like an exorcism—could it be that?

I like writing letters. Besides mere administrative ones, they tend to communicate personal views and opinions. In expounding my ideas, I somehow try to enlarge my private area into the external world. This requires, of course, to find a balance between what I know of the addressee and my own train of thought, a balance, so to say, between the outside and the inside. Attempting such balance necessarily contributes to both, understanding the other as well as clarifying myself, it makes the private and the public attuned to each other. In other words: it diminishes the alienness of the non-I.

Might it be the same for books? In a sense, yes. Books are like letters, but with a large number of anonymous addressees. Their message, no doubt, also extends the private realm, but does so, too, by vying for a balance. In as far as my writings address psychological problems, they try to take into account the thinking and knowledge of informed readers; but I also look at facts and problems in my own way, wanting to make science "in tune" not only with my private experience and existence, with the realities of daily life, but also with standards of humanity which should control scientific rules. This may, imperceptively or voluntarily, shift my writing towards expressing personal ideas and images, from scientific it might turn literary.

Or it may be, in a way, literary already from the start. Because writing means creating structures, transforming thoughts into language. Or, language is a recalcitrant medium, handled badly, it can be ugly, unpleasant to the eye, the ear as well as the mind. Writing, thus, means more than formulating a message—it requires to give the message a form which is pleasant no less than convincing. Beauty of form, sound, view and thought is what the poet, of course, strives at more intimately than the prosaic writer—who, however, should feel similarly responsible. In this sense, writing sentences whose content is not only clear, but sounds well, comes along in the right rhythm, both creates harmony for oneself, and makes one's message agreeable and understandable to the reader.

In a previous article I said that an artiste surrounding himself with beautiful paintings, symbolically erected a wall to protect his private area against the threats of the outside world. I compared it with the gardener who encloses his well tended garden with a wall in order to keep out weeds and pests. He will not completely succeed, nettles, moles and mice will always find a way in, yet the wall will make it easier to maintain the pleasantness of his private area. Endeavouring to maintain its beauty, he may, unconsciously, imagine a perfect harmony, somehow pursuing his private fantasm of paradise.[2] Could such not also be, unconsciously, the function of my writing? In some ways, I am "writing against," against an outside which, though pleasant or seductive at times, always appears to be threatened by chaos. I might even be writing against a similar inside danger. Creating something like beauty, be it in form, colour, sound, in attractive images or simply in balanced sentences, is indeed a kind of exorcism. It defeats chaos by form.

That is a too simple, perhaps also too ambitious formula. Yet, in a sense I do write less for communicating what I know, but for finding knowledge; more exactly, for organizing what is amorphous. Writing aims at giving form to what I feel to be unclear, even disturbing. Thus, writing is for me a process of exploration, of searching for the answer to a question. Not too rarely that answer may even differ from what I expected it to be—the search may lead astray, but what looks astray could at times be the right direction. Thus, I seem often to need writing in order to think clearly. Hence it turns into a curious interaction. I write down an idea, but the sentence or the paragraph somehow talks back at me, forces me to scrutinize it, urges my thoughts towards more clarity, perhaps, as I said, in an unforeseen direction. In a sense, writing incites a struggle between language and thought, uncovering now the inadequacy of language, then again the inadequacy of thought, and the result may finally be no more than provisionally satisfying—but satisfying all the same. Whatever that be, the study considered here is a place for inner organisation. And in this organisation all its contents play their role. They symbolize key experiences in my life, they somehow circumscribe the area of questions important to me, and thus the values they represent implicitly permeate my thinking and direct my writing.

All this shows that to consider only the "surface function" of my study, as a place for work and, intermittently, relaxation, in no way exhausts its meaning. We have uncovered, still incompletely, close interrelations between its location in a larger surrounding, its contents and its function. We have seen that its contents, results as well as reminders of positive moments in my life, form a meaningful whole. They have been selected and arranged with no plan in mind, and yet with the persistent purpose to create a significant surrounding for my writing. But this again, we have seen, is polyvalent and over-determined, it combines multiple origins and intentions into an action of complex meaning. The complexitiy of the action corresponds with the heterogeneity of the collected objects. Thus, the study appears to be a focus concentrating a past and its many ramifications with purposes and fantasms of becoming.

IV. Would this long consideration of my study now give us a clearer idea of what is meant by the word "meaning?" A twig breaks down in the garden, and Supanee says "message!"—does the event, although it "means something" to her, have a structure and a purpose? Or a child despairs about the broken arm of her doll—does its meaning "bundle" a past with anticipations? There are many little things which "mean something to us," do they really always relate a person to his or her world or action? The question, of course, could be answered only by analysing closely a number of such instance—I propose to look here only at one example, which I hope to be informative: A dream. Most of the time a dream is like a sealed "message," it both announces and conceals a meaning. The message reveals its "meaning" only when the seal is broken, when the dream is interpreted, either by oneself or by a more or less competent outsider. To interpret a dream, one has to relate its contents with ongoing and past experiences of the person. Once the dreamer feels this integration to "fit consistently" her or his view of themselves and their situation, the dream becomes meaningful. Otherwise, the interpretation, be it "true" or not, will be rejected (Let me note here, that no interpretation of a dream can be objectively true—individual situations are too complex for definite "deciphering"; therefore, the "feeling of consistent fit"—be it instant or delayed—remains a purely subjective evaluation, although perhaps useful to the dreamer.) Thus, a dream may be a message, but it turns meaningful only by relating it to a dreamer's experience and outlook.

Now, the breaking of the twig in front of my wife's garden window may be a message, but it is of course a "sealed" one. To interpret it, she has to relate it in some ways to herself. Which, basically, presupposes her being receptive to such "messages," due to, I think, a belief in the close connectedness between outside and inside, between I and world. Such receptivity and watchfulness would somehow arise from her whole history. Even such tiny events can become meaningful only by being integrated into an individual's subjective world. "Meaning," thus, relates an object, a situation or an action to the continuity of one's existence. We might say that it concentrates the "coming from" and the "going to" into an actual metaphor. Whereby "going to" seems to be more important. Memories provide security, the confidence of being able to cope, but such coping potential derives its sense from anticipations; should the future be curtailed, in imagination or in fact, coping is not needed anymore and reality looses its meaning.

V.   The things in my study have been designed, collected, selected by myself. Each of them has, of course, its own meaning, related in more or less close or distant ways with other objects, in or outside the study. All this has been constructed, but, as I said, not planned – it grew as my experience expanded. The network of its meanings is by far not exhausted by what I write here. This all the more, since meanings are often felt rather than analysed, difficult to verbalize, and may even change in my consciousness according to situation. In spite of that, I sit here and write about them. What for? Might it perhaps be for countering these changes, for stabilizing the meanings in my world? Whatever that be, speaking about the meanings in our world is important. It creates solid structures of valences, reliable orientations, stable contents for communication. We are, basically, "narrators," as I wrote elsewhere[3]—might it not even be that the "narrated" messages, rather than other experiences, create our values? Words create the world, said Saint John, although probably in a different vain.

The word creates the world. Indeed, all religions create their image or the world, political ideologists try the same, educators do it, philosophers, writers, even scientists compete for changing peoples' world view—by language. That is why manipulating words and images in information, politics, commerce and entertainment has developed into an important and rewarding skill. Man is easy to cheat, because she or he want to live in a meaningful world. Reality often appears chaotic, therefore words which seem to make it understandable, transparent and, before all, propitious to one's desires, will readily be believed. And we tend to think that what we believe is real, be it about our world or even ourselves.

And yet, we have to ask to what extent the word really creates meanings. After all, words are vague, unspecific markers of some kind of reality. A man tells a girl that he loves her, what does he mean? The girl, unless being naïve and gullible, will want to know more. Which may embarrass even an honest lover—how to say what he really means by love? All too often the right words fail us to describe so many things, a feeling, a colour, a sound, the taste of a food, the impression we gain from a person or so many others. The poet attempts precision by metaphors, rhymes, sounds, and still may discover that language fails him. Of course, this blurredness of the language plays into the hands of various proselytizers: Their message, interpretable in many ways, can please different listeners. Thus, words do not really specify meaning, they only mark limits within which meanings can be variably allotted. And so a verbal message may be heard by one in this, by another in a different way. A woman may say, "This poem moves me", and her friend "To me it's just empty words." So language, too, has to be made meaningful—but how?

The words we hear or use are of course understood in their common denominations. But they are loaded, too, with private experiences, expectations, emotional connotations, hopes, fears. Take again the word "study"—the contents enumerated in these pages plus others not mentioned enter my understanding of the word, but anybody else would give it a different meaning. Of course, a person whom I would invite to my study would understand the "surface meaning" of it—yet, the reaction of a young girl or of a seasoned gentleman might be quite different.

Everything in my study is personal, and so is, in a sense, also what I write about it. Yet, is not everything in it also cultural? Objects, pictures, books, of course the computer, all are cultural products, and the same is true, after all, of the language which I use—and even of myself. I am a "cultured individual," yet I transform culture, assimilate it, give it my personal form and meaning. About which I speak again in the cultural signs of language which, however, I use in a personal way. By evaluating and selecting, by assimilating and interpreting cultural contents, culture becomes meaningful for myself and I define in it by the same token my role and function. But all this is regulated and steered by a purpose. Which one? Are my goals not cultural again?

So we move in a circle. Culture suggests meanings in numerous ways, which. however, need to be understood, interpreted, qualified. So we seem to decide what they mean to us, seem to evaluate and select them according to our own intentions. Yet, how can we do that? Are we not ourselves mere cultural products, as some philosophers, sociologists and psychologists uphold? Is there anything personal that empowers us to form meanings beyond cultural dictates? Perhaps a look at a very intimate experience may give us some clues.[4]

VI.   I am walking. One step after the other, and each, potentially, carries a meaning. I may not notice it, yet I walk differently in a cheerful mood, in sorrow or in deep thoughts. Might we say that my mood somehow "commands" my style of walking? Of course, but the opposite is no less true: My walking commands my mood. Look at it more closely: Each step, whether consciously aware of it or not, sends me a message—a "feedback" in the more sober terminology of science: it tells me that I walk easily or with effort, lightly or laboriously. This contains both, the basic information that I am able to move, and the more circumstantial one about the actual quality of my moving. This feedback immediately translates itself into a mood, a feeling of ease or strain, and it extends and generalizes: It makes me confident or doubting about reaching my aim, not only the present one I am going to, but also others, possible ones. In other words, the feedback from my walking, imperceptibly perhaps, but unavoidably influences my action potential. In our usual walking such feedbacks may pass unnoticed, but fatigued by a long march or with a strained ankle, they will provide obvious messages. The Buddhist meditation, walking slowly with attention, intends to strengthen awareness of messages emanating from the movement of muscles and senses, from the contact with the earth, and to widen thereby the meditator's consciousness. What does that mean? What could be the messages he thus receives? Would they be cultural? Hardly. They are impressions before words, not yet conceptualized, the feeling of firmness of the ground he steps on, the caresses of wind and sun on his skin, somehow messages of belonging, of oneness with his world, a feeling of security or however one would awkwardly try to name them. They can be felt as being in tune, as an openness towards what surrounds the meditator, or simply as a rich inner firmness. Whatever it be, it is certainly genuinely personal.

This would be a special walking experience, but also our common walking commands mood, self-awareness, may be even a quality of I-world relationship. Of course, such immediate, intrinsically subjective messages accompany any of our actions, be they predominantly physical, like walking, be they mental, or even emotional. Emotions regulate actions, as we know since Pierre Janet,[5] but beyond that every emotion also signals an I-world relationship. Similarly, the ease or difficulties of my thinking reverberate on my self-feeling, they too are messages felt before words, spontaneously and intimately. All these, I would uphold, are pre-cultural messages, emanating from one's inner experience and—consciously or unconsciously—contributing to the way in which we interpret our world and act in it.

They will also colour the cultural influences. Take a lover on the way to his sweetheart—his steps will be light, he may even be humming a tune, while the next day, going apprehensively to an examination, he would be likely to walk with a hesitant, even heavy gait. In both cases, his mood is not formed by the ongoing, but by the anticipated action, the expectation of a positive goal lightens, of a feared one impedes the steps. But of course, both love and examination are strongly loaded with cultural values, promises and constraints. Yet, self-confidence or self-doubts gained from previous intrinsic action messages will give these cultural values a personal tone. Furthermore, walking will retain its feedback function: The lightfootedness of the lover would increase his cheerful mood, the heavy walking of the anxious candidate strengthen his self-doubts. Thus, the anticipated goal and the actual performance, cultural input and subjective experience coalesce to form their intrinsic message.

Naturally, not all messages are proprioceptive. The wind playing in the foliage of a tree, the birds singing, the sound of engines on the street and a thousand other impressions may be messages—most of them, however, already labelled by culture. Yet, those labels are flexible. Our surrounding culture is an immense pool of messages among which we search for those which promise adequate subjective-functional feedbacks. We select our food, choose where and how to relax, with whom to socialize. The world of music is almost inexhaustible, and yet my CDs comprise only a small section of it; the books I read are a just a minimal sample of the millions available. Often we tentatively choose messages before knowing their meaning. I may search a book for a moving poem, discarding many before finding one which pleases me. The message turns to meaning when it fits an inner orientation, a vague anticipation or hope waiting to find its fulfilling content. In this hope we "hunt for" promising messages, in leisure time, holidays, hobbies, friendships, and we feel at home in a culture which offers a sufficiently wide—or at least safe—range for our search. Messages are a promise, but they can also be a challenge, or even a threat. Therefore, interpreting them consists essentially in trying to balance the pre-cultural and the cultural, to equalize the relationship between me and the world. Meanings, thus, indicate the presence or absence of such balance.

VII.   Let us then, to make these rather abstract reflections more tangible, look again at my study. The meaning of the objects considered so far was all connected with manifold past experiences. Let me then look at one in no way related to my past. On the wall above the Sihing Buddha hangs a red Japanese tray, a flat lacquered circle, with no decoration except two small slots for carrying it. I had bought it for no other reason than its perfect simple beauty, and it just lay around at home without being used in any way. Then, when I put the Sihing Buddha statue on the music shelf, I spontaneously filled the empty space above it with this tray. It resembles the emblem of the Japanese flag, the rising sun, and I somehow felt that it belonged there. Yet, in fact, to put it above the Buddha's head is irreverential. It might however also be thought to be behind rather than above, as in medieval paintings distant figures have to be put above the ones in the foreground. And indeed, looked at from Europe, Japan lies far "behind" Thailand.

But what could it mean to put this Japanese emblem near the Buddha statue? I have never been in Japan, and do even not regret it. I have read enough about modern Tokyo, Kyoto or other big towns, about the oppressive school system, the hectic of Japanese life, or even the behaviour of its army during World War II. The few Japanese scholars I have met were meticulous, but uninspiring, and even Japanese women do not attract me particularly. All these, impressions from reading, films or occasional encounters are, of course, entirely subjective, yet, they suffice to limit my desire to know the reality of modern Japan.

But there is another Japan, corresponding in some ways to my personal fantasms. Its N-theatre, with its masks and costumes, evokes my old and at times active interest in the marionette theatre. It is the country which attracts me with its Zen wisdom, its art and temples, the tea ceremony, the flower aesthetics, or the garden culture. In its Haikus I discovered a poetry able to express in three simple lines a profound wisdom uncovered in inconspicuous daily details; and, in spite of noisy TV pictures, I imagine it to be a country of soft and smooth movements and of smiling communication. All this, although I know it to be a merely subjective image, creates a land where beauty permeates life, where Buddhism finds its concrete realization. Thus, the Japanese emblem near the Buddha statue makes already much sense.

There is more to it. Japan is Asia, and my own life has been profoundly affected by the Asian experience. Which, by the way, has stimulated and sustained my interest in two poet-writers who appeared also to have been influenced strongly by their contacts with Japan: the Dutch Cees Nooteboom and the Swiss Adolf Muschg. They appealed, of course, to my own writing ambitions, and the second, being of the same nationality and having married, too, an Asian wife, even fostered a tendency at identification.

I possess much literature about Japan, a few novels, some poetry, art books, writings on Zen Buddhism, and quite a few on Japanese gardens. In its garden culture my imaginary Japan found a perfect balance between nature and art. This appeals, I think, to my wishes—although contradictory—to integrate harmony and spontaneity; spontaneity in nature implies chaotic growth, harmony on the contrary imposes restraint, compromise or even sacrifice. The Japanese garden seems to succeed in combining both—through much work, of course. Zen practice, I feel, pursues about the same goal.

All this justifies the proximity of the Japanese tray to the Sihing Buddha. This statue, although acquired (as already told) in Saarbruecken, represents both my real and imaginary Thai experience. Thai Buddhism, being of the Hinayana line, differs much from the Mahayana Japanese Zen, but in my imagination this difference melts away, and they both symbolize a kind of perfect wisdom. A message, relating to personal imaginations and emotions, which had found their expression in short stories I wrote about more or less mythical events in Thailand.[6]

The two items in my study, in front of a wall, somehow open an imaginary window into far reaching other dimensions—they negate the spatial seclusion. They reach towards the past, back even to the younger years when I constructed string puppets and wrote a play for them (which I sent to Hermann Hesse, receiving a kind answer from the then already old man). Which, of course, connects me with the emotions, the wishes and secret hopes I harboured at that time. And they reach also towards more recent years when I started reading about Japanese culture and got interested in the writers Nooteboom and Muschg. Another thread includes even the glass carafe of my cousin Dora who had spent time in Japan. But the extensions reach out, too, towards a future, implying projects as well as memories (which, by colouring hopes or fears, concern the future, too).

VIII.   All this is woven in my daily perception of the Japanese tray and the Thai Buddha image. Although unconscious most of the time, it permeates it, like the different tones and their harmonics melt indistinguishably into a musical chord. Thus, objects, things of the outside world, by being amalgated with my past and outlook, turn subjective-functional, are loaded with meanings. Perception, therefore, is more than recognition of external facts; it produces feedbacks of idiosyncratic content. They mean something *to me*, thereby structuring relationships between I and world.

These relationships are, first of all, actional. In a strange world I feel lost, deprived of my action potential. But once familiarized with the meaning of objects, of gestures and words, I can adequately act again. Meanings, thus, are sign-posts for action. Being surrounded in our culture by meaningful things, we feel familiar, "at home," confident to master usual as well as contingent action requirements.

This sounds obvious and easy, and is of course sufficiently true for daily communications and interactions. Yet, on closer analysis, the things around us are only individually meaningful; whether others attribute them the same meanings, we will never know. Of course, usually it seems to be so. People act in similar ways, and therefore commerce can count on a large communality of tastes and preferences. Yet, when a wife cannot agree with her husband on the kinds of curtains or of china to buy, differences of meaning become obvious. The meaningfulness of my world depends on my personal action experience and outlook. There are large overlaps of meaning between persons, but also persistent differences. Of course, close community, constraints of interaction foster a harmonization of meanings. Their overlap may be enlarged, the individual meanings modified in the course of life. Yet, experience shows that even after a long partnership in marriage divergences persist. They are often concealed by concessions, compromises, submissive yielding, but may reveal their presence in apparently trivial quarrels, secret dissatisfactions or even neurotic conflicts.

Still, such individual idiosyncrasies do not abolish the action significance of meanings. Yet concretely, would this apply to the objects filling my study? What might be the action significance of a Thai picture or of a Picasso lithography on the wall, of a Buddha image on my desk or a glass carafe in a book case? Of course, in order to explain their meanings, I related their history and their associative links with events in my life—at some time they possessed an action value. Was that sufficient then, is it sufficient now for understanding their actual meaning?

All I wrote here about my study and its contents did, of course, by far not exhaust its associative links. To do that, would fill an autobiography. I had to limit my observations to the most obvious connections. But, to finish these considerations, let me point out an additional aspect. The Japanese tray, the Buddha statues, the Thai paintings and silver bowls are all not of my culture, and they apparently don't anymore have an action significance for me. They may have had when I was in Thailand, maybe also later when I wrote the Thai Naga stories, although less directly. But they come from that immense part of the world which is unknown, alien to us, an area of darkness which perhaps may beckon the adventurous, but more often is imagined to be threatening. And so these alien cultural objects are messengers from that far-away world, they reduce its threat, may even promise familiarity. They enliven my curiosity, my wish to learn, which increases to me the transparency of their world, enlarging thereby the one in which I feel at home.

But there hangs, near the Sihing Buddha, a Picasso lithography. It is, of course, not from a far-away world, yet also from a threatening one. Picasso was a chaotic man, destructive as much as creative, or destructive even in his creations. I studied much of his work, wrote about it, trying to unveil the sense behind his chaos. I believe to have been successful, and so the litho on the wall signifies to me something like a victory of order over the threat of destruction. It still hangs there enigmatically: The shadow of a young bovine behind a bowl of fruits which could as well symbolize the face of a black woman—Picasso's life-long obsessions? Maybe, but they have lost their fascination for me. Psychological analysis as exorcism? Anyhow, the picture reminds me that working about Picasso increased my insight into modern art. Another alien world loosing its strangeness.

It is not sufficient, as one usually tends to do, to understand action as a pursuit of concrete goals. Similarly important is its function of extending the transparency of our world. This, of course, is less practical than imaginative action, but it is of prevalent importance. We continuously need to create a world in which we feel at home, mentally even more than practically, Strangeness limits our action potential, and therefore tends to be felt as a threat. This is the main reason for our striving at meanings. We want to be able to relate ourselves to our world. Which implies to be aware of messages. Thus to ask what this or that means, is a basic question for human beings. We may forget it, may attach conventional labels to events and thus dull our perceptiveness for what might be surprising, even enriching—or dangerous. We need a live curiosity, ready to wonder at the apparently insignficant or common place, in order to open up a larger world. The action relevance of my study, thus, extends beyond writing, even in its polyvalent function we have considered. It is a place where messages converge which increase the transparency of my world and expand it beyond the confines of its physical walls and the daily restrictions of life.

A twig cracks, "a message," comments my wife. What does it say? Is it a warning? Does the tree and the wind know what will happen to me? What part of the universe, then, am I? And so the thoughts might run, unconsciously perhaps, and still probing, structuring, evaluating—the unending search for and the construction of meaning which accompany our days. Ours is a tiny section of the whole world, but by making it meaningful, we make it *our* world. A world of which we go on being a part, but which also becomes a part of us. And I wonder whether all this – we may know it or not – does not lastly express our longing for the basic meaning, the magic formula, which gives sense to our life and existence.

ANNOTATIONS

1. Bond, 1997, p. XVIII.
2. Kunst, Glaube, Terror. In Boesch, 2004.

3.   Homo narrator, der erzählende Mensch. In Boescdh, 2004.

4.   see also Boesch, 1992: Culture-individual-culture. The cycle of knowledge. In: v.Cranach et al., Social representations and the social basis of knowledge. Bern: Huber.

5.   See Boesch, E.E., The development of affective schemata. Human Development, 1984, 27.

6.   Boesch, E.E., Von Nagas, Drachen und Geistern. Bonn: Deutsch-Thailändische Gesellschaft, 1993.

CONCLUSION

The Authors

The intent of this book has been to honor Ernest E. Boesch, a scholar who has distinguished himself in the psychological study of culture. As noted earlier in this book, the project began in March, 2002, when the senior author of this book, Walter J. Lonner, learning during a visit at Professor Boesch's home that no one had written his biography, asked him if he might "have a go" at it. Ernest, at the time 85 years of age, accepted the offer and then the challenging task began. Soon realizing that a respectable overview of a nonagenerian's life could be a deeply absorbing and time-consuming project, WJL invited Susanna A. Hayes to join him in this effort and she agreed.

Early on it was thought that this project would be just as intended—an overview of Ernest Boesch's life, intermixed with commentaries about and highlights of his career. The idea that only modest attention would be given to his major contribution to cultural psychology, symbolic action theory, was based on both the initial perceived limitations of space in the project and the knowledge that the interested scholar could read many of his works that were previously published, and several that are in press. Fortunately, we modified our plans, the reasons for which will be explained presently.

Discovering Cultural Psychology: A Profile and Selected Readings of
Ernest E. Boesch, pp. 331–362
Copyright © 2007 by Information Age Publishing

When this chapter was being written, exactly 4 years had passed since the idea for the initial project was conceived. During that period many things happened in our respective careers and personal lives, some of which were seriously disruptive to a more relaxed and productive pace in completing the project. With no deadline or contract in hand dictating such parameters as the scope and length of the final manuscript, we forged ahead. At approximately the half-way point in this effort we realized that we should not write only a reasonably complete biographical sketch, as interesting as Ernest Boesch's life has been. Rather, we decided, that this project should also contain a selection of Ernest's readings. Without the latter, it might be analogous to applauding with one hand, for Boesch dedicated much of his life to writing on a wide range of topics. With Professor Boesch's guidance and enthusiastic cooperation, we therefore carefully selected 11 of his relatively brief writings. They are presented in Part II. These writings, which we think are among his very best *short* essays or reports, provide a representative sampling of the way in which Ernest has written about different topics and phenomena, all of which say important things about human beings and the cultures they have coconstructed.

In the Introduction we explained in some detail how the project started—that is, in more detail than was offered above—as well as the nature and scope of our interviews and other ways we gathered information. It is now appropriate to explain further why this effort is considered to be a meaningful contribution to the literature in both cultural psychology and cross-cultural psychology. We shall briefly review the ground we covered in this book and selectively mention a number of things we had to exclude. We shall also offer some comments on various aspects of Ernest Boesch's life, scholarly contributions, and what his work may mean to future generations of scholars who are drawn to the various psychological orientations where the nebulous and complex construct of "culture" is featured.

Ernest mentioned to us several times that anyone who has dedicated his or her life to the psychological study of culture merits the attention that a book such as this may bring to those who dare to extend his or her reach beyond the familiar borders of psychology. As he put it in one of our interviews, "Many psychologists have interesting stories to tell about their involvement with other people and places." There are indeed many scholars who have made significant contributions to psychology by journeying to other lands to ply their trade or who have otherwise expanded the theoretical and practical reach of psychology by going beyond their own conceptual and geographic borders. As we reminded the reader in the introduction, a search of the literature in cross-cultural and cultural psychology will result in an enormously long list of books, journal articles, conference proceedings and other material. This is especially true if one uses the mid-1960s as the starting point for such a search, for it was during that period that activities in both cross-cultural psychology and cultural psychology experienced an impressive and unprecedented flourishing. But it is equally true that Ernest Boesch is a genuine pioneer in the psychological study of culture. Only a handful of individuals, especially those who are still active (as Ernest certainly is), can make such a claim. Having no established guide to follow, no guild or association to instruct him or to validate what he was doing, and no particular template or research framework that he or anyone else developed that he might follow, his career has been one of a "journey of discovery." This phrase fits him well, because his career has been, and still is, propelled by a passion to look at phenomena differently, obliquely, and curiously, and to ask probing questions about human phenomena as they were occurring, and will continue to occur, in a wide spectrum of cultural contexts.

THE EARLY AND FORMATIVE YEARS

In Part I, chapters 1 and 2 we traced the development of Ernest Boesch. Born in St. Gallen when World War I was ravaging Europe and experiencing life in a somewhat difficult family, Ernest thrived by developing his many musical and literary talents. Hard economic times left his family poor and hungry. An uncertain future was exacerbated by his parent's divorce. His curiosity and excellent progress in school helped pull him through some complex times. As he wrote in a short autobiographical sketch (Boesch, 1997), his adolescent "fantasms of becoming" fueled his voracious reading habits and consequently his desire to become a writer. His love of literature and music helped him "to create a more harmonious world and to relieve anxiety and gloom" (p. 258). Much of his youth was spent dreaming of a more promising world. When many German writers whom he admired turned to Nazism, which he despised, he lost interest in their poetry and literature. Although he experienced some success as a novice author, he questioned if his abilities were such that he could make a living as a writer. Somewhat doubtful that this was the case, he decided that he could study medicine, become a physician, and write for his personal enjoyment. He decided to study medicine.

Ernest chose to study in Geneva because it was francophone and far from St. Gallen. Describing his Geneva years as his "second birth," circumstances and serious financial constraints soon found him as a new student in the Institut Jean-Jacques Rousseau. Little did he know at the time, but this spontaneous and fateful turn of events would help shape nearly everything he has said and done since. Under the tutelage of Edouard Claparede, Pierre Bovet, Pierre Janet, Andre Rey and of course Jean Piaget, who became a towering international figure, he received an outstanding introduction to important ways to study human beings. All of this intellectual activity instilled in him the kind of background and mentoring that, as he has said, "imprinted" itself on him. Although he did not study "culture" in Geneva (and even doubted he heard the word mentioned during his lectures and discussions), he was certain, in retrospect, that his studies "contained the seed" for his later thinking about the relationship between psychology and culture. Piaget's constructivist approach, his "clinical method" of testing, and Rey's process-oriented clinical method of assessment provided a solid foundation for his later work.

His preparation was further honed by post-Geneva work as a school psychologist in St. Gallen. He made the move back to his home town in large part because Ernest, with a strong attraction to anything humanitarian and of an applied nature, wanted to use the education he received in Geneva and not be constrained by laboratory-type research. That experience served him well for 8 years. Then he received a call to go to the new University of the Saar. The university, in pleasant and unpretentious Saarland with its significant francophone history, was to become his permanent academic home. In 1955 he was presented with an opportunity that would literally change his intellectual, philosophical, and personal life forever. What he has termed his "third birth" was about to begin. He left for Bangkok to direct a UNESCO-funded institute designed to study the development of children. Three years later he returned to Germany as a vastly reeducated, reenergized, enlightened and even converted person, ready to make his mark.

The Bangkok Years

His 3 years (1955-58) in an entirely new culture was, by his own accounts, an extraordinarily exciting period in his life. Still in his early 40s, he went from a somewhat mechanistic, stoic and material culture to one that was refreshingly different, highly interactive, and perpetually brightened by the legendary Thai smile. He worked exceptionally long and hard to learn the difficult Thai language so that he might feel a greater sense of awareness and belonging with the people. With the new institute to direct, he worked equally hard to design research projects and to secure funds to carry out the plans he developed. This demanded the training of assistants and the development of an organizational infrastructure. Early in his visit, a young and bright student was assigned to him as both a research assistant and a teacher of the Thai language. That student was Supanee with whom he fell in love and married 5 years after they first met. She continues to have a profound influence on Ernest's life and way of thinking.

Chapter 3 gives many details about his Bangkok years; chapter 4, written by his friend and colleague, Bob Textor, provides other Thai perspectives. However, one document he wrote while he was in Bangkok (and not mentioned earlier in this book) will be singled out here as an example of just how prescient his efforts were in the soon-to-flourish area of cross-cultural psychology. The undated document, mimeographed and with "limited" distribution, is titled "Expert Meeting on Cross-Cultural Research in Child Psychology." Subtitled "Working Paper I," it gives a detailed account of the meeting that took place from August 26 to September 6, 1958. Its focus on "Problems and Methods in Cross-Cultural Research" was well ahead of its time. As noted elsewhere in this book, the psychological study of culture started to blossom in the 1960s (see Segall, Lonner, & Berry, 1998). But some visionary individuals followed in the footsteps of numerous scholars in anthropology, linguistics, sociology and psychology, paving the way in studying the relationships between psychology and culture. They did so, however, largely as independent efforts and isolated sorties, loosely tied together with only occasional theoretical threads and cooperative ventures.

While the UNESCO effort that Boesch directed could be characterized as one of these "independent efforts," it did have an official sanctioning body with a mission, or goal, which assumedly would reach far into the future. The 1958 meeting in Bangkok was among the first, if not *the* first, meeting that focused on a wide range of methodological problems that faced, and continue to face, psychologists who dare to design and conduct research in other cultures. The introduction to the report is as current today as it was half a century ago in Thailand:

> The question is whether the traditional Western forms of education are suitable for other cultures. If education has to respect cultural traditions, and if, moreover, those traditions have a formative part to play in the educational process, the answer to the above question is likely in many instances to be no. The programme, therefore, will consist of the following points: to know, on the one hand, which particular aspects of culture contribute to the formation of personality, and on the other hand, how these aspects influence the shaping of human behaviour patterns; and, finally, to integrate this knowledge into a programme of education which does not simply follow patterns copied from elsewhere, but really is designed to serve the actual needs of the community.

In all respects, the remainder of the report could serve well as a guide in the design and implementation of contemporary cross-cultural research. It is truly a pioneering document. As such it is a pity that its circulation precluded getting it into the hands of those who organized somewhat similar meetings in different parts of the world 10 or 12 years later! Rich in methodological and conceptual details, and impressive by its depth and breadth of coverage, its influence would have been substantial during the flowering years that began nearly a decade later.

The Bangkok experience, however, was such an exciting and eye-opening period for Ernest that it can be viewed as the major impetus for his theoretical interest in human action. One might even assert that without Bangkok, which he understandably described as his "third birth," his symbolic action theory would not have been as richly textured and so universally adaptable to human behavior. His Bangkok experience served him well as a psychological and somewhat spiritual catalyst. Certainly it was a life-altering period for him.

Symbolic Action Theory

The centerpiece of Ernest Boesch's contributions to psychology is symbolic action theory. As he has noted elsewhere, as early as the 1950s he thought and taught in "action theoretical" terms. Affecting, in some way, nearly everything he has written, it is a grand attempt to explain the nature and scope of human activity. As a theoretical template or "map of the mind," it is among the relatively few attempts, by either cross-cultural or cultural psychologists, to develop a coherent framework that can be used to explain a broad range of human activity. Among its admirers is Gustav Jahoda (1991), one of the founding figures in cross-cultural psychology who also has made many impressive excursions into cultural psychology. While Ernest was in Bangkok in the mid-1950s, Jahoda was in Ghana conducting his own pioneering research. They did not know of each other at the time, thanks to rather primitive (by today's standards) communication networks and virtually no association or organization that might have brought them together. In his foreword to Boesch's 1991 *Symbolic Action Theory and Cultural Psychology*, Jahoda's comments on the essence of the theory could well have served as a miniature précis of chapter 3 in this book:

> In briefly indicating the nature of the theory, a reminder is appropriate that the Gestalt theorists distinguished between what they called the "geographical" and "behavioral" environments. In a similar vein, Boesch

started his work on action theory by realizing the cultural structuring of space. In his view, however, "behavior" becomes "action," and action takes place within a field and will be organized into hierarchies and systems of goals and means. This organization will of course be shaped by the cultural environment with its social, object and ideational contents, but it will necessarily have to be "constructed" (in a Piagetian sense) by the individual, who thus both assimilates culture and, by his action, transforms it. (p .vi)

An axiom used by all culturally-oriented psychologists is that the human being and his or her culture are "co-constructed" in a never-ending interplay of, in Piagetian terms, assimilation and accommodation. Jahoda (1991) went further in his foreword:

The complex integration of action gives it a "polyvalent" and "overdetermined" quality, which entails a pervasive symbolic 'connotation' of action – hence the name Symbolic Action Theory. Symbolism thus is a result of the structuring of action and not simply a cultural determination of meanings. This unusual conception of symbolism is carefully detailed in the text [and in Chapter 4 as well as the extensive foreword to this book], and the far-reaching implications of such a perspective constitutes the central theme [of the book], exemplified in various fields. (p. vi)

Jahoda also pointed out that running through much of Ernest Boesch's writings dealing with culture there has been an important pattern. That pattern can be described as a coalition in Boesch's breadth of knowledge covering anthropology, philosophy, literature, poetry, art, music, and any perspective coverings ways that people endeavor to make sense of their surroundings. For many years Boesch has been convinced that cultural psychology should not only enrich the discipline by going well beyond behaviorism and nomothetic proclivities, doing so in a broad range of settings where of course human action always takes place. As Jahoda said, "this makes him unafraid of speculative flights that have not been, and sometimes could not be empirically verified" The boldness of his interpretations and the creativity behind his speculations are nearly always thought-provoking.

Once again we want to thank Ernest for taking the time to assist as only he could to provide an outline of his symbolic action theory. Chapter 3 contains the nomenclature and basics of the theory. It is not often that the central figure in a profile of one's life, largely written by others, is in a position to explain his or her views exactly as he or she wishes. It is also not often that other parts of a book gives so much further insight and understanding of a theoretical position. We again thank Jürgen Straub and Arne Weidemann for providing their perspective on Boesch's theory, which they obviously admire.

An Impressive Range of Intellectual Accomplishments and Interests

There are many facets to Ernest Boesch. He could be regarded as a *theoretical psychologist,* especially in view of his symbolic action theory. In SAT he carefully and patiently put together a unique perspective concerning behavior and thought in cultural context. Echoing what Kurt Lewin once said, "There is nothing so practical as a good theory," Ernest could also be regarded as an applied psychologist—one who wanted to make a difference in the real world. His work as a school psychologist in St. Gallen demonstrated this, as did his research in Bangkok involving the systematic study of communication between doctors and patients. In Bangkok he was also involved in research focusing on the adjustment patterns of immigrants, in communication between doctors and patients, in the helping to design child welfare programs, and other applied areas. He is also a psychoanalyst, and at one point in his career was an active therapist. An examination of his bibliography will show that throughout his career, Boesch has extended his efforts to an impressive breadth of activities.

Ernest might also be regarded as an aficionado of poetry and the arts, and therefore an *aesthetic psychologist.* His life-long interest in playing musical instruments, especially the flute and the piano, and his keen knowledge and appreciation of fine music provides a glimpse at another of his talents. A privately published book, *Über musik,* is a compelling essay on one of his main avocations. His article, "The Sound of the Violin" (see chapter 8, Part II) is extraordinarily informative and insightful, as well as beautifully written. Just as we were completing the manuscript for this book, Ernest finished a small psychological novella about wisdom titled *Gregrorius und der Engel oder Erholung am Thunersee* (Boesch, 2006), which he explained can be viewed as an extension of his "Violin" article. This little "thought-piece" tells the story of a man who strives to fulfill his *Sehnsucht* (longing) for the "non-lived rest of life." When his quest fails he is led to understand that the answer has to be found in the inner self. Interestingly, Thunersee (Lake Thun, near Merligen) in Switzerland is a special place for Ernest and Supanee. It has served as a place for quiet thought and contemplation for both of them. In a nearby village is the master violin maker whose work fascinated Ernest.

In the front piece of the little book Ernest included a saying attributed to Laotse. Translated from his German rendition, it reads:

> If one does not go out the door,
> one knows the world.
> If one does not look out the window,

One sees Heaven's way.
The more one goes out,
the less one knows.

It is striking how much this well-known saying relates to Ernest's life, and it is equally striking how much this relates to the motives and aspirations of those who toil among the world's cultures in pursuit of knowledge.

Many people know Ernest not as a psychologist but as a *poet*. Some of his poetry has been well-received. He is an excellent writer, having shown his mettle in numerous ways from his birth. Boesch insists on precision in writing, frequently laboring over the "right" way to explain a concept or describe a situation. His creative stories about dragons and ghosts show another dimension of his literary skills, as do his analyses of pernicious social and international problems. Boesch is also a dedicated *humanist*, and many of his writings express his sincere concern about where the world is headed and, within that conundrum, how psychology may and should contribute to a more balanced and sane society. His "A Psychology of Concern," also included in Part II (chapter 12), which is essentially a brief reflective essay on what psychology should be doing, shows that he has always been worried about the highly fractionated and volatile world in which we live.

In the Company of Stellar Thinkers

Although his efforts during his "journey" were unique, independent, and the result of tenacious efforts, it is to our collective advantage that Ernest Boesch joined, and was joined by, a number of people who toiled in the same area. These connections were hardly ever planned, and in Boesch's case were never completely nurtured. Because this book has an educational function, we want to remind students that he is in good and illustrious company in the psychological study of culture. Along with scholars such as Jerome Bruner, Michael Cole, Richard Shweder, Jaan Valsiner, Jürgen Straub and others as part of the family of cultural scholars whose careers have been devoted to the study of how, why, when, and where culture affects all of us, Ernest Boesch can be regarded as a star in a galaxy of talented intellectuals.

In a special issue of the journal *Psychology and Culture* titled "The Legacy of Ernest E. Boesch in Cultural Psychology," which is a noteworthy record of the celebration of his 80th birthday in Berlin in 1996, Hubert Hermans (1997) gave an interesting summary of some important characteristics of two genuine scholars. It has almost certainly never been done before, but Hermans focused on what he considers to be the main commonalities in the perspectives of Ernest Boesch, the founder of the Saarbrücken School of Cultural Psychology, and Henry A. Murray (1940), an icon of American, and in several ways, world psychology. Murray's name has never been closely associated with either cultural or cross-cultural psychology. His main influence on these highly related fields was by way of the Thematic Apperception Test, a projective device that has been exceeded in use only by the Rorschach (which Ernest used, in abbreviated form, in his seminal investigations in Bangkok), as well as his dedication to the study of lives under the rubric of "personology." One of Murray's closest colleagues, David C. McClelland, used the TAT and other sources of data to measure achievement motivation, easily the most widely studied of what Murray called psychogenic needs. All, or many, of these needs have been classified as universal.

The manner in which Hermans (1997) drew parallels between Boesch and Murray (1940) is unprecedented and informative. We summarize and occasionally paraphrase or comment on Hermans' observations:

1. Both theorists are holistic thinkers, their overall aim being to arrive at an understanding of the whole person. In doing so, they are opposed to reductionistic methods and artificial laboratory experiments; their interest lies in studying persons in their own habitat.

2. Both of them give "explicit and systematic attention to the person-situation interaction" and assert that "no person exists separate from the situation" and that person and situation should be conceived as intrinsically connected in an arena of dynamic polarities in a "field" situation. Both, therefore, were either inspired by or reflective of Lewin's field theory.

3. Both have a tendency to use certain psychoanalytic concepts or, we assert, concepts reminiscent of psychoanalysis. For instance, they believe that "the unconscious is an indispensable part of understanding a person's daily life." Hermans (1997) noted that it is therefore "not surprising that both Boesch and Murray discuss fantasy, myths, fairy tales and other narratives in which unconscious motives come to the surface" (p. 397).

4. Both theorists made serious attempts to explain psychological phenomena as they interact with culture. For instance, anthropologist Clyde Kluckhohn and Henry Murray collaborated on a comparative project concerning socialization processes across different cultures. Their time-honored 1949 edited book, *Personality in nature, society and culture,* is among the most frequently-cited works in the

general area of "culture." It is in that book where one of the most famous phrases in the area of "culture and personality" appeared:

> Every man [sic] is in certain respects
> a. like all other men,
> b. like some other men,
> c. like no other man (p. 35)

Kluckhohn and Murray concluded that while socialization may vary from culture to culture, certain general aims remain constant everywhere. Similarly, Boesch's theoretical perspective includes some concepts that are culturally invariant (action potential, for instance, albeit under a different rubric, such as "competence") but that must also be understood in dynamic cultural contexts.

5. Both theorists used a tremendous range of material and in particular were "deeply involved in novelistic literature." We have already explained that Ernest Boesch has an affinity for literature and poetry, and has gifts in these areas that influenced his colorful, prose-like psychological writing. In a very real sense, inside Ernest Boesch there is a poet and a writer longing to be heard; these longings are manifested in almost everything he writes. As Hermans noted, many of Boesch's creative writings (about myths, dragons, and magic, for example) demonstrate that "his original novelistic and aesthetic inspiration (is) still alive and (that they) coexist with his scientific endeavors." Murray, by the same token but in a different way, used other voices in his creative and exploratory bent. He especially developed an affinity for the writings of Herman Melville. Murray's influential analysis of *Moby Dick* featured Captain Ahab representing evil forces of the id, the great sperm whale standing for the incarnation of the Protestant God and, therefore, a projection of the mighty superego.

6. Both have creative ideas on the nature of the self. For Boesch, the "I" plays a central role in SAT. There is, for him, a multiplicity of selves. The relationship between I and World may be varied according to potential numerous and changing functional modalities such as, using examples given by Hermans, "I-marching, I-hoping, I-fearing, I-tired, I-angry." The existence of different functional modalities, as Hermans points out, implies "a rejection of a separate, autonomous I as having an existence in and by itself" (1997, p. 398). In Murray's colorful language,

which matches the florid and flowing eloquence often used by Ernest Boesch, he agrees with the idea of the non-separation of I and World by "visualizing a whispering gallery in which voices echo from the distant past; a gulf stream of fantasies with floating memories of past events, currents of contending complexes, plots and counterplots, hopeful intimations and ideals" (Murray, 1940, p. 160).

Murray's influence was substantially aided by his being at Harvard University—arguably, at that time and perhaps even today, the most prestigious stage in the academic world—or many years as director of its psychological clinic. There he interacted with numerous influential scholars in psychology and other fields. Ernest Boesch, on the other hand, was engaged with a rather small number of scholars in Germany's Saarland, quite some distance from the major centers of psychological activity. In addition to unknowingly sharing wide interests with Murray, Ernest Boesch has kinship with him in the area of writing about human life—not detached as or fractionated life, partitioned for the sake of some experimental design, but for the purpose of explaining how life unfolds in specific environments. Their writing is rich, colorful, captivating, poetic, impassioned, and rife with examples in many fields. Henry Murray could have had a stellar career as a scholar in one of several different fields, especially those that required the precise use of language and a riveting intensity and depth of knowledge. We suggest that Ernest Boesch can be described the same way. It is a pity that they never met. But it is also uplifting that parallels emerged. In his article, Hermans has shown how these parallels can be made. However, we suggest that, in the development of psychological theories, a return to Kluckhohn and Murray's (1949) axiomatic statement is appropriate:

Every psychological theory is, in certain respects,

a. like all other theories,

b. like some other theories,

c. like no other theory

In Ernest Boesch's case, the third alternative is easily the most appropriate. He developed symbolic action theory on no one else's terms than his own, always insisting that it is based on his own observations and "working it out" as logically as possible. In the paths he has taken during his career, however, he did not stray far from the canons of science. But he ventured far enough from them to create a unique perspective and explanation for the various ways that active individuals in complex environments are mutually interactive and coconstructed.

Personal Observations and Reflections

Productive and visionary thinkers like Ernest Boesch will not necessarily be known by the totality of their work but by selected parts of many contributions. In Boesch's case, some may regard him as a theorist, a poet, a story teller, or a commentator on current world events. Though gentle and polite to a fault, he is certainly an indomitable spirit with a demanding and commanding presence. We are reasonably certain that Ernest would prefer to be remembered as a person who developed a unique theory, a theory of human action that interacts with highly personal symbols that can only be understood in cultural contexts. We are also convinced that one of Ernest's most fervent hopes is that psychologists will pay much more attention to the detailed context and meaningfulness of human behavior and not continually bow before the obligatory rules of statistics and empiricism. Ernest has no quarrel with these aspects of the discipline. Remember that initially he was on course toward a career in the realm of experimental psychology. However, we are confident that he would agree with the view that psychology is too important to leave it exclusively in hands of rampant quantification. Someone has to ask the uniquely sensitive and deeply compelling questions that surface in a troubled and complex world. Why shouldn't these activities become standard among psychologists?

Reflecting on what we, the authors, have experienced during the process of writing what we hope is a respectful treatment of Ernest Boesch's life and career, we can only describe it as enriching and challenging. Boesch cannot be separated from a Gestalt-like aura of dedicated scholarship. His verbal and analytic skills are remarkable. He is at his best when he is dissecting some conceptual, methodological, or moral problem or difficulty. His mind works much like that of an engineer. Instead of working with motors, stone, or electrical systems, he analyzes complex human intellectual and physical behavior. His inductive and deductive skills are phenomenal, as is his intense concentration on the task at hand. One day when asked why he doesn't write and listen to music at the same time, since he has great love of Bach, Chopin, Brahms, and others, he launched into a lengthy discourse on why the two are incompatible, or mutually distracting. To paraphrase him: "One must focus on the task at hand and not compromise one's concentration by dividing mental loyalties." This changed both authors' music-listening, and writing, habits forever. Another example, reported earlier, concerns his life-long love of the violin: Once when Ernest visited a renowned Swiss violin maker in a Swiss village, he engaged the expert in detailed and interesting questions for nearly two hours (See his "The Sound of the Violin" in Part II). With a mind so fascinated with the intricate details of how things work, it is no wonder why Ernest's perspectives on the juxtaposition of human action and human culture are so intricately structured. This is the kind of analytical thinking that cannot be reduced to a tabular presentation or a facile statistical treatment. Human behavior, a wonderful example of which is designing and making exquisite violins, is complex and intricate. As such, it deserves the kind of deep probing that cultural psychologists demand.

A Touching Tribute by Paul B. Baltes[1]

Ernest's influence on many scholars seems remarkably similar to what one of Ernest's distinguished students, the late Paul Baltes, wrote in the above-mentioned special issue of *Psychology and Culture*. Part of what Baltes (1997) wrote captures the essence of what the Boesch's legacy may be for many scholars who are deeply involved in cultural psychology. As Baltes noted,

> We benefited tremendously from Boesch's originality, from watching a creative mind in action and unfold, and observing someone who valued thinking by himself more than communicating the work of others. Boesch, as he taught and interacted with us, developed his own action and cultural theory, his own view on things, and he pressed all of us to be equally autonomous, except, of course, for the attention we need to pay to his mind and his concepts. (p. 252)

Baltes (1997) went on to pay his mentor a fitting tribute. Recounting the roots of Ernest's effect on his students, Baltes wrote the following:

> Boesch's voice, then, typically asked for more than I was able to deliver. And my hunch is that my fellow students felt similarly from time to time. Not surprisingly, therefore, I was quickly attracted to a biographical account when I read it for the first time a couple of years ago—a story about the famous Nobel-winning physicist Wolfgang Pauli. For me, this story told by several of Pauli's student is as authentic as personal truth can be.
> The inner voice of Wolfgang Pauli in the heads of his students constantly followed them around, mostly, but not always, in productive ways. The voice was there when planning experiments, when interpreting data, even when

out on a date or listening to a piece of music: What would Pauli think about this? What questions would he now ask? What would he do next? Which control experiments would he now perform? Which flaw would he now point out? Which person would he think that I should marry? Indeed, when reading this story about Pauli, I had no problem whatsoever understanding what was meant. All I had to do was to substitute Boesch for the name of Pauli – easy in my case: in my childhood I was called Pauli by my parents and siblings. (p. 252)

Since meeting Ernest Boesch we, the authors, have had a growing similar tendency to think along the same lines. Neither of us, of course, had the good fortune to be a student in one of his classes (which they may not have "passed"). Nor were we able to be with him in Thailand or anywhere else he plied his career. However, we did have a number of opportunities to listen to him and understand with increasing depth and fidelity how he thinks and works—often in action-theoretical terms but frequently by simply reflecting on some problem or issue and dissecting it logically, carefully, and always respectful of the work of others. A scholar and gentleman to the core, the only voices Ernest has ever tried to stifle are those that work against the grain of human decency.

As noted earlier in this book, Ernest Boesch leaves a strong and lasting impression of a gentleman scholar in the grandest of European traditions. And indeed there is a European tradition of scholarship, especially when compared, for instance, with the strident and often scientifically perfunctory research and scholarship practices of the "new world." He is a deeply probing and profoundly concerned scholar. Never taking the easy path, he toils in his efforts to explain complexities of human life in a rapidly changing, complex, and troubled world. He labors intensely to refine and expand his professional efforts. He has often explained how much he dislikes and distrusts facile, quick, and often shallow experimental studies just for the sake of a generating a few promotion-oriented publications. His symbolic action theory reflects his view of how truly complex human behavior is. Why, then, he has often asked, should we not think extremely carefully and comprehensively about the various and often intricately complex relationships between the person and his or her environment?

Cultural and Cross-Cultural Psychology Need Each Other

One of the authors, WJL, has been a dedicated cross-cultural psychologist for about 40 years. Like many of his colleagues, his involvement in this area of the discipline was initially energized by a gnawing feeling, starting in graduate school or in the early stages of their careers, that psychology may be too enthralled by statistical analyses, careful laboratory research that often seemed to be quite unlike the "real world" that experimentalists were trying to approximate in contrived settings. The discipline seemed too duty-bound to go much beyond extensive experimentation with college sophomores, and too enslaved by intricate theories and parsimonious procedures. Cross-cultural psychologists have great respect for the many psychologists who have contributed in important ways to an increasingly informed picture of how humans live individually and collectively. It would be unthinkable for cross-cultural psychologists to abandon the core tenets of the discipline. However, questions frequently asked are "Will Theory A or Finding B transfer well to the rest of the world?" "Why do most Western-trained psychologists tend to ignore the rest of the world?" "Why is it that curricular offerings in most psychology departments are almost completely devoid of courses that feature culture's influence on thought and behavior?"

Most cross-cultural psychologists would like nothing more than to see their discipline transformed into one that is truly universal. Actually, it can be argued that the main mission of cross-cultural psychology is, or could be, to make itself obsolete. The only way this might be done is for the discipline, world wide, to become more or less unified by deciding on what is truly necessary to understand human thought and behavior. Of course, this may be a long way off. It was against this backdrop that an unforeseen, interesting and productive little venture occurred. It resulted in the articulation of one of the readings reproduced in Part II titled "The Seven Flaws of Cross-Cultural Psychology: The Story of a Conversion" (see chapter 11).

The following is a short history of that reading. We explained that about 10 years ago WJL was writing an invited chapter for a book that featured conceptual and methodological considerations in cross-cultural research. In an attempt to make a basic point about how many cross-cultural research projects are designed, he contrived a "fictional" experiment that could be used to make certain points. The "experiment" was concerned with the extent to which levels of interpersonal and social support contributed to the onset of depression in old age. Part of the design was to select three groups of people that differed on levels of such support—high, medium, and low. Moreover, the groups were to come not from just one society or culture but potentially many. The rationale for such a design is obvious: level of interpersonal and social support either does or does not contribute in uniform ways to the onset of depression, regardless of culture or the nature of any social setting that was selected.

A tentative draft of that chapter was sent to Ernest Boesch. He was asked if he might find time to comment on the paper. This resulted in his authoring the "Seven Flaws" paper. Briefly recounting the general nature of the correspondence, Ernest criticized the various ways in which the study could be considered "flawed." Of course, these "flaws" were clearly articulated in the article. As a pedagogical exercise, this example worked well. However, as was pointed out later to Ernest, the use of "flaws" in the title, and the way in which they were explained, may be somewhat misleading. Perhaps a better word to use in the context of the little exercise would have been "challenges." That is, the problems or "flaws" that Boesch articulated are, to most cross-cultural psychologists, primarily challenges. They try to meet these challenges to the best of their ability.

But the main issue to be emphasized is one that Boesch addressed toward the end of the article. He wrote,

> Well, so far goes the story. It might appear to be a plea for cultural and against cross-cultural psychology. This is only partly so. The relationship between cultural and cross-cultural psychology is not one of either-or, one of simply choosing to be or the other, because, at their appropriate place, each is needed. But we should be aware of their respective functions and qualities. (p. 257, chapter 11)

That wise perspective, to me, is an excellent example of the wisdom Boesch has brought to the psychological study of culture. We might summarize the situation in this manner: The best that cross-cultural psychology has to offer—conceptualizing research projects, addressing the challenges of numerous methodological concerns, using the results to enrich psychology—can only happen if the best of cultural psychology—deep and probing cultural analysis, a solid understanding of the intricacies in cultures in any project—is made available to cross-cultural psychologists. Both approaches to the study of culture are, ideally, mutually relevant. They truly need each other. This, we believe, is one of the most important legacies of Ernest Boesch.

A Consideration of Other Factors

What would most people do with their life if delivered the varied circumstances that were allotted to Professor Boesch as a child and adolescent? From his position as an accomplished scholar, he wrote and spoke of the importance of psychology as an applied study and assumed an active voice by expressing his deep concern for human life. He fully recognized that his childhood and adolescence was a time of deep emotional pain inflicted largely by his parents' divorce and the oppressive wartime conditions of early twentieth century Europe. How ironic and counter-intuitive that one who suffered hardship became a staunch advocate for compassion and concern of others. Would it not be more likely that a highly talented and sensitive young boy becomes very angry, rebellious, and seeks ways to gain power so as never to endure the wiles of aggression again, unrealistic as that aspiration might be? There is much to learn about the ideals of Ernest Boesch's scholarship by examining the various choices he made in his life when presented with distinct options at crucial junctures of time and space. What valence system led him to choose the actions he did when he clearly had rich and diverse action potential within reach?

Many times while researching and writing this biography the mind's eye has watched a little boy intensely observing pigeons strutting along the walkway in front of a stately old Church in St. Gallen. He was fascinated and wished so much that he could touch those illusive creatures. In response to his father's suggestion, he believed he might actually catch a bird and hold it if he could get close enough to sprinkle salt on its tail. Why would a 4-year-old child doubt his father when he offered a strategy to achieve something he greatly desired? Yet, when the child carefully stepped toward a pigeon, he heard his father laughing as he tried so hard to approach the bird. He realized then that he had been tricked, and it was hurtful enough so the event was recalled more than 80 years later. He had been manipulated; trust was compromised if not lost. Who can return to trusting someone who mocks you because you believed him? Ironically, Ernest's father apprehended a child who bullied his son. He gave the boy a harsh lecture about his wrongful behavior, and then sent him away without so much as a swat across his bottom. What psychologist would not expect that a child exposed to such behaviour be somewhat confused about the value and purpose of human relationships? Such inconsistency could become resentful about the injustices he endured and seek retribution? At 12 years of age, Ernest's world collapsed around him when his parents divorced and the family broke up. Not until he became a young adult would Ernest be free enough to visit his mother and sister again. Adding insult to injury, the boy recognized that his mother had left him for life with a new husband who was neither a pleasant nor accomplished person. Where was her compassion and empathy? What were the prospects of living even a modestly happy life when one is living with a father who struggled to earn a living in a seriously depressed economy?

Without considering the pain of hunger and poor health the adolescent boy endured, how did school life complement or counter-balance a difficult personal life? School offered one of the greatest sources of hope in Ernest's young life. He was a voracious reader as a child and a regular patron of the school library. Recognizing the kind of books he selected on his own, an attentive librarian offered resources that expanded his knowledge and awareness. He heeded the suggestions and found the pursuit of literature a highly satisfying way to nourish his inquisitiveness and imagination. Entering the world of books probably offered a psychological reprieve from negative conditions at home and in the community. Ernest could create his own mental space by reading and writing.

The more he read, the more he wanted to create his own stories and poems. Ernest Boesch's interest in all forms of literature grew with his education and personal development. Even as he approached his 90th year, despite severely impaired vision, he was writing and publishing books (as noted earlier, he was working on a psychological novel that used some aspects of "The Sound of the Violin" in the plot). Written language was a means of personal expression and a mode of exploring the world of others who shared their intellectual and personal lives with readers. Despite brief spates of academic rebellion, formal education provided a means of successfully associating with the wider world, demonstrating his abilities, and finding a mode of direction for his talents and energy. Simply put, school success was a crucially important way that Boesch demonstrated his action potential that expanded his sense of accomplishment and life purpose.

Music was one of the most universally positive areas of expression that Ernest shared with his family, fellow students, and community. It was a source of delight in his early family experiences, and an aspect of life that his grandparents and parents shared with their children. His natural talents were acknowledged and nurtured, particularly by his father. As Ernest grew older, his interest and mastery increased. Performing at community events in school bands and symphonies provided happy and encouraging experiences. In his more quiet and personal time, playing guitar and singing was an outlet shared with small groups of friends whom he met at school. Music allowed Ernest safe, liberating, and rewarding expressions individually and collectively. Like his reading habits, the more Ernest knew of music, the more he sought to learn. As with his literary interests, music was a means by which feelings and energy were channeled into forms that could be shared, positively received, and establish connections with others. Picture the gaily decorated streets of St. Gallen, crowds gathered along the parade route for the community festival, and Ernest leading the band playing his trumpet. With zest and confidence born of practice and acknowledgement that he was a talented musician worthy of his place as parade leader, he embraced the excitement. Music and academic abilities were strongly endorsed by the child, his teachers, family, and peers. They offered hope for the present and the future.

When Ernest Boesch spoke of nurturing family members in his childhood, his maternal grandmother was clearly a person who was consistently positive and offered him a loving relationship. "Cheerful," a rather infrequent description in his lexicon, was the word he used to describe her. She was also generous, warm, and happy in the simple activities of home and community life. Ernest's grandfather was described as caring.

He taught his grandson woodworking skills that may have been mutually enjoyable outlets for artistic talents he otherwise applied as an embroidery designer. However, there was a cloak of tragedy about grandfather Boesch that related to his financial difficulties that meant hardship and loss for his family. He conveyed a feeling of guilt that Ernest detected when he attended church services with his grandfather. The environment and messages delivered at church were remembered as dour, heavy, and conveyed a sense that life was experienced in the shadow of guilt and humiliation. There was nothing inspiring, interesting, or spirited about church-going for Ernest. However, his introduction to Buddhism while in Thailand offered a more positive religious experience.

Although Ernest's father turned his anger outward and tended to inflict it on others, his grandfather turned his distress inward, seemingly to punish himself. While there is no way to be certain, Ernest's exposure to males was much less nurturing than the females he knew, primarily his grandmother. It would not be until university studies that he met men of great ability who were positive models for such a dedicated and accomplished student. At Geneva he encountered men who were open, warm, interesting, and encouraging. It is remarkable that he patiently endured until his university life began.

Surely there are many students who have succeeded in advanced studies and academic careers despite lacking a role model among family members for such ambitious endeavors. However, Ernest's situation was much more complicated given that he and his father were in economic distress. Basic sustenance was meager, sometimes leaving them poorly nourished. They rented a sleeping room for their shelter. While his father tried to overcome poverty, employment was scarce and his efforts proved ineffective. In keeping with Ernest's practical nature, after completing the commercial branch of high school, he immediately sought work. Yet, surprisingly, his high score on a personnel test did not result in an immediate job offer. Rather, he and his father were told that someone with the ability to score as Ernest belonged in the university. Basically, he was considered ineligible for a job because of his high abilities. This closed one narrow option and opened an array of new ones. Ironically, an objective recommendation offered by a person who had very little to do with Ernest other than reading a test score changed his life dramatically.

The negative consequences of his rebellion against Latin classes registered immediately in as much as Ernest was ineligible for university without them. Fortunately, a tutor, who worked for a modest stipend, was found and Ernest was transformed into a willing Latin student. Were the stars, the fates, and undeniable motivation the coaligned forces that produced a new path? How much easier and practical it would have been to persuade the carpet manufacturer that a job and steady income was far more important than academics at that time. "Unique by destiny" as Ernest would say. Talent pointed the way to higher education.

What did he mean when Professor Boesch referred to arriving at Geneva as a "rebirth?" Not only did he enter a new and very beautiful physical environment. He became an independent person except for a friend from St. Gallen who was also university bound. The war had not ceased, economic hardship was only slightly relieved. Yet Ernest himself was transformed by the changes that took place in his environment and circumstances. He realized that context mattered greatly. Previous events of his childhood and youth lay behind him, sad and uninspiring as many of them were. He was in a place and time that invited him to seize the moment. "Cognitive Restructuring" was not officially invented. Yet that is an apt description of the very process of "rebirth" Ernest experienced in Geneva. The creative force of human mind and will that is at the core of Boesch's SAT was at work. If he could be reborn once, why couldn't that happen again?

Once again, practicality dictated the program of study Ernest selected, despite his strong preference to become a child psychiatrist. He could not afford the cost medical studies required, so he selected what seemed a next-best option. Perhaps there were feelings of regret, but he launched his studies in the Rousseau Institute with determination. Piaget "was like a mountain," and Ernest was in awe of him. Through the faculty at Geneva, Ernest was lead on a fascinating study of children's psycho-linguistic and cognitive development. His studies were rewarding, but a personal relationship eventually became problematic.

When Ernest discussed his relationship with Claire, it appeared that there were many elements of their situation that were not adequately assessed before marriage. One was that they were both of a marriageable age when they met. As their relationship developed, the expectation that they would marry increased for Claire. Even though there was much about her that Ernest respected and admired, he deeply questioned the possibility that they could ever share an enduring and happy relationship. His initial doubts proved to be accurate. However, despite serious misgivings they married and had three children. One might question why they started raising a family, especially considering the reservations Ernest had expressed to Claire. Ernest was starting a new career as a school psychologist and also had to write a defendable dissertation. He was fully occupied with his professional responsibilities. Claire had aspirations for a musical career and care for an infant forced her to set her goals aside. From the description of their life that Ernest provided, the time they seemed to share most easily was their interaction when Ernest accompanied Claire as she practiced her violin. Not unlike Ernest's parents, the young couple tried to find a point of contact through shared musical interests. Yet that did not compensate for the tensions and dissatisfactions each experienced.

When Andre was born in 1943, Ernest's life was keenly focused on professional accomplishments. Even when discussing his life with his us, he infrequently spoke of personal concerns and relationships after he reached adulthood. He did not mention extended family relationships with his or Claire's parents, nor did he mention the emotional impact (or lack thereof) of his parents' death on himself or members of his family. In his discussions, his writing, research, and teaching were of utmost importance. He spoke enthusiastically and consistently about the development of SAT, his psychological theory. But when reflecting on relationships with his children, he indicated they were somewhat strained. However, his children have achieved considerable success as accomplished adults.

After living in St. Gallen for more than eight years, Professor Boesch decided to move his family to Saarbrücken when he was offered the chair of psychology at the newly established university. Being closer to Paris was positive for Claire and her parents, however that was a secondary consequence of the goal of securing a professional position that suited Ernest. Unlike his earlier move from St. Gallen to Geneva, he did not speak of his arrival at Saarbrucken as anything close to a personal or professional rebirth. It seemed to be a strategic "next step" in his career development but was not regarded with unabated enthusiasm.

With his dissertation completed and well received, leaving the intense schedule of work as a school psychologist for a position as chair of psychology would seem to have allowed for a more balanced personal and professional life. However, Professor Boesch soon became involved in UNESCO programs of a global scope. It is not difficult to recognize that such an affiliation was very appealing to him considering his intellectual curiosity and concern for people particularly those from undeveloped or third world nations. When UNESCO offered Professor Boesch the position as director of a new research institute in Bangkok, his university endorsed it as a way to increase its status as an educational institution. On a personal level, the Bangkok assignment afforded Earnest and Claire a period of separation in which they could evaluate what might be done about their unhappy and unfulfilling marriage.

However, there were three young children in the family in 1955. Given that Boesch's primary focus in psychology to date was on child development and assessment strategies, it would seem he must have thought of how his absence from the family might affect his children's development, especially their emotional life. This might be of particular concern since he indicated that Claire was not highly rewarded in the role of mother and homemaker. When she asked about the family going to Bangkok together, it was finally decided that Ernest would go alone. From our perspective, this was a very important personal as well as professional decision. It meant that when he arrived in Bangkok, the primary emphasis was on his professional responsibilities and personal adaptation to a very new and different cultural environment. His time and attention could be dedicated to developing working relationships with his staff and associates, and conducting a complex research agenda.

Experientially, Thailand presented a riot of diversity in all aspects of living. Ernest entered into an ecological system unlike anything he had previously experienced. Climate, language, food, clothing, accommodations, sights, sounds, smells, were all radically different from what he had known before. Rather than being overwhelmed by the changes, it seemed to be energizing and exciting to him. His reference to arriving in Bangkok as a rebirth, the same term used to describe his personal evolution when he arrived in Geneva, was very revealing. He anticipated, and was on the cusp of major developments in his personal and professional life. Bangkok represented a new cultural and professional life that was very agreeable to Ernest. Given that his SAT was in a nascent stage, a totally new context allowed for constant observations to assess how well it withstood the test of universality.

For a highly imaginative and creative young man, there was something missing in his new life and that was romance. With whom could he share his excitement and intrigue about all that he was experiencing? That person was Supanee, a staff member of the institute who was assigned to spend many hours each day teaching Ernest the Thai language. For those who are honored by meeting Supanee, even as an elderly woman, she is intelligent, spontaneous, warm, beautiful, charmingly humorous, and high spirited. One only has to see the photos of her as a young woman to understand how easily Ernest came to like her and eventually love her. Being from a large and prominent Bangkok family, Supanee was able to introduce Professor Boesch into an extensive, interesting, and happy social life. Through her he was able to satisfy his desire to gain a sense of belonging, and becoming "one of them" as he referred to one of his goals as an emerging cultural psychologist.

When the time came to leave Thailand it must have been emotionally wrenching for both Ernest and Supanee. Neither had any assurance of what lay ahead in terms of their relationship. For Ernest, returning to Claire and his children had to feel quite daunting. He knew that it was not possible to return home and resume life with Claire as though they would continue as before or with renewed dedication to their marriage. When he told Claire of his relationship with Supanee, she was not willing to accept her husband's proposed resolution to the complicated situation. Claire preferred that they end the marriage in divorce, which they did. Again a great distance was created between Professor Boesch and his children.

Claire left with them for Paris and later moved to Geneva which became her permanent home until her death. With his active professional life and his marriage to Supanee in 1960, visits with his children were not frequent. This was complicated further by the barriers that Claire placed between herself and her former husband. Eventually, Claire became estranged from Ernest, thus affecting his relationship with his children as well. She died in 2004.

In the midst of personal changes, professionally Ernest was advancing as a cultural psychologist. With cultural norms of the Saar at the time being quite ethnocentric, Ernest and Supanee were an unusual couple. They shared an adapted Thai lifestyle at home including speaking Thai and enjoying Thai food. Ernest's professional role consisted of teaching, research, and administration of the institute adjacent to the university. In time, Supanee adapted to life as the "foreign" person in a rather provincial German city. Now in their 46th year of marriage, one can only conclude that they shared a meaningful and happy life that sustained them in the early years of cultural and personal challenges. It is impossible to estimate how much Supanee influenced Ernest's life and vice-versa. However, when visiting their home, Thai culture is immediately obvious in the art, furnishings, and rhythm of their life together.

As he clearly articulated in his "Seven Flaws" essay, Ernest Boesch's thoughtful insights into the complexity of conducting research across cultures was largely based on his Bangkok years. Furthermore, he also gained awareness of how many layers of differences there are among people living within an identified cultural group as he spent more time and studied Thai society more carefully. Ernest identified many crucial points that any researcher who conducted studies with multiple human subjects needs to take into careful consideration. Interactions between researchers and subjects may affect the responses that are given to survey or interview questions. He identified differences in value systems, language usage, and interpretations across socioeconomic classes even within one city, such as Bangkok. After 1958 Professor Boesch deeply questioned the assumptions and methods of what may be considered mainstream Euro-American psychology.

A Final Word and the Reprise of an Epilogue

We hope that those who read this text and dedicate time to reflect on its constituent parts will gain an appreciation for the immense influence that culture has on all human endeavors. This influence includes the nature, purpose and scope of psychological research involving forays into cultures and societies unlike our own. Indeed, the ways we think about and package the elusive construct of culture is central to our intellectual inquiries. Neither Professor Boesch nor we, the authors, have the desire to invoke change or to alter the thinking or work of their readers purposely. What he hoped to accomplish in a career highlighted by a wide range of writings, and what we have hoped to accomplish in this book, is to join him in contributing to an increased awareness and appreciation for what cultural and cross-cultural psychologists can do. The intense questioning and study that Ernest Boesch brought to his work as a psychologist who experienced substantial changes in his personal life and in his productive professional life, and in the way he thought that psychology should be used, commands respect and invites emulation. Those who recognize and respect the powerful influence that culture has on all aspects of human life will find much food for thought in the life and work of Ernest Boesch. We especially hope that readers will reflect on the journey that led to discovering himself to be a cultural psychologist.

As our lengthy work on this book was drawing to a close, Ernest sent us an e-mail that contained a slightly apologetic eleventh-hour idea. He said that he had been thinking about his career, about the topical coverage contained in this book, and mainly about what the reader should remember regarding his contributions. Clearly, he has reflected a great deal about his heartfelt and passionately-driven attempt to help explain the intricate dance between human activity and culture. Paraphrasing him, he said the more he thought about it, the more he would be grateful if the epilogue that appeared in his 387-page 1991 *Symbolic Action Theory and Cultural Psychology* could be included. In making this request, he noted that it "really summarizes well the reasons for action theory," and above all contains basically important considerations that may not be sufficiently explicit in the previous sections. We agree that it is a fine summary of his main reasons for developing symbolic action theory and for writing a book about it. Because this book is primarily an effort to acquaint the reader with highlights of the life and work of a dedicated student of human behavior (and often a worried one because of the perils and pernicious perturbations of the world), we took the necessary last-minute steps to include the epilogue that appeared in a book that is now out of print. Information Age Publishing kindly agreed to accommodate, through us, Ernest's request. The epilogue closed his 1991 book. Still timely, we take pleasure in using it in its entirety as a fitting way to close this one.

EPILOGUE (BOESH, 1991)

We have now somehow closed the circle of our deliberations. We started with a look at the experience of alien cultures, and we finished by looking at the experience of the other person. Taking into account our preceding discussions, the two problems appear not to be basically different. The other, the self, our and the alien culture, all emerge from complex processes of construction, partly succeeding each other, partly parallel, but basically pursuing the same goal: to place the individual within a world which appears to be ordered, "transparent," as I said, providing the space, the opportunities and the rules for action. It is action which relates the individual to his or her environment, action which leads him or her to assimilate their world, to identify with it, submit to it, dissociate from it or rebel against it. In the course of these various forms of interaction, the individual's reality will be influenced or even transformed, and his self will be structured. These processes are interrelated in complex ways, but the basic concept for analyzing them is "action."

I therefore started by looking at action in its simplest form—initiation, execution, goal. Indeed, pursuing goals appeared to be the general common property of the multitude of possible actions. Yet, we soon discovered that these goals were embedded within goal-sequences and systems, regulated by dominant orientations, so that isolating the single action became a kind of analytical "trick," useful, but not sufficient in itself. In addition, we discovered that action goals were not always easy to specify or delimit: first, because there are, so to speak "permanent" goals, the most basic of these appearing to be the strengthening and improving of our "action potential." The testing, expanding, and reinforcing of this potential is a life-long motive, and it requires, as a consequence, other goal orientations: it needs surroundings in which we can orient ourselves, anticipate events, localize our goals. In other words, the action potential depends upon an ordered environment. This need for orientation somehow integrates actions into a continuous activity of creating order out of what potentially could become chaotic. Yet, in pursuing order, we are like a navigator: we structure objective bearings, but we do so according to the goals we want to reach.

There is a second difficulty in defining goals. Goals are integrated in action *sequences*; therefore, they have a history and aim toward a future. They are integrated in action *spheres*; therefore, they are interlaced with goals of others and related to a material, social and ideational environment. Moreover, action will always achieve objective as well as subjective results. All this combines to imbue our actions with complex meanings: they are polyvalent.

"Polyvalent" means three things: first, actions, aiming at composite goals, are "over-determined"; second, they connote different areas of experience; and, third, they draw their justifications not simply from the concrete specific results they (tend to) achieve, but also from the subjective experiences implied, from personal fantasms, cultural rules and values. In this multidimensional way actions become symbolic, and this symbolism applies not simply to single actions, but to the environment as well, and to the acting individuals. Symbolism, we found, pervasive; we live in a world which throughout is both real and symbolic, and both, reality and symbolism, derive from processes of structuring.

I do not want, in this epilogue, to summarize further the long discussions of this volume, or to justify again the conclusions offered. After all, the general course of my argumentation has already been outlined in the introductory chapter; to repeat it here would be uselessly redundant. I do wish to stress, though, some additional general points concerning, on the one hand, questions of methodology, and on the other concerns about the rationale this type of psychology implies.

In 1971 I published a book whose subtitle was *"Prolegomena to an ecological psychology."* I could as well have named it "cultural psychology," since I defined "culture" to be the "biotope" of human beings (Boesch, 1980, p. 19)—but at that time the term culture would not yet have appealed much to potential (Germanophone) readers. Yet, rereading today the introductory chapter, it seems to me as pertinent as it did twenty years ago. Its main thrust was that psychology as an experimental science was unable to study man as a maker of history—meaning culture. The being, I wrote, whose perception, memory, thinking, emotions and motivations we analyze patiently in long series of experiments, "is also the one who invents electricity, nylons, atom bombs, who carries the names of Mozart, Picasso, Einstein, Churchill or Hitler, is the one who researches, nurtures, builds, plans, tortures, kills, kidnaps and seduces. Little of what the object of our studies does in reality, and little of what our society profits or suffers from it, appears in psychological publications. It seems as if there were two kinds of human beings: those in the aseptic laboratories of psychologists, and those in whose realities we participate as partners, friends or opponents" (1971, pp. 9-10). I then contrast the methodologies of experimental and "naturalistic" psychology. Experiments, to be sure, produce highly controlled and precise results, which, however, lose much of their validity when generalized beyond the experimental situation. On the other hand, "naturalistic" (or "biotic," as I tend to call it) research has to forego the systematic control of situations, variables and subjects, yet is able to compensate for the resulting imprecision by multiplying the biotic observations and by its closeness to the areas of reality on which its results should bear. Experimental and naturalistic research, each with its own qualities and limitations, should therefore complement each other.

At that time I still assumed that researchers were mainly motivated by a quest for truly understanding reality. Yet, like any other action, research also is polyvalent. The goal of researchers may, indeed, be truth, but only among a number of other goal components, not the least of them being social recognition. This explains why methodology tends to become an ideology, opposing, sometimes quite violently, different "schools"—meaning ingroups—of thought. Thus, even the most liberal experimentalist would consider naturalistic methods as mere preliminaries to "serious" research, and while I grant that these rigid positions have been somewhat softened in recent years, in the scientific community of our universities nomothetic psychology still commands the highest prestige.

This, I am convinced today, has to be reversed. Experimental research will be useful mainly in selectively checking the findings of biotic research amenable to this method of investigation. It will control the generality of biotic findings, the conditions of their emergence and development - but biotic research will have to lead the way. The reason is obvious: *Each experiment, however "controlled" the setting, represents a cultural situation.* The relationships between experimenter and subject differ from culture to culture, and so do the connotations of tasks, of question-answer interactions, so do the oughts and the interdictions, the self-other-aspirations or anxieties. Thus, the sense of an experiment, the meaning of its results and its external validity depend upon cultural understanding which has to be provided by biotic research. It is therefore useless—although often practised—to export our experimental techniques to cultures with which we are not intimately familiar.

The question then arises as to how to conduct such biotic research. I cannot in this short epilogue go into details of methodology. Basically, Barker's "natural settings" paradigm (1968) will gain importance here; anthropological techniques of systematic (participant) observation will provide models; unobtrusive interviewing in natural settings will have to be developed as a special skill and will have to precede, accompany—and often also to follow up—more formal questioning; key-informants will have to be used extensively, albeit with more sophistication than is often the case: in-depth analysis of their own goal structures and I-world-relationship, as well as systematic comparison with other informants, would have to become standard practice. And in all this, of course, proficiency in the local language will become imperative.

However, the main methodological requisite will be an adequate theoretical framework. "Participant observation" must decide *what* to observe; interviewing, however unobtrusive, will have to decide *whom* to interview on *what*. In analogy to his clinical colleague, whose inquiry is guided by a taxonomy of behavior deviations, the cultural psychologist needs a theoretical framework of cultural forms and conditions of action. Therefore, in planning as well as in performing research, our most frequent question was: What kind of action is this for the actor within his specific context and situation? Thus, when planning an investigation on future anticipations of Thai villagers (Sripraphai & Sripraphai, 1988), we had to specify under what conditions a person started future planning, in which form and along which dimensions. We had to ask, too, what it meant to talk to an investigator about future anticipations (this being an action in its own right); which, then, brought up the question of how, when and why an individual tended to protect his private imaginations, fears or hopes—and so on. Inquiring about the nature of an action will necessarily lead to action networks within an action field. Hence, action theory proved most adequate because it allowed one to remain close to the natural situation of the involved actors—whose own perspective, I should stress, it takes systematically into account.

These, of course, are only cursory comments concerning problems which would better be treated in a new book. Allow me just one additional point. The members of our "Socio-psychological Research Center" have carried out, over a period of about twenty years, a number of projects in Thailand, Afghanistan and different African countries. Of course, in these projects we tried out various methodological approaches and time schedules. Ultimately, we concluded that the anthropological routine of staying with the target group for a longish period (we chose it to be a year) offered the best conditions for psychological research. Of course, financial constraints made this an optimum we could achieve only exceptionally. To psychologists, who are accustomed to collecting their data speedily, a full year in the field would sound like an unnecessary luxury—or even a waste of time. For anthropologists, though, it is normal (or even minimal, if we consider their frequent *second* field trip for verifying or completing initial findings). For animal ethologists—studying for instance chimpanzees in the wild—a year is even much too short. Maybe that we should start looking more seriously at the problem of "biotic—read cultural—validity": short field trips are, of course, cheaper, but the low validity of their findings makes them *too* cheap.

Cultural psychology is not infrequently considered to be a branch of general psychology applied to alien cultures. This, of course, is an error. Cultural psychology is no less relevant in our *own* cultures and subcultures, and in fact is already practised to some extent under names such as "social psychology," "environmental psychology," "consumer psychology," or "political psychology." It certainly is going to make inroads, too, in clinical psychology, counseling and psychotherapy (where, by the way, action theory will be of significant importance). Yet, these branches tend to be considered as mere specializations subsumable under the "basic" discipline of general psychology. It is my contention that in the future the prestige of psychological investigations which disregard the cultural context should and will be reduced to the level of biotic validity they can claim—and prove.

Cultural psychology is a "systemic" science. We have seen in the preceding pages the enormously complex interrelations into which the individual action is embedded. In other words, the paradigm of "independent-dependent variables" will no longer be of great use; this use will be even less when we remember the ubiquitous and considerable symbolic variance of reality and experience which makes the "operationalization" of variables a futile endeavor. Necessarily, then, progress in cultural psychology will come about less by an increased sophistication of measurements than by a continuous to and fro between observation and theory: Theory will guide observation, observation will check and modify theory, and progress will consist in multiplying and differentiating observations which can consistently be integrated into a refined theoretical framework. Improving the fit between observation and theory will thus become the dominant methodological concern. This, in a nutshell, would be how I define a methodology which might be qualified as hermeneutic, provided that the term is not taken as a licence for freewheeling speculation. On the contrary, this conception requires that a theory be made explicit from the *outset*, as a framework for specifying problems and directing observations, and that the interchange between findings and theory remain an "overarching goal." Action theory would, I assert, be suited for fulfilling such a function.

But there is more to it. Action theory, in the constructivist conception I have proposed in this book, is based on a dynamic philosophy of the human being. As I see it, historically psychology has tended to adopt three paradigms of human nature, which can be succinctly formulated as follows: a first, exemplified by the Gestalt perspective, considered human behavior to be determined by the structures of the brain; for a second, behaviorism, man was the product of a succession of conditionings; and a third, psychoanalysis, saw man as being shaped by imprintings and reaction-formations during childhood. All based their scientific status on a strict determinism, and of course, all are right: the Gestalt laws are real, conditionings do occur, and we all are influenced by childhood experiences. Yet, all three are wrong in the generalization of their findings to the nature of man. Although psychoanalysis (and some Gestaltists) have tried, none of them proved able to explain the main human achievement: *culture*.

In constructivist action theory, by contrast, human beings interact with the environment in a dynamic way, thereby structuring the objectal and social world as well as the self and its action potentialities. Of course, this ontogenetic construction is neither unguided nor arbitrary. The successive structures the human child achieves are in part determined by his constitutional endowment, following a universal course; in part they are guided by cultural impacts. Yet there remain leeways, degrees of freedom, due both to culture and to the elasticity of our endowment, which individuals may fill out according to their inclinations and orientations. Of course, the gifted ones, the privileged ones, will enjoy more of those opportunities than others, yet, potentially, human beings are, within limits, creators of situations. This is the deeper sense of the concept of action. Action implies the possibility of choice, and the potential of the actor to effect those choices. I am aware of the philosophical problems this raises—it is my choice to disregard them. We cannot solve unsolvable problems—like the one of freedom—before taking a stand.

Such a conception, necessarily, implies responsibility. Culture is a creation of human beings, a result of choices made over generations, but also a result of continuous interactions between individuals and their group and environment. Man is the perceiver, interpreter, transformer and, to some extent, also the maker of his world, and so he becomes also responsible for it—each in his or her smaller or bigger ways. Trying to understand man as a cultural being forced me to see the diversity of cultures as a proof of human *creativity*. Then, however, a strictly deterministic theoretical framework could not be appropriate anymore. For all these reasons, although having undergone quite a few theoretical influences, I unhesitatingly opted for the one which not only allows inclusion of man's creativity, but also promises to restore his dignity.

NOTE

1. Paul B. Baltes died on November 7, 2006, shortly after the manuscript for this book was completed. Baltes, a brilliant student of Ernest Boesch, received his doctorate from the University of the Saar in 1967. After some years at the University of Virginia, he became director of the Center of Lifespan Psychology at the Max Planck Institute for Human Development, Berlin, and professor of psychology at the Free University of Berlin. There he instituted and conducted, together with a group of devoted students and colleagues, for many years a research program on aging known throughout the world. The research projects in which he was involved, besides their methodological merits, greatly contributed to restoring the social importance, the self-confidence, and the dignity of elderly people. This is a lasting and important contribution made by Paul Baltes in times prone to complaining about the over-aging of society. He died at the early age of 67, but his work will remain.

REFERENCES

Baltes, P. B. (1997). Ernst E. Boesch at 80: Reflections from a student on the culture of psychology. *Culture & Psychology, 3,* 247-256.

Barker, R. G. (1968). *Ecological psychology.* Stanfordm CT: Stanford University Press.

Boesch, E. E. (1980). *Kultur und Handlung.* Bern: Huber.

Boesch, E. E. (1997). The story of a cultural psychologist: Autobiographical observations. *Culture & Psychology, 3,* 257-275.

Boesch, E. E. (2006). *Gregorius und der Engel oder Erholung am Thunersee.* Saarbrükken: Private Printing.

Hermans, H. J. M. (1997). Commonalities in Boesch and Murray: Bridging between a European and an American thinker. *Culture & Psychology, 3,* 395-404.

Jahoda, G. (1991). Foreword. In E. E. Boesch (Ed.), *Symbolic action theory and cultural psychology* (pp. v-vi) Berlin, Germany: Springer.

Kluckhohn, C. & Murray, H.A. (1949). *Personality in nature, society, and culture.* New York: A. A. Knopf.

Murray, H. A. (1940). What should psychologists do about psychoanalysis? *Journal of Abnormal and Social Psychology, 35,* 150-175.

Sripraphai, P., & Sriprahphai, K. 1988). *Future anticipations in a Thai village.* Fort Lauderdale, FL: Breitenbach.

Segall, M. H., Lonner, W. J., & Berry, J. W (1998). Cross-cultural psychology as a scholarly discipline: On the flowering of culture in behavioral research. *American Psychologist, 53,* 1101-1110

SCHRIFTENVERZEICHNIS/ BIBLIOGRAPHY

BOOKS

1946: L'organisation d'un service de psychologie scolaire. St. Gallen: Tschudy. (Phil.Diss., Genève), 134 p.

1952: L'exploration du caractère de l'enfant. Paris: Editions du Scarabée. 165 p. (Italian and Portuguese translations; bibl. of which lacking)

1965: (in collaboration with H. -J. Koebnik, B. Joerges, S. Paul): Das Problem der Alphabetisierung in Entwicklungsländern. Stuttgart: Klett. 146 p.

1970: Zwiespältige Eliten. Eine sozialpsychologische Untersuchung über administrative Eliten in Thailand. Bern: Huber, 333 p.

1971: Zwischen zwei Wirklichkeiten. Prolegomena zu einer ökologischen Psychologie. 499 p.. Bern: Huber. (Content: See 3.ARTICLES, 1971, and reprint 1971)

1973: Arzt und Patient in Thailand. In: Hochschule des Saarlandes, Aus Forschung und Lehre, 5, 61 p.

1975: Zwischen Angst und Triumph. Über das Ich und seine Bestätigung. Bern: Huber, 87 p.

1976: Psychopathologie des Alltags. Zur Ökopsychologie des Handelns und seiner Störungen. Bern: Huber, 525 p.

1980: Kultur und Handlung. Einführung in die Kulturpsychologie. 270 p. Bern: Huber.

1983: Das Magische und das Schöne. Stuttgart: Frommann-Holzboog, 335 p.

1991: Symbolic action theory and cultural psychology. 356 p. Berlin/New York: Springer.

1993: Von Nagas, Drachen und Geistern. Ein siamesisches Fabulierbuch. Bonn: Deutsch-Thailändische Gesellschaft.

1995: L'action symbolique. Fondements de psychologie culturelle. Paris: L'Harmattan. (French translation and revision of 1991).
1998: Sehnsucht—Von der Suche nach Glück und Sinn. Bern: Huber. 278 p.
2000a: Das lauernde Chaos. Mythen und Fiktionen im Alltag. Bern: Huber. 176 p. 2005: Von Kunst bis Terror. Über den Zwiespalt in der Kultur. Göttingen: Vandenhoeck + Ruprecht. 272 p.

BOOKS, MIMEOGRAPHED, OR PRIVATE PRINTINGS

1956: Research plan of the International Institute for ChildStudy. Bangkok (mimeogr.)
1958: Problems and methods in cross-cultural research. Bangkok: UNESCO, Working Paper I, Ed./4., Expert Meeting on Cross-Cultural Research in Child Psychology (mimeogr., 53 p.).
1958: First research plan of the International Institute for Child Study, parts II and III. Bangkok: UNESCO, Working Paper III, Expert Meeting on Cross Cultural Research in Child Psychology (mimeogr., 61 p.).
1972: Communication between doctors and patients in Thailand. 157 p. Saarbrücken: Sozialpsychologische Forschungsstelle für Entwicklungsplanung.
1989: Das Andere. 21 p. Saarbrücken: Private printing.
2000: Feinde. Nachdenkliches zum Jahrhundertwechsel. Saarbrücken: Private printing
2001: Über Musik. Saarbrücken: Private printing.
2004: Adam und Eva, oder die Hoffnung des Erzengels und die Unruhe des Don Juan. Private printing
2005: Reime und Bilder. Gedichte. Private printing,
2006a: Konnotationsanalyse. Zur Verwendung der freien Ideenassoziation in Diagnostik und Therapie. Überarbeitung und Erweiterung von 1977. Private printing. 101 p.
2006b: Gregorius und der Englel oder Erholung am Thuner see. Private printing.

ARTICLES

1942: (avec J. Piaget, M. Lambercier, B. v. Albertini), Introduction à l'étude des perceptions chez l'enfant et analyse d'une illusion relative à la perception visuelle de cercles concentriques. Archives de Psychologie, Genève, 29, 111. (Diplomarbeit)
1943-1951: Schulpsychologische Sprechstunde. St.Gallen: St.Galler Tagblatt. (various articles concerning school-psychological problems; detailed bibl. lacking)
1949: Un test par le dessin. In: L. Klages et al. (ed), Le diagnostic du caractère. Paris: Presses Universitaires de France.

1951: Schule und Psychologie. Bern: Schweizerische Erziehungsrundschau. (bibl. lacking)

1951: Das schwachbegabte Kind in der Normalschule. Bern: Schweizerische Erziehungsrundschau. (bibl. lacking)

1951: Das erziehungsgefährdete Kind. Bern: Pro Juventute. (bibl. lacking)

1952a: Die Gewohnheit und das Unbewusste. Saarbrücken: Annales Universitatis Saraviensis, 1, 110-113.

1952b: L'UNESCO et l'enseignement européen. Saarbrücken: Annales Universitatis Saraviensis, 1, 379-385.

1952c: Zum Problem der psychischen Projektionen. Saarbrücken: Annales Universitatis Saraviensis, 1, 286-302.

1953: Persönlichkeit und Gemeinschaft. In: A.Wellek (ed.), *Bericht über den 19. Kongress der Deutschen Gesellschaft für Psychologie*, 204-205. Köln.

1954: Über die klinische Methodik in der psychologischen Diagnostik. Zeitschrift für diagnostische Psychologie und Persönlichkeitsforschung, 2, 275-292.

1954: Brandverhütungspropaganda bei Kindern. St. Gallen: Mitteilungen der Vereinigung kantonal-schweizerischer Feuerversicherungsanstalten, 33, 167-172.

1955a: Soziabilität, Sozialverhalten und Sozialleistung. Schweiz. Zeitschrift für Psychologie und ihre Anwendungen, 14, 278-296.

1955b: Erziehung zum internationalen Verständnis als psycho-hygienisches Problem. Saarbrücken: Hefte des Europa-Instituts der Universität des Saarlandes, 1, 10-26.

1960a: Projektion und Symbol. Psychologische Rundschau, 11, 73-91.

1960b: Research in child life as a basis for child welfare programmes. In: International Union for Child Welfare, Geneva (ed.), The child and the family. International Study Conference on Child Welfare (Tokyo).

1960c: The Thailand project, step one. In: Vita humana, No.3, 123-142. Basel: Karger.

1962a: Jugend in Asien. In: A. Wellek (ed.), Bericht über den 16. Internationalen Kongress für Psychologie in Bonn, 1960. Amsterdam, 281-186.

1962b: Auswahl und Vorbereitung von Experten für Entwicklungshilfe. Forum der freien Welt, 4.

1962c: Autorität und Leistungsverhalten in Thailand. In: Thailandstudien. Hamburg: Schriften des Instituts für Asienkunde, vol. 15 (reprint 1971).

1962d: Soziologische und sozialpsychologische Überlegungen zum Aufbau von Gewerbeschulen in Entwicklungsländern. Mondo, Schweizerische Zeitschrift für Entwicklungsfragen, 2, 1-6.

1962e: Education et culture. Etudes Pédagogiques, 17-32.

1963a: Raum und Zeit als Valenzsysteme. In: Hiltmann & Vonessen (eds.), Dialektik und Dynamik der Person. (p. 135-154) Köln: Kiepenheuer & Witsch. (reprint 1971)

1963b: Industrialisierung und sozialer Wandel in Entwicklungsländern. In: Friedrich Ebert Stiftung (ed.), Probleme der Entwicklungshilfe. Hannover: Verlag
Literatur und Zeitgeschehen. (reprint 1971)

1963c: Psychological basis for the education of the physician. In: WHO (ed.), Preparation of the physician for general practice. Geneva: WHO Public Health Paper 20.

1963d: Sozialpsychologische Aspekte der Erziehungshilfe in Thailand. Zeitschrift für Ethnologie, 87/2.

1963e; Adapting education to society. Paris: Working Paper UNESCO/SS/PP/It.9. (reprint 1971, p. 226-267; Italian translation and reprint see here 1965).

1964a: Erziehung und Kultur. In. I. Schindler (ed.), Pädagogisches Denken in Geschichte und Gegenwart. Ratigen: Alois Henn. (reprint 1971)

1964b: Die diagnostische Systematisierung. In: R. Heiss (ed.), Handbuch der Psychologie. vol. 6., p. 930-960. Göttingen: Hogrefe.

1964c: Psychologische Überlegungen zum Rassenvorurteil. In: Vorurteile und ihre Erforschung und Bekämpfung. Politische Psychologie, Bd.3. Frankfurt: Europäische Verlagsanstalt. (reprint 1971; Spanish translation 1972).

1965: Adattare l'instruzione alla società. In: UNESCO (ed.), La metodologia della planificazione dell instruzione nei programmi di sciluppo. Milano:? (Translation of 1963e, reprint in 1971and in: Education, Vol. 1. Tübingen: German Institute for Scientific Cooperation).

1966a: Psychologische Theorie des sozialen Wandels. In: H. Besters & E. E. Boesch (eds.), Entwicklungspolitik. Handbuch und Lexikon. p. 335-416. Stuttgart/Mainz: Kreuz-Verlag/Mathias-Grünewald-Verlag.

1966b: Generationen. In: H. Besters & E.E.Boesch (eds.), Entwicklungspolitik (see 1966a). p. 1177-1179.

1967a: Die Schulpsychologie vor sozialpsychologischen Problemen unserer Zeit. In: E. Bauer (ed.), Ein schulpsychologischer Dienst. p. 65-84. St. Gallen: Verlag und Druckerei Goldach.

1967b: Vorwort. In: D. McClelland: Motivation und Kultur. p. 7-11. Bern: Huber.

1968a: Entwicklungsprozessforschung: Zur Relation von Problem und Methode der Untersuchung. In: Methodische Probleme bei der Entwicklungsländerforschung mit besonderer Berücksichtigung der Stichprobenauswahl. p. 15-35. Berlin: Deutsche Stiftung für Entwicklungsländer.

1968b: (mit P. Baltes & L. Schmidt) Preference for different auditory stimulus sequences in various age groups. In: Psychon. Sci., 10 (6).

1968c: (mit P. Baltes & L. Schmidt) Preference for different visual stimulus sequences in children, adolescents and young adults. In: Psychon. Sci., 11 (8).

1970: Vorwort. In: H. -J. Kornadt & E. Voigt, Situation und Entwicklungsprobleme des Schulwesens in Kenia, II. p. 9-18. Stuttgart: Klett.

1972: Entwicklungshilfe in Forschung und Lehre. In: Dritte Welt, I/3, p. 357-371.

1971: (articles included in book 1971, in addition to the previous ones marked "reprint 1971"):
- Die zwei Wirklichkeiten der Psychologie. p. 9-34.
- Organisation und Regulation. p. 39-49.
- Information, Aspiration und Leistung. p. 138-186.
- Educational assistance to developping countries and disarmement. p. 268-334.
- Überlegungen zum Eliteproblem in Entwicklungsländern. p. 335-390.
- Methodenprobleme der kulturvergleichenden Psychologie. p. 397-445.

- Empirie und Theorie in der Psychologie. p. 446-488.

1975: La détermination culturelle du soi. In: Association de psychologie scientifique de langue française (ed.), Psychologie de la connaissance de soi. p. 99-119. Paris: Presses Universitaires de France.

1976: Fantasmes et réalité. Psychologica Belgica, XVI, 1976-2, p. 171-184.

1977a: The medical interaction. A study in Thailand. In: The German Journal of Psychology, I/1.

1977b: Konnotationsanalyse—zur Verwendung der freien Ideenassoziation in Diagnostik und Therapie. In: Materialien zur Psychoanalyse und analytisch orientierten Psychotherapie. Göttingen/Zürich: Vandenhoeck & Ruprecht, Heft 4, p. 6-72. (Reviewed and completed as privat printing 2006)

1977c: "Mai pen arai"? Überlegungen zur thailändischen Mentalität. Hamburg: Merian, Oktober 1977, p. 28-35.

1977d: Probleme des sozialen Wandels: 15 Jahre Sozialpsychologische Forschungsstelle für Entwicklungsplanung. Ein orschungsbericht. Saarbrücken: Universität des Saarlandes. 62 p.

1977e: Psychological research and social development, illustrated by a study in Thailand. In: Institut für Auslandsbeziehungen (ed.), Cultures in Encounter: Germany and the Southeast Asian Nations. Materialien zum internationalen Kulturaustausch, Bd. 6, p. 118-123. Tübingen: Horst Erdmann.

1978a: Die Flucht in den Rezeptblock. In: Curare, 1, p. 55-63.

1978b: Kultur und Biotop. In: C.F.Graumann (ed.), Ökologische Perspektiven in der Psychologie. p. 11-32. Bern: Huber.

1978c: Pädagogische Hochschule und Universität. In: CAMPUS, Nr.2, Saarbrücken: Universität des Saarlandes.

1980a: Loss of culture through industrialization. In: R.E.Vente & S.J. Chen (eds.): Culture and industrialization. Baden-Baden: Nomos.

1980b: Spiegelverhalten. In: Sozialpsychiatrisches Institut Saar (ed.): Vor und hinter der Kliniktür. Saarbrücken: Schriftenreihe im Sozialpsychiatrischen Institut Saar, p. 23-39.

1980c: Action et objet, deux sources de l'identité du moi. In: P. Tap (ed.), Identité individuelle et personnalisation.Toulouse: Edition Privat, p. 23-37.

1981a: Möglichkeiten und Grenzen psychotherapeutischen Handelns. In: W. R. Minsel & R. Scheller (eds.), Brennpunkte der klinischen Psychologie. p. 11-38. München: Kösel.

1981b: Das persönliche Objekt. In: E.D. Lantermann (ed.), Wechselwirkungen - Psychologische Analysen der Mensch-Umwelt-Beziehung. p. 29-41. Göttingen: Hogrefe.

1981c: Can modern education make use of traditional values? In: R.E.Vente, R. S. Bhathal & R. M. Nakhooda (eds.), Cultural heritage versus technological development, challenges to education. p. 103-136. Singapore: Maruzen Asia.

1981d: Zum Problem der Wertentwicklung, illustriert am Beispiel des traditionellen thailändischen Dorfes. In: R. Oerter (ed.), Bericht über die 5. Tagung Entwicklungspsychologie. p. 10-13. Augsburg: Dokumentation der Universität Augsburg, Bd. 1.

1982a: Fantasmus und Mythus. In: J. Stagl (ed.), Aspekte der Kultursoziologie. p. 59-86. Berlin: Dietrich Reimer.

1982b: Normen und Werte der Körperlichkeit. In: F. Hiller (ed.), Normen und Werte. p. 69-82. Heidelberg: C. Winter.

1982c: Ritual und Psychotherapie. In: Zeitschrift für klinische Psychologie und Psychotherapie, 3/30, p. 214-234.

1983a: A psychologist's look at the refugee problem. In: E. E.Boesch & A .Goldschmidt (eds.), The world refugee problem—refugees and development. p. 11-74. Baden-Baden: Nomos.

1983b: Die psychologische Bedeutung der Hautfarbe. In: R. Kurzrock (ed.), Farbe: Material, Zeichen, Symbol. Schriftenreihe der RIAS-Funkuniversität. p. 131-140. Berlin: Colloquium.

1983c: The personal object. In: Education, vol. 27, p. 99-113. Tübingen: Institute for Scientific Cooperation. (translation of 1981b).

1983d: Von der Handlungstheorie zur Kulturpsychologie. Saarbrücken: Universität des Saarlandes. (Abschiedsvorlesung Juni 1982, 29 p.).

1983e: Die Kulturbedingtheit des Menschen. In: P. Gordan (ed.), Menschwerden, Menschsein. p. 339-369. Kevelaer: Butzon & Bercker.

1983f: Thailand research: Problems of method and theory. In: E. E. Boesch (ed.), Thai culture. Report on the second Thai-European research seminar 1982. p. 3-23. Saarbrücken: Socio-psychological Research Centre on Development Planning.

1984a: Moderne Erziehung und traditionelle Werte. In: G. Trommsdorff (ed.), Jahrbuch für empirische Erziehungswissenschaft. p. 171-190. Düsseldorf: Schwann-Bagel.

1984b: The development of affective schemata. In: Human Development, 3-4, p. 173-183.

1984c: Frontières et comportement. In: Revue Frontières, Merlebach, 1, p. 19-21.

1985a: Qu'est-ce que le dessin ? In: Bulletin de Psychologie, tome XXXVII, no. 369, p. 181-185.

1985b: Verhaltensort und Handlungsbereich. In: G. Kaminski (ed.), Ordnung und Variabilität im Alltagsgeschehen. p. 129-134. Göttingen: Hogrefe.

1986a: Überlegungen zur Genese der Zukunftsperspektive. In: R. Feig & H.D. Erlinger (eds.), Zeit - Zeitlichkeit, Zeiterleben. Siegener Studien, Vol. 39. p. 9-19. Essen: Die blaue Eule.

1986b: Science, culture and development. In: K. Gottstein & G. Link (eds), Cultural development, science and technology in Sub-Saharan Africa. p. 19-29. Baden-Baden: Nomos.

1987a: Die Situation des Handelnden. In: Dr. Margrit Egnèr Stiftung, Festschrift. Zürich, p. 33-45

1987b: Zur Psychologie des magischen Handelns. In: J. Albertz (ed.), Wissen—Glaube—Aberglaube. p. 171-189. Wiesbaden: Freie Akademie.

1987c: Cultural Psychology in action theoretical perspective. In: Ç. Kagitçibasi (ed.), Growth and progress in cross-cultural psychology. p. 41-52. Lisse: International Association for Cross-Cultural Psychology.

1988: Handlungstheorie und Kulturpsychologie. In: Psychologische Beiträge, 30, 3, p. 233-247. Meisenheim/Glan.

1990: Wahrnehmung und Bedeutung im Design. / Perception and meaning in design. (German/English). In: Internationales Forum für Gestaltung Ulm (ed.), Kulturelle Identität und Design / Cultural identity and design. p. 50-56. Berlin: Ernst & Sohn.

1991a: Die Metapher des Käfigs oder die Gedanken von Vaclav Havel. In: DU, Zeitschrift für Kultur, Juni 1991. Zürich: Tages-Anzeiger.

1991b: Skizze zur Psychologie des Heimwehs. In: P. Rück (ed.), Grenzerfahrungen. p. 17-36. Marburg a.L.: Basilisken- Presse.

1992a: Culture—individual—culture: The cycle of knowledge. In: M. v. Cranach, W. Doise & G. Mugny (eds.), Social representations and the social bases of knowledge. p. 89-95. Lewiston, Toronto, Bern, Göttingen: Hogrefe & Huber.

1992b: Ernst Boesch, 1916. In: E.G.Wehner (ed.), Psychologie in Selbstdarstellungen, Bd. 3. p. 67-106. Bern: Huber.

1993a: La patrie construite: vers une psychologie européenne ? In: Psychologie Europe, II, Nr. 2, 1992/1993. p.55-61.

1993b: The sound of the violin. In: The Quarterly Newsletter of the Laboratory of Comparative Human Cognition, Vol. 15, I, p. 6-16. Idem, in: Schweizerische Zeitschrift für Psychologie, 52, No. 2, p. 70-81. Deutsch in book 1998.

1993c: Coda. In: Hommage à Bärbel Inhelder. Archives de Psychologie, Vol. 61, No. 238, Sept. 1993. Genève: Ed. Médecine et Hygiène. p. 253-257.

1993d: Bärbel Inhelder: Ein Blumenstrauss zum 80. Geburtstag. Psychoscope 7, Vol. 14. Bern: Hans Huber.

1993e: First experiences in Thailand. In: W.J. Lonner & R. Malpass (eds.), Psychology and culture. p. 47-51. Boston: Allyn and Bacon.

1994a: La réalité comme métaphore. Journal de la psychanalyse de l'enfant 15, 155-180. Paris: Ed. Bayard.

1994b: Das Haus an Soi Wathana. Bonn, Thailand Rundschau, Dez. 1994.

1995a: Action, champ d'action et culture. In: Festschrift für Albert Leemann, Zürich.

1996a: The seven flaws of cross-cultural psychology. The story of a conversion. In: Mind, Culture and Activity. Vol 3, 1., p. 2-10. Mahwah: Laurence Erlbaum.

1996b: Das Fremde und das Eigene. In: Thomas, A. (ed.), Psychologie interkulturellen Handelns. Göttingen: Hogrefe.

1996c: Das neue Buddhabild. Bonn: Thailand Rundschau, April 1996.

1996d: Ein thailändischer Tempel in der Schweiz. Bonn, Thailand-Rundschau, Dezember 1996.

1997a: The story of a cultural psychologist: Autobiographical observations. in: Culture and Psychology, Vol. 3, Nb.3, Sept 1997. London: Sage.

1997b: Reasons for a symbolic concept of action. In: Culture & Psychology, Vol. 3, Nb. 3.

1997c: Bärbel Inhelder, 1913-1997. In: Psycholog. Rundschau,

1997d: What kind of game in a far-away forest ? In: M. Bond (ed.), Working at the interface of cultures. London: Routledge.

2000: Homo narrator – der erzählende Mensch. In: Handlung, Kultur, Interpretation. IX, 2.

2001: Symbolic Action Theory in Cultural Psychology. In: Culture & Psychology, VII,4, Dec. 2001.

2002: Psychologie der Betroffenheit, In: Verhaltenstheorie und psychosoziale Praxis. XXXIV, 2.

2003: "Why does Sally never call Bobby 'I'?" In: Culture & Psychology, Vol. 9(3).
2006a: Meditation on message and meaning.In: The pursuit of meaning. Edit. Jürgen Straub.
2006b; The enigmatic other. In: ?, ed. By Livia Simao und Jaan Valsiner.
2006c: Kultur in Evolution. In: Handlung, Kultur, Interpretation. 2006, Heft 1

ABOUT THE AUTHORS

Walter J. Lonner is professor emeritus of psychology, Western Washington University, Bellingham, Washington. A charter member, past president, and Honorary Fellow of the International Association for Cross-Cultural Psychology (founded in 1972), he has been continuously involved in cross-cultural psychology for more than 40 years. Cofounder in 1969 of the Center for Cross-Cultural Research at WWU, he is the founding and special issues editor of the *Journal of Cross-Cultural Psychology*, which was inaugurated in 1970.

Susanna A. Hayes is associate professor emeritus of psychology, Western Washington University. She was a key member of WWU's graduate program in school psychology. Early in her career she spent eight years on the Colville Indian Reservation in Western Washington. For 4 years she was director of the Center for Indian Education Specialists at WWU. She recently completed a four-month assignment in Rome where she taught in Loyola University of Chicago's study abroad program.

Printed in the United States
79904LV00001B/64-69